# Contents

# Preface

## WHY THIS DICTIONARY?

This dictionary represents a commitment to American Sign Language, known familiarly as ASL—a commitment to its authenticity as a living, evolving, fully functional language and to its role as a cohesive force among the large numbers of its regular deaf and hearing users known as the Deaf community.

Numbering more than 16 million, people with hearing loss form the largest disability group in this country. Adding to this number are the 4,000 to 5,000 babies who are born deaf every year, countless numbers of people who suffer injuries or illnesses that cause deafness, and those whose hearing is deteriorating as a natural result of the aging process.

After a long and controversial history, American Sign Language has emerged in recent decades not only as the standard means of communication for deaf people and for their families, friends, and colleagues, but also as a symbol of cultural unity. Sign language is in fact the native language—that is, the language learned before any other—of some 300,000 to 500,000 users in North America. At any given time there are roughly 100,000 people actively learning ASL, both in formal institutions of learning and in classes conducted by social agencies, churches, and other groups. It is estimated that 13 million people, including members of both the deaf and hearing populations, can now communicate to some extent in sign language. If we count all of them, this would make ASL the fourth most commonly used language in the United States.

American Sign Language is becoming even more important as federal law increasingly mandates acceptance and accommodation of deaf people in the workplace, the education system, and public accommodations. Most recently, the landmark Americans with Disabilities Act (ADA), which became law on July 26, 1990, has extended to deaf people what may be the world's strongest civil rights legislation for the disabled. Businesses and public entities of all kinds must now be prepared to communicate effectively—through sign language if necessary—with job applicants, employees, customers, and service users who are deaf.

Clearly, the need for reference materials in sign language is great. To help meet this need, the *Random House Webster's Concise American Sign Language Dictionary* offers a comprehensive and up-to-date treasury of signs, faithfully recording their formation and usage. In addition to the standard signs used in day-to-day communication throughout the nation, this book features signs from an expanding technical vocabulary. Thus this dictionary is a broad reference designed to be useful to a wide range of users, from novices seeking "survival signs" for rudimentary communication to sophisticated users already fluent in ASL and looking to enlarge their vocabularies. This compendium is drawn from an ever-growing collection, maintained by the author and continually augmented by contributions from members of the Deaf community.

The formation of each sign in this dictionary is depicted in relation to the entire upper torso, in illustrations prepared by Deaf artists using models from the Deaf community. Each illustration is accompanied by a complete verbal description of how the sign is made and, often, by a "hint" to help the reader remember the sign.

As with any other living, growing language, American Sign Language can never be fully and finitely documented: it constantly evolves and changes; it has variant forms that shift according to individual, group, or regional usage; and most saliently, as a language transmitted not by writing but by gesture, it is in many respects a language to which no printed reference book can fully do justice. What this dictionary can do, however, is provide the fundamental building blocks of this language: a basic vocabulary of ASL signs.

And so, welcome to the beautiful visual language called American Sign Language! Enjoy the physical character of each sign and the messages that its gestures convey. Through interaction with its community of users, add the nuances of the language that come so naturally to its native speakers. Above all, put aside inhibitions, physically and emotionally entering into the essential conceptual nature of the language.

# Guide

## HOW TO USE THIS DICTIONARY

### What This Dictionary Contains

*Requirements of a Lexicon of Sign Language*

Like any specialized dictionary, such as a legal or medical lexicon, this one contains a specialized vocabulary. Rather than embracing the full spectrum of terms from common to technical that one finds in a standard dictionary of English, this book focuses on the body of signs most responsive to the needs of users and students of American Sign Language (ASL).

This means that while a broad range of concepts is covered, many English words are not included. In some cases this is simply because their signs are used infrequently. Other terms do not have a corresponding sign; their meanings are communicated quite differently in sign language—for example, as an integrated component of some other sign, as a nonmanual cue accompanying a sign, as a pointing (or "indexing") movement, or by fingerspelling.

Conversely, there are strings of words in this book, phrases and entire clauses that would be out of place in a standard dictionary. Here they represent concepts expressed in one unified signing gesture in ASL. Examples are **I love you** and **Now I remember**.

*Sources of Signs*

For the most part, the signs in this dictionary are firmly established elements of American Sign Language. Some signs from systems of Manually Coded English have also been included, to reflect recent borrowings into ASL. In addition, the dictionary includes a few finger-spelled forms, like **ha ha**, which are considered to be ASL signs, although no attempt is made to give a comprehensive listing of these terms.

Although some regional variation is represented, the signs have been collected primarily from up and down the East coast. The general tendency is for these signs to spread westward.

### Usage Levels: The Social Appropriateness of Signs and Their English Translations

Like English and every other language, American Sign Language contains its share of terms that would be inappropriate in polite conversation. If a dictionary is to present an accurate picture of a language, it must include even vulgar or disparaging terms. In this dictionary, to prevent the novice from inadvertently insulting a conversational partner by unwittingly using a sign that would cause offense, cautionary notations or labels have been included for such signs. For example, a note at the end of the description of the sign might indicate that the sign is used disparagingly, or a cautionary usage label may be added to an English translation.

## How to Find a Sign

### Complete Entries

All entries, whether words or phrases and whether common terms or proper nouns, are presented in large boldface type in a single alphabetical listing, following a strict letter-by-letter order that disregards spaces between words, for example **ever, everlasting, ever since.** An exception to this order is made for verb phrases, which are shown as a group.

Most signs can be found by looking them up under any of several English words or phrases. Only one of these, however, will set forth a complete description of the sign. That complete entry usually includes one or more part-of-speech labels (*n.* for *noun,* *v.* for *verb,* etc.), and a description of how to make the sign.

Additional words for concepts covered by that sign are often listed within the entry in small boldface type, although the list of words with equivalent or related meanings is by no means exhaustive. Typical examples may be seen at the entry for **confident,** which lists the related form **confidence** as another meaning for that sign, and the entry for **earn,** which notes that the same sign is used for **deserve, income, salary,** and **wages.** Where appropriate, these additional words are given usage labels (e.g., *informal, slang, vulgar, diminutive*) to emphasize that the sign portrayed in that entry may be interpreted in those various ways depending upon the context and manner in which it is used, and that it should therefore be used with some caution.

### Cross References

A cross-reference entry, at its own alphabetical listing, simply sends the reader to one or more complete entries, where appropriate signs will be found. An example is the entry for **fatigue**, which states: See signs for TIRED, WEAK.

An additional type of cross reference, signaled by the instruction to "See also sign for...," is found within complete entries. This occurs when the signs for two different words are interchangeable. For example, at **achieve** there is an instruction to "See also sign for SUCCESSFUL," while at **successful** we find a matching instruction to "See also sign for ACHIEVE." This means that either sign may be used to represent either concept.

Because the range of meanings for a sign may differ widely from the meaning of its closest English translation, the relationship between a main entry and its cross references all of which share the same sign is sometimes obscure to a person who is not fluent in ASL. Although a cross reference may be virtually synonymous with the main entry (**officer** refers to entries for **captain** and **chief**), it is more likely to be linked to the main entry in some more nebulous, conceptual fashion, without being directly substitutable for it in an English sentence (at **farm** the reader is referred not only to the noun **agriculture**, but also to the adjective **sloppy**). Occasionally, the dictionary suggests a connection, as at the entry for **alert**, which reads: "See sign for INSOMNIA. Shared idea of remaining awake."

### Multiple Entries for the Same Word

Often there are two or more separate entries for the same word, each marked by a small identifying superscript number. These numerically sequenced groups of entries are of three sorts:

(1) Entries that have different signs because they differ in meaning (**country**[1] "foreign nation" and **country**[2] "rural land") or in part of speech (**fish**[1] a noun and **fish**[2] a verb). Each one is handled separately as a complete entry.

(2) Separate entries for a word that, though not varying in meaning or part of speech, may be expressed by two or more interchangeable signs. In these cases each numbered entry includes a sign and sign

description, but only the first entry in the group is defined; those that follow are simply labeled "alternate sign." See, for example, the two interchangeable signs at the entries **nosy**[1] and **nosy**[2].

(3) Entries with at least one of the terms in the group are cross referenced to a different sign elsewhere in the alphabet e.g., **pile**[1], a complete main entry, and **pile**[2], a cross reference to **amount** and **stack**. Cross-reference entries are always shown last in any such sequence.

## How to Make a Sign

### *Illustrations*

Formation of the sign is illustrated at every complete entry and at every entry labeled "alternate sign," sometimes by a single picture but more often by a series of full-torso line drawings that take the reader step by step through a sequence of movements. Arrows show the direction in which the hands move, and the accompanying description gives any special instructions needed on how to execute the movement.

All the illustrations demonstrate how a right-handed signer would execute each sign as seen by the listener; the model's right hand is on the reader's left. A left-handed signer should transpose the illustrated hands as well as the arrows when forming the sign—in other words, treating the picture as if it were the reader's mirror image.

In a sequence of pictures, the illustrations in a circle focus on some significant portion of the movement, often the final position of the hands. The reader should execute the signs in the order shown, from left to right.

### *Descriptions*

Each illustration is supplemented by a verbal description giving detailed instructions for making the sign. The formation of the sign is described in terms of the four component parts of a sign. These four parts are: (1) handshape, (2) location in relation to the body, (3) movement of the hands, and (4) orientation of the palms.

In cases where the rhythm of the movement is a critical component of the sign's formation, the description may state that, for example, the hands "move quickly" or the sign is "made with deliberate movement." An indication is also given when a double movement is required or when a movement is to be "repeated"—that is, made two or more times.

Within the description, italicized terms such as *A hand* and *C hand* refer to handshapes shown in the chart of the Manual Alphabet (p. 511). Terms such as *1 hand* or *10 hand* refer to handshapes for numbers. Other special handshapes, such as *bent hand*, *open hand*, and *flattened C hand*, are shown on page xii.

## Hints

Beginning most descriptions is a bracketed memory aid, or *hint*. These hints use a number of devices to help the reader understand the nature of the sign and better remember how it is made. For a *pantomimic sign*, for example, the reader may be instructed to perform an appropriate imitative action, as at **golf**: [Mime swinging a golf club]. The hint for an *iconic sign* might point out the sign's resemblance to the thing depicted or to some aspect of that thing, as at **camp** [Shape of a tent], or at **ear**: [Location of an ear].

The hint for a *compound sign* (one formed by combining two or more independent signs) tells the reader which signs are to be combined, as at **income**[1], where the hint is: [**money** + **earn**]. Superscript numbers specify which of the multiple entries for the same word the reader may use in forming the compound. For example, the hint [**gather**[1] + **meeting**] at **conference**[1] reveals that one may form conference using either of the two signs for **gather**, although both the description and the illustration refer only to **gather**[1]. The sign for a compound often involves some streamlining of the component signs, which is reflected in the description.

An *initialized sign* is formed with the handshape for the relevant letter in the English term, taken from the American Manual Alphabet (see chart on p. 511). The hint for **hum** is: [Initialized sign using **m** indicating the sound that is made when humming].

*Fingerspelled signs* use the Manual Alphabet to spell out a short word or abbreviation, as indicated by such hints as: [Fingerspell **n-o**] at **no**.

Two special notations used in the hints need a word of explanation. First, an occasional reference is made to "the finger used for feelings." Signs made with the bent middle finger often refer to concepts of sensitivity, feelings, or personal contact; examples include the signs for **mercy**, **sick**, and **network**. Second, allusions to the "male" and "female" areas of the head relate to the fact that signs referring to men, such as **father** and **uncle**, begin at or are made near the forehead, whereas signs referring to women, such as **mother** and **aunt**, begin at or are made near the chin. A clear example of the importance of this distinction may be seen in the signs for **cousin**, made near the temple for a male cousin and near the lower cheek to refer to a female cousin.

# Abbreviations Used in This Dictionary

| | |
|---|---|
| *adj.* | adjective |
| *adv.* | adverb |
| *conj.* | conjunction |
| *interj.* | interjection |
| *n.* | noun |
| *pl. n.* | plural noun |
| *prep.* | preposition |
| *pron.* | pronoun |
| *v.* | verb |
| *v. phrase* | verb phrase |

# Handshapes Used in This Dictionary

*Open*

*Bent*

*Curved 5*

*Flattened C*

*Bent V*

*Modified X*

*Flattened O*

*Modified C*

*Curved 3*

**abandon** *v.* Related form: **abandonment** *n.* See also sign for FORSAKE[1].
Same sign used for: **discard, evict, expel, throw out.**

- [Natural gesture of giving up hope] Beginning with both *S hands* in front of the chest, both palms facing in and the right hand above the left hand, quickly throw the hands upward to the right while opening into *5 hands* in front of the right shoulder, ending with the palms facing back and the fingers pointing up.

---

**abbreviate** *v.* See sign for BRIEF.

---

**abdomen** *n.* See sign for STOMACH.

---

**ability** *n.* Same sign as for **able**[1] but made with a double movement. See also sign for SKILL.

---

**able**[1] *adj.*

- [Both hands sign **yes**, indicating ability to do something] Move both *A hands*, palms facing down, downward simultaneously in front of each side of the body.

---

**able**[2] *adj.* See sign for SKILL.

---

**abolish**[1] *v.* See sign for DAMAGE. Shared idea of destruction.

---

**abolish**[2] *v.* See signs for ELIMINATE[1], REMOVE[1].

---

**abort** *v.* See signs for ELIMINATE[1], REMOVE[1]. Related form: **abortion** *n.*

---

**abortion** *n.*

- [Represents removing the fetus and throwing it away] Beginning with the palm of the left *open hand*, palm facing down, resting on the palm side of the right *A hand*, palm facing up, turn the right hand over and move it outward to the right while opening into a *5 hand* in front of the right side of the body, palm facing down.

---

# about

**about**[1] *prep.* Same sign used for: **concerning.**

■ [One thing moving about another] Move the extended right index finger, palm facing in and finger pointing left, around the fingertips of the left *flattened O hand*, palm facing in and fingers pointing right.

**about**[2] *adv.* See signs for ALMOST[1], APPROXIMATELY.

**above** *prep., adv.* Same sign used for: **over.**

■ [Indicates area above] Beginning with the right *open hand* on the back of the left *open hand*, both palms facing down, bring the right hand upward in an arc, ending several inches above the left hand.

**abrupt** *adj.* Related form: **abruptly** *adv.* Same sign used for: **accelerate, quick, quickly, snap.**

■ [A sudden action] Snap the thumb of the right hand off the right middle finger, forming an *A hand* in front of the right shoulder.

**absent** *adj., v.* Related form: **absence** *n.* See also signs for DISAPPEAR[1], SKIP[1]. Same sign used for: **drain, extinct, gone, miss, missing.**

■ [Something seems to go down the drain] Pull the right *flattened C hand*, palm facing in, downward through the left *C hand*, palm facing right, while closing the fingers and thumb of the right hand together.

**absent-minded** *adj.* See sign for BLANK[1].

**absolute** *adj.* Related form: **absolutely** *adv.* Same sign used for: **certain, truly.**

■ [**true** + a gesture that is used when one gives a promise] Beginning with the thumb side of the extended right index finger against the chin, palm facing left and finger pointing up, move the hand forward while opening into an *open hand*, palm facing forward and fingers pointing up.

**absorb**[1] *v.* Related forms: **absorbent** *adj.*, **absorption** *n.*
Same sign used for: **attract, magnetic.**

- [The hands seem to be pulled together as if by a magnet] Beginning with both *5 hands* in front of each side of the body, palms facing down and fingers pointing forward, bring the hands back while forming *flattened O hands,* ending with the fingers of both hands touching in front of the chest.

**absorb**[2] *v.* See sign for RAPTURE.

**abstain** *v.* Related form: **abstinence** *n.*

- [Initialized sign sealing the lips closed] Move the fingertips of the right *F hand,* palm facing in, from left to right across the mouth.

**absurd** *adj.*

- [Coming from one's imagination] Beginning with the index finger of the right *4 hand* touching the right side of the forehead, palm facing left, bring the hand forward in a series of small arcs.

**abuse** *v.* See signs for BEAT[3], BEAT UP, TORTURE.

**accelerate** *v.* See sign for ABRUPT.

**accept** *v.* Related form: **acceptance** *n.* Same sign used for: **adopt, adoption, approval, approve.**

- [Bring something that is accepted toward oneself] Beginning with both *5 hands* in front of the chest, fingers pointing forward, bring both hands back toward the chest while pulling the fingers and thumbs of each hand together.

**accident**[1] *n.* Same sign used for: **collide, collision, crash.**

- [Two things collide with each other] Move both *5 hands* from in front of each side of the chest, palms facing in and fingers pointing toward each other, while changing into *A hands,* ending with the knuckles of both *A hands* touching in front of the chest.

**accident**[2] *n.* See signs for HAPPEN, MISTAKE.

# accidentally

**accidentally** *adv.* Alternate form: **by accident.** Related form: **accidental** *adj.* Same sign used for: **amiss.**
- [Similar to sign for **mistake** except made with a twisting movement] Twist the knuckles of the right *Y hand*, palm facing in, on the chin from right to left.

**acclaim** *v.* See sign for ANNOUNCE.

**acclamation** *n.* See sign for PRAISE.

**accompany** *v.* See sign for GO WITH.

**accomplish** *v.* See sign for SUCCESSFUL. Related form: **accomplishment** *n.*

**according to** Same sign used for: **proportion, ratio.**
- [Initialized sign similar to sign for **proportion** showing two similar things] Move both *P hands*, palms facing down, from in front of the left side of the body to the right side of the body by bring the hands upward simultaneously in a large arc.

**accredit** *v.* Related forms: **accreditation** *n.*, **accredited** *adj.* Same sign used for: **adopt, certify.**
- [Stamping something with a seal] Beginning with the right *S hand* in front of the right shoulder, palm facing down, twist the wrist to hit the little-finger side of the upturned left *open hand* with a deliberate movement.

**accumulate**[1] *v.* Related form: **accumulation** *n.* Same sign used for: **amass.**
- [More and more of something being piled up on top of other things] Beginning with the right *U hand*, palm facing left, beside the left *U hand*, palm facing down, flip the right hand over with a double movement, tapping the right fingers across the left fingers each time.

**accumulate**[2] *v.* See signs for ADD[1], COLLECT.

**accurate** *adj.* See signs for PERFECT, RIGHT[3].

**accuse**[1] *v.*

- [Similar to sign for **blame**[1] except formed with a double movement] Push the little-finger side of the right *A hand*, palm facing left, forward with a double movement across the back of the left *A hand*, palm facing down.

**accuse**[2] *v.* See sign for FAULT[2].

**accustomed to** See sign for HABIT.

**ache** *v., n.* See signs for HURT[1], PAIN[1].

**achieve** *v.* Related form: **achievement** *n.* See also sign for SUCCESSFUL. Same sign used for: **chalk up, success.**

- [An accumulation of something] Beginning with the left *bent hand* over the right *bent hand* in front of the chest, both palms facing down, move the hands with an alternating movement over each other to in front of the face.

**acid** *n.* Related form: **acidic** *adj.* Same sign used for: **eat up.**

- [Action of acid eating something] Open and tightly close the fingers of the right *curved 5 hand* as it moves with a crawling movement from the heel to the fingertips of the left *open hand*, palm facing right.

**acquaint** *v.* See sign for ASSOCIATE.

**acquire** *v.* See signs for GET, LEARN, TAKE.

**across** *prep., adv.* Same sign used for: **after, afterward, cross, over.**

- [Movement across another thing] Push the little-finger side of the right *open hand*, palm facing left, across the back of the left *open hand*, palm facing down.

# act

**act¹** *v., n.* Related forms: **action** *n.*,
**activity** *n.* Same sign used
for: **deed.**

- [The hands seem to be
  actively doing something]
  Move both *C hands,* palms
  facing down, simultaneously
  back and forth in front of the body with a swinging movement.

**act²** *v.* Same sign used for: **drama, perform,
play, show, theater.**

- [Initialized sign] Bring the thumbs of both *A hands,*
  palms facing each other, down each side of the
  chest with alternating circular movements.

**active¹** *adj.* Related forms: **action,** *n.*,
**activity,** *n.* Same sign used for: **deed, labor.**
See also sign for WORK.

- [The hands seem to be actively doing something]
  Move both *C hands,* palms facing down, back
  and forth in front of the body in opposite
  directions with a double swinging movement.

**active²** *adj.* See sign for AMBITIOUS¹.

**actual** *adj.* See signs for REAL, TRUE.

**actually** *adv.* See sign for TRUE.

**adapt** *v.* See sign for CHANGE¹.

**add¹** or **add up** *v.* or *v. phrase.* Related form: **addition** *n.*
Same sign used for: **accumulate, plus, sum, total.**

- [Hands bring two quantities together] Beginning with the right
  *5 hand* from above the right shoulder, palm facing down, and
  the left *5 hand* near the left side of the waist, palm facing up,
  bring the hands toward each other while changing into
  *flattened O hands,* ending with the fingertips touching
  each other in front of the chest.

**add²** *v.* Related form: **addition** *n.* Same sign used for:
**amend, bonus, extra, supplement.**

- [One hand brings an additional amount to the other hand] Swing
  the right *5 hand* upward from the right side of the body while
  changing into a *flattened O hand,* ending with the right index
  finger touching the little-finger side of the left *flattened O hand*
  in front of the chest, both palms facing in.

**addition** *n.* See sign for PLUS[1].

**addicted** *adj.* Related form: **addiction** *n.*
Same sign used for: **hooked.**
- [Gesture indicates that one is "hooked"] With the index finger of the right *X hand* hooked in the right corner of the mouth, pull the cheek outward to the right.

**address**[1] *n., v.*
- [Initialized sign similar to sign for **live**] Move both *A hands,* palms facing in, upward on each side of the chest with a double movement.

**address**[2] *v.* See sign for SPEAK[2].

**adept** *adj.* See sign for ADROIT.

**adequate** *adj.* See sign for ENOUGH.

**adhere** *v.* See signs for APPLY[3], STICK[1].

**adhesive** *n., adj.* See sign for STICK[1].

**adjust** *v.* See sign for CHANGE[1].

**administer** *v.* See sign for MANAGE. Alternate form: **administrate.**

**admission** *n.* Alternate form: **admittance.**
Same sign used for: **enter, entrance, entry.**
- [Similar to sign for **enter** except formed with a double movement] Move the back of the right *open hand* forward in a downward arc under the palm of the left *open hand,* both palms facing down, with a double movement.

**admit**[1] *v.* Related form: **admission** *n.* Same sign used for: **confess, confession, submit, willing.**
- [Hand seems to bring a confession from the chest] Move the right *open hand,* palm facing in, from the chest forward in an arc while turning the palm slightly upward.

# admit

**admit²** *v.* See sign for ENTER.

**admonish** *v.* See sign for SCOLD.

**adopt** *v.* See signs for ACCEPT, ACCREDIT, APPROVE, TAKE. Related form: **adoption** *n.*

**adore** *v.* See sign for WORSHIP¹.

**adrift** *adj.* See sign for ROAM.

**adroit** *adj.* Same sign used for: **adept, expert, skillful, whiz** (*informal*).

- [Similar to sign for **serious**] Beginning with the fingertips of the right *F hand* touching the chin, palm facing forward, twist the hand to turn the palm inward.

**adult** *n., adj.*

- [Initialized sign formed in the traditional male and female positions; can be formed with an opposite movement] Move the thumb of the right *A hand*, palm facing forward, from the side of the forehead to the lower cheek.

**adultery** *n.*

- [Initialized sign indicating moving from one partner to another] Tap the knuckles of the right *A hand*, palm facing down, first on the index fingertip and then on the middle fingertip of the left *V hand*.

**advance** *v.* Same sign used for: **exalt.**

- [Moving to a more advanced position] Beginning with the back of the right *bent hand* touching the palm of the left *open hand*, both palms facing in, move the right hand upward and forward of the left hand.

**advanced** *adj.* Same sign used for: **elevate, elevated, elevation, exalt, exalted, exaltation, higher, prominent, promote, promotion, supreme.**

- [Moving to a more advanced position] Move both *bent hands*, palms facing each other, from near each side of the head upward a short distance in a deliberate arc.

**advantage**[1] *n.* Same sign used for: **take advantage of.**

- [Represents "an easy touch"] Flick the bent middle finger of the right *5 hand* upward off the heel of the left *open hand.*

**advantage**[2] *n.* See sign for BENEFIT.

**advertise** *v.* Related form: **advertisement** *n.* Same sign used for: **broadcast, commercial, propaganda, publicity, publicize.**

- [Suggests "blowing one's own horn" in order to advertise] Beginning with the thumb side of the right *S hand*, palm facing left, against the little-finger side of the left *S hand*, palm facing right, move the right hand forward and back with a double movement.

**advice** *n.* Same sign used for: **effect.**

- [Sending information to another] Beginning with the fingertips of the right *flattened O hand* on the back of the left *open hand*, palm facing down, move the right hand forward while spreading the fingers into a *5 hand.*

**advise** *v.* See sign for COUNSEL.

**advocate** *v.* See sign for SUPPORT.

**aerial** *n.* See sign for ANTENNA.

**affect** *v.* See signs for COUNSEL, INFLUENCE.

**affection** *n.* See sign for HUG. Related form: **affectionate** *adj.*

**affiliation** *n.* See sign for COOPERATION.

**affix** *v.* See sign for APPLY[3].

**afford** *v.* Same sign used for: **debt, due, owe.**

- [Indicates that money should be deposited in the palm] Tap the extended right index finger on the palm of the left *open hand* with a double movement.

# affront

**affront** *v.* See sign for INSULT.

---

**afraid** *adj.* Same sign used for: **fright, frightened, panic, scared, timid.**

■ [Hands put up a protective barrier] Beginning with both *A hands* in front of each side of the chest, spread the fingers open with a quick movement, forming *5 hands,* palms facing in and fingers pointing toward each other.

---

**after a while** See sign for LATER.

---

**after**[1] *prep., conj., adv.* Same sign used for: **afterward, beyond, from now on, rest of.**

■ [A time frame occurring after another thing] Beginning with the palm of the right *bent hand* touching the back of the fingers of the left *open hand,* both palms facing in, move the right hand forward a short distance.

---

**after**[2] *prep.* See sign for ACROSS.

---

**afternoon** *n.* Same sign used for: **matinee.**

■ [The sun going down in the afternoon] With the bottom of the right forearm resting on the back of the left *open hand,* palm facing down, move the right *open hand* downward with a double movement.

---

**afterward** *adv.* See signs for ACROSS, AFTER[1], LATER.

---

**again** *adv.* Same sign used for: **reiterate, repeat.**

■ [The movement indicates wanting something to be repeated] Beginning with the right *bent hand* beside the left *curved hand,* both palms facing up, bring the right hand up while turning it over, ending with the fingertips of the right hand touching the palm of the left hand.

---

**against** *prep.* Same sign used for: **anti-** [prefix], **opposed to, prejudice.**

■ [Demonstrates making contact with a barrier] Hit the fingertips of the right *bent hand* into the left *open hand,* palm facing right.

---

**age** *n.*

- [An old man's beard] Move the right *O hand,* palm facing left, downward a short distance from the chin while changing into an *S hand.*

---

**agency** *n.* See sign for ASSOCIATION.

---

**agenda** *n.*

- [Initialized sign similar to sign for **list**] Move the palm side of the right *A hand* from first touching the fingers and then the heel of the left *open hand,* palm facing right.

---

**aggravate** *v.* Related form: **aggravation** *n.*

- [Mixing up emotions] Move both *curved 5 hands,* palms facing in, in large alternating circles on each side of the chest.

---

**aggravated** *v.* See sign for DISGUSTED[1].

**aggressive** *adj.* See sign for AMBITIOUS[1].

**agile** *adj.* See sign for SKILL.

**ago** *adj.* Same sign used for: **last, past, was, were.**

- [Indicates a time in the past] Move the right *bent hand* back over the right shoulder, palm facing back.

---

**agree**[1] *v.* Same sign used for: **compatible, compromise, in accord, in agreement, suit.**

- [**think**[1] + lining up two things to show they agree with each other] Move the extended right index finger from touching the right side of the forehead downward to beside the extended left index finger, ending with both fingers pointing forward in front of the body, palms facing down.

---

# agree

### agree² *v.*

- [Directional sign showing that two people share the same opinion] Move the right *Y hand,* palm facing left, from the right shoulder forward and back with a double movement.

---

**agriculture** *n.* See sign for FARM.

---

**ahead** *adv.* Same sign used for: **forward, further.**

- [The hand moves to a position ahead] Beginning with the palm sides of both *A hands* together, move the right hand forward in a small arc.

---

**aid** *n.* See sign for HELP.

---

**aide** *n.* See sign for ASSISTANT.

---

**aim** *v.* See sign for GOAL.

---

**air conditioning** *n.* Related form: **air conditioner.**

- [Abbreviation **a-c** + a gesture showing air blowing at one's face] Form an *A* and then a *C* in front of the right shoulder. Then with both *open hands* near each side of the face, palms facing back and fingers pointing up, bend the fingers up and down with a double movement.

---

**airplane** *n.* Same sign used for: **airport, jet, plane.**

- [Shape and movement of an airplane] Move the right hand with the thumb, index finger, and little finger extended, palm facing down, forward with a short repeated movement in front of the right shoulder.

---

**airport** *n.* See sign for AIRPLANE.

---

**airtight** *adj.* See sign for SEAL².

---

**alarm** *n.* Same sign used for: **alert, drill.**

- [Action of clapper on alarm bell] Tap the extended index finger of the right hand, palm facing forward, against the left *open hand,* palm facing right, with a repeated movement.

**alas** *interj.* Same sign used for: **drat, shoot.**

- [Natural gesture] Snap the middle finger off the thumb of the right *3 hand*, palm facing in, while swinging the right hand in toward the center of the chest.

---

**alert**[1] *n.* See sign for ALARM.

---

**alert**[2] *n.* See sign for INSOMNIA. Shared idea of remaining awake.

---

**algebra** *n.*

- [Initialized sign similar to sign for **arithmetic**] With a repeated movement, brush the palm side of the right *A hand* as it moves left in front of the chest, palm facing down, against the palm side of the left *A hand*, palm facing up, as it moves right.

---

**align**[1] *v.*

- [Putting something into alignment with another thing] Move the little-finger side of the right *B hand*, palm facing left and fingers pointing forward, forward with a wavy movement along the extended left index finger, palm facing right and finger pointing forward.

---

**align**[2] *v.* See sign for LINE UP.

---

**alike**[1] *adj., adv.* See also signs for LIKE[3], SAME. Same sign used for: **also, identical, look alike, similar.**

- [Sign moves between two people or things that are similar] Move the right *Y hand*, palm facing down, from side to side with a short repeated movement in front of the body.

---

**alike**[2] *adj., adv.* See also signs for LIKE[3], SAME[1]. Same sign used for: **similar, uniform.**

- [Sign shows things that are similar] Move the right *Y hand*, palm facing down, in a flat circle in front of the body.

---

**alive** *adj.* See sign for LIVE.

# all

---

**all** *pron.* Same sign used for: **entire, whole.**

■ [The hand encompasses the whole thing] Move the right *open hand* from near the left shoulder in a large circle in front of the chest, ending with the back of the right hand in the left *open hand* held in front of the body, palms facing in.

---

**all afternoon** *adv.*

■ [**afternoon** formed with a continuous movement indicating duration] With the right forearm on the back of the left *open hand,* palm facing down, move the right *B hand* smoothly downward from in front of the right shoulder.

---

**all along** *adv.* See signs for GO ON[1], SINCE[1].

---

**all day** *adv.*

■ [Shows movement of the sun through the day] With the fingers of the left *open hand* in the crook of the right arm, move the right *B hand* smoothly from the right side of the body in a large arc in front of the body, ending with the right hand, palm facing down, on the back of the left arm near the elbow.

---

**all gone** *adj.* See signs for NOTHING[5], RUN OUT OF.

---

**all morning** *adv.*

■ [**morning** formed with a continuous movement indicating duration] With the fingers of the left *open hand* in the crook of the right arm, move the right *B hand* smoothly upward from in front of the right side of the body to in front of the right shoulder, palm facing back.

---

**all night** *adv.* Same sign used for: **overnight.**

■ [**night** formed with a continuous movement indicating duration] With the fingers of the left *open hand* in the crook of the right arm, move the right *B hand* smoothly downward from in front of the right side of the chest, ending under the left arm, palm facing back.

---

**all over** *adv.* Same sign used for: **overall.**

■ [Surrounds entire thing] Move the right *5 hand* from in front of the right side of the body, palm facing forward, in a large arc in front of the face, ending in front of the left side of the body.

---

**all right** *adv.* See sign for RIGHT[2].

**all the time** *adv.* Same sign used for: **ever since, total.**

■ [Hands bring together a total amount of time] Move both *curved 5 hands* from in front of each shoulder, palms facing each other, toward each other while closing the fingers, ending with the fingertips of both *flattened O hands* touching in front of the chest.

**alligator** *n.* Same sign used for: **jaws.**

■ [Mime action of alligator's jaws] Beginning with the fingertips and heels of both *curved 5 hands* touching, right hand on top of the left hand and fingers forward, bring the hands apart and together again with a double movement.

**allegiance** *n.* See sign for SUPPORT.

**allow** *v.* See sign for LET.

**allowance** *n.* See sign for PENSION.

**ally** *n.* See sign for RELATIONSHIP.

**almost**[1] *adv.* Same sign used for: **about, barely, nearly.**

■ [The fingers almost touch the other hand] Brush the fingertips of the right *open hand* upward off the back of the left fingers, both palms facing up.

**almost**[2] *adv.* See sign for CLOSE CALL.

**alone**[1] *adv., adj.* Same sign used for: **isolated, lone, only, solely.**

■ [Shows one thing alone] With the right index finger extended up, move the right hand, palm facing back, in a small repeated circle in front of the right shoulder.

**alone**[2] *adj.* See sign for SINGLE.

**a lot** *adv.* See signs for MANY, MUCH.

**aloud** *adv.* See sign for NOISE.

### alphabet *n.*

- [a-b-c + **fingerspell**] With the right hand, palm facing forward, sequentially form the first three manual alphabet letters in front of the right shoulder, moving the hand slightly to the right after each letter. Then move the right *5 hand*, palm facing down, to the right in front of the right shoulder while wiggling the fingers.

**already** *adv.* See sign for FINISH[1].

**also** *adv.* See sign for ALIKE[1].

### altar *n.*

- [Initialized sign showing the shape of an altar] Beginning with the thumbs of both *A hands* touching in front of the body, palms facing down, move the hands apart and then down in front of each side of the body.

**alter** *v.* See sign for CHANGE[1].

**alternate** *v.* See sign for TURN[1].

**alternative** *n.* See sign for EITHER[1].

**altitude** *n.* See sign for HIGH.

### alumnus *n.*

- [Initialized sign similar to sign for **year**] Beginning with the right *A hand*, palm facing left, over the left *A hand*, palm facing right, move the right hand forward in a complete circle around the left ending with the little-finger side of the right hand on the thumb side of the left hand.

### always *adv.* Same sign used for: **ever.**

- [A continuous circle signifying duration] Move the extended right index finger, palm facing in and finger angled up, in a repeated circle in front of the right side of the chest.

**amass** *v.* See sign for ACCUMULATE[1].

**amaze** *v.* See signs for SURPRISE, WONDERFUL. Related form: **amazement** *adj.*

# American Sign Language

**amazed** *v.* See sign for INCREDIBLE[1].

**ambiguous** *adj.* See sign for VAGUE.

**ambitious**[1] *adj.* Related form: **ambition** *n.* Same sign used for: **active, aggressive.**

■ [Initialized sign] Move both *A hands,* palms facing in, in large alternating circles upward on each side of the chest.

**ambitious**[2] *adj.* See sign for GOAL.

**ambulance** *n.* Same sign used for: **siren.**

■ [Represents flashing light on an ambulance] Move the right *flattened O hand* in a circular movement near the right side of the head by repeatedly twisting the wrist and opening the fingers into a *5 hand* each time.

**amen** *interj.* Same sign used for: **pray, prayer.**

■ [Natural gesture for folding one's hands to pray] Bring the palms of both *open hands* together, fingers angled upward, while moving the hands down and in toward the chest.

**amend** *v.* See sign for ADD[2].

**America** *n.* Related form: **American** *adj., n.*

■ [The rail fences built by settlers] With the fingers of both hands loosely entwined, palms facing in, move the hands in circle in front of the chest.

## American Sign Language *n.*

■ [Initialized sign similar to **gesture + language**] With both *A hands* in front of chest, palms facing forward and right hand higher than the left, move the hands in an alternating circular movement toward the chest. Then move both *L hands* from together in front of the chest, palms facing down, simultaneously apart to each side of the chest.

# amid

**amid** or **admidst** *prep.* See sign for AMONG.

**amiss** *adj.* See sign for ACCIDENTALLY.

**among** *prep.* Same sign used for: **amid, admidst, midst.**

- [Shows one moving among others] Move the extended right index finger in and out between the fingers of the left *5 hand,* both palms facing in.

**amount** *n.* Same sign used for: **heap, lump, pile.**

- [Shows a small amount in a pile] Move the extended right index finger, palm facing down, in an arc from near the heel to the fingers of the upturned left *open hand,* ending with the right palm facing in toward the chest.

**amuse** *adj.* See sign for FUNNY.

**analyze** *v.* Related form: **analysis** *n.* Same sign used for: **diagnose, diagnosis.**

- [Taking something apart to analyze it] With both *bent V hands* near each other in front of the chest, palms facing down, move the fingers apart from each other with a downward double movement.

**ancestor** *n.*

- [Shows moving back into the past] Beginning with both *open hands* in front of the right shoulder, palms facing in and right hand above the left hand, roll the hands over each other with an alternating movement while moving the hands back over the right shoulder.

**anchor** *n.*

- [Represents unhooking an anchor and dropping it] Beginning with the thumb side of the right *X hand,* palm facing down, against the palm of the left *3 hand,* palm facing right and fingers pointing forward, bring the right hand downward in an arc, ending with the palm facing left.

**ancient** *adj.* See sign for LONG TIME AGO.

**and** *conj.*
- [Stretching one part of a sentence to connect it to the rest] Move the right *curved 5 hand,* palm facing left, to the right in front of the body while closing the fingers to the thumb, ending in a *flattened O hand.*

**and so forth** See sign for VARIETY.

**angel** *n.* Same sign for: **wings.**
- [Shows movement of an angel's wings] Beginning with the fingertips of both *bent hands* touching each shoulder, palms facing down, twist the hands forward and outward and bend the fingers up and down with a repeated movement.

**anger** *n.* Related form: **angry** *adj.* See also sign for CROSS[2]. Same sign used for: **enrage, fury, mad, outrage, rage.**
- [Hands bring up feeling of anger in the body] Beginning with the fingertips of both *curved 5 hands* on the lower chest, bring the hands upward and apart, ending in front of each shoulder.

**angle** *n.*
- [Shape of an angle] With the extended right index finger, trace along the index finger and thumb of the left *L hand,* palm facing forward.

**angry** *adj.* See sign for CROSS[2].

**animal** *n.* Same sign used for: **beast.**
- [Shows an animal breathing] Beginning with the fingertips of both *curved 5 hands* on the chest near each shoulder, roll the fingers toward each other on their knuckles with a double movement while keeping the fingers in place.

**annex** *v.* See sign for BELONG[1].

### anniversary *n.*

■ [**annual** + **celebrate**] Beginning with the little-finger side of the right *S hand* on the thumb of the left *S hand*, flick the right index finger forward and back with a double movement. Then move both modified *X hands* in large simultaneous circles, palms facing back, near each side of the head.

### announce *v.* Related form: **announcement** *n.* Same sign used for: **acclaim, declaration, declare, proclaim, proclamation, reveal, tell.**

■ [**tell**[1] with a movement that shows a general announcement] Beginning with the extended index fingers of both hands pointing to each side of the mouth, palms facing in, twist the wrists and move the fingers forward and apart from each other, ending with the palms facing forward and the index fingers pointing outward in opposite directions.

### annoy *v.* Same sign used for: **bother, disturb, interfere, interrupt, irritate.**

■ [A gesture showing something interfering with something else] Sharply tap the little-finger side of the right *open hand*, palm facing in at an angle, at the base of the thumb and index finger of the left *open hand* with a double movement.

### annual *adj.* Related form: **annually** *adv.* Same sign used for: **every year, per annum.**

■ [Formed like **year** as it moves into the future] Beginning with the little-finger side of the right *S hand* on the thumb side of the left *S hand*, palms facing in opposite directions, flick the right index finger forward and back with a double movement.

### anoint *v.*

■ [Mime pouring oil on something] Move the extended thumb of the right *10 hand*, palm facing right, and thumb pointing down, in a flat circle over the left *S hand*, palm facing down, with a double movement.

### another *adj., pron.* Same sign used for: **other.**

■ [Points away to another] Beginning with the right *10 hand* in front of the body, palm facing down and thumb pointing left, flip the hand over to the right, ending with the palm facing up and the thumb pointing right.

**answer** *n., v.* Same sign used for: **react, reply, response.**

■ [Indicates directing words of response to another] Beginning with both extended index fingers pointing up in front of the mouth, right hand nearer the mouth than the left and both palms facing forward, bend the wrists down simultaneously, ending with fingers pointing forward and the palms facing down.

**ant** *n.*

■ [Initialized sign showing the movement of an ant's legs] With the heel of the left *A hand* on the back of the right *curved 5 hand,* palm facing down, move the right hand forward while wiggling the fingers.

**antagonism** *n.* See sign for STRUGGLE.

**antagonistic** *adj.* See sign for CONTRARY[1].

**antenna** *n.* Same sign used for: **aerial.**

■ [Shape of an antenna] Place the palm of the right *3 hand* on the extended left index finger pointing up, palm facing right.

**anti-** *prefix.* See signs for AGAINST, RESIST.

**anxiety** *n.* See signs for CONCERN[2], NERVOUS.

**anxious** *adj.* See signs for NERVOUS, TROUBLE[1].

**any** *adj., pron.*

■ [Initialized sign pointing to a selection of things] Beginning with the right *10 hand* in front of the chest, palm facing left, twist the wrist and move the hand down and to the right, ending with the palm facing down.

**anybody** *pron.*

■ [any + you] Beginning with the right *10 hand* in front of the chest, palm facing left, twist the wrist and move the hand down and to the right, ending with the palm facing down. Then move the extended right index finger, palm facing left and finger pointing forward, in an arc from left to right in front of the body.

# anyone

**anyone** *pron.*

■ [**any + one**] Beginning with the right *10 hand* in front of the chest, palm facing left, twist the wrist and move the hand down and to the right, ending with the palm facing down. Then hold the extended right index finger up in front of the chest, palm facing in.

**anything** *pron.*

■ [**any + thing**] Beginning with the right *10 hand* in front of the chest, palm facing left, twist the wrist and move the hand down and to the right, ending with the palm facing down. Then move the right *curved hand* from the right side of the body, palm facing up, outward to the right in a double arc.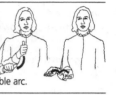

**anyway** *adv.* Same sign used for: **despite, doesn't matter, even though, however, hardly, nevertheless, whatever.**

■ [Flexible hands signify no firm position] Beginning with both *open hands* in front of the body, fingers pointing toward each other and palms facing in, move the hands forward and back from the body with a repeated alternating movement, striking and bending the fingers of each hand as they pass.

**anywhere** *adv.*

■ [**any + where**] Beginning with the right *10 hand* in front of the chest, palm facing left, twist the wrist and move the hand down and to the right, ending with the palm facing down. Then move the extended right index finger, pointing up in front of the chest and palm facing forward, back and forth with a repeated movement.

**apart** *adv.* See sign for PART[2].

**ape** *n.* See signs for GORILLA, MONKEY.

**apologize** *v.* See sign for SORRY. Related form: **apology** *n.*

**apostrophe** *n.* Same sign used for: **comma.**

■ [Mime drawing an apostrophe in the air] Draw an apostrophe in the air with the extended right index finger, pointing forward, by twisting the wrist in front of the right shoulder.

**apparently** *adv.* See sign for SEEM.

**appeal** *v.* See sign for SUGGEST.

**appear** *v.* See signs for SEEM, SHOW UP.

**appearance** *n.*
- [Shows area of facial appearance] Move the right *5 hand*, palm facing in, in a large circle in front of the face.

**appease** *v.* See sign for SATISFY.

**appendix** *n.*
- [Shape and location of appendix] Bend the extended right index finger, palm facing back, forward and back with a double movement near the right side of the waist.

**appetite**[1] *n.*
- [**hungry + eat**] Beginning with the fingertips of the right *C hand* touching the chest, palm facing in, move the hand downward a short distance. Then bring the fingertips of the right *flattened O hand,* palm facing down, to the lips with a double movement.

**appetite**[2] *n.* See sign for HUNGRY.

**applaud** *v.* Related form: **applause** *n.*
Same sign used for: **clap.**
- [Natural gesture for clapping] Pat the palm of the right *open hand* across the palm of the left *open hand* with a double movement.

**apple** *n.*
- [Shows action of chewing an apple] With the knuckle of the right *X hand* near the right side of the mouth, twist the wrist downward with a double movement.

# apply

**apply**¹ *v.* Related form: **applicable** *adj.* Same sign used for: **charge, file, install, post.**

- [Put messages on a spindle] Move the fingers of the right *V hand,* palm facing forward, downward on each side of the extended left index finger, pointing up in front of the chest.

---

**apply**² *v.* Related form: **application** *n.* Same sign used for: **candidate, eligible, nominate, volunteer.**

- [Seems to pull oneself forward to apply for something] Pinch a small amount of clothing on the right side of the chest with the fingers of the right *F hand* and pull forward with a short double movement.

---

**apply**³ *v.* Same sign used for: **adhere, affix.**

- [Mime applying tape or a label] Tap the fingers of the right *H hand,* palm facing left, against the palm of the left *open hand,* palm facing right, first near the fingers and then near the heel.

---

**apply**⁴ *v.* See sign for LABEL.

---

**appoint**¹ *v.* See also sign for SELECT. Same sign used for: **choose, elect.**

- [Fingers seem to pick someone] Beginning with the thumb side of the right *G hand,* palm facing down and fingers pointing forward, against the left *open hand,* palm facing right and fingers pointing up, pull the right hand in toward the chest while pinching the index finger and thumb together.

---

**appoint**² *v.* Related form: **appointment** *n.* Same sign used for: **assign.**

- [Hand seems to grab someone and set that person aside] Beginning with the right *curved 5 hand* in front of the right side of the body, palm facing left, move the hand to the left while closing into an *S hand.* Then move the right *S hand* forward and to the left in a short arc.

---

**appointment** *n.* Same sign used for: **assignment, book, reservation.**

■ [The hands are bound by a commitment] Move the right *S hand*, palm facing down, in a small circle and then down to the back of the left *A hand*, palm facing down in front of the chest.

**appreciate**[1] *v.* Related form: **appreciation** *n.*

■ [Similar to sign formed for **enjoy**] Move the bent index finger of the right *5 hand* in a small circle on the chest.

**appreciate**[2] *v.* See sign for ENJOY. Related form: **appreciation** *n.*

**appreciative** *adj.* See sign for GRATEFUL.

**apprehend** *v.* See sign for UNDERSTAND.

**approach**[1] *v., n.* Same sign used for: **close to, near.**

■ [One hand moves to approach the other] Move the back of the right *bent hand* from near the chest forward with a double movement toward the palm of the left *bent hand*, both palms facing in and fingers pointing in opposite directions.

**approach**[2] *v.* See sign for CLOSE[1].

**appropriate** *adj.* See sign for REGULAR[1]. Related form: **appropriately** *adv.*

**approve** *v.* See sign for ACCEPT. Related form: **approval** *n.*

**approximate** *adj.* See sign for ROUGH.

**approximately** *adv.* Related form: **approximate** *adj.* Same sign used for: **about, around.**

■ [Natural gesture of vagueness] Move the right *5 hand*, palm facing forward, in a circle in front of the right shoulder with a double movement.

**arc** *n.* See sign for ARCH.

# arch

**arch** *n.* Same sign used for: **arc, curve.**

■ [Shape of an arch] Beginning with the right *B hand* in front of the chin, palm facing forward and fingers pointing to the left, move the hand in a large arc, ending in front of the right side of the body, palm facing left.

**arctic** *n., adj.* Same sign used for: **bitter cold, frigid.**

■ [Natural gesture used when one is very cold] Beginning with both *S hands* in front of each shoulder, palms facing down, move the hands downward toward each other in front of the chest with a sharp deliberate movement, ending with the palms facing in.

**area**[1] *n.* Same sign used for: **place, space.**

■ [Indicates an area] Move the right *5 hand,* palm facing down and fingers pointing forward, in a flat forward arc in front of the right side of the body.

**area**[2] *n.* See sign for DISTRICT.

**argue** *v.* Related form: **argument** *n.* Same sign used for: **fight, quarrel, squabble.**

■ [Represents opposing points of view] Beginning with both extended index fingers pointing toward each other in front of the chest, palms facing in, shake the hands up and down with a repeated movement by bending the wrists.

**argument** *n.* See sign for DISCUSS.

**arithmetic** *n.* Same sign used for: **estimate, figure, figure out, multiplication.**

■ [Movement suggests combining things] Brush the back of the right *V hand* across the palm side of the left *V hand,* both palms facing up, as the hands cross with a double movement in front of the chest.

**army** *n.*
- [Holding a gun while marching] Tap the palm side of both *A hands* against the right side of the chest, right hand above the left hand, with a repeated movement.

**around**[1] *adv., prep.* Same sign used for: **revolve, rotary, surrounding.**
- [Demonstrates moving in a circle around something] Move the extended right index finger, pointing down, in a small circle around the extended left index finger, pointing up in front of the chest.

**around**[2] *prep.* See sign for APPROXIMATELY.

**arouse** *v.* See sign for AWAKE[1].

**arrange** *v.* See signs for PLAN, PREPARE.

**arrest** *v.* See signs for CAPTURE, CATCH[2].

**arrive** *v.* Same sign used for: **reach.**
- [Hand moves to arrive in other hand] Move the right *bent hand* from in front of the right shoulder, palm facing left, downward, landing the back of the right hand in the upturned left *curved hand*.

**arrogant** *adj.* See signs for CONCEITED, PROUD.

**art** *n.* Same sign used for: **drawing, illustration, sketch.**
- [Demonstrates drawing something] Move the extended right little finger with a wiggly movement down the palm of the left *open hand* from the fingers to the heel.

**article** *n.* Same sign used for: **journal.**
- [Shape of a column of newspaper type] Move the right *modified C hand* down the palm of the left *open hand* from the fingers to the heel with a double movement.

# artificial

**artificial** *adj*. See sign for FAKE[2].

**ascend**[1] *v*. Related form: **ascent** *n*.

- [Represents climbing upward] Beginning with both *H hands* in front of the chest, right palm up and left palm down, repeatedly flip the hands over to place the right *H hand* across the fingers of the left *H hand* as the hands move upward in front of the face.

**ascend**[2] *v*. See sign for CLIMB.

**ashamed** *adj*. Same sign used for: **shame, shameful, shy.**

- [Blood rising in the cheeks when ashamed] Beginning with the back of the fingers of both *curved hands* against each cheek, palms facing down, twist the hands forward, ending with the palms facing back.

**aside** *adv*. Same sign used for: **put aside, put away.**

- [Natural gesture for pushing something aside] Beginning with both *open hands* in front of the body, both palms facing right and fingers pointing forward, push the hands deliberately to the right.

**ask** *v*. Same sign used for: **pray, request.**

- [Natural gesture used for asking] Bring the palms of both *open hands* together, fingers angled upward, while moving the hands down and in toward the chest.

**ASL** *n*. See sign for AMERICAN SIGN LANGUAGE.

**asleep** *adv*. See sign for FALL ASLEEP.

**aspire** *v*. See sign for ZEAL. Related form: **aspiration** *n*.

**assemble**[1] *v*. Same sign used for: **put together.**

- [Mime putting parts together] Bring the fingertips of both *flattened O hands* together, palms facing down, with a double movement in front of the chest changing the angle of the hands each time.

**assemble**[2] *v*. See signs for GATHER[1,2].

28

**assembly**[1] *n.*

- [Initialized sign] Tap the side of the right thumb of the *A hand* on the back of the left *open hand*, palm facing down, with a repeated movement.

---

**assembly**[2] *n.* See sign for MEETING.

---

**assembly line** *n.* Same sign used for: **mass-produce.**

- [Pushing things along on an assembly line] With both *4 hands* near each other in front of the chest, right palm facing down and left palm facing up, push the hands off to the right with a double movement.

---

**assign** *v.* See signs for APPOINT[2], CHOOSE[1].

---

**assignment** *n.* See sign for APPOINTMENT.

---

**assist** *v.* See sign for HELP.

---

**assistant** *n., adj.* Same sign used for: **aide.**

- [Initialized hand showing giving a boost or aid to another] Use the thumb of the right *A hand* under the little-finger side of the left *A hand* to push the left hand upward in front of the chest.

---

**associate** *v., n.* Same sign used for: **acquaint, brother-hood, each other, fellowship, fraternity, interact, mingle, one another, socialize.**

- [Represents mingling with each other] With the thumb of the left *A hand* pointing up and the thumb of the right *A hand* pointing down, circle the thumbs around each other while moving the hands from left to right in front of the chest.

---

**association** *n.* Related form: **associate** *v.* Same sign used for: **agency.**

- [Initialized sign similar to sign for **class**] Beginning with the thumbs of both *A hands* touching in front of the chest, palms facing each other, move the hands apart and forward in a circular movement by twisting the wrists until the little fingers touch and the palms face in.

---

# assume

**assume** *v.* See signs for GUESS, TAKE. Related form: **assumption** *n.*

**assure** *v.* See sign for VOW. Related form: **assurance** *n.*

**astonish** *v.* Related form: **astonishment** *n.*

■ [Represents jumping up with bent legs and falling
over in astonishment] Beginning with the fingertips
of the right *V hand,* palm facing in, on the palm of
the left *open hand* held in front of the chest, palm
facing up, bring the right hand upward in front of
the chest while crooking the fingers and then down
again, landing with the back of the *bent V hand* on the left palm.

**astound** *v.* See signs for FLABBERGAST, SURPRISE.

**astounded** *adj.* See sign for SHOCK[1].

**astray** *adv., adj.* Same sign used for: **backside, estranged,
offshoot, off the point, off track, out of the way,
sidetracked, stray.**

■ [Shows one hand veering off the path] Beginning with both
index fingers touching in front of the chest, palms facing
down, slide the right index finger forward along the side
of the left index finger, moving the right hand off to the
right as it moves forward.

**at fault** *adj.* See sign for BLAME[1].

**at last** *adv. phrase.* See sign for FINALLY.

**at odds** *adj.* See sign for STRUGGLE.

**atop** *prep.*

■ [Indicates location of something atop another thing] Place the
fingertips of the right *curved hand,* palm facing down, on the
back of the left *S hand* held in front of the chest,
palm facing down.

**attach** *v.* See sign for BELONG[1].

**attack**[1] *v., n.*

■ [**hit**[1] + forcing another down] Bring the knuckles of
the right *S hand,* palm facing in, forward from in
front of the right shoulder to hit against the
extended left index finger, palm facing
forward, forcing the left finger downward
in front of the body.

**attack**[2] *v.* See sign for HIT[1].

**attain** *v.* See sign for GET.

**attempt** *v.* See sign for TRY[1].

**attend** *v.* See also sign for GATHER[2]. Same sign used for:
**go to.**

- [**go** formed with a directed movement] Beginning with
  both extended index fingers pointing up in front of
  the chest, right hand closer to the chest than the left
  and both palms facing forward, move both hands
  forward simultaneously while bending the wrists so
  the fingers point forward.

**attention** *n.* Related form: **attend** *v.* Same sign
used for: **concentrate, concentration, focus on,
pay attention, watch.**

- [Forms blinkers to direct one's attention] Move both
  *open hands* from near each cheek, palms facing
  each other, straight forward simultaneously.

**attitude** *n.*

- [Initialized sign similar to sign for **character**[1]] Move
  the thumb of the right *A hand* in a circular movement
  around the heart, palm facing left, ending with the
  thumb against the chest.

**attract**[1] *v.* Same sign used for: **draw.**

- [Hands pull something to oneself] Beginning with
  both *curved hands* in front of each side of the
  body, palms facing up, bring the hands back
  toward the body while closing into *A hands.*

**attract**[2] *v.* See sign for ABSORB[1].

**attractive** *adj.* Related form: **attracted to.**

- [Taking in something attractive and holding it]
  Beginning with the right *C hand* in front of the
  face, palm facing left, and the left *C hand*
  somewhat forward, palm facing right, move
  both hands forward while closing into *S
  hands,* ending with the little-finger side
  of the right hand near the thumb side
  of the left hand.

# auction

**auction** *n., v.* Same sign used for: **bid.**

- [Mime raising one's hand to bid at an auction] Move both *open hands*, palms facing forward, in an alternating upward movement beside each side of the head.

**audience** *n.* See also sign for HORDE. Same sign used for: **crowd.**

- [**people** + movement indicating large crowd of people] Move both *P hands*, palms facing down, in alternating forward circular movements in front of each side of the body. Then move both *curved 5 hands*, palms facing down, from in front of each side of the body forward with a simultaneous movement.

**audit** *n., v.*

- [Initialized sign similar to sign for **count**] Swing the palm side of the right *A hand* with a double movement from the fingers to the heel of the left *open hand* held in front of the body, palm facing up.

**aunt** *n.*

- [Initialized sign formed near the right cheek] Shake the right *A hand*, palm facing forward, near the right cheek.

**authority** *n.*

- [Shows muscle in arm symbolizing strength and authority] Beginning with the extended right thumb of *A hand*, palm facing left, near the left shoulder, move the hand down in an arc while twisting the right wrist, ending with the little-finger side of the right hand in the crook of the left arm, bent across the body.

**automatic**[1] *adj.* Same sign used for: **automatic transmission.**

- [Indicates repetitive movement of something operating automatically] Move the extended right curved index finger, palm facing in, back and forth on the back of the left *open hand*, palm facing in, with a repeated movement.

**automatic**[2] *adj.* See sign for FAST.

**automobile** *n.* See sign for CAR.

**autopsy** *n.*

- [**die + operate**[1]] Beginning with both *open hands* in front of the body, right palm facing up and left palm facing down, flip the hands to the left, turning the right palm down and the left palm up. Then move the thumbs of both *10 hands* downward on each side of the chest, in short alternating movements.

**autumn** *n.* See sign for FALL[2].

**available** *adj.* See sign for EMPTY.

**avenge** *v.* See sign for REVENGE.

**average** *adj.*

- [Shows split down the middle] Beginning with the little-finger side of the right *open hand* across the index-finger side of the left *open hand,* palms angled down, twist the wrists down, bringing the hands apart a short distance with a double movement, palms facing down.

**avoid** *v., adj.* Same sign used for: **back out, elude, evade, fall behind, get away, shirk.**

- [One hand moves away from the other to avoid it] Beginning with the knuckles of the right *A hand,* palm facing left, near the base of the thumb of the left *A hand,* palm facing right, bring the right hand back toward the body with a wiggly movement.

**awake**[1] *v.* Related form: **awaken** *v.* Same sign used for: **arouse, wake up.**

- [Indicates eyes opening when becoming awake] Beginning with the *modified X hands* near each eye, palms facing each other, quickly flick the fingers apart while widening the eyes.

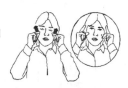

**awake**[2] *adj.* See sign for INSOMNIA.

# award

---

**award**[1] *n.*

- **[trophy + gift]** Tap the thumbs and little fingers of both *Y hands,* palms facing in, against each other with a double movement in front of the chest. Then, beginning with both *X hands* in front of the chest, palms facing each other, move the right hand forward in a small arc.

---

**award**[2] *n.* See signs for GIFT, TROPHY[1].

---

**aware**[1] *adj.* Same sign used for: **familiar, knowledge.**

- [Shows location of awareness] Tap the fingertips of the right *bent hand,* palm facing in, against the right side of the forehead with a double movement.

---

**aware**[2] *adj.* See sign for NOTICE[1].

---

**away** *adj., adv.* Same sign used for: **get away, go, gone.**

- [Natural gesture as if shooing something away] Flip the fingers of the right *open hand* from pointing down near the right side of the body outward to the right by flicking the wrist upward with a quick movement.

---

**awesome** [*slang*] *adj.* See signs for FINEST, FLABBERGAST.

---

**awful** *adj.* Same sign used for: **disastrous, dreadful, fierce, horrible, sordid, terrible.**

- [Natural gesture used when indicating something terrible] Beginning with both *8 hands* near each side of the head, palms facing each other, flip the fingers open to *5 hands* while twisting the palms forward.

---

**awkward** *adj.* Same sign used for: **clumsy.**

- [Represents walking awkwardly] Beginning with both *3 hands* in front of the body, right hand higher than the left and both palms facing down, raise the left and then the right hand in alternating movements.

---

34

---

**babble** *v.* See sign for BLAB.

---

**baby** *n.* Same sign used for: **infant.**

- [Action of rocking a baby in one's arms] With the bent right arm cradled on the bent left arm, both palms facing up, swing the arms to the right and the left in front of the body with a double movement.

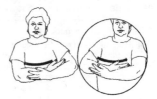

---

**bachelor** *n.* Related form: **bachelorette** *n.*

- [Initialized sign] Move the index finger of the right *B hand* from touching the left side of the chin, palm facing left, in an arc to touch the right side of the chin.

---

**back** *n.* Same sign used for: **rear.**

- [Natural gesture indicating location] Pat the fingertips of the right *open hand* behind the right shoulder with a repeated movement.

---

**back and forth** *adv.* See sign for COMMUTE.

---

**background** *n.*

- [Initialized sign] In quick succession tap the index-finger side of the right *B hand* and then *G hand*, palm facing forward, against the left *open hand*, palm facing right.

---

**back out** *v. phrase.* See signs for AVOID, RESIGN.

---

# backpack

### backpack *n., v.*

■ [Action of putting on a backpack] Move the thumbs of both *curved 3 hands,* palms facing forward, downward toward each shoulder with a double movement.

---

### backslide *v.* See signs for ASTRAY, BEHIND.

### backup[1] *n., adj., v.* **back up.**

■ [Hand moves to provide support for the other hand] Beginning with the right *10 hand,* palm facing down, beside the left *10 hand,* palm facing right, move the right hand clockwise in an arc and then forward to the heel of the left hand, ending with the right palm facing left.

---

### backup[2] *n.* See sign for SUPPORT.

### bacon *n.*

■ [Hands indicate wavy shape of fried bacon] With the thumbs of both hands pointing up and fingers of both *U hands* touching in front of the chest, palms facing in, bring the hands apart while bending the fingers back into each palm with a double movement.

---

### bad *adj.* Related form: **badly** *adv.* Same sign used for: **evil, nasty, naughty, wicked.**

■ [Gesture tosses away something that tastes bad] Move the fingers of the right *open hand* from the mouth, palm facing in, downward while flipping the palm quickly down as the hand moves.

---

### badge[1] *n.* Same sign used for: **emblem.**

■ [Putting on a badge] Bring the index-finger side of the right *F hand,* palm facing left, against the left side of the chest with a double movement.

---

**badge**[2] *n*. See sign for POLICE.

**bag** *n*. See also sign for BASKET. Same sign used for: **sack.**
- [Shows shape of filled bag] Beginning with the little fingers of both *curved hands* touching in front of the body, palms facing up, bring the hands apart and upward in an arc while spreading the fingers, ending with both *curved 5 hands* in front of each side of the chest, palms facing each other.

**baggage** *n*. Same sign used for: **luggage.**
- [Shows carrying a bag in each hand] Shake both *S hands*, palms facing in, up and down with a short movement near each side of the waist with the elbows bent.

**bake**[1] *v*.
- [Putting something in the oven] Move the fingers of the right *open hand*, palm facing up, forward under the left *open hand* held in front of the chest, palm facing down.

**bake**[2] *v*. See sign for COOK.

**balance** *v*., *n*.
- [Action shows trying to balance something] With a simultaneous movement bring the right *open hand* and the left *open hand*, both palms facing down, up and down in front of each side of the chest, shifting the entire torso slightly with each movement.

**bald** *adj*. Related form: **baldness** *n*. Same sign used for: **bareheaded, scalp.**
- [Indicates bare area of head] Move the bent middle finger of the right *5 hand*, palm facing down, in a circle around the top of the head.

# ball

## ball *n.*

- [The shape of a ball] Touch the fingertips of both *curved 5 hands* together in front of the chest, palms facing each other.

## balloon *n.* Same sign used for: **expand.**

- [Shows shape of balloon as it expands] Beginning with the left fingers cupped over the back of the right *S hand* held in front of the mouth, move the hands apart while opening the fingers, ending with both *curved 5 hands* near each side of the face, palms facing each other.

## ban *v.* See signs for FORBID, PREVENT.

## banana *n.*

- [Mime peeling a banana] With the extended left index finger pointing up in front of the chest, palm facing forward, bring the fingertips of the right *curved 5 hand* downward, first on the back and then on the front of the index finger, while closing the right fingers to the thumb each time.

## band *n.* Same sign used for: **choir.**

- [**music + class**] Swing the little-finger side of the right *open hand,* palm facing in, back and forth across the length of the bent left forearm. Then, beginning with the thumbs of both *C hands* near each other in front of the body, palms facing, bring the hands apart and outward in an arc, ending with the hands in front of the chest, palms facing in.

## bandage *n.* Same sign used for: **Band-Aid** (*trademark*).

- [Mime putting on a bandage] Pull the right *H fingers,* palm facing down, across the back of the left *open hand,* palm facing down.

## banquet *n.* Same sign used for: **feast, reception.**

- [Indicates continuous eating] Bring the fingertips of both *flattened O hands,* palms facing down, to the mouth with repeated alternating movements.

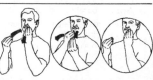

**banter** *v.*, *n.* See sign for STRUGGLE.

**bare**[1] *adj.*
- [Indicates a bare area] Move the bent middle finger of the right *5 hand,* palm facing down, in a double circle on the back of the left *open hand,* palm facing down.

**bare**[2] *adj.* See signs for EMPTY, NUDE.

**bareheaded** *adj.* See sign for BALD.

**barely** *adv.* See signs for ALMOST[1], CLOSE CALL.

**bark** *v.*
- [The movement of a dog's jaws when barking] Beginning with the fingertips of both *open hands* touching, palms facing each other and heels apart, bring the fingers apart and then together again with a repeated movement.

**barrier** *n.* See sign for PREVENT.

**base** *n.* Related forms: **basic** *adj.*, **basis** *n.*
- [Initialized sign] Move the right *B hand,* palm facing left, in a flat circle under the left *open hand,* palm facing down.

**baseball** *n.* Same sign used for: **softball.**
- [Natural gesture of swinging a baseball bat] With the little finger of the right *S hand* on the index finger of the left *S hand,* palms facing in opposite directions, move the hands from near the right shoulder downward in an arc across the front of the body with a double movement.

**based on** *v.* See sign for ESTABLISH.

# basement

**basement** *n.* Same sign used for: **beneath, cellar.**
- [Indicates an area beneath a house] Move the right *10 hand,* palm facing in, in a flat circle under the left *open hand* held across the chest, palm facing down.

**bashful** *adj.*
- [Shows a blush rising in the face] Move the palms of both *open hands* slowly upward from each side of the chin to each side of the forehead, palms facing in and fingers pointing up.

**basket** *n.* See also sign for BAG. Same sign used for: **suitcase.**
- [Initialized sign showing where a basket hangs from the arm] Move the index-finger side of the right *B hand* from the wrist to near the elbow of the bent left arm.

**basketball** *n.*
- [Mime tossing a basketball] Move the *curved 5 hands* from in front of the chest, palms facing each other, upward with a double movement by twisting the wrists upward.

**batch** *n.* See sign for PILE¹.

**bath** *n.* Related form: **bathe** *v.*
- [Washing oneself when bathing] Rub the knuckles of both *10 hands,* palms facing in, up and down on each side of the chest with a repeated movement.

**bathroom¹** *n.*
- [**bath + box**] Rub the knuckles of both *10 hands,* palms facing in, up and down on each side of the chest with a repeated movement. Then, with both *open hands* in front each side of the chest, palms facing each other and fingers pointing forward, move hands in opposite directions, ending with the left hand near the chest and the right hand several inches forward, both palms facing in.

**bathroom**[2] *n.* See sign for TOILET.

**bathtub** *n.*

- [**bath** + a sign similar to **sit**] Rub the knuckles of both *10 hands,* palms facing in, up and down on each side of the chest with a repeated movement. Then bring the fingers of the right *H hand,* palm facing down and fingers pointing forward, down on the palm of the left *open hand,* palm facing up.

**batter** *n.* See sign for BEAT[1].

**battery** *n.* See sign for ELECTRIC.

**battle** *n., v.* Same sign used for: **war.**

- [Indicates opponents in warlike maneuvers] Beginning with both *5 hands* in front of the right shoulder, palms facing down and fingers pointing toward each other, move the hands toward the left shoulder and then back toward the right shoulder.

**bawl out** *v.* Same sign used for: **burst, burst out.**

- [Represents a sudden burst of words] Beginning with the little finger of the right *S hand* on the top of the index-finger side of the left *S hand,* flick the hands forward with a deliberate double movement while opening the fingers into *5 hands* each time.

**beads** *pl. n.* Same sign used for: **necklace.**

- [Location and shape of a necklace of beads] Move the index-finger side of the right *F hand,* palm facing left, from the left side of the neck smoothly around to the right side of the neck.

**bean** *n.*

- [Shape of a string bean] Beginning with the extended left index finger, palm facing in and finger pointing right, held between the index finger and thumb of the right *G hand,* palm facing left, pull the right hand outward to the right with a double movement.

# bear

**bear**[1] *n.*

- [Action of a bear scratching itself] With the arms crossed at the wrist on the chest, scratch the fingers of both *curved hands* up and down near each shoulder with a repeated movement.

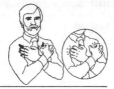

**bear**[2] *v.* See signs for BURDEN, HURT[2], PATIENT[1].

**bear up** *v. phrase.* See sign for ENCOURAGE.

**beard** *n.*

- [Location and shape of beard] Beginning with the right *C hand* around the chin, palm facing in, bring the hand downward while closing the fingers to the thumb with a double movement.

**beast** *n.* See sign for ANIMAL.

**beat**[1] *v.* Same sign used for: **batter, mix, stir.**

- [Mime beating using a spoon in a bowl] Move the right *A hand,* palm facing the chest, in a quick repeated circular movement near the palm side of the left *C hand,* palm facing right.

**beat**[2] *n.* Same sign used for: **vibrate, vibration.**

- [Feeling the rhythm of music] Move both *5 hands,* palms facing down, from side to side with a short repeated alternating movement in front of each side of the body.

**beat**[3] *v.* Same sign used for: **abuse, hit, strike.**

- [Indicates beating something] Hit the back of the right *S hand,* palm facing in, against the palm of the left *open hand,* palm facing right, with a double movement.

**beat**[4] *v.* See also sign for DEFEAT.

■ [Directing a single blow] Beginning with the right *S hand* in front of the right shoulder, palm facing left, move the hand quickly forward while opening the fingers to form a *H hand*.

**beat up** *v.* Same sign used for: **abuse, hit, strike.**

■ [Indicates beating something repeatedly] Swing the right *S hand*, palm facing in, in a large arc in front of the chest, repeatedly striking the extended left index finger, palm facing right, each time it passes and returns.

**beau** *n.* See sign for SWEETHEART.

**beautiful** *adj.* Related form: **beauty** *n.* See also sign for PRETTY. Same sign used for: **lovely.**

■ [Hand encircles a beautiful face] Move the right *5 hand* in a large circular movement in front of the face while closing the fingers to the thumb, forming a *flattened O hand*. Then move the hand forward while spreading the fingers quickly into a *5 hand*.

**because** *conj.* Same sign used for: **since.**

■ Bring the index finger of the right *L hand* with a sweeping movement across the forehead from left to right, changing to a *10 hand* near the right side of the head.

**beckon** *v.* Same sign used for: **come on, recruit.**

■ [Natural beckoning gesture] Beginning with the extended right index finger pointing forward in front of the chest, palm facing up, bend the index finger into an *X hand* while bringing the hand back toward the chest, with a double movement.

**become** *v.* Same sign used for: **turn into.**

■ [Hands reverse positions as if to change one thing into another] Beginning with the palm of the right *open hand* laying across the upturned palm of the left *open hand*, rotate the hands, exchanging positions while keeping the palms together.

## become successful

**become successful** See sign for SHOOT UP.

**bed** *n.*
- [Mime laying the head against a pillow] Rest the right cheek at an angle on the palm of the right *open hand*.

**bedroom** *n.*
- [**bed** + **box**] Rest the right cheek at an angle on the palm of the right *open hand.* Then, beginning with both *open hands* in front of each side of the chest, palms facing each other and fingers pointing forward, move the hands in opposite directions, ending with the left hand near the chest and the right hand several inches forward of the left hand, both palms facing in.

**bee** *n.* Same sign used for: **mosquito.**
- [The biting action of an insect and then a natural gesture of brushing it away] Press the index finger and thumb of the right *F hand* against the right cheek. Then brush the index-finger side of the right *B hand*, palm facing forward, from near the right ear forward by bending the wrist.

**been** *v.* See sign for SINCE[1].

**been (there)** Same sign used for: **finish.**
- [Similar to sign for **touch** except made more quickly] Bring the bent middle finger of the right *5 hand* downward to tap quickly the back of the left *open hand* held across the chest, both palms facing down.

**beer** *n.*
- [Initialized sign] Slide the index-finger side of the right *B hand*, palm facing forward, downward on the right cheek with a double movement.

**before**[1] *adv.* Same sign used for: **last, past, previous, prior.**

- [Indicates a time or place in the past] Move the fingertips of the right *open hand,* palm facing back, from near the right cheek back and down to touch the right shoulder.

**before**[2] *prep.* Same sign used for: **pre-, preceding, prior.**

- [Indicates a time or place experienced in the past] Beginning with the back of the right *open hand,* palm facing in and fingers pointing left, touching the back of the left *open hand,* palm facing forward and fingers pointing up, move the right hand in toward the chest.

**beg**[1] *v.* Same sign used for: **implore, plead.**

- [Mime extending a hand while begging] While holding the wrist of the upturned right *curved 5 hand* in the left palm, constrict the right fingers with double movement.

**beg**[2] *v.* See sign for WORSHIP[1].

**beginning** *n.* See sign for START[1].

**behind** *prep.* Same sign used for: **backslide.**

- [Indicates a position behind another] Move the right *10 hand,* palm facing left, from in front of the left *10 hand,* palm facing right, back toward the chest in a large arc.

**belch** *v., n.* Same sign used for: **burp.**

- [Indicates gas moving up from the stomach] Move the fingertips of the right *bent hand,* palm facing in, up and down on the chest with a double movement.

**believe** *v.* Related form: **belief** *n.*

- [mind + clasping one's beliefs close] Move the extended right index finger from touching the right side of the forehead downward while opening the hand, ending with the right hand clasping the left *open hand,* palm facing up, in front of the body.

# bell

**bell** *n.* Same sign used for: **reverberate, ring.**

- [Indicates the striking of a bell's clapper and the sound reverberating] Hit the thumb side of the right *S hand,* palm facing down, against the palm of the left *open hand.* Then move the right hand to the right while opening the fingers into a *5 hand,* wiggling the fingers as the hand moves.

**belong**[1] *v.* Same sign used for: **annex, attach, combine, connect, fasten, hook up, join, joint, link, unite.**

- [Two things coming together] Beginning with both *curved 5 hands* in front of each side of the body, palms facing each other, bring the hands together while touching the thumb and index fingertips of each hand and intersecting with each other.

**belong**[2] *v.* Same sign used for: **entitle.**

- [**true + your**] Move the extended right index finger, palm facing left, from in front of the mouth forward while changing into an *open hand,* palm facing forward.

**below**[1] *prep., adv.* Same sign used for: **beneath, bottom.**

- [Indicates a position below] Beginning with the left *open hand* on the back of the right *open hand,* both palms facing down, bring the right hand downward in an arc, ending several inches below the left hand.

**below**[2] *prep.* See sign for MINIMUM.

**belt** *n.*

- [Location of a belt] Move both *H hands* from each side of the waist around toward each other until the fingers overlap in front of the waist.

**bend**[1] *v.* Related form: **bent** *adj.*

- [Indicates the ability to bend] Grasp the fingers of the left *open hand,* palm facing right, with the fingers of the right *flattened O hand,* and then bend the left fingers downward until both palms are facing down and hands are bent.

46

**bend**[2] *v.* See signs for BOW[1], DENT.

**beneath** *prep., adv.* See signs for BASEMENT, BELOW[1].

**benefit** *n.* Same sign used for: **advantage.**

- [Pocketing a beneficial item] Push the thumb side of the right *F hand* downward on the right side of the chest, palm facing down, with a short double movement.

**bent** *adj.* See sign for DENT.

**berry** *n.*

- [Twisting a berry to pick it from the vine] Grasp the extended little finger of the left hand, palm facing in, with the fingertips of the right *O hand* and twist the right hand outward with a double movement.

**beside** *prep.* Same sign used for: **next to.**

- [Indicates a location beside another] Beginning with the palm of the right *bent hand,* palm facing in and fingers pointing left, touching the back of the left *bent hand,* palm facing in and fingers pointing right, move the right hand forward in a small arc.

**best** *adj., adv.*

- [Modification of **good,** moving the sign upward to form the superlative degree] Bring the right *open hand,* palm facing in and fingers pointing left, from in front of the mouth upward in a large arc to the right side of the head, changing to a *10 hand* as the hand moves.

**bet** *n., v.* Same sign used for: **bid, gamble, wager.**

- [Initialized sign showing the turning of dice] Beginning with both *B hands* in front of each side of the body, palms facing each other and fingers pointing forward, turn the hands toward each other, ending with the palms facing down.

# betray

**betray**[1] *v.* Same sign used for: **con, deceive, fib, fool, swindle.**

- Strike the knuckles of the right *A hand,* palm facing forward, against the extended left index finger, palm facing forward, with a double movement.

**betray**[2] *v.* See sign for CHEAT.

**better** *adj., adv.*

- [Modification of **good,** moving the sign upward to form the comparative degree] Bring the right *open hand,* palm facing in and fingers pointing left, from in front of the mouth upward in an arc to the right side of the head, changing to a *10 hand* as the hand moves.

**between** *prep.* Same sign used for: **gap, lapse.**

- [Indicates space between two things] Brush the little-finger side of the right *open hand,* palm facing left, back and forth with a short repeated movement on the index-finger side of the left *open hand,* palm angled right.

**beverage** *n.* See sign for DRINK[1].

**bewilder** *v.* See sign for SURPRISE.

**bewildered** *adj.* See sign for PUZZLED.

**beyond** *prep., adv.* See sign for AFTER[1].

**biannual** *adj.* Same sign used for: **semiannual, six months.**

- [**six** handshape used to sign **month**] Move the right *6 hand,* palm facing forward and fingers pointing up, downward with a double movement on the extended left index finger held in front of the chest, palm facing right and finger pointing up.

**bicycle** *n.*

- [Shows action of pedaling a bicycle] Move both *S hands* in alternating forward circles, palms facing down, in front of each side of the body.

**bid** *n.*, *v.* See signs for AUCTION, BET, SUGGEST.

**big** *adj.* See also sign for LARGE. Same sign used for: **enlarge.**

■ [Shows big size] Move both *L hands* from in front of the body, palms facing each other and index fingers pointing forward, apart to each side in large arcs.

**big-headed** *adj.* See sign for CONCEITED.

**big shot** *n.* See sign for CONCEITED.

**bill** *n.* See sign for DOLLAR.

**billiards** *n.* See sign for POOL.

**billion** *n.*, *adj.*

■ [Initialized sign similar to sign for **million**] Tap the fingertips of the right *bent B hand*, palm facing in, first on the heel and then on the fingers of the left *open hand*, palm facing up.

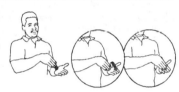

**bimonthly** *adj.* Same sign used for: **every two months.**

■ [**month** formed with a **two** handshape] Move the back of the right *2 hand*, palm facing in and fingers pointing left, downward on the extended left index finger held in front of the body, palm facing right and finger pointing up.

**bind** *v.* Same sign used for: **bondage, bound, locked into.**

■ [Shows wrists bound together] Beginning with the wrists of both *S hands* crossed in front of the chest, but slightly apart, palms facing in, bring the wrists against each other.

**binoculars** *n.*

■ [Mime looking through binoculars] Beginning with both *C hands* near each side of the face, palms facing each other, twist the hands upward and toward each other in a double arc.

---

**biology** *n.*

- [Initialized sign similar to sign for **science**] Move both *B hands*, palms facing forward, in large alternating inward circles in front of the chest.

---

**bird** *n.* Same sign used for: **chicken, coward, fowl.**

- [Mime the action of a bird's beak] Close the index finger and thumb of the right *G hand*, palm facing forward, with a repeated movement in front of the mouth.

---

**birth** *n.* Same sign used for: **born.**

- [Indicates the birth of a baby] Bring the right *open hand*, palm facing in, from the chest forward and down, ending with the back of the right hand in the upturned palm of the left *open hand*.

---

**birthday** *n.*

- [**birth** + **day**] Bring the right *open hand*, palm facing in, from the chest forward and down, ending with the back of the right hand in the upturned palm of the left *open hand*. Then, with the right elbow resting on the back of the left hand held across the body, palm down, bring the extended right index finger downward toward the left elbow in a large sweeping arc.

---

**biscuit** *n.* See sign for COOKIE.

---

**bite** *v.*

- [Mimes teeth biting into something] Bring the fingertips of the right *C hand*, palm facing down, down to close around the index-finger side of the left *open hand*.

---

**bitter** *adj.* See sign for SOUR.

---

**bitter cold** *adj. phrase.* See sign for ARCTIC.

---

**biweekly** *adj., adv.* Same sign used for:
**every two weeks, two weeks.**

- [**week** formed with a **two** handshape] Move
  the palm side of the right *2 hand* from the
  heel to the fingertips of the left *open hand*
  held in front of the body, palm facing up.

---

**bizarre** *adj.* See sign for STRANGE.

---

**blab** *v.* Same sign used for: **babble, chat,
chatter, gab, gossip, talk, talkative.**

- [Action of the mouth opening and closing]
  Beginning with both *flattened C hands*
  near each side of the face, palms facing
  each other, close the fingers and thumbs
  together simultaneously with a
  double movement.

---

**black** *adj., n.*

- [Shows a black eyebrow] Pull the side of the extended
  right index finger, palm facing down and finger
  pointing left, from left to right across the forehead.

---

**blackboard** *n.* See sign for BOARD¹.

---

**blah** *n.* See sign for NEVER MIND.

---

**blame**¹ *v.* Same sign used for: **at fault.**

- [Shoves blame at someone] Push the little-finger side of
  the right *A hand,* palm facing left, forward across the
  back of the left *A hand,* palm facing down.

---

**blame**² *v.* See sign for FAULT².

---

**blank**¹ *adj.* Same sign used for: **absent-minded.**

- [Indicates a blank mind] Bring the bent middle finger
  of the right *5 hand,* palm facing in, from left to right
  across the forehead.

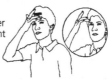

# blank

**blank**[2] *adj*. See sign for EMPTY.

**blanket** *n*.

- [Initialized sign miming pulling up a blanket to the chest] Move both *B hands* from in front of the body, palms facing down and fingers pointing toward each other, upward, ending with both index fingers against the upper chest.

---

**blend** *v*. See signs for CIRCULATE, COMBINE[1], MAINSTREAM, MESH, MIX[1].

**bless** *v*. Related form: **blessed** *adj*.

- [Taking a blessing from the lips and distributing it] Beginning with the thumbs of both *A hands* touching the lips, palms facing each other, move the hands down and forward while opening into *5 hands* in front of each side of the chest.

---

**blind** *adj*.

- [Poking out the eyes] Jab the fingertips of the right *bent V hand* back toward the eyes with a short, deliberate movement.

---

**blinds** *n*. Same sign used for: **venetian blinds.**

- [Represents opening the slats of venetian blinds] Beginning with the little fingers of both *B hands* touching in front of the chest, palms facing in and fingers pointing in opposite directions, move the left hand down to bring the hands slightly apart while spreading the fingers into *5 hands*.

---

**blizzard** *n*.

- [**snow + wind**] Beginning with both *5 hands* in front of the face, palms facing out and fingers pointing upward, wiggle the fingers while moving the hands downward with a wavy movement. Then, beginning with both *5 hands* over the right shoulder, palms facing forward and fingers angled up, bring the hands downward to the left with a double movement.

---

**block**[1] *n.* Same sign used for: **cube.**

■ [Shape of a cube or block] Beginning with both *B hands* in front of each side of the chest, palms facing each other and fingers pointing up, bend the hands sharply, ending with the left hand above the right hand, both palms facing down.

**block**[2] *v.* See sign for PREVENT. Related form: **blockage** *n.*

**blond** or **blonde** *adj.*

■ [yellow + hair] Wiggle the right *Y hand*, palm facing left, near the right side of the head. Then grasp a small strand of hair with the thumb and index finger of the right *F hand*, palm facing left.

**blood** *n.* Related form: **bloody** *adj.* Same sign used for: **shed.**

■ [red + a gesture representing the flow of blood from a wound] Brush the extended right index finger, palm facing in, downward on the lips. Then open the right hand into a *5 hand* and bring it downward while wiggling the fingers, palm facing in, past the open left hand held across the chest, palm facing in and fingers pointing right.

**bloom** *v., n.* Same sign used for: **blossom.**

■ [Shows a bloom opening up] Beginning with the fingertips and heels of both curved *5 hands* touching in front of the chest, palms facing each other, while keeping the heels together, move the fingers away from each other while opening slightly.

**blossom** *n.* See sign for BLOOM.

**blouse** *n.*

■ [Location and shape of woman's blouse] Touch the bent middle fingers of both *5 hands* on each side of the upper chest, and then bring the hands down in an arc, ending with the little fingers of both hands touching the waist, palms facing up and fingers pointing toward each other.

# blow

**blow¹** *v.* Same sign used for: **fool.**

■ [Mimes blowing one's nose] Squeeze the nose with the thumb and index finger of the right *A hand* while pulling the hand slightly forward.

**blow²** *v.*

■ [Indicates the flow of air through the mouth] Beginning with the back of the *flattened O hand* at the mouth, palm facing forward and fingers pointing forward, move the hand forward a short distance while opening the fingers into a *5 hand.*

**blowup** *n., v.* Same sign used for: **blow one's top, burst, bust, erupt.**

■ [Demonstrates the top blowing off of something] Beginning with the palm of the right *5 hand,* palm facing down, on the thumb side of the left *S hand,* palm facing right, bring the right hand upward and back down again.

**blue** *adj.*

■ [Initialized sign] Move the right *B hand,* fingers angled up, back and forth by twisting the wrist in front of the right side of the chest.

**bluff** *v.* See sign for FLATTER. Shared idea of insincerity.

**blur** *v.*

■ [Obstructing the view] Beginning with the fingertips of both *flattened O hands* touching in front of the upper chest, left palm facing in and right palm facing out, move the hands in opposite directions across each other while opening into *5 hands,* palms facing each other.

**blurry** *adj.* See sign for VAGUE.

**blush** *v.* Same sign used for: **flush.**

- [Blood rising in the face when blushing] Beginning with both *flattened O hands* near each cheek, palms facing in and fingers pointing up, spread the fingers slowly upward, forming *5 hands.*

---

**board**¹ *n.* Same sign used for: **blackboard, chalkboard, wall.**

- [Initialized sign showing the flatness of a chalkboard or a wall] Beginning with the index-finger sides of both *B hands* together in front of the chest, palms facing forward and fingers pointing up, move the hands apart to in front of each shoulder.

---

**board**² *n.*

- [Initialized sign formed similar to sign for **member**] Touch the index-finger side of the right *B hand*, palm facing left, first to the left side of the chest and then to the right side of the chest.

---

**boast** *v.* See sign for BRAG.

**boat** *n.* Same sign used for: **cruise, sail, sailing, ship.**

- [Shows the shape of a boat's hull] With the little-finger sides of both *curved hands* together, palms facing up, move the hands forward in a bouncing double arc.

---

**body** *n.*

- [Location of the body] Touch the fingers of both *open hands*, palms facing in and fingers pointing toward each other, first on each side of the chest and then on each side of the waist.

---

**boiling mad** *adj.* Same sign used for: **burning mad, flare up, fume, furious, seethe.**

- [**fire**¹ formed close to the body as if boiling inside] Wiggle the fingers of the right *5 hand*, palm facing the chest, in a flat circle under the left *open hand*, held close to the chest, palm facing down.

---

# bold

**bold** *adj.* See signs for BRAVE, CONFIDENT, STRICT, WELL[1].

**bologna** *n.*
- [The shape of sausage links] Beginning with the thumbs and index fingers of both *C hands* touching in front of the chest, palms facing down, move the hands apart while closing the fingers, ending with both *S hands* in front of each side of the chest.

**bolt** *n.* See sign for LIGHTNING.

**bomb** *n.* See sign for EXPLODE.

**bond** *n.* See sign for RELATIONSHIP.

**bondage** *n.* See sign for BIND.

**bone**[1] *n.*
- [**rock**[1] + **skeleton**] Tap the palm side of the right *A hand*, palm facing down, against the back of the wrist of the left *A hand.* Then, with the hands crossed at the wrists, tap the fingers of both *bent V hands* on the opposite side of the chest, palms facing in.

**bone**[2] *n.* See sign for SKELETON.

**bonus** *n.* See sign for ADD[2].

**book**[1] *n.*
- [Represents opening a book] Beginning with the palms of both *open hands* together in front of the chest, fingers angled forward, bring the hands apart at the top while keeping the little fingers together.

**book**[2] *v.* See sign for APPOINTMENT.

**boom** *v.* See sign for EXPLODE.

**boost** *n.* See sign for SUPPORT.

**boots** n. Same sign used for: **galoshes.**

- [Mime pulling on boots] Beginning with both *A hands* in front of the left side of the waist, palms facing each other, bring the hands sharply back and upward toward the body by twisting the wrists. Repeat in front of the right side of the waist.

**boring**[1] *adj.* Related forms: **bore** *v.*, **bored** *adj.* Same sign used for: **dull.**

- [Boring a hole on the side of the nose] With the tip of the extended right index finger touching the side of the nose, palm facing down, twist the hand forward.

**boring**[2] *adj.* See sign for DRY.

**born** *adj.* See sign for BIRTH.

**borrow** *v.* Same sign used for: **lend me.**

- [Bring borrowed thing toward oneself; opposite of movement for **lend**] With the little-finger side of the right *V hand* across the index-finger side of the left *V hand,* bring the hands back, ending with the right index finger against the chest.

**bosom** *n.* See sign for BREAST.

**boss** *n.* See signs for CAPTAIN, CHIEF[1].

**both** *adj., pron.* Same sign used for: **pair.**

- [Two things pulled together to form a pair] Bring the right *2 hand,* palm facing in, downward in front of the chest through the left *C hand,* palm facing in and fingers pointing right, closing the left hand around the right fingers as they pass through and pulling the right fingers together.

**bother** *v.* See sign for ANNOY.

**bottle** *n.* Same sign used for: **glass.**

- [Shape of a bottle] Beginning with the little-finger side of the right *C hand,* palm facing left, on the upturned left *open hand,* raise the right hand.

## bottom

**bottom** *n.* See sign for BELOW[1].

**bounce** *v.* Same sign used for: **dribble.**
- [Mime bouncing a ball] Move the right *open hand,* palm facing down, up and down in front of the right side of the body with a repeated movement.

**bound** *v.* See sign for BIND.

**boundary** *n.*
- [Demonstrates the boundary of something] Beginning with the little-finger side of the right *B hand,* palm facing left and fingers pointing forward, on the index-finger side of the left *B hand,* palm facing right and fingers pointing forward, tip the right hand from side to side with a double movement.

**bow**[1] *v.* Same sign used for: **bend, nod.**
- [Represents bowing one's head] Beginning with the forearm of the right *S hand,* palm facing forward, against the thumb side of the left *B hand,* palm facing down and fingers pointing right, bend the right arm downward while bending the body forward.

**bow**[2] *n.* Same sign used for: **ribbon.**
- [The shape of a hair bow] With both *S hands* crossed on the right side of the head, palms facing in, flip the *H fingers* of both hands outward with a deliberate movement.

**bow**[3] *v.* See sign for HAIL[2].

**bowl** *n.* Same sign used for: **pot.**
- [The shape of a bowl] Beginning with the little fingers of both *C hands* touching, palms facing up, bring the hands apart and upward, ending with the palms facing each other.

**bowling** *n.* Related form: **bowl** *v.*

- [Mime throwing a bowling ball] Swing the right *bent 3 hand,* palm facing forward and fingers pointing down, from near the right hip forward and upward in an arc.

**box** *n.* See also sign for ROOM. Same sign used for: **package, present.**

- [Shape of a box] Beginning with both *open hands* in front of each side of the chest, palms facing each other and fingers pointing forward, move the hands deliberately in opposite directions, ending with the left hand near the chest and the right hand several inches forward of the left hand, both palms facing in. (This sign may also be formed with the hands beginning in the final position and then changing to the first position.)

**boy** *n.* Same sign used for: **male.**

- [Grasping the visor of a baseball cap] Beginning with the index-finger side of the right *flattened C hand* near the right side of the forehead, palm facing left, close the fingers to the thumb with a repeated movement.

**boycott** *v.* See sign for COMPLAIN.

**bracelet** *n.*

- [The location of a bracelet] With the right thumb and middle finger encircling the left wrist, twist the right hand forward with a double movement.

**bracket** *n.* See sign for CLASS.

**brag** *v.* Same sign used for: **boast, show off.**

- [Natural gesture while bragging] Tap the thumbs of both *10 hands,* palms facing down, against each side of the waist with a double movement.

**braid** *n., v.*

- [Represents hair being braided] Beginning with both *X hands* near the left side of the head, palms facing each other, twist the wrists with a repeated alternating movement while moving the hands downward.

# brain

**brain** *n*. See sign for MIND.

**brake** *n*., *v*.
- [Shows action of stepping on the brake] Push the right *A hand* downward in front of the right side of the body, palm facing forward, with a double movement.

**brand** *n*. See signs for LABEL, STAMP².

**brandy** *n*. See sign for WHISKEY.

**brat** *n*. See sign for CONCEITED.

**brave** *adj*. Same sign used for: **bold, courage.**
- [Hands seem to take strength from the body] Beginning with the fingertips of both *5 hands* on each shoulder, palms facing in and fingers pointing back, bring the hands deliberately forward while closing into *S hands*.

**bread** *n*.
- [Slicing a loaf of bread] Move the fingertips of the right *bent hand* downward on the back of the left *open hand* with a repeated movement, both palms facing in.

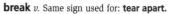

**break** *v*. Same sign used for: **tear apart.**
- [Mime breaking something] Beginning with both *S hands* in front of the body, index fingers touching and palms facing down, move the hands away from each other while twisting the wrists with a deliberate movement, ending with the palms facing each other.

**break down** *v*. Same sign used for: **collapse, destruction, fall through, tear down.**
- [Indicates things crumbing down] Beginning with the fingertips of both *curved 5 hands* touching in front of the chest, palms facing each other, allow the fingers to loosely drop, ending with the palms facing down.

### breakfast *n.*

■ **[eat + morning]** Bring the fingertips of the right *flattened O hand* to the lips. Then, with the left *open hand* in the crook of the bent right arm, bring the right *open hand* upward, palm facing in.

### breast *n.* Same sign used for: **bosom, bust.**

■ [Location of breasts] Touch the fingertips of the right *bent hand* first on the right side of the chest and then on the left side of the chest.

### breath *n.* Related form: **breathe** *v.* Same sign used for: **expel, inhale, pant, respiration.**

■ [Indicates the movement of the lungs when breathing] With the right *5 hand* in front of the chest above the left *5 hand,* fingers pointing in opposite directions and palms in, move both hands forward and back toward the chest with a double movement.

### breed *v.* See signs for CONFLICT¹, PREGNANT¹.

### breeze *n.*

■ [Shows movement of the wind] Beginning with both *4 hands* in front of the body, palms in and fingers pointing toward each other, swing the hands forward then back with a double movement by bending the wrists.

### bride *n.* Same sign used for: **bridesmaid.**

■ [Mime walking with a bride's bouquet] With the little-finger side of the right *S hand* on the thumb-side of the left *S hand,* move the hands forward a short distance and then forward again.

### bridesmaid *n.* See sign for BRIDE.

### bridge *n.*

■ [Shows the structure of supports for a bridge] Touch the fingertips of the right *V hand,* palm facing left, first to the bottom of the wrist and then near the elbow of the left arm held in front of the chest, palm facing down.

# brief

**brief** *adj.* See also sign for SHORT[1]. Same sign used for: **abbreviate, condense, reduce, squeeze, summarize.**

- [Squeeze information together as if to condense] Beginning with both *5 hands* in front of the chest, right hand above the left hand and fingers pointing in opposite directions, bring the hands toward each other while squeezing the fingers together, ending with the little-finger side of the right *S hand* on top of the thumb side of the left *S hand*.

**bright** *adj.* Same sign used for: **clarify, clear, light, radiant.**

- [Hands spread to reveal brightness] Beginning with the fingertips of both *flattened O hands* touching in front of the chest, palms facing each other, move the hands quickly upward in arcs to above each shoulder while opening to *5 hands.*

**brilliant** *adj.* See sign for SMART.

**bring** *v.* Same sign used for: **carry, deliver, return, transport.**

- [Moving an object from one location to another] Move both *open hands,* palms facing up, from in front of the left side of the body in large arcs to the right side of the body. (This sign may be formed in the direction of the referent or its proposed new location.)

**broad** *adj.* See signs for GENERAL[1], WIDE.

**broad-minded** *adj.* Same sign used for: **liberal, open-minded, tolerant.**

- [The mind is open wide] Beginning with both *open hands* near each other in front of the forehead, palms angled toward each other, move the hands forward and outward away from each other.

**broadcast** *v., n.* See sign for ADVERTISE.

**brochure** *n.* See sign for MAGAZINE.

**broke** *adj. Informal.* See sign for PENNILESS.

**broom** *n.* Same sign used for: **sweep.**

- [Mime sweeping] Beginning with both *S hands* in front of the right side of the body, right hand above the left hand and palms facing in, move the hands to the right with a double swinging movement.

### brother *n.*

■ [The male area of the head plus a sign similar to **same**[1] indicating a boy in the same family] Beginning with the thumb of the right *L hand* touching the right side of the forehead, palm facing left, move the right hand downward, landing across the thumb side of the left *L hand*, palm facing right.

**brotherhood** *n.* See sign for ASSOCIATE.

### brother-in-law *n.*

■ [**brother + law**] Beginning with the thumb of the right *L hand* touching the right side of the forehead, palm facing left, move the right hand downward, placing the palm side of the right *L hand* first on the fingers and then on the heel of the palm of the left *open hand*, palm facing up and fingers pointing forward.

### brown *adj.*

■ [Initialized sign] Slide the index-finger side of the right *B hand*, palm facing left, down the right cheek.

**browse** *v.* See sign for LOOK OVER.

### brush[1] *n., v.*

■ [Mime brushing one's hair] Move the palm of the right *A hand* down the right side of the head with a repeated movement.

**brush**[2] *n.* See sign for PAINT.

### bubble *n.*

■ [Shows action of bubbles] Wiggle the fingers of both *curved 5 hands*, palms facing down, while moving them upward a short distance.

### bucket *n.* Same sign used for: **pail, pot.**

■ [Shape of a bucket + mime holding a bucket's handle] Beginning with both *C hands* in front of each side of the chest, palms facing each other, move them upward a short distance. Then move the right *S hand* upward a short distance in front of the right side of the body with a double movement.

# buckle

**buckle** *n., v.* Same sign used for: **seat belt.**

■ [Mime fastening a seat belt] Bring both *bent V hands* from in front of each side of the waist, palms facing each other, around to mesh the fingers together in front of the waist.

---

**budget**[1] *n., v.* Same sign used for: **exchange.**

■ [Shows moving money around] Beginning with both *flattened O hands* in front of each side of the body, palms facing each other, move the right hand in a circle back toward the body, over the left hand, and forward to return to its original position.

---

**budget**[2] *n.* See sign for TRADE.

---

**bug** *n.* Same sign used for: **insect.**

■ [Represents a bug's antennas] With the extended thumb of the right *3 hand* on the nose, palm facing left, bend the extended index and middle fingers with a repeated movement.

---

**build** *v.* Related form: **building** *n.* Same sign used for: **construct, construction.**

■ [Shows putting one thing upon another to build something] Beginning with the fingers of the right *bent hand* overlapping the fingers of the left *bent hand* in front of the chest, palms facing down, reverse the position of the hands with a repeated movement as the hands move upward.

---

**bulk** *n.* See sign for PILE[1].

---

**bulletin board** *n.* Same sign used for: **post, post a notice, poster.**

■ [Mime posting something on a wall] Push the thumbs of both *10 hands*, palms facing each other, forward with a short movement, first in front of each shoulder and then in front of each side of the body.

---

**bullheaded** *adj.* See sign for CONTRARY[1].

---

**bully** *n.* See sign for CONCEITED.

**bum** *n. Informal.* See sign for FARM. Shared idea of a country bumpkin.

**bump** *n.* See also sign for LUMP¹.

- [Shape of a bump on the head] Beginning with the fingertips of the right *curved 5 hand* on the right side of the head, palm facing in, move the hand upward a short distance.

**bumper-to-bumper** *adj.*

- [Demonstrates a vehicle very close behind another vehicle] Beginning with the right *open hand* near the base of the thumb of the left *open hand,* both palms facing down and fingers pointing forward, move the hands forward with a short double movement.

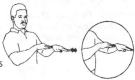

**bunch** *n.* See sign for CLASS.

**bunk beds** *n.*

- [**bed** + the location of one bunk bed above another] Rest the right cheek at an angle on the palm of the right *open hand.* Then place the left *H hand* above the right *H hand,* both palms facing down and fingers pointing forward.

**burden** *n.* Same sign used for: **bear, fault, liability, obligation, responsible, responsibility.**

- [The weight of responsibility on the shoulder] With the fingertips of both *bent hands* on the right shoulder, push the shoulder down slightly.

**burglary** *n.* See signs for ROB, SHOPLIFT, STEAL.

**burn¹** *v.*

- [Flames leaping up from a fire] Wiggle the fingers of both *curved 5 hands* with a repeated movement in front of each side of the body, palms facing up.

# burn

**burn²** *v.* See sign for FIRE¹.

**burning mad** *adj.* See sign for BOILING MAD.

**burp** *n., v.* See sign for BELCH.

**burst** *v.* See signs for BAWL OUT, BLOWUP.

**burst out** *v. phrase.* See sign for BAWL OUT.

**bury** *v.* Same sign used for: **grave.**
■ [Shape of a mound of dirt on a grave] Move both *curved hands,* palms facing down and fingers pointing down, back toward the body in double arcs.

**bus** *n.*
■ [Initialized sign] Beginning with the little-finger side of the right *B hand* touching the index-finger side of the left *B hand,* palms facing in opposite directions, move the right hand back toward the right shoulder.

**bust¹** *v.* See sign for BLOWUP.

**bust²** See sign for BREAST.

**bust³** *v.* See sign for MEAN¹.

**busy¹** *adj.*
■ [Initialized sign] Brush the base of the right *B hand,* palm facing forward, with a repeated rocking movement on the back of the left *open hand,* palm facing down.

**busy²** *adj.* (alternate sign) Same sign used for: **lots to do.**
■ [Fingerspelling **d-o** in a continuous pattern] With both *D hands* in front of the chest, palms facing up, pinch the index fingers and thumbs together repeatedly while moving the hands in repeated circles. [Note: the number of repetitions increases to reflect an increase in things to be done.]

**but** *conj.* Same sign used for: **however.**

- [Indicates opinions moving in opposite directions] Beginning with both extended index fingers crossed in front of the chest, palms facing forward, bring the hands apart with a deliberate movement.

**butt in** *v.* See sign for NOSY².

**butter** *n.* Same sign used for: **margarine.**

- [Mime spreading butter] Wipe the extended fingers of the right *U hand,* palm facing down and thumb extended, across the palm of the left *open hand* with a repeated movement, drawing the right fingers back into the palm each time.

**butterfly** *n.*

- [Symbolizes shape of butterfly's wings] With the thumb of the right *open hand* hooked around the thumb of the left *open hand,* both palms facing the chest, bend the fingers of both hands in and out with a repeated movement.

**button** *n.*

- [Shape and location of buttons] Touch the index-finger side of the right *F hand,* palm facing left, first in the center of the chest, and then lower on the chest.

**buy** *v.* Same sign used for: **purchase.**

- [Shows taking money from the hand to buy something] Beginning with the back of the right *flattened O hand,* palm facing up, in the upturned palm of left *open hand,* move the right hand forward in an arc.

**by** *prep.* See sign for PASS.

**by accident** *prep. phrase.* See sign for ACCIDENTALLY.

**bye** *interj.* See sign for GOOD-BYE.

### cab *n.* Same sign used for: **taxi.**
- [Represents the lighted dome on top of a taxi] Tap the fingertips of the right *C hand,* palm facing down, on the top of the head with a double movement.

### cabbage *n.*
- [The head represents a head of cabbage] Tap the heel of the right *curved hand* against the right side of the head with a repeated movement.

### cabinet *n.*
- [Demonstrates opening and closing of multiple cabinet doors] Beginning with the index-finger sides of both *B hands* together in front of the left side of the head, palms facing forward, bring the hands apart by twisting the wrists in opposite directions, ending with the palms facing back. Repeat in front of the right side of the head.

### cafeteria *n.* Alternate form: **café.**
- [Initialized sign similar to sign for **restaurant**] Touch the index-finger side of the right *C hand,* palm facing left, first on the right side of the chin and then on the left side.

### cage *n.*
- [Shape of a wire cage] Beginning with the fingertips of both *4 hands* touching in front of the chest, palms facing in, bring the hands away from each other in a circular movement back toward the chest, ending with the palms facing forward.

### cake *n.*

- [Represents a cake rising] Beginning with the fingertips of the right *curved 5 hand* on the palm of the left *open hand*, raise the right hand upward in front of the chest.

### calculator *n.*

- [Mime using a calculator] Alternately tap each fingertip of the right *5 hand* while moving up and down the upturned left *open hand* held in front of the body.

### calculus *n.* Related form: **calculate** *v.*

- [Initialized sign similar to sign for **arithmetic**] Beginning with both *C hands* in front of each side of the chest, palms facing each other, move the hands past each other with a repeated movement.

### calendar *n.*

- [Initialized sign indicating turning pages on a calendar] Move the little-finger side of the right *C hand*, palm facing left, from the heel upward in an arc over the fingertips of the left *open hand*, palm facing in and fingers pointing up.

### call[1] *v.* Same sign used for: **summon.**

- [Tap on the hand to get one's attention] Slap the fingers of the right *open hand* on the back of the left *open hand*, palm facing down, dragging the right fingers upward and closing them into an *A hand* in front of the right shoulder.

### call[2] or **call out** *v.* or *v. phrase.* Same sign used for: **cry, holler, yell.**

- [Natural gesture of cupping the mouth when yelling] Place the index-finger side of the right *C hand* against the right side of the chin.

## call

**call³** *v.* Same sign used for: **name.**

- [Similar to sign for **name**[1]] With the middle-finger side of the right *H hand* across the index-finger side of the left *H hand,* move the hands forward in an arc in front of the body.

**call⁴** *v.* See sign for TELEPHONE.

**calm** *adj., v.* See signs for QUIET, SETTLE, SILENT.

**calm down** *v. phrase.* See signs for QUIET, SETTLE, SILENT.

**camcorder** *n.* See sign for VIDEOTAPE².

**camera¹** *n.*

- [Mime taking a picture with a camera] Beginning with the *modified C hands* near the outside of each eye, palms facing each other, bend the right index finger up and down with a repeated movement.

**camera²** *n.* See sign for MOVIE CAMERA.

**camp** *n.* Same sign used for: **tent.**

- [Shape of a tent] Beginning with the extended index fingers and little fingers of both hands touching at an angle in front of the chest, bring the hands downward and apart with a repeated movement.
The same sign is used for the verb, as in *to camp on the beach for the weekend,* but the sign is made with a single movement.

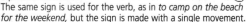

**camper** *n.*

- [Represents a camper on top of a truck] Tap the fingertips of the right *flattened C hand* on the back of the left *open hand,* palm facing down, with a double movement.

---

**can**[1] *auxiliary v.* Same sign used for **may.**

■ [Similar to sign for **able**[1]] Move both *S hands*, palms facing down, downward simultaneously with a short double movement in front of each side of the body.

---

**can**[2] *n.* See sign for CUP.

---

**cancel** *v.* Same sign used for: **condemn, correct, criticize.**

■ [Finger crosses out something to cancel it] With the extended right index finger, draw a large X across the upturned left *open hand.*

---

**candidate** *n.* See sign for APPLY[2].

---

**candle** *n.* Same sign used for: **flame, glow.**

■ [Represents the flame on a candle] With the extended right index finger touching the heel of the left *5 hand*, palm facing right, wiggle the left fingers.

---

**candy**[1] *n.* Same sign used for: **sugar.**

■ [Similar to sign for **sweet**] Bring the fingers of the right *U hand* downward on the chin with a repeated movement, bending the fingers down each time.

---

**candy**[2] *n.* (alternate sign)

■ [As if tasting candy] Twist the extended right index fingertip in the right cheek with a repeated movement.

---

**cannabis** *n.* See sign for MARIJUANA.

---

**can't** *contraction.* Alternate form: **cannot.**

- [One finger is unable to move the other finger] Bring the extended right index finger downward in front of the chest, striking the extended left index finger as it moves, both palms facing down.

---

**cantankerous** *adj.* See sign for CONTRARY[1].

---

**cap** *n.*

- [Mime tipping a cap with a visor] Bring the right modified *X hand* from in front of the head, palm facing left, back to the top of the head.

---

**capable** *adj.* See sign for SKILL.

---

**capital**[1] *adj., n.*

- [Shows size of capital letter] Hold the right *modified C hand,* palm facing forward, in front of the right side of the body.

---

**capital**[2] *n.*

- [Initialized sign] Tap the thumb of the right *C hand,* palm facing left, on the right shoulder with a double movement.

---

**captain** *n.* Same sign used for: **boss, chief, general, officer.**

- [Location of epaulets on captain's uniform] Tap the fingertips of the right *curved 5 hand* on the right shoulder with a repeated movement.

---

**capture** *v.* Same sign used for: **arrest, catch, claim, conquer, nab, occupy, possess, repossess, seize, takeover.**

- [Mime grabbing at something to capture it] Beginning with both *curved 5 hands* in front of each shoulder, palms facing forward, move the hands downward while closing into *S hands.*

---

**car** *n.* Same sign used for: **automobile.**

■ [Mime driving] Beginning with both *S hands* in front of the chest, palms facing in and the left hand higher than the right hand, move the hands in an up-and-down motion with a repeated alternating movement.

**card**[1] *n.* Same sign used for: **check, envelope.**

■ [Shows shape of a rectangular card] Beginning with the fingertips of both *L hands* touching in front of the chest, palms facing forward, bring the hands apart to in front of each shoulder, and then pinch each thumb and index finger together.

**card**[2] *n.* Same sign used for: **credit card.**

■ [Initialized sign showing shape of credit card] With the fingers of the right *C hand* curved around the left *open hand,* palm facing in and fingers pointing right, pull the right hand from the base of the left thumb to the fingertips with a double movement.

**cards** *n.* Same sign used for: **play cards.**

■ [Mime dealing cards] Beginning with both *A hands* in front of the body, palms facing each other, flick the right hand to the right with a repeated movement off the left thumb.

**care**[1] *n.* Same sign used for: **monitor, patrol, supervise, take care of.**

■ [Represents eyes watching out in different directions] With the little finger side of the right *K hand* across the index finger side of the left *K hand,* palms facing in opposite directions, move the hands in a repeated flat circle in front of the body.

**care**[2] *v.* See sign for TROUBLE[1].

**careful** *adj.* Same sign used for: **cautious.**

■ [Eyes looking attentively] Tap the little-finger side of the right *K hand* with a double movement across the index-finger side of the left *K hand,* palms facing in opposite directions.

**carefully** *adv.* Same sign used for: **cautiously.**

- [Eyes looking in all directions] With the little-finger side of the right *K hand* across the index finger side of the left *K hand,* palms facing in opposite directions, move the hands upward and forward in large double circles.

**careless** *adj.* Related form: **carelessly** *adv.* Same sign used for: **reckless.**

- [Misdirected eyes] Move the right *V hand* from near the right side of the head, palm facing left and fingers pointing up, down to the left in front of the eyes with a double movement.

**carry**[1] *v.* Alternate forms: **carry on** or **onto.**

- [Having something in one's hands to transfer to another place] Beginning with both *curved hands* in front of the right side of the body, move the hands in a series of simultaneous arcs to the left, ending in front of the left side of the body.

**carry**[2] *v.* See sign for BRING.

**cart** *n.*

- [Mime pushing a cart] Beginning with both *S hands* in front of the body, palms facing down, push the hands forward.

**carton** *n.*

- [Initialized sign showing shape of carton] Beginning with the fingertips of the index fingers and thumbs of both *C hands* touching in front of the chest, palms facing forward, bring the hands apart to in front of each side of the body.

**cartoon** *n.*

- [Initialized sign similar to sign for **funny**] Move the right *C hand,* palm facing left, downward with a double movement from in front of the nose.

**carve** *v.* Same sign used for: **engrave, sculpt.**

- [Mime action of carving] Flick the right thumb of the right *10 hand* upward off the heel of the upturned left *open hand*.

**cash register** *n.*

- [Mime action of using a cash register] Move the right *open hand*, palm facing down, from in front of the right shoulder downward with a repeated movement while wiggling the fingers.

**cast** *v.* See sign for THROW.

**casual** *adj.* See signs for DAILY, FARM.

**cat** *n.*

- [Cat's whiskers] Move the fingertips of both *F hands*, palms facing each other, from each side of the mouth outward with a repeated movement.

**catch[1]** *v.*

- [Mime catching ball] Beginning with both *5 hands* in front of the body, palms facing each other, bring the hands back toward the body while constricting the hands into *curved 5 hands*.

**catch[2]** *v.* (alternate sign) Same sign used for **arrest, convict, nab.**

- [Hand moves to "catch" the finger on the other hand] Move the right *C hand* from in front of the right shoulder, palm facing left, forward to meet the extended left index finger, palm facing right and finger pointing up, while changing into an *A hand*.

**catch[3]** *v.* Same sign used for: **prone.**

- [One's fingers receive something and bring it to oneself] With an alternating movement, move first the right *curved 5 hand* and then the left *curved 5 hand* from in front of the chest, palms facing down and fingers pointing forward, back to the chest while changing into *flattened O hands*.

# catch

**catch**[4] *v.* See sign for CAPTURE.

**catch up** *v. phrase.*
- [One hand catches up with the other hand] Bring the right *A hand* from near the right side of the chest, palm facing left, forward to the heel of the left *A hand,* palm facing right, held in front of the body.

**category** *n.* See sign for CLASS.

**catsup** *n.* See sign for KETCHUP.

**cattle** *n.* See sign for COW.

**cause** *v.*
- [Something moving out from the body to affect others] Beginning with both *S hands* near the body, palms facing up and left hand nearer the body than the right hand, move both hands forward in an arc while opening into *5 hands.*

**caught in the act** See sign for NAB[1].

**caution** *v.* See sign for WARN.

**cautious** *adj.* See sign for CAREFUL.

**cautiously** *adv.* See sign for CAREFULLY.

**cease** *v.* See sign for STOP[1].

**celebrate** *v.* Related form: **celebration** *n.* Same sign used for: **festival, gala, rejoice.**
- [Waving flags in celebration] With *modified X hands* in front of each shoulder, move both hands in large repeated outward movements, palms angled up.

**celery** *n.*
- [**green** + action of eating celery stalk] Beginning with the right *G hand* in front of the right shoulder, palm facing in, twist the hand back and forth with a double movement. Then move the right *G hand* from near the right side of the mouth, palm facing up, in toward the mouth while moving the mouth as if eating.

**cellar** *n*. See sign for BASEMENT.

**cemetery** *n*. Same sign used for: **graveyard**.

■ [Shape of mounds of dirt on graves] Move both *curved hands,* palms facing down and fingers pointing forward, with a double movement back toward the body in double arcs.

**cent** *n*. Same sign used for: **penny**.

■ [Symbolizes the head on a penny] With a double movement, move the extended right index finger forward at an outward angle from touching the right side of the forehead, palm facing down.

**center** *n*. Related form: **central** *adj*. See also sign for MIDDLE.

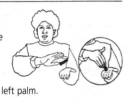

■ [Indicates location in center of something] Move the right *open hand,* palm facing down, in a circular movement over the upturned left *open hand,* bending the right fingers as the hand moves and ending with the fingertips of the right *bent hand* touching the middle of the left palm.

**cereal** *n*.

■ [Action of scooping cereal from bowl to mouth] Move the right curved hand, palm facing up, from the palm of the left *open hand,* palm facing up, upward to the mouth with a double movement.

**certain** *adj*. See signs for ABSOLUTE, SURE[1], TRUE.

**certainly** *adv*. See sign for TRUE.

**certificate** *n*. Related form: **certify** *v*.

■ [Initialized sign showing shape of certificate] Tap the thumbs of both *C hands* together in front of the chest with a repeated movement, palms facing each other.

**certify** *v*. See sign for ACCREDIT.

# chain

**chain** *n.* Same sign used for: **Olympics.**

■ [Shape of chain] Beginning with the index fingers and thumbs of both *F hands* intersecting in front of the left side of the chest, palms facing each other and the right hand above the left hand, release the fingers, flip the hands in reverse positions, and connect the fingers again with a repeated alternating movement as the hands move across the front of the body from left to right.

**chair** *n.* Same sign used for: **seat.**

■ [Fingers represent legs hanging down when sitting] With a double movement, tap the fingers of the right *curved U hand* across the fingers of the left *U hand,* both palms facing down.

**chalkboard** *n.* See sign for BOARD[1].

**chalk up** *v. phrase.* See sign for ACHIEVE.

**challenge** *v., n.* Same sign used for: **versus.**

■ [Hands seem to confront each other] Swing both *10 hands,* palms facing in, from in front of each side of the chest toward each other, ending with the knuckles touching in front of the chest, thumbs pointing up.

**champagne** *n.* See sign for COCKTAIL.

**champion** *n.* Same sign used for: **trophy.**

■ [Symbolizes placing crown on head of winner] With the fingers of the right *curved 3 hand,* tap the right palm on the extended left index finger pointing up in front of the chest.

**chance** *n.*

■ [Initialized sign formed like turning over dice] Beginning with both *C hands* in front of each side of the body, palms facing up, flip the hands over, ending with the palms facing down.

**change**[1] *v.* See also sign for TURN. Same sign used for: **adapt, adjust, alter, justify, modify, shift, switch.**

- [Hands seem to twist something as if to change it] With the palm sides of both *A hands* together, right hand above left, twist the wrists in opposite directions in order to reverse positions.

**change**[2] *n.* See sign for SHARE. Shared idea of dividing an amount of money to be shared.

**change places** See sign for TRADE PLACES.

**change the subject** Same sign used for: **change the topic.**

- [One hand moves away to another topic] Beginning with both *bent V* hands near each other in front of the chest, palms facing down, swing the right hand to the right.

**change the topic** See sign for CHANGE THE SUBJECT.

**chant** *n.* See sign for MUSIC.

**chaos** *n.* See sign for MESSY.

**chapped** *adj.* See sign for CRACK[1].

**chapel** *n.* See sign for CHURCH.

**chapter** *n.*

- [Initialized sign showing a column of text] Move the fingertips of the right *C hand* down the upturned left *open hand* with a repeated movement.

**character**[1] *n.* Related form: **characteristic** *n.*

- [Initialized sign similar to sign for **personality**] Move the right *C hand,* palm facing left, in a small circle and then back against the left side of the chest.

# character

**character**[2] *n.* (alternate sign for the character in a story, play, or film)

- [Initialized sign similar to sign for **role**] Move the right *C hand*, palm facing left, in a small circle against the left *open hand*, palm facing forward.

**charge**[1] *v.* Same sign used for: **credit card.**

- [Represents getting impression of credit card charge] Rub the little-finger side of the right *S hand*, palm facing in, back and forth on the upturned left *open hand*.

**charge**[2] *v.* See signs for APPLY[1], COST[1].

**charity**[1] *n.* Same sign used for: **contribute, contribution, donate, donation.**

- [**gift** formed repeatedly to indicate frequent contributions] With the right *X hand* closer to the chest than the left *X hand,* move each hand, palms facing each other, forward from the chest with a double alternating movement.

**charity**[2] *n.* See sign for GIFT.

**chart** *n.* See sign for SCHEDULE[1].

**chase** *v.* Same sign used for: **pursue.**

- [One hand seems to pursue the other hand] Move the right *A hand,* palm facing left, in a spiraling movement from in front of the chest forward, to behind the left *A hand* held somewhat forward of the body.

**chat**[1] *v.* Same sign used for: **talk.**

- [Exchanging dialogue between two people] Move both *5 hands,* palms angled up, from in front of each shoulder downward at an angle toward each other with a repeated movement.

**chat**² *v.* See sign for BLAB.

**chatter** *v.* See signs for BLAB, JABBER.

**cheap** *adj.*
- [Pushing down the cost] Brush the index-finger side of the right *B hand* downward on the palm of the left *open hand,* bending the right wrist as it moves down.

**cheat** *v.* Same sign used for: **betray, deceive, fraud.**
- [Splitting the truth] Slide the right *3 hand* between the index and middle fingers, palm facing in, onto the index-finger side of the left *B hand,* palm facing down, with a double movement.

**check**¹ *v.* Same sign used for: **examine, inspect.**
- [Bringing one's attention to something to inspect it] Move the extended right index finger from the nose down to strike sharply off the upturned palm of the left *open hand,* and then upward again.

**check**² *n.* See sign for CARD¹.

**checkers** *n.*
- [Action of moving a checker on a checkerboard] Move the fingers of the right *curved 3 hand,* palm facing down, in a small arc to the right and then to the left, in front of the right side of the body.

**check for** *v. phrase.* See sign for LOOK FOR.

**cheek** *n.*
- [Location of cheek] Touch the fingertips of the right *flattened C hand* against the right cheek.

# cheer

**cheer** *n.* See sign for HAPPY.

**cheerful** *adj.* See signs for FRIENDLY, HAPPY.

**cheese** *n.*
- [Pressing cheese in a cheese press] With the heel of the right *open hand* pressed on the heel of the upturned left *open hand,* palms facing each other and perpendicular to each other, twist the right hand forward and back slightly with a repeated movement.

**cherish** *v.* See sign for PRECIOUS.

**cherry** *n.*
- [The stem of a cherry] Move the fingertips of the right *F hand,* palm facing left, from near the mouth forward and downward with a wavy movement.

**chest** *n.*
- [Location of chest] Rub the fingertips of both *open hands,* palms facing in and fingers pointing toward each other, up and down on the chest with a repeated movement.

**chew** *v.* Same sign used for: **grind.**
- [Represents grinding motion of teeth when chewing] With the palm sides of both *A hands* together, right hand on top of the left hand, move the hands in small repeated circles in opposite directions, causing the knuckles of the two hands to rub together.

**chewing gum** *n.* Same sign used for: **gum.**
- [Action of jaw when chewing gum] With the fingertips of the right *V hand* against the right side of the chin, palm facing down, move the hand toward the face with a double movement by bending the fingers.

**chewing tobacco** *n.* See sign for TOBACCO.

**chicken**[1] *n.* Same sign used for: **hen.**

- [Represents a chicken's comb] Tap the thumb of the right *3 hand,* palm facing left and fingers pointing up, against the chin with a repeated movement.

**chicken**[2] *n.* See sign for BIRD.

**chief**[1] *n., adj.* Same sign used for: **boss, officer, prominent, superior.**

- [Shows higher location] Move the right *10 hand* upward from in front of the right side of the chest, palm facing in and thumb pointing up.

**chief**[2] *n.* See sign for CAPTAIN.

**child** *n.*

- [Patting child on the head] Pat the right *bent hand* downward with a short repeated movement in front of the right side of the body, palm facing down.

**children** *pl. n.*

- [Patting a number of children on their heads] Pat the right *open hand,* palm facing down, in front of the right side of the body and then to the right with a double arc.

**chilly** *adj.* See sign for COLD[2].

**chimpananzee** *n.* See sign for MONKEY.

**chip in** *v. phrase.* Same sign used for: **pool.**

- [Similar to sign for **spend** but directed toward a common pool of shared funds] Beginning with both *flattened O hands* in front of each side of the body, palms facing up and fingers pointing toward each other, bring the hands toward each other while sliding the fingers so that they close into *A hands.*

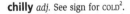

# chocolate

**chocolate** *n., adj.*
- [Initialized sign] Move the thumb side of the right *C hand,* palm facing forward, in a repeated circle on the back of the left *open hand* held in front of the chest, palm facing down.

**choice** *n.* See sign for EITHER[1].

**choir** *n.* See sign for BAND.

**choose**[1] *v.* Related form: **choice** *n.* See also sign for SELECT. Same sign used for: **assign, draw, pick.**
- [Hand picks from alternatives] Beginning with the bent thumb and index finger of the right *5 hand* touching the index finger of the left *5 hand,* palms facing each other, pull the right hand back toward the right shoulder while pinching the thumb and index finger together.

**choose**[2] *v.* See sign for APPOINT[1].

**chop**[1] *v.*
- [Mime chopping food] Sharply hit the little-finger side of the right *open hand,* palm facing left, on the upturned left *open hand* with a triple movement.

**chop**[2] *v.* See sign for HARVEST.

**Christmas** *n.*
- [Initialized sign showing the shape of a wreath] Move the right *C hand,* palm facing forward, in a large arc from in front of the left shoulder to in front of the right shoulder.

**church** *n.* Same sign used for: **chapel.**
- [Initialized sign similar to sign for **rock**[1]] Tap the thumb of the right *C hand,* palm facing forward, on the back of the left *S hand,* palm facing down.

### cigarette *n.*

■ [Tapping a cigarette to settle the tobacco] Tap the extended index finger and little finger of the right hand with a double movement on the extended left index finger, both palms facing down.

### circle[1] *n.* Same sign used for: **cycle, round.**

■ [Shape of circle] Draw a circle in the air in front of the right side of the chest with the extended right index finger, palm facing down and finger pointing forward.

### circle[2] *n.*

■ [Represents a number of people sitting in a circular pattern] Beginning with both *4 hands* in front of the chest, palms facing forward, bring the hands away from each other in outward arcs while turning the palms in, ending with the little fingers together.

### circulate *v.* Related form: **circulation** *n.* Same sign used for: **blend, merge, mix, random.**

■ [Movement of circulating similar to sign for **mix**] Beginning with the right *5 hand* hanging down in front of the chest, palm facing in and fingers pointing down, and the left *5 hand* below the right hand, palm facing up and fingers pointing up, move the hands in circles around each other.

### circumcise *v.* Related form: **circumcision** *n.*

■ [**operate** around a thumb representing a penis] Move the thumb of the right *10 hand* in a circle around the thumb of the left *10 hand*, both palms facing down.

### circumstance *n.* See sign for CONDITION.

### city *n.* Same sign used for: **community.**

■ [Multiple housetops] With the palms of both *bent hands* facing in opposite directions and the fingertips touching, separate the fingertips, twist the wrists, and touch the fingertips again with a double movement.

# claim

## claim[1] *v.*

- [**my** + pointing to possession] Pat the palm of the right *open hand* on the chest with a double movement while pointing the extended index finger of the left hand downward.

## claim[2] *v.* See sign for CAPTURE.

## clap *v.* See sign for APPLAUD.

## clarify *v.* See sign for BRIGHT.

## class *n.* Same sign used for: **bracket, bunch, category, group, mass, section, series.**

- [Initialized sign showing an identifiable group] Beginning with both *C hands* in front of the chest, palms facing each other, bring the hands away from each other in outward arcs while turning the palms in, ending with the little fingers near each other.

## classical *adj.* See sign for FANCY.

## classified *adj.* See sign for SECRET.

## clean *v.* Alternate form: **clean up.**

- [Wiping dirt off something to clean it] Slide the palm of the right *open hand* from the heel to the fingers of the upturned palm of the left *open hand* with a repeated movement. For the adjective, the same sign is used, but made with a double movement.

## cleaners *n.* Same sign used for: **dry cleaners.**

- [Action of a presser] Bring the palm of the right *open hand,* palm facing down and fingers pointing left, with a double movement down on the palm of the left *open hand,* palm facing up and fingers pointing right.

## clear *adj.* See sign for BRIGHT.

## clever *adj.* See sign for SMART.

**client** *n.* Same sign used for: **customer.**

- [Initialized sign similar to sign for **person**] Move both *C hands*, palms facing each other, downward on each side of the chest.

**climb** *v.* Same sign used for: **ascend, ladder.**

- [Mime climbing a ladder] Beginning with both *curved 5 hands* in front of the chest, palms facing forward and right hand higher than the left, move the hands upward one at a time with an alternating movement.

**cling to** *v. phrase.* See sign for DEPEND.

**clippers** *pl. n.* See sign for SCISSORS.

**clock** *n.*

- [time$^2$ + round shape of a clock's face] Tap the curved right index finger on the back of the left wrist. Then hold both *modified C hands* in front of each side of the face, palms facing each other.

**close**$^1$ *adv.* Same sign used for: **approach, near.**

- [Moves one hand close to the other] Beginning with the right *bent hand* somewhat forward of the chest and the left *bent hand* near the chest, palms facing in and fingers pointing in opposite directions, move the right palm to the back of the left hand, pushing the left hand toward the chest.

**close**$^2$ *adv.* (alternate sign) Same sign used for: **approach, near.**

- [Moves one hand close to the other] Bring the back of the right *bent hand* from the chest forward toward the left *bent hand*, both palms facing in and fingers pointing in opposite directions.

# close call

**close call** Alternate form: **close shave.** Same sign used for: **almost, barely.**

- [As if removing sweat from the brow] Beginning with the fingertips of the right *F hand* against the right side of the forehead, palm facing left, bring the hand forward a short distance.

**closet**[1] *n.*

- [**clothes + door**] Brush the thumbs of both *5 hands* downward on each side of the chest with a double movement. Then, beginning with the index-finger side of both *B hands* touching in front of the chest, palms facing forward and fingers pointing up, swing the right hand back toward the right shoulder with a double movement by twisting the wrist.

**closet**[2] *n.* (alternate sign) Same sign used for **locker.**

- [Represents hangers] Beginning with the fingers of both *H hands* crossed in front of the left shoulder, twist the wrists to alternate positions.

**close to** *adj.* See sign for APPROACH[1].

**close up** *adv.*

- [Location of something close up to the face] Move the right *open hand,* palm facing in and fingers pointing up, back toward the face.

**clothes** *pl. n.* Same sign used for: **costume, dress, suit.**

- [Location of clothes on body] Brush the thumbs of both *5 hands* downward on each side of the chest with a double movement.

**cloud** *n.*

- [Shape and location of clouds] Beginning with both *C hands* near the left side of the head, palms facing each other, bring the hands away from each other in outward arcs while turning the palms in, ending with the little fingers close together. Repeat the movement near the right side of the head.

**clown** *n.*

- [Shape of clown's big nose] Put the fingertips of the right *curved 5 hand* on the nose.

**clumsy**[1] *adj.* Same sign used for: **inexperienced.**

- [Similar to sign for **unskilled** but moving in the opposite direction] While holding the thumb of the right *5 hand* tightly in the left *S hand*, twist the right hand forward and down.

**clumsy**[2] *adj.* See signs for AWKWARD, UNSKILLED.

**coach** *n.*

- [Initialized sign similar to sign for **captain**] Tap the thumb of the right *C hand*, palm facing left, against the right shoulder with a double movement.

**coarse** *adj.* See sign for ROUGH.

**coat** *n.* Same sign used for: **jacket.**

- [A coat's lapels] Bring the thumbs of both *A hands* from near each shoulder, palms facing in, downward and toward each other, ending near the waist.

**cocktail** *n.* Same sign used for: **champagne, drink.**

- [Mime drinking from a small glass] Beginning with the thumb of the right *modified C hand* near the mouth, palm facing left, tip the index finger back toward the face.

## coffee *n.*

- [Grind coffee beans] Move the little-finger side of the right *S hand* with a circular movement on the index-finger side of the left *S hand,* palms facing in opposite directions.

**cogitate** *v.* See sign for MULL.

## coin *n.*

- [Shape of coin held in the hand] Move the extended right index finger, palm facing in and finger pointing down, in a double circular movement on the left *open hand,* palm facing up.

**coincidence** *n.* See sign for HAPPEN.

## Coke *n.* Trademark. Alternate form: **Coca-Cola** (*trademark*).

- [Mime injecting a drug] With the index finger of the right *L hand,* palm facing in, touching the upper left arm, move the right thumb up and down with a double movement.

## cold[1] *n.*

- [Mime blowing one's nose] Grasp the nose with the thumb and index finger of the right *A hand,* palm facing in, and pull the hand forward off the nose with a double movement.

## cold[2] *adj.* Same sign used for: **chilly, frigid, shiver, winter.**

- [Natural gesture when shivering from cold] Shake both *S hands* with a slight movement in front of each side of the chest, palms facing each other.

**collapse** *n.* See sign for BREAK DOWN.

**collar** *n.*

- [Shape and location of a collar] Move the fingertips of the right *G hand*, palm facing in, from the right side of the neck around to the front.

**collate** *v.*

- [Shows filing things in order] Beginning with the palms of both *open hands* together in front of the chest, fingers pointing forward, move the right hand in a series of double arcs to the right.

**collect** *v.* Related form: **collection** *n.* Same sign used for: **accumulate, gather.**

- [Pulling money to oneself] With a double movement, bring the little-finger side of the right *curved hand*, palm facing left, across the palm of the left *open hand*, palm facing up, from its fingertips to the heel while changing into an *S hand*.

**college** *n.*

- [Similar to sign for **school** but moves upward to a higher level] Beginning with the palm of the right *open hand* across the palm of the left *open hand* in front of the chest, move the right hand upward in an arc, ending in front of the upper chest, palm angled forward and fingers angled upward toward the left.

**collide** *v.* See sign for ACCIDENT[1]. Related form: **collision** *n.*

**color**[1] *n.*

- [The fingers represent the colors of the rainbow] Wiggle the fingers of the right *5 hand* in front of the mouth, fingers pointing up and palm facing in.

# color

**color²** *v., n.* Same sign used for: **crayon.**

- [Action of coloring with a crayon] Rub the extended right little finger, palm facing down, back and forth on the upturned left *open hand* with a repeated movement.

**column¹** *n.*

- [Shape of a column] Move the right *C hand* from in front of the right side of the chest, palm facing forward, downward a short distance, ending with the palm facing left.

**column²** *n.* See sign for PILLAR.

**comb** *n.*

- [Mime combing hair] Drag the fingertips of the right *curved 5 hand* through the hair on the right side of the head with a short double movement.
  The verb is the same sign as the noun, but made with a longer double movement.

**combat** *n.* Same sign used for: **fight.**

- [Represents two people hitting each other] Beginning with both *S hands* in front of each shoulder, palms facing each other, move the hands toward each other with a double movement by bending the wrists.

**combination** *n.*

- [**1-2-3** + mime twisting a combination on a lock] With the heel of the right hand on the left *open hand*, palm facing right, form a 1-2-3 with the right hand. Then move the right *curved 5 hand*, palm facing left, with a double movement by twisting the wrist forward near the palm of the left *open hand*, palm facing right and fingers pointing forward.

**combine**[1] *v.* Same sign used for: **blend.**

- [**match**[1] + **mix**[1]] Beginning with both *curved 5 hands* in front of each side of the chest, palms facing in, bring the hands together, ending with the fingers meshed together in front of the chest. Then, with the right *curved 5 hand* over the left *curved 5 hand,* palms facing each other, move the hands simultaneously in repeated circles around each other.

**combine**[2] *v.* See signs for BELONG[1], MATCH[1], MESH.

**come** *v.*

- [Indicates direction for another to come toward oneself] Beginning with both extended index fingers pointing up in front of the body, palms facing in, bring the fingers back to each side of the chest.

**come back** *v. phrase.* See sign for REFUND.

**come on**[1] or **come in** *v. phrase.*

- [Natural gesture beckoning someone] Move the right *open hand,* palm angled up, back toward the right shoulder.

**come on**[2] *v. phrase.* See sign for BECKON.

**come up** *v. phrase.* See sign for SHOW UP.

**comfortable** *adj.* Same sign used for: **convenient, cozy.**

- [Stroking as a gesture of comfort] Wipe the palm of the right *curved hand* down the back of the left *curved hand,* and then repeat with the palm of the left *curved hand* on the back of the right *curved hand,* both palms facing down.

**comical** *adj.* See sign for HUMOROUS.

**comma** *n.* See sign for APOSTROPHE.

# command

**command** *n., v.* See sign for ORDER.

**comment** *v.* See sign for SAY.

**commercial** *n.* See sign for ADVERTISE.

**commit** *v.* See signs for DO, PROMISE, VOW.

**committee** *n.*

■ [Initialized sign similar to sign for **member**] Touch the fingertips of the right *curved 5 hand* first to the left side of the chest and then to the right side of the chest, palm facing in.

**common sense** *n.*

■ [Initials **c-s** formed near the brain for "common sense"] Beginning with the right *C hand* in front of the right side of the forehead, palm facing left, move the right hand forward while changing into an *S hand*.

**common** *n., adj.* See sign for STANDARD.

**communication** *n.* Related form: **communicate** *v.* Same sign used for: **conversation, converse.**

■ [Initialized sign indicating words moving both to and from a person] Move both *C hands*, palms facing each other, forward and back from the chin with an alternating movement.

**community** *n.* See signs for CITY, TOWN.

**commute** *v.* Same sign used for: **back and forth.**

■ [Demonstrates movement to and from] Move the right *10 hand*, palm facing left, from in front of the right side of the body to in front of the left side of the body with a double movement.

**companion** *n.* See sign for STEADY[1].

**compare** *v.* Related form: **comparison** *n.*

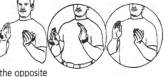

- [Holding something in one hand and comparing it with something in the other hand] With both *curv_d hands* in front of each side of the chest, palms facing, alternately turn one hand and then the other toward the face while turning the other hand in the opposite direction, keeping the palms facing each other and the fingers pointing up.

---

**compatible**[1] *adj.* Related form: **compatibility.**

- [Bringing something to combine with something else] Beginning with both *curved 5 hands* in front of each side of the chest, palms facing in, move the right hand to the left to mesh the fingers with the bent fingers of the left hand.

---

**compatible**[2] *adj.* See sign for AGREE[1].

---

**complain** *v.* Same sign used for: **boycott, gripe, grumble, object, protest, riot, strike.**

- [Natural gesture used when complaining] Tap the fingertips of the right *curved 5 hand* against the center of the chest.

---

**complaint** *n.* See sign for PROTEST[1].

---

**complete** *v., adj.* See signs for END[1], FINISH[1], FULL[2].

---

**complex**[1] *adj.* Same sign used for: **complicated.**

- [Thoughts moving through the brain in opposite directions] Beginning with both extended index fingers point toward each other in front of each side of the face, both palms facing down, continuously bend the fingers up and down as the hands move past each other in front of the face.

---

**complex**[2] *adj.* See sign for MIX[1].

---

**compliment** *v., n.* See sign for PRAISE.

---

**comprehend** *v.* See sign for UNDERSTAND.

# compromise

### compromise[1] *n.*

- [Initialized sign indicating two minds coming into agreement] Beginning with both *C hands* near each side of the head, palms facing each other, turn the hands downward, ending with the palms facing down and fingers pointing forward.

### compromise[2] *n.* See sign for AGREE[1].

### computer *n.*

- [Initialized sign] Move the thumb side of the right *C hand,* palm facing left, from touching the lower part of extended left arm upward to touch the upper arm.

### comrade *n.* See sign for FRIEND.

### con *v.,n.* See signs for BETRAY[1], TRICK.

### conceal *v.* See sign for HIDE.

### conceited *adj.* Same sign used for: **arrogant, big-headed, big shot, brat, bully.**

- [**big** formed near the head, signifying a person with a "big head"] Beginning with both *L hands* in front of each side of the forehead, index fingers pointing toward each other and palms facing in, bring the hands outward away from each other a short distance.

### conceive *v.* See sign for PREGNANT[1].

### concentrate *v.* See sign for ATTENTION. Related form: **concentration** *n.*

### concept *n.* Same sign used for: **creative.**

- [Initialized sign similar to sign for **invent**] Move the right *C hand,* palm facing left, from the right side of the forehead forward and slightly upward in a double arc.

**concern**[1] *v.* Same sign used for: **consider, think.**

- [Thoughts moving through the brain] Beginning with both extended index fingers in front of each side of the forehead, palms facing in and fingers angled up, move the fingers in repeated alternating circular movements toward each other in front of the face.

**concern**[2] *v.* Same sign used for: **anxiety.**

- [The finger used to show feeling repeatedly touches the heart] Beginning with the bent middle fingers of both *5 hands* pointing to each side of the chest, left hand closer to the chest than the right hand and palms facing in, bring the hands forward and back to the chest with a repeated alternating movement.

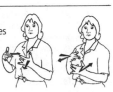

**concern**[3] *n.* See sign for TROUBLE[1].

**concerning** *prep.* See sign for ABOUT[1].

**concise** *adj.* See sign for PRECISE.

**conclude** *v.* See sign for END[1].

**condemn** *v.* See signs for CANCEL, CURSE.

**condense** *v.* See sign for BRIEF.

**condition** *n.* Same sign used for: **circumstance, culture.**

- [Initialized sign showing area around a thing] Beginning with the right *C hand,* palm facing left, near the extended left index finger, palm facing right, move the right hand in a circle forward and around the left finger.

**conduct** *v.* See signs for DO, LEAD.

**conference**[1] *n.*

- [gather[1] + meeting] Beginning with both *5 hands* in front of each side of the chest, palms facing each other, bring the hands together in front of the chest, fingers pointing down. Then, beginning with both *5 hands* in front of each shoulder, palms facing each other and fingers pointing up, close the fingers into *flattened O hands* while moving the hands together with a double movement.

**conference**[2] *n.* See sign for MEETING.

---

**confess** *v.* See sign for ADMIT[1]. Related form: **confession** *n.*

---

**confident** *adj.* Related form: **confidence** *n.*
Same sign used for: **bold, trust.**

- [Holding firmly to one's beliefs] Beginning with both *curved 5 hands* in front of the chest, right hand above the left and palms facing in, bring both hands downward a short distance with a deliberate movement while closing into *S hands.*

---

**confidential** *adj.* See sign for SECRET.

---

**confined** *adj.* See sign for STUCK.

---

**conflict**[1] *n., v.* Same sign used for: **breed, cross-purposes, fertilize.**

- [Represents a crossing of opinions] Beginning with both extended index fingers in front of each side of the body, palms facing in and fingers angled toward each other, move the hands toward each other, ending with the fingers crossed.

---

**conflict**[2] *v., n.* See sign for STRUGGLE.

---

**confuse**[1] *v.* Related form: **confusion** *n.* Same sign used for: **mixed up.**

- [**think** + **mix**[1]] Bring the extended right index finger from touching the right side of the forehead, palm facing in, down to in front of the chest, changing into a *curved 5 hand.* Then, with the right *curved 5 hand* over the left *curved 5 hand,* palms facing each other, move the hands simultaneously in repeated circles going in opposite directions.

---

**confuse**[2] *v.* See sign for MIX[1].

---

**congratulate** *v.* Related form: **congratulations** *pl. n., interj.*

- [Mime clasping hands to congratulate another] Clasp both *curved hands* together in front of the body and shake them with a repeated movement.

---

**Congress** *n.*

- [Initialized sign similar to sign for **committee**] Touch the thumb of the right *C hand,* palm facing left, first on the left side of the chest and then on the right side.

---

**connect** *v.* See sign for BELONG[1].

---

**connection** *n.* See sign for RELATIONSHIP.

---

**conquer** *v.* See signs for CAPTURE, DEFEAT.

---

**consider** *v.* See signs for CONCERN[1], WONDER.

---

**consistent** *adj.* Related form: **consistently** *adv.*
Same sign used for: **faithful, regular.**

- [Similar to sign for **right**[2] formed with a continuous movement] With the little-finger side of the right *1 hand* across the index-finger side of the left *1 hand,* palms facing in opposite directions, move the hands downward in front of the chest.

---

**constant**[1] *adj.* Same sign used for: **continuous, momentum.**

- [Similar to sign for **alike**[2] but formed with two hands] Beginning with both *Y hands* in front of each side of the chest, palms facing down, move the hands in simultaneous circles, moving inward in opposite directions.

---

**constant**[2] *adj.* Same sign used for: **even, steady.**

- [Indicates a steady movement] Beginning with the right *open hand* in front of the right shoulder, palm facing down and fingers pointing forward, move the hand straight forward in a slow movement.

---

**constant**[3] *adj.* Same sign used for: **continual, persistent, steadfast, steady.**

- [Indicates continuing movement] Beginning with the thumb of the right *10 hand* on the thumbnail of the left *10 hand,* both palms facing down in front of the chest, move the hands downward and forward in a series of small arcs.

# construct

**construct** *v.* See sign for BUILD. Related form: **construction** *n.*

**consult** *v.* See sign for COUNSEL. Related form: **consultation** *n.*

**consume** *v.* Related form: **consumption** *n.*
Same sign used for: **devour, eat up, gullible.**

- [Represents food entering the mouth to be consumed]
Move the right *bent hand,* palm facing in, past the
right cheek with a deliberate movement.

**contact** *n., v.* Same sign used for: **in touch with.**

- [Indicates two things coming into contact with
each other] With the right hand above the left
hand in front of the chest, touch the bent
middle finger of the right *5 hand* to the
bent middle finger of the left *5 hand*
with a double movement, palms
facing each other.

**contact lens** *n.*

- [Action of putting in contact lenses] Bring the
bent middle finger of the right *5 hand,* palm
facing in, first toward the right eye, and then
toward the left eye.

**contained in** See sign for INCLUDE.

**contemplate** *v.* See sign for WONDER.

**contempt** *n.* Same sign used for: **look
down at** or **on, scorn.**

- [Represents eyes looking down on
another] Beginning with both
*V hands* in front of each side
of the chest, palms facing
forward and fingers pointing
up, twist the wrists downward
to point the fingers forward with
a slow movement.

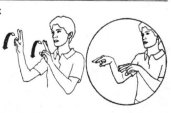

conversion

**content** *adj.* See signs for RELIEF, SATISFY. Related form: **contentment.** *n.*

**continual** *adj.* See sign for CONSTANT.

**continue**[1] *v.* Same sign used for: **last, remain.**
■ [Indicates continuous movement] Beginning with the thumb of the right *10 hand* on the thumbnail of the left *10 hand,* both palms facing down in front of the chest, move the hands downward and forward in an arc.

**continue**[2] *v.* See sign for GO ON.

**continuous** *adj.* See sign for CONSTANT[1].

**contrary**[1] *adj.* Same sign used for:
**antagonistic, bullheaded, cantankerous.**
■ [Two opposing things meeting head-on] Bump the heels of both *Y hands* sharply against each other and then apart in front of the chest.

**contrary**[2] *adj.* See sign for OPPOSITE.

**contrast** *v.* See signs for DISAGREE, OPPOSITE.

**contribute** *v.* See signs for CHARITY[1], GIFT, GIVE. Related form: **contribution** *n.*

**control**[1] *v.* Same sign used for: **restrain, suppress, tolerate.**
■ [The hands seem to suppress one's feelings] Beginning with the fingertips of both *curved 5 hands* against the chest, palms facing in, bring the hands downward while forming *S hands,* palms facing up.

**control**[2] *v.* See sign for MANAGE.

**controversy** *n.* See sign for STRUGGLE.

**convenient** *adj.* See signs for COMFORTABLE, EASY.

**convention** *n.* See sign for MEETING.

**converse** *v.* See sign for COMMUNICATION. Related form: **conversation** *n.*

**conversion** *n.* See sign for UPDATE.

# convertible

**convertible** *n.*

- [Represents lowering and raising a convertible top] Beginning with both X hands in front of each shoulder, palms facing each other, bring the hands upward and backward, and then forward again, in a simultaneous double arc.

---

**convey** *v.* See sign for NARROW DOWN.

---

**convict** *v.* See sign for CATCH[2].

---

**convince**[1] *v.*

- [The hands come from both sides to influence someone] Beginning with both *open hands* in front of each shoulder, palms angled upward, bring the hands down sharply at an angle toward each other.

---

**convince**[2] *v.* (alternate sign, used especially when referring to convincing one other person.)

- [One hand hits the other hand to influence it] Move the little-finger side of the right *open hand*, palm facing up, sharply against the extended left index finger held up in front of the chest.

---

**convince**[3] *v.* (alternate sign, used especially when referring to being convinced by the influence of another or others.)

- [Strike the sides of the neck to convince someone] Hit the little-finger sides of both *open hands*, palms facing down and fingers pointing back, against each side of the neck with a sharp movement.

---

**convocation** *n.* See sign for MEETING.

---

**cook** *v.* Same sign used for: **bake, flip, fry, turn over.**

- [As if turning food in a frying pan] Beginning with the fingers of the right *open hand,* palm facing down, across the palm of the left *open hand,* flip the right hand over, ending with the back of the right hand on the left palm.

---

**cookie** *n.* Same sign used for: **biscuit.**

- [Mime using a cookie cutter] Touch the fingertips of the right *C hand,* palm facing down, on the upturned palm of the left *open hand.* Then twist the right hand and touch the left palm again.

**cool** *adj.* Same sign used for: **pleasant, refresh.**

- [As if fanning oneself] With both open hands above each shoulder, palms facing back and fingers pointing up, bend the fingers up and down with a repeated movement.

**cooperation** *n.* Related form: **cooperate** *v.* Same sign used for: **affiliation, union, unity, universal.**

- [One thing is linked to another] With the thumbs and index fingers of both *F hands* intersecting, move the hands in a flat circle in front of the chest.

**coordinate** *v.* Same sign used for: **relate.**

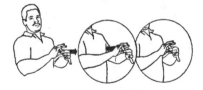

- With the thumbs and index fingers of both *F hands* intersecting, move the hands forward and back with a double movement.

**cop** *n.* See sign for POLICE.

**copy**[1] *v.* Same sign used for: **duplicate, imitate, impose.**

- [Represents taking information and recording it on paper] Move the right *curved hand* in front of the chest, palm facing forward, down to touch the palm of the left *open hand* while closing the right fingers and thumb into a *flattened O hand.* The noun is formed in the same way except with a double movement.

# copy

**copy²** *v., n.* Same sign used for: **duplicate, imitate, impose, photocopy.**

■ [Represents the action of a photocopy machine] Move the fingers of the right *curved hand,* palm facing up, downward from touching the palm of the left *open hand* while closing the right fingers and thumb into a *flattened O hand.*

**copy³** *n.* See sign for EXCERPT.

**cord** *n.* Same sign used for: **thread, wire.**

■ [Shape of a coiled cord] Beginning with both extended little fingers pointing toward each other in front of the chest, palms facing in, move the fingers in circular movements while moving the hands away from each other.

**corn** *n.*

■ [Mime eating corn on the cob] With both *flattened C hands* held near each side of the face, palms facing each other, twist both hands forward simultaneously with a repeated movement.

**corner¹** *n.*

■ [Hands form the shape of a corner] Move the fingertips of both *open hands,* palms angled toward each other, to touch each other at an angle with a repeated movement.

**corner²** *v.* See sign for NAB¹.

**correct** *v.* See signs for CANCEL, EDIT¹, RIGHT³.

**correspond** *v.* Related form: **correspondence** *n.*

■ [Represents the sending and receiving of letters] Beginning with *modified X hands,* palms facing each other and the right hand closer to the chest than the left, flick the index fingers toward each other with a repeated alternating movement.

**corridor** *n.* See sign for HALL.

**cosmetics** *pl. n.* See sign for MAKE-UP[1].

**cost**[1] *n., v.* Same sign used for: **charge, fare, fee, fine, price, tax.**

- [Making a dent in one's finances] Strike the knuckle of the right *X hand*, palm facing in, down the palm of the left *open hand*, palm facing right and fingers pointing forward.

**cost**[2] *n.* (alternate sign) Same sign used for: **price, value, worth.**

- [The price tag on an item] Tap the fingertips of both *F hands* together, palms facing each other, with a repeated movement.

**costly** *adj.* See sign for EXPENSIVE.

**costume** *n.* See sign for CLOTHES.

**couch** *n.* Same sign used for: **pew, sofa.**

- [**sit** + **loaf** to indicate the elongated shape of a couch] Place the fingers of the right *curved U hand* across the fingers of the left *U hand*, both palms facing down. Then, beginning with the index-finger sides of both *C hands* touching, palms facing down, bring the hands apart to each side of the body.

**cough** *v., n.*

- [Location of the origin of a cough in the chest] With the fingertips of the right *curved 5 hand* on the chest, palm facing in, lower the wrist with a repeated movement while keeping the fingertips in place.

**council** *n.* See sign for MEETING.

**counsel** *v.* Same sign used for: **advise, affect, consult, consultation.**

- [Represents the spreading of one's counsel to others] Beginning with the fingertips of the right *flattened O hand* on the back of the left *flattened O hand*, palm facing down, move the right hand forward with a double movement while spreading the fingers into a *5 hand* each time.

# count

## count v.

- [Counting beads on an abacus] Move the fingertips of the right *F hand*, palm facing down, across the upturned palm of the left *open hand* from the heel to the fingers.

**counter** *adj.* See sign for OPPOSITE.

**counterfeit** *n.* See sign for FAKE².

## country¹ *n.*

- [Similar to sign for **country²** but formed with a *Y hand*] Rub the bent fingers of the right *Y hand*, palm facing in, in a circle near the elbow of the bent left arm with a repeated movement.

## country² *n.* (alternate sign)

- [The tattered elbows of a farm worker] Rub the palm of the right *open hand* in a circle near the elbow of the bent left arm with a repeated movement.

## couple *n.* Same sign used for: **pair.**

- [Pointing to two people making up a couple] Move the right *V fingers,* palm facing up and fingers pointing forward, from side to side in front of the right side of the body with a repeated movement.

**courage** *n.* See sign for BRAVE.

## course *n.* Same sign used for: **lesson.**

- [Initialized sign similar to sign for **list**] Move the little-finger side of the right *C hand*, palm facing in, in an arc, touching first on the fingers and then near the heel of the upturned left hand.

**court** *n.* See sign for JUDGE.

**courteous** *adj.* See sign for POLITE. Related form: **courtesy** *n.*

**cousin** *n.*

- [Male cousin: Initialized sign formed near the male area of the head] Move the right *C hand,* palm facing left, with a shaking movement near the right side of the forehead.
- [Female cousin: Initialized sign near the female area of the head] Move the right *C hand,* palm facing left, with a shaking movement near the right side of the chin.

male      female

**cover**[1] *n., v.*

- [Demonstrates pulling a cover over something] Move the right *open hand,* palm facing down, from in front of the right side of the body in a large circular movement over the bent left arm held across the body.

**cover**[2] *n.* See signs for LID.

**cover-up** *n., v. phrase.* **cover up**

- [Hands seem to try to blur the truth] Beginning with the left *5 hand* in front of the chest, palm facing in, and the right *5 hand* by the right side of the body, palm facing forward, bring the right hand in an arc past the left hand, ending with the wrists crossed.

**covetous** *adj.* See sign for GREEDY.

**cow** *n.* Same sign used for: **cattle.**

- [A cow's horns] With the thumbs of both *Y hands* on both sides of the forehead, palms facing forward, twist the hands forward.

**coward** *n.* See signs for BIRD, FEAR.

**cozy** *adj.* See sign for COMFORTABLE.

**crack**[1] *n.* Same sign used for: **chapped, split.**

- [Shape of a crack] Move the little-finger side of the right *open hand,* palm facing left, down the palm of the left *open hand,* palm facing up, with a jagged movement.

# crack

**crack**[2] *n.* See sign for RAGGED. Related form: **cracked** *adj.*

**cracker** *n.*

- [The old-world custom of breaking a cracker with the elbow] Strike the palm side of the right *A hand* near the elbow of the bent left arm with a repeated movement.

**cramp** *n., v.* Related form: **cramps** *pl. n.*

- [A gesture indicating a cramp] Beginning with both *A hands* in front of each side of the body, right palm facing down and left palm facing up, twist the hands in opposite directions.

**cramped** *adj.* See sign for CROWDED[1].

**crash**[1] *n., v.*

- [Shows impact of a crash] Beginning with the right *5 hand* near the right side of the chest, palm facing down and fingers angled forward, move the hand deliberately to hit against the palm of the left *open hand,* bending the right fingers as it hits.

**crash**[2] *n.* See sign for ACCIDENT[1].

**crave** *v.* See signs for DROOL, HUNGRY.

**crawl** *v.*

- [Represents movement of crawling] Beginning with the back of the right *bent V hand,* palm facing up, on the inside of the bent left forearm, move the right hand down the forearm toward the left hand while crooking the finger of the *bent V hand* with a repeated movement.

**crayon** *n.* See sign for COLOR[2].

**crazy** *adj.* Same sign used for: **wacky** (*slang*).

■ [Indicates that things are confused in one's head] Twist the *curved 5 hand,* palm facing in, forward with a repeated movement near the right side of the head.

**cream** *n.*

■ [Initialized sign representing skimming cream from the top of milk] Bring the little-finger side of the right *C hand,* palm facing left, back toward the chest in a circular movement across the palm of the left *open hand.*

**create** *v.* See signs for INVENT, MAKE.

**creative** *adj.* See sign for CONCEPT.

**credit card** *n.* See signs for CARD², CHARGE¹.

**cross¹** *n.*

■ [Shape of a cross] Bring the right *C hand,* palm facing forward, first downward in front of the right side of the body and then from left to right.

**cross²** *adj.* See also sign for ANGER.
Same sign used for: **angry, mad.**

■ [Hand seems to pull the face down into a scowl] With the palm of the right *5 hand* in front of the face, fingers pointing up, bring the hand slightly forward while constricting the fingers into a *curved 5 hand.*

**cross³** *prep., adv.* See sign for ACROSS.

**crossing** *n.* See sign for INTERSECTION.

**cross-purposes** *n.* See sign for CONFLICT¹.

**crowd** *n.* See signs for AUDIENCE, HORDE.

# crowded

**crowded**[1] *adj.* Same sign used for: **cramped, crushed.**

■ [The hands are crushed tightly together] Beginning with the palms of both *A hands* together in front of the chest, twist the hands in opposite directions.

**crowded**[2] *adj.* See sign for JAM[1].

**cruel** *adj.* See signs for MEAN[1], MEANNESS, ROUGH.

**cruise** *n.* See signs for BOAT, SHIP.

**crushed** *adj.* See sign for CROWDED[1].

**cry**[1] *v.* Same sign used for: **weep.**

■ [Tears flowing down the cheeks] Bring both extended index fingers, palms facing in and fingers pointing up, downward from each eye with an alternating movement.

**cry**[2] *v.* See signs for CALL[2], SCREAM.

**culture** *n.* See sign for CONDITION.

**cube** *n.* See sign for BLOCK[1].

**cup** *n.* Same sign used for: **can.**

■ [Shape of a cup] Bring the little-finger side of the right *C hand,* palm facing left, down to the upturned left *open hand* with a double movement.

**cure** *n., v.* See sign for WELL[1].

**curious** *adj.* Related form: **curiosity** *n.*

■ [Pulling the neck forward out of curiosity] With the fingertips of the right *F hand* against the neck, palm facing left, twist the hand downward with a double movement.

**curly** *adj.*

- [Shape of curly hair] Move both *curved 5 hands,* palms facing in, in alternating circles near each ear.

**current** *adj.* See sign for NOW.

**curse** *n., v.* Same sign used for: **condemn, swear.**

- [Threatening words are directed toward God] Beginning with the right *curved 5 hand* near the mouth, palm facing in, bring the hand upward with a deliberate movement while closing into an *S hand.*

**curtain** *n.*

- [Shape of curtains hanging on a window] Beginning with both *4 hands* in front of the face, palms facing forward, bring the hands downward in an arc to about shoulder width and then straight down, ending with the palms facing down.

**curve**[1] *n.*

- [Shape of a curve] Move the right *B hand* from in front of the right shoulder, palm facing left, downward in an arc, ending with the palm facing up and the fingers pointing forward.

**curve**[2] *n.* See sign for ARCH.

**customer** *n.* See sign for CLIENT.

**cut**[1] *v.* Same sign used for: **haircut.**

- [Mime cutting hair] Move both *V hands,* palms facing down, back over each shoulder while opening and closing the fingers of the *V hands* repeatedly as the hands move.

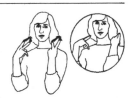

# cut

### cut[2] *v.*

- [Represents cutting across a piece of paper] Move the right *V hand*, fingers pointing left, across the fingertips of the left *open hand*, palm facing down, with a deliberate movement while closing the *V fingers* together.

### cut[3] *v.* Same sign used for: **cut out.**

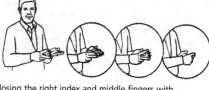

- [Represents cutting around a clipping] Move the right *V hand*, palm facing left, around the fingertips of the left *open hand*, palm facing up, while opening and closing the right index and middle fingers with a repeated movement as the hand moves.

**cut down** *v. phrase.* See sign for HARVEST.

### cute *adj.*

- [Similar to the sign for **sweet** but formed with a *U hand*] With the right thumb extended, brush the fingers of the right *U hand*, palm facing down, downward on the chin while changing into a *10 hand*.

**cut off** *v. phrase.* See sign for INTERCEPT.

**cut out** *v. phrase.* See sign for CUT[3].

**cutthroat** *adj.* See sign for RISK[1].

**cycle** *n.* See signs for CIRCLE[1], YEAR-AROUND.

**dad** *n.* See sign for FATHER. Related form: **daddy** *n.*

**daily** *adj., adv.* Same sign used for: **casual, domestic, everyday, every day, ordinary, routine, usual.**

- [Similar to sign for tomorrow, only repeated to indicated recurrence] Move the palm side of the right *A hand* forward on the right side of the chin with a repeated movement.

**damage** *n., v.* Same sign used for: **abolish, demolish, destroy, ruin.**

- [Hands seem to take something and pull it apart] Beginning with both *curved 5 hands* in front of the chest, right hand over the left, right palm facing down and left palm facing up, bring the right hand in a circular movement over the left. Then close both hands into *A hands* and bring the knuckles of the right hand forward past the left knuckles with a deliberate movement.

**damp** *adj.* See sign for WET.

**dance** *v., n.* Same sign used for: **disco, gala.**

- [Represents legs moving in rhythm to dance music] Swing the fingers of the right *V hand,* palm facing in and fingers pointing down, back and forth over the upturned left *open hand* with a double movement.

**danger** *n.* Related form: **dangerous** *adj.* Same sign used for: **endanger, harassment, harm, hazard, risk, threat.**

- [Represents hidden danger coming at a person] Move the thumb of the right *10 hand,* palm facing left, upward on the back of the left *A hand,* palm facing in, with a repeated movement.

# dare

**dare** *v.* See sign for GANG.

**dark** *adj.* Related form: **darkness** *n.* Same sign used for:
**dim, dusk.**

- [Hands shade the eyes from light] Beginning with both *open hands* in front of each shoulder, palms facing back and fingers pointing up, bring the hands past each other in front of the face, ending with the wrists crossed and the fingers pointing in opposite directions at an angle.

**darken** *v.* See sign for DIM[1].

**darn** *adj., adv., interj.* Same sign used for: **drat.**

- Forcibly insert the thumb of the right *5 hand,* palm facing forward, into the opening of the left *5 hand* held in front of the chest.

**daughter** *n.*

- [Begins at the female area of the head + **baby**] Beginning with the index-finger side of the right *B hand,* palm facing left, touching the right side of the chin, swing the right hand downward, with the bent right arm cradled in the bent left arm held across the body.

**dawn** *n.* See sign for SUNRISE.

**day** *n.*

- [Symbolizes the movement of the sun across the sky] Beginning with the bent right elbow resting on the back of the left hand held across the body, palm facing down, bring the extended right index finger from pointing up in front of the right shoulder, palm facing left, downward toward the left elbow.

**daydream** *v., n.* See sign for DREAM.

**dead** *adj.* See sign for DIE.

**deadline** *n.*

- [**die** + **line**] Beginning with both *open hands* in front of the body, right palm facing down and left palm facing up, flip the hands to the right, turning the right palm up and the left palm down. Then, beginning with both extended little fingers pointing toward each other in front of the chest, palms facing in, move the hands away from each other.

**deaf** *adj.*

- [Points to the ear and mouth to indicate that a person cannot hear or talk] Touch the extended right index finger first to near the right ear and then to near the right side of the mouth.

---

**deal** *v.* See signs for PASS AROUND, PASS OUT[1].

---

**death** *n.* See sign for DIE.

---

**debate** *v., n.*

- [**discuss** formed while moving toward another person] Tap the side of the right extended index finger, palm facing in and finger pointing left, across the upturned left *open hand,* first on the palm and then again on the fingers as the left hand moves forward slightly.

---

**debt** *n.* See sign for AFFORD.

---

**decal** *n.* See sign for LABEL.

---

**decay** *v.* See sign for WEAR OUT.

---

**deceive**[1] *n.* Related forms: **deceit** *v.,* **deceitful** *adj.*
Same sign used for: **defraud, fraud.**

- [An underhanded movement] Slide the palm side of the right *Y hand,* palm facing down, from the wrist forward on the back of the left *Y hand,* palm facing down.

---

**deceive**[2] *v.* See signs for BETRAY[1], CHEAT.

---

**decide** *v.* Related form: **decision** *n.* Same sign used for: **determine, make up your mind, officially.**

- [**think**[1] + laying one's thoughts down decisively] Move the extended right index finger from the right side of the forehead, palm facing left, down in front of the chest while changing into an *F hand,* ending with both *F hands* in front of the body, palms facing each other.

---

**declare** *v.* See sign for ANNOUNCE. Related form: **declaration** *n.*

# decline

**decline**¹ *v., n.* Same sign used for: **deteriorate**.

- [Hands move downward in location] Beginning with both *10 hands* in front of each shoulder, palms facing in and thumbs pointing up, move both hands down in front of each side of the chest.

**decline**² *v., n.* (alternate sign) Same sign used for: **deteriorate**.

- [Shows a movement downward] Touch the little-finger side of the right *open hand*, palm facing in, first near the shoulder, then near the elbow, and finally near the wrist of the extended left arm.

**decline**³ *v.* Same sign used for: **drop, refuse, turn down**.

- [**true** + **excuse**¹] Move the extended right index finger from pointing up in front of the mouth, palm facing left, downward while opening the hand, ending with the fingers of the right *open hand* wiping forward across the length of the upturned left *open hand*.

**decorate** *v.* Related form: **decoration** *n.*

- [Hands seem to arrange ornamental items] Beginning with both *flattened O hands* in front of each side of the chest, palms facing forward, move them in alternating circles with a repeated movement.

**decrease**¹ *n., v.* Same sign used for: **lessen, lose, reduce, reduction**.

- [Taking some off to decrease it] Beginning with the fingers of the right *U hand* across the fingers of the left *U hand*, both palms facing down, take the right fingers off by flipping the right hand over.

**decrease**² *n., v.* (alternate sign, used especially to indicate a total reduction or depletion) Same sign used for: **deflate, reduce, shrink**.

- [Shows amount decreasing in size] Beginning with the thumb of the right *C hand*, palm angled forward, on the back of the left *curved hand*, palm facing down, close the right fingers to the thumb, forming a *flattened O hand*.

**decrease**[3] *n., v.* (alternate sign) Same sign used for: **lessen, reduce.**

■ [Shows decreasing size] Beginning with both extended index fingers pointing forward in front of the chest, right hand over the left hand and palms facing each other, bring the hands toward each other.

---

**deduct** *v.* See sign for SUBTRACT.

---

**deed** *n.* See signs for ACT[1], ACTIVE, DO.

---

**deep** *adj.* Same sign used for: **depth, detail.**

■ [Indicates direction of bottom of something deep] Move the extended right index finger, palm facing down, downward near the fingertips of the left *5 hand,* palm facing down.

---

**deer** *n.* Same sign used for: **reindeer.**

■ [A deer's antlers] Tap the thumbs of both *5 hands,* palms facing forward, against each side of the forehead with a repeated movement.

---

**defeat** *v.* See also sign for BEAT[4]. Same sign used for: **conquer, overcome, subdue, vanquish.**

■ [Represents forcing another down in defeat] Move the right *S hand* from in front of the right shoulder, palm facing forward, downward and forward, ending with the right wrist across the wrist of the left *S hand,* both palms facing down.

---

**defend** *v.* Related forms: **defense** *n.,* **defensive** *adj.* Same sign used for: **protect, security, shield.**

■ [Blocking oneself from harm] With the wrists of both *S hands* crossed in front of the chest, palms facing in opposite directions, move the hands forward with a short double movement.

---

**defensive** *adj.* See sign for RESIST.

---

# defer

**defer**[1] *v.* Same sign used for **delay, procrastinate, put off.**

- [Represents taking something and putting it off several times] Beginning with both *F hands* in front of the body, palms facing each other and the left hand nearer to the body than the right hand, move both hands forward in a series of small arcs.

**defer**[2] *v.* See sign for POSTPONE.

**define** *v.* See sign for DESCRIBE. Related form: **definition** *n.*

**deflate** *v.* See sign for DECREASE[2].

**defraud** *v.* See sign for DECEIVE[1].

**degree** *n.* See sign for DIPLOMA.

**delay** *n., v.* See signs for DEFER, LATE, POSTPONE.

**delegate** *n., v.*

- [Initialized sign] Brush the fingers of the right *D hand,* palm facing in and index finger pointing up, downward on the right side of the chest with a double movement.

**delete** *v.* See sign for ELIMINATE[1].

**deliberate** *v.* See sign for MULL.

**delicious** *adj.* Same sign used for: **tasty.**

- [Something is tasted appreciatively] Touch the bent middle finger of the right *5 hand* to the lips, palm facing in, and then twist the right hand quickly forward.

**delighted** *adj.* See sign for HAPPY.

**deliver** *v.* See sign for BRING.

**deluxe** *adj.* See sign for FANCY.

**demand** *v.* Same sign used for: **insist, require.**

- [Something is dragged in on a hook] With the extended right index finger, palm facing in, touching the palm of the left *open hand* bring both hands back toward the chest.

**Democrat** *n.*

- [Initialized sign] Shake the right *D hand,* palm facing forward, from side to side in front of the right shoulder.

**demolish** *v.* See sign for DAMAGE.

**demon** *n.* See sign for DEVIL.

**demonstrate** *v.* See sign for SHOW[1]. Related form: **demonstration** *n.*

**demote** *v.* See sign for LOW.

**dent** *v., n.* Same sign used for: **bend, bent.**

- [Bending of a surface] Beginning with the fingertips of both *open hands* touching in front of the chest, palms facing in, bend the fingers in toward the chest while keeping fingertips together.

**dentist** *n.*

- [Initialized sign formed similar to **tooth**] Tap the fingers of the right *D hand,* palm facing in and index finger pointing up, against the right side of the teeth with a repeated movement.

**dentures** *pl. n.* See sign for FALSE TEETH.

**deny**[1] *v.*

- [**not**[1] with a repeated movement] Beginning with the thumb of the right *A hand* under the chin, palm facing left, and the left *A hand* held somewhat forward, palm facing right, move the right hand forward while moving the left hand back. Repeat the movement with the left hand.

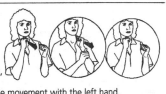

# deny

**deny**[2] *v.* (alternate sign)

- [Hand seems to hold oneself back or suppress oneself] Beginning with the fingertips of the right *C hand* on the upper chest, palm facing in, bring the hand straight down while quickly closing into an *S hand*.

**deodorant** *n.*

- [Mime spraying on deodorant] With the left arm raised above the head, bend the extended right index finger up and down with a double movement near the left armpit.

**depart** *v.* See signs for FORSAKE[1], GO[1], LEAVE[1], PARTING. Related form: **departure** *n.*

**department** *n.* Same sign used for: **division.**

- [Initialized sign similar to sign for **class**] Beginning with the fingertips of both *D hands* touching in front of the chest, palms facing each other, bring the hands away from each other in outward arcs while turning the palms in, ending with the little fingers together.

**depend** or **depend on** *v.* Related forms: **dependency** *n.*, **dependent** *adj.* Same sign used for: **cling to, rely.**

- [Represents resting on another] With the extended right index finger across the extended left index finger, palms facing down, move both fingers down slightly with a double movement.

**deplete** *v.* See sign for RUN OUT OF.

**deposit**[1] *v., n.*

- [Sealing a deposit envelope with the thumbs] Beginning with the thumbs of both *10 hands* touching in front of the chest, both palms facing down, bring the hands downward and apart by twisting the wrists.

**deposit**[2] *n., v.* See sign for INVEST.

**depressed** *adj.* Related forms: **depressing** *adj.*, **depression** *n.*
Same sign used for: **despair, discouraged.**

■ [Feelings moving downward in the body] Beginning with
the bent middle fingers of both *5 hands* on each side of
the chest, palms facing in and fingers pointing toward
each other, move the hands downward with a
simultaneous movement.

**depth** *n.* See sign for DEEP.

**descend** *v.*

■ [Movement of someone or something to a lower place]
Move the extended right index finger, palm facing
down, downward with a wavy movement from
near the right side of the head to in front
of the body.

**describe** *v.* Related form: **description** *n.*
Same sign used for: **define, definition,
direct, direction, explain, explanation,
instruct, instruction.**

■ [Bringing something before one's eyes
to describe it] Beginning with the
fingers of both *F hands* in front of the
chest, palms facing each other and index fingers pointing
forward, move the hands forward and back with an alternating movement.

**desert** *v.* See sign for LEAVE¹.

**deserve** *v.* See sign for EARN.

**design** *v.* Same sign used for: **draw, drawing, draft.**

■ [Initialized sign similar to sign for **art**] Move the
fingertips of the right *D hand*, palm facing left,
down the palm of the left *open hand* with a
wavy movement.

**desire** *v.* See signs for WANT, WISH.

**desist** *v.* Same sign used for: **stop.**

■ [Natural gesture used when asking another to stop doing
something] Beginning with the fingers of both *5 hands*
in front of each side of the chest, palms facing in, twist
the wrists to flip the hands in a quick movement, ending
with the palms facing down.

# desk

**desk** *n.* Same sign used for: **table.**

■ [**table**[1] + shape of a desk] Pat the forearm of the bent right arm with a double movement on the bent left arm held across the chest. Then, beginning with the fingers of both *open hands* together in front of the chest, palms facing down, move the hands apart to in front of each shoulder and then straight down, ending with the palms facing each other.

---

**despair** *n., v.* See sign for DEPRESSED.

---

**desperate** *adj.*

■ [**must** + **have**] Move the bent index finger of the right *X hand,* palm facing forward, downward with a deliberate movement in front of the right side of the body while bending the wrist down. Then bring the fingertips of both *bent hands,* palms facing in, back to touch each side of the chest.

---

**despise** *v.* See signs for DETEST[1], HATE.

---

**despite** *prep.* See sign for ANYWAY.

---

**dessert** *n.*

■ [Initialized sign] Tap the fingertips of both *D hands,* palms facing each other, together with a repeated movement in front of the chest.

---

**destroy** *v.* See sign for DAMAGE.

---

**destruction** *n.* See sign for BREAK DOWN.

---

**detach** *v.* See sign for DISCONNECT.

---

**detail** *n.* See sign for DEEP. Shared idea of careful attention to important matters.

---

**detective** *n.* Same sign used for: **private eye** (*informal*).

■ [Initialized sign similar to sign for **police**] Move the right *D hand,* palm facing left, in a circular movement on the left side of the chest.

---

**deteriorate** *v.* See signs for DECLINE[1,2].

---

**determine** *v.* See sign for DECIDE.

---

**detest**[1] *v.* Same sign used for: **despise, loathe.**

- [Similar to sign for **vomit**] Beginning with the right *5 hand* near the chin, palm facing left, and the left *5 hand* somewhat forward, palm facing right, move both hands forward with a deliberate movement.

---

**detest**[2] *v.* See sign for HATE.

---

**detour** *n., v.*

- [Shows changing the course of movement] Beginning with the right *B hand* in front of the right shoulder, palm facing in and fingers pointing left, move the fingers toward the extended left index finger, palm facing right, and then twist the wrist to bring the right hand back outward to the right, ending with the palm facing forward.

---

**develop** *v.*

- [Initialized sign moving upward to represent growth or development] Move the fingertips of the right *D hand,* palm facing left, upward from the heel to the fingers of the left *open hand,* fingers pointing up and palm facing right.

---

**devil** *n.* Related form: **devilish** *adj.* Same sign used for: **demon, mischief, mischievous, rascal, Satan.**

- [Represents a devil's horns] With thumbs of both *3 hands* on each side of the forehead, palms facing forward, bend the index and middle fingers of both hands downward with a double movement.

---

**devour** *v.* See sign for CONSUME.

---

**dew** *n.* See sign for WET.

---

**diagnose** *v.* See sign for ANALYZE. Related form: **diagnosis** *n.*

# diamond

**diamond** *n.*

- [Initialized sign showing location of a diamond ring] Tap the right *D hand*, palm facing down, with a double movement on the base of the ring finger of the left *5 hand*, palm facing down.

**dice** *n.* See sign for GAMBLE[1].

**dictionary**[1] *n.*

- [Initialized sign formed similar to **page**] Move the fingertips of the right *D hand*, palm facing down, upward with a double movement on the heel of the upturned left *open hand*.

**dictionary**[2] *n.* See sign for PAGE.

**didn't mean that** See sign for SHUT UP[2].

**didn't say that** See sign for SHUT UP[2].

**die** *v.* Same sign used for: **dead, death, perish.**

- [Represents a body turning over in death] Beginning with both *open hands* in front of the body, right palm facing down and left palm facing up, flip the hands to the right, turning the right palm up and the left palm down.

**diet** *n.* Same sign used for: **lean, shrink, slim, thin.**

- [Shows slimmer body] Beginning with both *L hands* in front of each side of the chest, palms facing in, swing the hands downward by twisting the wrists, ending with the hands in front of each side of the waist, both palms facing down.

**different** *adj.* Related form: **difference** *n.*

- [Moving things apart that are not the same] Beginning with both extended index fingers crossed in front of the chest, palms facing forward, bring the hands apart from each other with a deliberate movement.

124

**difficult** *adj.* Same sign used for: **hard, problem, trouble.**

- [The bent fingers impede each other, making movement difficult] Beginning with both *bent V hands* in front of the chest, right hand higher than the left hand, palms facing in, move the right hand down and the left hand upward with an alternating movement, brushing the knuckles of each hand as the hands move in the opposite direction.

**dig**[1] *v.* Same sign used for: **shovel.**

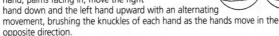

- [Mime using a shovel to dig] Beginning with both modified *X hands* in front of each side of the waist, left hand lower than right, palms facing each other, move the hands downward with a deliberate movement and then upward in a large arc over the right shoulder.

**dig**[2] *v.* See sign for SPATULA.

**dignity** *n.*

- [Holding one's head up with dignity] Place the extended right index finger, palm facing left, against the bottom of the chin.

**digress** *v.* Same sign used for: **distracted, off the point, off the subject, off track.**

- [Begins similarly to sign for **goal** and then veers off to the side] Move the extended right index finger from in front of the right shoulder, palm facing left, forward toward the extended left index finger held up in front of the chest, turning sharply to the left near the left index finger.

**dim**[1] *adj., v.* Same sign used for: **darken, tint.**

- [Represents headlight beams going down to dim] Beginning with both *5 hands* in front of each shoulder, palms facing forward, bring the hands downward while constricting the fingers into *curved 5 hands.*

**dim**[2] *adj.* See sign for DARK.

# dime

**dime** *n.* Same sign used for: **ten cents.**

- [**cent + ten**] Beginning with the extended right index finger touching the right side of the forehead, palm facing down, bring the right hand forward while changing into a *10 hand*. Then slightly twist the right *10 hand* with a repeated movement, palm facing in and thumb pointing up.

**dimple** *n.*

- [Location of dimples in the cheeks] Beginning with both extended index fingers touching the cheeks on each side of the mouth, twist the hands forward with a double movement.

**dining room** *n.*

- [**eat + box**] Tap the fingertips of the right *flattened O hand* to the lips with a double movement. Then, beginning with both *open hands* in front of each side of the body, palms facing each other, turn the hands sharply in opposite directions by bending the wrists, ending with both palms facing in.

**dinner** *n.*

- [**eat + night**] Tap the fingertips of the right *flattened O hand* to the lips with a double movement. Then tap the heel of the right *bent hand,* palm facing down, with a double movement against the index-finger side of the left *B hand* held in front of the chest, palm facing down.

**dinosaur** *n.*

- [Initialized sign showing the long neck typical of some dinosaurs] Move the right *D hand* up and back in an arc from the forehead, ending with the hand above the head, palm facing left.

**dip** *v.* See sign for DYE.

**diploma** *n.* Same sign used for: **degree.**

- [Shape of rolled diploma] Beginning with the index-finger sides of both *F hands* in front of the chest, palms facing forward, move the hands apart to in front of each side of the chest.

---

**direct** *v., adj.* See signs for DESCRIBE, MANAGE, ORDER, STRAIGHT[1]. Related form: **direction** *n.*

---

**dirt** *n.* Same sign used for: **ground, land, soil.**

- [Feeling the texture of dirt] Beginning with both *flattened O hands* in front of each side of the body, palms facing up, move the thumb of each hand smoothly across each fingertip, starting with the little fingers and ending as *A hands.*

---

**dirty** *adj.* Same sign used for: **filthy, nasty, pollution, soiled.**

- [Represents a pig's snout groveling in a trough] With the back of the right *curved 5 hand* under the chin, palm facing down, wiggle the fingers.

---

**disagree** *v.* Same sign used for: **contrast, object.**

- [**think**[1] + **opposite**] Move the extended right index finger from touching the right side of the forehead downward to meet the extended left index finger held in front of the chest. Then, beginning with both index fingers pointing toward each other, palms facing in, bring the hands apart to each side of the chest.

**disappear**[1] *v.* Related form: **disappearance** *n.* See also sign for ABSENT. Same sign used for: **vanish.**

- [Moving out of sight] Beginning with the extended right index finger, palm facing left, pointing up between the index and middle fingers of the left *5 hand*, palm facing down, pull the right hand straight down a short distance.

---

**disappear**[2] *v.* See sign for DISSOLVE.

---

# disappointed

**disappointed** *adj.* Related form: **disappointment** *n.*
Same sign used for: **miss.**

- [Symbolizes "Take it on the chin," a result of disappointment]
  Touch the extended right index finger to the chin,
  palm facing down.

---

**disastrous** *adj.* See sign for AWFUL.

**discard** *v.* See sign for ABANDON.

**discharge** *v.* See sign for DISMISS.

**disco** *n.* See sign for DANCE.

**disconnect** *v.* Same sign used for: **detach,
loose, part from, withdraw.**

- [Demonstrates releasing of a connection] Beginning with the thumb and index fingertips of each
  hand intersecting with each other, palms facing
  each other and right hand nearer the chest than
  the left hand, release the fingers and pull the
  left hand forward and the right hand back toward the right shoulder.

---

**discount**[1] *n.*

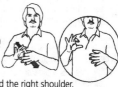

- [Initialized sign showing reduction] Beginning with
  both *D hands* in front of the chest, right hand
  above the left hand, palms facing each other,
  and index fingers pointing forward, bring the
  hands toward each other.

---

**discount**[2] *v.* See sign for SUBTRACT.

**discouraged** *adj.* See sign for DEPRESSED[1].

**discover** *v.* See sign for FIND.

**discriminate** *v.* Related form:
**discrimination** *n.*

- [Initialized sign similar to sign for
  **cancel**] With the fingertips of the
  right *D hand*, palm facing left and
  index finger pointing up, draw a
  large X across the palm of the
  left *open hand*.

---

128

**discuss** *v.* Related form: **discussion** *n.* Same sign used for: **argument, dispute.**

- [Natural gesture used when making a point] Tap the side of the extended right index finger, palm facing in, on the upturned left *open hand* with a double movement.

**disgusted**[1] *adj.* Related form: **disgust** *n.*, *v.*
Same sign used for: **aggravated, nausea, stomachache, upset.**

- [Represents one's stomach churning in disgust] Move the fingertips of the right *curved 5 hand* in a repeated circle on the stomach.

**disgusted**[2] *adj.* (alternate sign, used especially when referring to one's own actions or mistakes) Same sign used for: **I should have thought of it before** and **Now I remember.**

- [Represents internal grumbling because of an oversight] Move the fingertips of the right *curved 5 hand,* palm facing in, in a double circle on the chest.

**dish** *n.*

- [Shape of a dish] Beginning with the fingertips of both *curved hands* touching in front of the chest, palms facing in, move the hands away from each other in a circle, ending with the heels together close to the chest.

**disk** *n.*

- [Initialized sign representing recording on a disk] Move the fingertips of the right *D hand,* palm facing down and index finger pointing forward, in a double circle on the upturned left *open hand.*

**dislike** *v.* See sign for DON'T LIKE.

**dismiss** *v.* Related form: **dismissal** *n.* Same sign used for: **discharge, lay off, pardon, parole, waive.**

- [Movement seems to wipe person away] Wipe the right *open hand,* palm down, deliberately across the upturned left *open hand* from the heel off the fingertips.

# disobey

**disobey** *v.*

- [Hands move as in protest] Beginning with the thumbs of both *A hands* touching each side of the forehead, palms facing down, swing the hands outward to each side of the head by twisting the wrists, ending with both palms facing forward.

**disorder** *n.* See signs for MESSY, MIX[1].

**dispute** *v.* See sign for DISCUSS.

**disseminate** *v.* See sign for SPREAD.

**dissolve** *v.* Same sign used for: **disappear, evaporate, fade away, melt, perish.**

- [Something in the hands seems to melt away to nothing] Beginning with both *flattened O hands* in front of each side of the body, palms facing up, move the thumb of each hand smoothly across each fingertip, starting with the little fingers and ending as *10 hands* while moving the hands outward to each side.

**distance** *n.* See sign for FAR. Related form: **distant** *adj.*

**distracted** *adj.* See sign for DIGRESS.

**distribute** *v.* See signs for SELL, SPREAD.

**district** *n.* Same sign used for: **area.**

- [Indicates an area] Beginning with the left *open hand* held in front of the body, palm facing down, bring the right *open hand* in a large arc from the right side of the body forward and back over the left hand, ending with the right fingertips on the left wrist.

**disturb** *v.* See sign for ANNOY.

**dive** *v., n.*

- [Mime hand position when diving] Beginning with the palms of both *open hands* together in front of the chest, fingers pointing up, move the hands forward and downward in a large arc.

**divide** *v.* Same sign used for: **split, split up.**

■ [Split something as if to divide it] Beginning with the little-finger side of the right *B hand* at an angle across the index-finger side of the left *B hand,* palms angled in opposite directions, move the hands downward and apart, ending with the hands in front of each side of the body, palms facing down.

**division** *n.* See sign for DEPARTMENT.

**divorce** *v., n.*

■ [Initialized sign representing two people moving apart] Beginning with the fingertips of both the *D hands* touching in front of chest, palms facing each other and index fingers pointing up, swing the hands away from each other by twisting the wrists, ending with the hands in front of each side of the body, palms facing forward.

**dizzy** *adj.*

■ [Indicates confusion or a spinning sensation in the head] Beginning with the right *curved 5 hand* near the right side of the head, palm facing left, move the hand in a double circular movement.

**do** *v.* Related form: **done** *adj.* Same sign used for: **commit, conduct, deed, perform, performance.**

■ [Hands seem to be actively doing something] Move both *C hands,* palms facing down, from side to side in front of the body with a repeated movement.

**doctor** *n.* Same sign used for: **medical, physician.**

■ [Formed at the location where one's pulse is taken] Tap the fingertips of the right *M hand,* palm facing left, on the wrist of the upturned left *open hand* with a double movement.

**document** *v.* See sign for PUT DOWN[1].

**doesn't** or **does not** See sign for DON'T[1].

**doesn't matter** See sign for ANYWAY.

### dog *n.*

- [Natural gesture for signaling or calling a dog] With a double movement, snap the right thumb gently off the right middle finger, palm facing up, in front of the right side of the chest.

### doll *n.*

- [A doll's nose] Bring the index finger of the right *X hand,* palm facing left, downward on the nose with a repeated movement.

### dollar *n.* Same sign used for: **bill.**

- Beginning with the fingertips of the right *flattened C hand* holding the fingertips of the left *open hand,* both palms facing in, pull the right hand to the right with a double movement while changing to a *flattened O hand.*

### dolphin *n.* See sign for PORPOISE.

### domestic *adj.* See sign for DAILY.

### dominoes *n.*

- [Represents moving two dominoes end to end with each other] Bring the fingertips of both *H hands,* palms facing in, together in front of the body with a double movement.

**donate** *v.* See signs for CHARITY[1], GIFT, GIVE. Related form: **donation** *n.*

**done** *adj.* See sign for FINISH[1].

### donkey *n.* Same sign used for: **mule, stubborn.**

- [Represents a donkey's ears] With the thumb side of the right *B hand* against the right side of the forehead, palm facing forward, bend the fingers up and down with a repeated movement.

# don't want

**don't**[1] *contraction.* Same sign used for: **doesn't, does not.**

- [Natural gesture of denial] Beginning with both *open hands* crossed in front of the chest, palms angled in opposite directions, swing the hands downward away from each other, ending at each side of the body, palms facing down.

---

**don't**[2] *contraction.* See signs for NOT[1,2].

---

**don't believe** See sign for DOUBT[1].

---

**don't care** Same sign used for: **don't mind, indifferent, nonchalant.**

- [Outward movement indicates the negative] Beginning with the extended right index finger touching the nose, palm facing down, swing the hand forward by twisting the wrist, ending with the index finger pointing forward in front of the right shoulder.

---

**don't know** Same sign used for: **unaware, unconscious, unknown.**

- [**know** + an outward gesture indicating the negative] Beginning with the fingers of the right *open hand* touching the right side of the forehead, palm facing in, swing the hand forward by twisting the wrist, ending with the fingers pointing forward in front of the right shoulder.

---

**don't like** Same sign used for: **dislike.**

- [**like**[1] formed with an outward gesture indicating the negative] Beginning with the fingertips of the right *8 hand* touching the chest, palm facing in, swing the hand forward by twisting the wrist, and then release the fingers into a *5 hand,* palm facing down.

---

**don't mind** See sign for DON'T CARE.

---

**don't want** Same sign used for: **unwanted.**

- [**want** formed with an outward gesture indicating the negative] Beginning with both *curved 5 hands* in front of the body, palms facing up, swing the hands downward by twisting the wrists, ending with the palms facing down.

# door

**door** *n.*
- [Shows movement of a door being opened] Beginning with the index-finger sides of both *B hands* touching in front of the chest, palms facing forward, swing the right hand back toward the right shoulder with a double movement by twisting the wrist.

**doubt**[1] *v., n.* Same sign used for: **don't believe.**
- [As if one is blind to what is doubted] Beginning with the fingers right *bent V hand* in front of the eyes, palm facing in, pull the hand downward a short distance while constricting the fingers with a single movement.

**doubt**[2] *n.* See sign for INDECISION.

**doubtful** *adj.* Same sign as for DOUBT[1] but made with a double movement. See also sign for SKEPTICAL.

**down** *adv., prep.*
- [Shows direction] Move the extended right index finger downward in front of the right side of the body.

**downstairs** *adv.* Same sign as for DOWN but made with a double movement. Same sign used for: **downward.**

**doze** *v.* See signs for FALL ASLEEP, SLEEP.

**draft**[1] *v.* See signs for DESIGN, DRAW[1].

**draft**[2] *n.* See signs for ROUGH, SKETCH[1].

**drafting** *v.* See sign for ENGINEER.

**drag** *v.* Same sign used for: **draw, haul, pull, tow.**
- [Mime pulling something] Beginning with the right *curved hand* in front of the body and the left *curved hand* somewhat forward, both palms facing up, bring the hands back toward the right side of the body while closing them into *A hands*.

**drain** *adj.* See signs for ABSENT, LEAK.

**drama** *n.* See sign for ACT².

**drapes** *pl. n.*
- [Shape of drapes] Beginning with both *4 hands* in front of each shoulder, palms facing forward, drop the hands downward while turning the palms down.

**drat** *interj.* See signs for ALAS, DARN.

**draw¹** *v.* Same sign used for: **draft, sketch.**
- [Initialized sign similar to sign for **art**] Move the extended right little finger, palm facing left, down the palm of the left *open hand.*

**draw²** *v.* See signs for ATTRACT¹, CHOOSE, DESIGN, DRAG, FIND.

**draw back** *v. phrase.* See sign for RESIGN.

**draw blood** Same sign used for: **give blood.**
- [Hand seems to extract blood from the arm] Beginning with the fingers of the right *curved 5 hand,* palm facing up, near the crook of the left arm held extended in front of the left side of the body, pull the right hand to the right while closing the fingers to the thumb, forming a *flattened O hand.*

**drawer** *n.* Same sign used for: **dresser.**
- [Mime opening a drawer] With the fingers of both *A hands* tightly curled in front of each side of the body, palms facing up, pull the hands back toward the body with a repeated movement.

**drawing¹** *n.* Same sign as for DRAW¹ but made with a double movement.

**drawing²** *n.* See signs for ART, DESIGN, SKETCH¹.

# dreadful

**dreadful** *adj.* See sign for AWFUL.

**dream** *v., n.* Same sign used for: **daydream.**
- [Represents an image coming from the mind] Move the extended right index finger from touching the right side of the forehead, palm facing down, outward to the right while bending the finger up and down.

**dress¹** *v.*
- [Location of dress] Brush the thumbs of both *5 hands* downward on each side of the chest.

**dress²** *n.* See sign for CLOTHES.

**dresser** *n.* See sign for DRAWER.

**dribble** *v.* See signs for BOUNCE, DRIP.

**drill** *n.* See sign for ALARM.

**drink¹** *n., v.* Same sign used for: **beverage.**
- [Mime drinking from a glass] Beginning with the thumb of the right *C hand* near the chin, palm facing left, tip the hand up toward the face, with a single movement for the noun and a double movement for the verb.

**drink²** *n.* Same sign used for: **drinking.**
- [Initialized sign made with **a** to represent an alcoholic drink] Move the thumb of the right *A hand,* palm facing left, back toward the mouth with a double circular movement.

**drink³** *n.* See sign for COCKTAIL.

**drip** *n.*, *v.* Same sign used for: **dribble, drop, leak.**

■ [Represents action of water dripping] Beginning with the right *S hand*, palm facing down, near the fingertips of the left *open hand*, palm facing down and fingers pointing right, flick the right index finger downward with a repeated movement.

**drive** *v.*

■ [Similar to the sign for **car** except made with a larger movement] Beginning with both *S hands* in front of the chest, palms facing in and one hand higher than the other hand, move the hands in an up-and-down repeated alternating movement.

**drive to** *v. phrase.*

■ [Represents continuous driving] Beginning with both *S hands* in front of the chest, palms facing in, move the hands forward with a deliberate movement.

**drool** *v.* Same sign used for: **crave.**

■ [Indicates saliva running from corner of mouth] Beginning with the index finger of the right *4 hand* near the right side of the mouth, palm facing in and fingers pointing left, bring the hand downward in front of the chest.

**drop¹** *v.*

■ [Represents dropping something held in the hands] Beginning with both *flattened O hands* in front of the body, palms facing in and fingers pointing toward each other, drop the fingers of both hands downward while opening into *5 hands,* ending with both palms facing in and fingers pointing down.

**drop²** *v.* See sign for DECLINE³.

**drop³** *n.* See sign for DRIP.

# drop out

**drop out** *v. phrase.* See sign for RESIGN.

## drown *v.*
- [Symbolizes a person's head going under the water] Beginning with the thumb of the right *10 hand,* palm facing in, extended up through the index finger and middle finger of the left *open hand,* palm facing down and fingers pointing right, pull the right hand straight down.

## drug *n.*
- [Represents injecting a drug] Pound the little-finger side of the right *S hand,* palm facing up, with a double movement near the crook of the extended left arm.

## drum *n.*
- [Mime playing a snare drum] Move both modified *X hands,* palms facing in and knuckles pointing toward each other, up and down in front of the chest with a repeated alternating movement.

## drunk *adj.* Same sign used for: **intoxicated.**
- [Pouring alcohol into the mouth] Move the thumb of the right *10 hand,* palm facing left, in an arc from right to left past the chin.

## dry *adj.* Related form: **dried** *adj.* Same sign used for: **boring.**
- [Wiping the chin dry] Drag the index-finger side of the right *X hand,* palm facing down, from left to right across the chin.

**dry cleaners** *n.* See sign for CLEANERS.

**duck** *n.*

- [A duck's bill] Close the extended index and middle fingers of the right hand, palm facing forward, to the right thumb with a repeated movement in front of the mouth.

**due** *adj.* See sign for AFFORD.

**dull** *adj.* See sign for BORING[1].

**dumb** *adj.* Same sign used for: **stupid.**

- [Natural gesture] Hit the palm side of the right *A hand* against the forehead.

**dump** *v.* See sign for THROW.

**duplicate** *v., n.* See signs for COPY[1,2].

**during** *prep.* Same sign used for: **meanwhile, while.**

- [Shows two events occurring simultaneously] Beginning with both extended index fingers in front of each side of the body, palms facing down, move them forward in parallel arcs, ending with the index fingers angled upward.

**dusk** *n.* See sign for DARK.

**dwell** *v.* See sign for LIVE.

**dye** *n., v.* Same sign used for: **dip, rinse.**

- [Dipping cloth in dye] Move both *F hands,* palms facing down, with a slight up and down repeated movement in front of each side of the body.

**each** *adj., pron., adv.* Same sign used for: **per.**
- [Emphasizes one] Bring the knuckle side of the right *10 hand* down the knuckles of the left *10 hand,* palms facing each other and thumbs pointing up.

---

**each other** *pron.* See sign for ASSOCIATE.

**eager** *adj.* See sign for ZEAL.

**eagle** *n.*
- [Represents an eagle's beak] Tap the back of the index finger of the right *X hand,* palm facing forward, against the nose with a double movement.

---

**ear** *n.*
- [Location of an ear] Wiggle the right earlobe with the thumb and index finger of the closed right hand.

---

**earache** *n.*
- [**hurt**¹ formed near the ear] Jab both extended index fingers toward each other with a repeated movement near the right ear or near the ear with an earache.

---

**early** *adv., adj.*

■ [Represents a bird hopping around looking for the early worm] Push the bent middle finger of the right *5 hand* across the back of the left *open hand*, both palms facing down.

**earn** *v.* Same sign used for: **deserve, income, salary, wages.**

■ [Bringing earned money toward oneself] Bring the little-finger side of the right *curved hand*, palm facing left, across the upturned left *open hand* from fingertips to heel while changing into an *S hand*.

**earphones** *pl. n.*

■ [Putting on earphones] Tap the fingertips of both *curved 5 hands*, palms facing in, on each side of the head around each ear with a repeated movement.

**earring** *n.*

■ [Location of earring] Shake the right earlobe with the index finger and thumb of the right *F hand* with a repeated movement. For the plural, use the same sign but made with both hands, one at each ear.

**earth** *n.* Same sign used for: **geography.**

■ [The earth rotating on its axis] Grasp each side of the left *S hand*, palm facing down, with the bent thumb and middle finger of the right *5 hand*, palm facing down. Then rock the right hand from side to side with a double movement.

**east** *n., adj., adv.*

■ [Initialized sign showing an easterly direction on a map] Move the right *E hand*, palm facing forward, a short distance to the right in front of the right shoulder.

# easy

---

**easy** *adj.* Same sign used for: **convenient, simple.**

■ [The fingers are moved easily] Brush the fingertips of the right *curved hand* upward on the back of the fingertips of the left *curved hand* with a double movement, both palms facing up.

---

**eat** *v.*

■ [Putting food in the mouth] Bring the fingertips of the right *flattened O hand,* palm facing in, to the lips with a repeated movement.

---

**eat up** *v. phrase.* See signs for ACID, CONSUME.

---

**eavesdrop** *v.* See sign for LISTEN.

---

**edge** *n.*

■ [Shows edge of fingers] Slide the palm of the right *open hand,* palm facing left and fingers pointing forward, back and forth with a double movement on the fingertips of the left *B hand,* palm facing down and fingers pointing right.

---

**edit**[1] *v.* Same sign used for: **correct.**

■ [Crossing out text in order to correct it] With the extended right index finger, palm facing forward, make small repeated crosses on the palm of the left *open hand,* palm facing in, in front of the chest.

---

**edit**[2] *v.* See sign for WRITE.

---

**educate** *v.* See signs for LEARN, TEACH. Related form: **education** *n.*

---

**education** *n.* Related form: **educate** *v.*

■ [Initialized sign **e-d** similar to sign for **teach**] Beginning with both *E hands* near each side of the head, palms facing each other, move the hands forward a short distance while changing into *D hands.*

---

**effect** *n.* See signs for ADVICE, INFLUENCE.

---

**efficient** *adj.* See sign for SKILL.

**effort** *n.*

- [Initialized sign similar to sign for **try**] Move both
  *E hands* from in front of each side of the body,
  palms facing each other, downward and forward
  simultaneously in an arc.

**egg** *n.*

- [Represents cracking eggs] Beginning with the middle-finger side
  of the right *H hand* across the index-finger side of the left *H
  hand*, palms angled toward each other, bring the hands downward and away from each other with a double movement by
  twisting the wrists each time.

**egotistic** or **egotistical** *adj.*
Related forms: **ego** *n.*,
**egotism** *n.*

- [The repeated **I** sign
  represents concentrating
  on oneself] Beginning with
  the right *I hand* in front of
  the right side of the chest
  and the left *I hand* somewhat forward of the
  left side of the chest, palms facing in opposite directions, bring the right hand
  forward and the left hand back to the chest with an alternating movement.

**either**[1] *adj., pron., conj.* See also sign for OR. Same sign used for: **alternative,
choice.**

- [Shows alternative choices] Tap the fingertips
  of the right *V hand* with a repeated alternating
  movement on the fingertips of the left *V hand*,
  palms facing each other.

**either**[2] *adj., pron., conj.* See sign for WHICH.

# elaborate

**elaborate** *v.* Same sign used for: **extend.**

■ [Stretching out the facts] Beginning with the thumb side of the right *S hand* against the little-finger side of the left *S hand,* move the right hand forward with a wavy movement.

**elastic** *adj.* See sign for STRETCH[1].

**elect** *v.* See signs for APPOINT[1], VOTE. Related form: **election** *n.*

**electric** or **electrical** *adj.* Related form: **electricity** *n.* Same sign used for: **battery.**

■ [An electrical connection] Tap the knuckles of the index fingers of both *X hands* together, palms facing in, with a double movement.

**elegant** *adj.* See sign for FANCY.

**elementary** *adj.*

■ [Initialized sign similar to sign for **base**] Move the right *E hand,* palm facing forward, from side to side with a repeated movement below the left *open hand,* palm facing down and fingers pointing right, in front of the chest.

**elephant** *n.*

■ [Shape of elephant's trunk] Beginning with the back of the right *bent B hand* against the nose, palm facing down, move the hand downward and forward with a large wavy movement.

**elevate** *v.* See sign for ADVANCED. Related forms: **elevated** *adj.*, **elevation** *n.*

**elevator** *n.*

■ [Initialized sign showing movement of elevator] Move the index-finger side of the right *E hand,* palm facing forward, up and down with a repeated movement against the left *open hand,* palm facing right and fingers pointing up.

**eligible** *adj.* See sign for APPLY[2].

**eliminate[1]** *v.* Same sign used for: **abolish, abort, delete, omit, remove, repel, rid, terminate.**

- [Natural gesture] Beginning with the back of the right *modified X hand*, palm facing in, touching the extended left index finger, palm facing in and finger pointing right, bring the right hand upward and outward to the right while flicking the thumb upward, forming a *10 hand.*

**eliminate[2]** *v.* See sign for SUBTRACT.

**else** *adj., adv.* See sign for OTHER[1].

**elude** *v.* See sign for AVOID.

**embarrass** *v.* Related form: **embarrassed** *adj.*

- [Indicates blood rising in the face when embarrassed] Move both *5 hands,* palms facing each other, in repeated alternating circles near each cheek.

**emblem** *n.* See sign for BADGE[1].

**embrace** *v.* See sign for HUG.

**emerge** *v.* See sign for MAINSTREAM.

**emergency** *n.*

- [Initialized sign] Move the right *E hand,* palm facing forward, back and forth with a double movement in front of the right shoulder.

**emery board** *n.* See sign for PUMICE.

**emit** *v.*

- [Represents a beam of light] Beginning with the left *S hand* on the back of the right *S hand,* both palms facing down, move the right hand forward with a double movement, opening into a *5 hand* each time.

# emotional

**emotional** *adj.* Related form: **emotion** *n.*

■ [Initialized sign showing feeling welling up in the body] Move both *E hands,* palms facing in and knuckles pointing toward each other, in repeated alternating circles on each side of the chest.

**emphasis** *n.* See sign for IMPRESSION.

**employ** *v.* See sign for INVITE.

**employment** *n.* See sign for WORK.

**empty** *adj.* Same sign used for: **available, bare, blank, naked, vacancy, vacant, void.**

■ [Indicates a vacant space] Move the bent middle fingertip of the right *5 hand* across the back of the left *open hand* from the wrist to off the fingertips, both palms facing down.

**enable** *v.* See sign for SKILL.

**encourage** *v.* Related form: **encouragement** *n.* Same sign used for: **bear up.**

■ [Hands seem to give someone a push of encouragement] Beginning with both *open hands* outside each side of the body, palms and fingers angled forward, move the hands toward each other and forward with a double pushing movement.

**end**[1] *v.* Same sign used for: **complete, conclude, finish, over, wind up.**

■ [Demonstrates going off the end] Beginning with the little-finger side of the right *open hand,* palm facing left, across the index-finger side of the left *open hand,* palm facing in, bring the right hand deliberately down off the left fingertips.

**end**[2] *n.* See sign for LAST[1].

**endanger** *v.* See sign for DANGER.

**enemy** *n.* Same sign used for: **foe, opponent, rival.**

■ **[opposite + person marker]** Beginning with both extended index fingers touching in front of the chest, palms facing down, pull the hands apart to in front of each side of the chest. Then move both *open hands,* palms facing each other, downward along each side of the body.

**engaged** *adj.* Related form: **engagement** *n.*

■ [Initialized sign showing the location of an engagement ring] Beginning with the right *E hand* over the left *open hand,* both palms facing down, move the right hand in a small circle and then straight down to land on the ring finger of the left hand.

**engineer** *n.* Related form: **engineering** *n.* Same sign used for: **drafting, measuring.**

■ [Similar to sign for **measure**] With the thumbs of both *Y hands* touching in front of the chest, right palm facing forward and left palm facing in, twist the hands in opposite directions with a double movement.

**engrave** *v.* See sign for CARVE.

**enjoy** *v.* Related form: **enjoyment** *n.* Same sign used for: **appreciate, leisure, like, please, pleasure.**

■ [Hands rub the body with pleasure] Rub the palms of both *open hands* on the chest, right hand above the left hand and fingers pointing in opposite directions, in repeated circles moving in opposite directions.

**enlarge** *v.* See signs for BIG, EXPAND[1].

**enough** *adj., pron., adv.* Same sign used for: **adequate, plenty, sufficient.**

■ [Represents leveling off a container filled to the top] Push the palm side of the right *open hand,* palm facing down, forward across the thumb side of the left *S hand,* palm facing in.

# enrage

**enrage** *v.* See sign for ANGER.

**enroll** *v.* See sign for ENTER.

**enter** *v.* Related forms: **entrance** *n.*, **entry** *n.*
Same sign used for: **enroll, immigrate, into.**

- [Represents movement of entering] Move the back of the right *open hand* forward in a downward arc under the palm of the left *open hand,* both palms facing down.

**enthusiastic** *adj.* See sign for ZEAL.

**entice** *v.* See sign for TEMPT.

**entire** *adj.* See sign for ALL.

**entitle** *v.* See signs for BELONG², TITLE.

**entrance** *n.* See sign for ADMISSION. Related form: **entry** *n.*

**envelope** *n.* See sign for CARD¹.

**envy** *n., v.* Related form: **envious** *adj.*

- [Natural gesture used when a person envies another's possessions] Touch the teeth on the right side of the mouth with the right bent index fingertip.

**equal** *adj., v.* Same sign used for: **even, fair, get even.**

- [Demonstrates equal level] Tap the fingertips of both bent hands, palms facing down, together in front of the chest with a double movement.

**equipment** *n.*

- [Initialized sign similar to sign for **thing**] Move the right *E hand,* palm facing up, from lying on the upturned palm of the left *open hand* to the right in a double arc.

**erupt** *v.* See sign for BLOWUP.

**escape** *v.* See also sign for RUN AWAY. Same sign used for: **estranged, get away.**

- [Represents one person going off alone] Beginning with the extended right index finger, palm facing down and finger pointing forward, under the palm of the left *open hand,* palm facing down and fingers pointing forward, move the right hand straight forward.

**especially** *adv.* See sign for SPECIAL.

**essential** *adj.* See sign for IMPORTANT.

**establish** *v.* See also sign for SET UP. Same sign used for: **based on, founded.**

- [Represents setting something up firmly] Beginning with the right *10 hand* in front of the right shoulder, palm facing down, twist the wrist upward with a circular movement and then move the right hand straight down to land the little-finger side on the back of the left *open hand,* palm facing down.

**estimate** *n., v.* See signs for ARITHMETIC, GUESS, MULTIPLY, ROUGH.

**estranged** *adj.* See signs for ASTRAY, ESCAPE.

**eternal** *adj.* See sign for FOREVER.

**evade** *v.* See sign for AVOID.

**evaluate** *v.* Related form: **evaluation** *n.*

- [Initialized sign with a movement that signifies weighing choices] Move both *E hands,* palms facing forward, up and down with a repeated alternating movement in front of each side of the chest.

**evaporate** *v.* See signs for DISSOLVE, RAPTURE.

**even**[1] *adj.* Same sign used for: **fair, level.**

- [Shows things of equal level] Beginning with the fingertips of both bent hands touching in front of the chest, both palms facing down, bring the hands straight apart from each other to in front of each shoulder.

# even

**even**[2] *adj., v.* See signs for CONSTANT[2], EQUAL.

**evening** *n.*

■ [Represents the sun low on the horizon] Tap the heel of the right *bent hand,* palm facing forward, with a double movement against the thumb side of the left *open hand* held across the chest, palm facing down.

**event**[1] *n.*

■ [The fingers used for feeling move upward in excitement] Beginning with the bent middle fingers of both *5 hands* touching the chest, palms facing in, bring the hands upward and to the sides with a quick double movement.

**event**[2] *n.* See sign for HAPPEN.

**even though** *conj.* See sign for ANYWAY.

**ever** *adv.* See sign for ALWAYS.

**everlasting** *adj.* See sign for FOREVER.

**ever since** See signs for ALL THE TIME, SINCE[1].

**everyday** *adj.* See sign for DAILY.

**everything**[1] *pron.*

■ [each + thing] Beginning with both *A hands* held in front of each side of the body, palms facing up, bring the knuckles of the right hand to the left, brushing across the top of the left hand and back again to the right while opening into a *5 hand.*

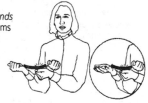

**everything**[2] *pron.* See sign for INCLUDE.

**every three months** See sign for QUARTERLY.

**every two months** See sign for BIMONTHLY.

**every two weeks** See sign for BIWEEKLY.

**every year** See sign for ANNUAL.

**evict** *v.* See sign for ABANDON.

**evidence**[1] *n.*
- [Initialized sign similar to sign for **proof**] Move the right *E hand* from near the right eye, palm facing left, downward to land the back of the right *E hand* in the left *open hand*, both palms facing up.

**evidence**[2] *n.* See sign for PROOF.

**evil** *adj.* See sign for BAD.

**exact** *adj.* See sign for PRECISE.

**exaggerate** *v.* Same sign used for: **prolong, stretch.**
- [Hands seem to stretch the truth] Beginning with the thumb side of the right *S hand*, palm facing left, against the little-finger side of the left *S hand*, palm facing right, move the right hand forward with a large wavy movement.

**exalt** *v.* See signs for ADVANCE, ADVANCED. Related forms: **exalted** *adj.*, **exaltation** *n.*

**examine** *v.* See signs for CHECK[1], INVESTIGATE, LOOK FOR, TEST. Related form: **examination** *n.*

**examination** *n.* See signs for INVESTIGATE, TEST.

**example**[1] *n.* Same sign used for: **exhibit.**
- [Initialized sign similar to sign for **show**[1]] With the index-finger side of the right *E hand*, palm facing forward, against the left *open hand*, palm facing right and fingers pointing up, move the hands forward together a short distance.

**example**[2] *n.* See sign for SHOW[1].

**exceed** *v.* See signs for EXCESS, OVER.

**excellent** *adj.* See signs for FINEST, SUPERB, WONDERFUL.

# excerpt

**excerpt** *n.*, *v.* Same sign used for: **copy, quotation.**

■ [Similar to sign for **quotation**[1]] Beginning with both *bent V hands* in front each side of the body, palms facing each other, bring the hands back toward the chest while constricting the fingers.

**excess** *n.*, *adj.* Related form: **excessive** *adj.* Same sign used for: **exceed, massive, more than, too much.**

■ [Demonstrates an amount that is more than the base] Beginning with the right *bent hand* on the back of the left *bent hand,* both palms facing down, bring the right hand upward in an arc to the right.

**exchange** *n.*, *v.* See signs for BUDGET, TRADE.

**excite** *v.* Related form: **excited** *adj.*, **exciting** *adj.*

■ [The finger used to show feeling brings up feeling in the body] Move the bent middle fingers of both *5 hands,* palms facing in and fingers pointing toward each other, in repeated alternating circles on each side of the chest.

**exclude** *v.* To keep out: *excluded from the meeting.* See also sign for REJECT[2].

■ [Shoving something away to exclude it] Beginning with the heel of the right *curved hand,* palm facing forward, against the heel of the left *open hand,* palm facing up, move the right hand across the left hand and off the fingertips.

**excuse**[1] *n.*

■ [The hand seems to wipe away a mistake] Wipe the fingertips of the right *open hand* across the upturned left *open hand* from the heel off the fingertips.

**excuse**[2] *v.* See sign for FORGIVE.

**excuse me** Same sign as **excuse**[1] except made with a shorter double movement.

**execute** *v.* Same sign used for: **run.**

- [Represents the parts of a machine running] Slide the palm of the right *open hand,* palm facing up, at an angle across the palm of the left *open hand,* palm facing down, with a double movement.

**exempt** *v.* See sign for SUBTRACT.

**exercise**[1] *n., v.* Same sign used for: **work out.**

- [Mime exercising] Beginning with both *S hands* near each shoulder, palms facing each other, bring both arms up and down with a double movement.

**exercise**[2] *n., v.* See sign for PRACTICE.

**exhausted** *adj.* See sign for TIRED.

**exhibit**[1] *v.* Related form: **exhibition** *n.*

- [Initialized sign similar to sign for **show**[2]] Beginning with the index-finger side of the right *E hand,* palm facing forward, against the palm of the left *open hand,* palm facing right and fingers pointing up, move both hands in a flat circle in front of the chest.

**exhibit**[2] *n., v.* See signs for EXAMPLE, SHOW[2].

**expand**[1] *v.* Related form: **expanse** *n.*
Same sign used for: **enlarge, explosion.**

- [Demonstrates something expanding] Beginning with the little-finger side of the right *S hand* on top of the index-finger side of the left *S hand,* palms facing in opposite directions, bring the hands apart while opening into *curved 5 hands* in front of each side of the chest, palms facing each other.

**expand**[2] *v.* See sign for BALLOON.

**expect** *v.* See sign for HOPE. Related form: **expectation** *n.*

# expel

**expel**[1] *v.t.*

- [Initialized sign similar to sign for **fire**[2]] Swing the knuckles of the right *E hand*, palm facing up, across the index-finger side of the left *B hand*, palm facing in and fingers pointing right.

**expel**[2] *v.* See signs for ABANDON, BREATH.

**expensive** *adj.* Same sign used for: **costly.**

- [**money** + a gesture of throwing it away] Beginning with the back of the right *flattened O hand* on the upturned left *open hand*, bring the right hand upward to the right while opening into a *5 hand* in front of the right shoulder, palm facing down.

**experience** *n., v.* Same sign used for: **ordeal.**

- [The grey sideburns of an experienced man] Beginning with the fingertips of the right *5 hand* on the right cheek, palm facing in, bring the hand outward to the right while closing the fingers into a *flattened O hand.*

**experiment** *n., v.*

- [Initialized sign similar to sign for **science**] Beginning with both *E hands* in front of the chest, palms facing forward and the right hand higher than the left hand, move the hands in repeated alternating circles.

**expert** *adj.* See signs for ADROIT, GOOD AT, SKILL.

**explain** *v.* See sign for DESCRIBE. Related form: **explanation** *n.*

**explode** *v.* Related form: **explosion** *n.* Same sign used for: **bomb, boom.**

- [Demonstrates something blowing up] Beginning with the fingers of both *flattened O hands* together in front of the chest, palms facing each other, move the hands suddenly upward and outward while opening into *5 hands*, ending with the palms angled upward near each side of the head.

**explosion** *n.* See sign for EXPAND.

**expose** *v.* See signs for SHOW[1], STICK[1].

**exposure** *n.*
- [Represents the shutter of a camera opening and closing while taking a picture] Beginning with the fingertips of the right *flattened O hand,* palm facing left, against the extended left index finger, palm facing right, bring the right hand back and then forward again to the index finger while changing into a *5 hand.*

**expression** *n.*
- [Indicates the face's movement when changing expression] Move both *modified X hands,* palms facing forward, up and down with a repeated alternating movement in front of each side of the face.

**extend** *v.* See sign for ELABORATE.

**external** *n., adj.* See sign for OUTSIDE.

**extinct** *adj.* See sign for ABSENT.

**extra** *n.* See sign for ADD[2].

**eye** *n.*
- [Location of the eye] Point the extended right index finger, palm facing in, toward the right eye with a double movement. For the plural, point to each eye.

**eyeglasses** *pl. n.* See sign for GLASSES.

### face *n.*
- [Location and shape of face] Draw a large circle around the face with the extended right index finger, palm facing in.

---

**face to face** See sign for IN FRONT OF.

**facing** *adj., v. (pres. participle of* FACE) See sign for IN FRONT OF.

**fact** *n.* See sign for TRUTH.

**factory** *n.* See sign for MACHINE.

**fade** *v.* See sign for VAGUE.

**fade away** *v. phrase.* See sign for DISSOLVE.

---

### fail¹ *v.* Related form: **failure** *n.*
- [Falling off the edge] Beginning with the back of the right *V hand* on the heel of the left *open hand,* palm facing up, move the right hand across the left palm and off the fingers.

---

**fail²** *v.* See sign for FLUNK.

---

### faint *v.*
- [Losing consciousness and falling forward] Touch both extended index fingers, palms facing down, to each side of the forehead. Then drop the hands down while opening into *5 hands,* ending with both palms facing in and fingers pointing down in front of each side of the chest.

---

**fair**[1] *adj.*

■ [Initialized sign] Tap the middle finger of the right *F hand,* palm facing left, against the chin with a repeated movement.

**fair**[2] *adj.* Same sign used for: **sort of, so-so.**

■ [Natural gesture showing ambivalence] Rock the right *5 hand,* palm facing down, from side to side with a repeated movement in front of the right side of the body.

**fair**[3] *adj.* See signs for EQUAL, EVEN[1].

**faith** *n.*

■ [**think**[1] + initialized sign similar to sign for **confident**] Move the extended right index finger from touching the right side of the forehead downward while changing into an *F hand,* ending with the index finger of the right *F hand* on top of the index finger of the left *F hand* in front of the body, palms facing each other.

**faithful** *adj.* See sign for CONSISTENT.

**fake**[1] *n., adj.* Same sign used for: **fiction.**

■ [Indicates a source in the imagination rather than reality] Beginning with the index-finger side of the right *4 hand* touching the right side of the forehead, palm facing left, move the hand forward in a double arc.

**fake**[2] *adj.* Same sign used for: **artificial, counterfeit, pseudo, sham.**

■ [Formed similar to sign for **false** indicating pushing the truth aside.] Brush the extended right index finger, palm facing left, with a double movement across the tip of the nose from right to left by bending the wrist.

**fake**[3] *adj.* See sign for HYPOCRITE.

# fall

**fall¹** *v., n.*

- [Represents legs slipping out from under a person] Beginning with the fingertips of the right *V hand* pointing down, palm facing in, touching the up-turned palm of the left *open hand*, flip the right hand over, ending with the back of the right *V hand* lying across the left palm.

**fall²** *n.* Same sign used for: **autumn.**

- [Leaves falling from a tree] Brush the index-finger side of the right *B hand*, palm facing down, downward toward the elbow of the left forearm, held bent across the chest.

**fall asleep** Same sign used for: **asleep, doze.**

- [Represents the head falling forward when dozing off] Beginning with the right *5 hand* in front of the face, palm facing in and fingers pointing up, bring the hand down while changing into an *A hand*, ending with the right hand, palm down, on top of the left *A hand*, palm up, in front of the body.

**fall behind** *v. phrase.* See sign for AVOID.

**fall through** *v. phrase.* See sign for BREAK DOWN.

**false** *adj.*

- [Similar to sign for **fake²** indicating pushing the truth aside] Brush the extended right index finger, palm facing left, across the tip of the nose from right to left by bending the wrist.

**false teeth** *pl. n.* Same sign used for: **dentures.**

- [Mime putting in false teeth] Push upward on the front top teeth with the fingers of the right *flattened O hand*, palm facing in.

**familiar** *adj.* See sign for AWARE[1].

**family** *n.*

- [Initialized sign similar to sign for **class**] Beginning with the fingertips of both *F hands* touching in front of the chest, palms facing each other, bring the hands away from each other in outward arcs while turning the palms in, ending with the little fingers touching.

**famished** *adj.* See sign for HUNGRY.

**famous** *adj.* Related form: **fame** *n.* Same sign used for: **notorious.**

- [Similar to sign for **tell**, except spreading the words far and wide] Beginning with both extended index fingers pointing to each side of the mouth, palms facing in, move the hands forward and outward in double arcs, ending with the index fingers pointing upward in front of each shoulder.

**fancy** *adj.* Same sign used for: **classical, deluxe, elegant, formal, grand, luxury.**

- [The ruffles on an old-fashioned shirt] Move the thumb of the right *5 hand,* palm facing left, upward and forward in a double circular movement in the center of the chest.

**fantastic** *adj.* See signs for SUPERB, WONDERFUL.

**far** *adv., adj.* Related form: **farther** *adv., adj.* Same sign used for: **distance, distant, remote.**

- [Moves to a location at a far distance] Beginning with the palm sides of both *A hands* together in front of the chest, move the right hand upward and forward in a large arc.

**far-out** *adj.* *Slang.*

- [Represents something getting smaller as it moves farther away] Beginning with the thumb of the right *C hand,* palm facing left, on the back of the left *open hand,* palm facing down, bring the right hand across the left fingers and outward to the right while changing into an *S hand.*

# fare

**fare** *n.* See sign for COST[1].

**farewell** *interj., n.* See sign for GOOD-BYE.

**farm** *n.* Same sign used for: **agriculture, bum, casual, ranch, sloppy.**

- [An unshaven farmer] Drag the thumb of the right *5 hand,* fingers pointing left, from left to right across the chin.

**fascinating** *adj.* See sign for INTEREST[1].

**fast** *adj., adv.* Same sign used for: **automatic, quick, sudden.**

- [Demonstrates quickness] Beginning with both extended index fingers pointing forward in front of the body, palms facing each other, pull the hands quickly back toward the chest while constricting the index fingers into *X hands.*

**fasten** *v.* See signs for BELONG[1], STICK[1].

**fat** *adj.*

- [Shows shape of fat body] Move both *curved 5 hands* from in front of each side of the chest, palms facing in and fingers pointing toward each other, outward in large arcs to each side of the body.

**father** *n.* Same sign used for: **dad, daddy, papa.**

- [Formed in the male area of the head, indicating the head of the household] Tap the thumb of the right *5 hand,* palm facing left and fingers pointing up, against the middle of the forehead with a double movement.

**father-in-law** *n.*

- [**father + law**] Tap the thumb of the right *5 hand* against the forehead, palm facing left, with a repeated movement. Then place the palm side of the right *L hand* first on the fingers and then on the wrist of the left *open hand* held in front of the body, palm facing up.

**fatigue** *n.* See signs for TIRED, WEAK.

**faucet** *n.*

- [Mime turning on faucets] Beginning with both *curved 3 hands* in front of each side of the body, palms facing down, turn the fingers outward and away from each other with a double movement.

**fault**[1] *n.*

- [Weight of faults on one's shoulders] Beginning with the fingers of the right *bent hand* on the right shoulder, palm facing down, pivot the hand downward while keeping the fingers in place.

**fault**[2] *n.* Same sign used for: **accuse, blame.**

- [Pushes blame toward another] Push the little-finger side of the right *10 hand,* palm facing left, forward and upward in an arc across the back of the left *S hand,* palm facing down.

**fault**[3] *n.* See sign for BURDEN.

**favor** *v.* See sign for PET[1].

**favorite**[1] *adj., n.* Related form: **favor** *v.* Same sign used for: **flavor, prefer, preference, rather, type, typical.**

- [Taste something on the finger] Touch the bent middle finger of the right *5 hand,* palm facing in, to the chin with a double movement.

**favorite**[2] *adj.* See sign for PARTIAL TO.

**fear** *n., v.* Same sign used for: **coward, frightened, scared.**

- [Natural gesture of protecting the body from the unknown] Beginning with both *5 hands* in front of each side of the chest, palms facing in and fingers pointing toward each other, move the hands toward each other with a short double movement.

# feast

**feast** *n.* See sign for BANQUET.

**federal** *adj. phrase.* See sign for GOVERNMENT.

**fed up** *adj. phrase.* See sign for FULL[1].

**fee** *n.* See sign for COST[1].

**feeble** *adj.* See sign for WEAK.

**feed** *v.* Same sign used for: **supply.**
- [Offering something to another] Beginning with both *flattened O hands* in front of each side of the body, palms facing up and right hand somewhat forward of the left hand, push the hands forward a short distance with a double movement.

**feedback** *n.* Same sign used for: **impeach.**
- [Initialized sign indicating information going both ways] Beginning with both *F hands* in front of each side of the chest, right palm facing forward and left palm facing in, move the hands with a double movement in opposite directions to and from the chest.

**feel** *v.* Related form: **feeling** *n.* Same sign used for: **motive, sensation, sense.**
- [Bent middle finger indicates feeling in sign language] Move the bent middle finger of the right *5 hand,* palm facing in, upward on the chest. Sometimes formed with a repeated movement.

**fellowship** *n.* See sign for ASSOCIATE.

**female** *n.* See sign for LADY.

**fence** *n.*
- [Shape of interlocking fence rails] Beginning with both *4 hands* in front of the chest, fingers pointing in opposite directions and overlapping, both palms facing in, move the hands outward to in front of each shoulder.

**fertilize** *v.* See sign for CONFLICT[1].

**festival** *n.* See sign for CELEBRATE.

**few** *adj.* Same sign used for: **several.**
- [A small number of items is revealed at a time] Beginning with the right *A hand* held in front of the right side of the chest, palm facing up, slowly spread out each finger from the index finger to the little finger, ending with an upturned *4 hand.*

**few days ago, a** *n. phrase.*
- [The fingers move into the past] Beginning with the thumb of the right *A hand* on the right cheek, palm facing down, twist the hand up while changing into a *3 hand* and keeping the thumb in place on the cheek.

**few minutes ago, a** *n. phrase.* See sign for WHILE AGO, A.

**fib** *v.* See signs for BETRAY[1], LIE.

**fiction** *n.* See sign for FAKE[1].

**fiddle** *n.* See sign for VIOLIN.

**field**[1] *n.*
- [Initialized sign similar to sign for **specialize**] Move the fingertips of the right *F hand,* palm facing down, forward along the length of the index finger of the right *B hand,* palm facing right, from the base to the tip.

**field**[2] *n.* See sign for SPECIALIZE.

**fierce** *adj.* See sign for AWFUL.

**fight**[1] *n., v.*
- [Mime two people striking at each other] Beginning with both *S hands* in front of each shoulder, palms facing each other, move the hands deliberately toward each other, ending with the wrists crossed in front of the chest.

# fight

**fight²** *v.* See sign for ARGUE.

**fight³** *n.* See sign for COMBAT.

**figure** *n., v.* See signs for ARITHMETIC, MULTIPLY.

**figure out** *v. phrase.* See signs for ARITHMETIC, MULTIPLY.

**file¹** *v.* Same sign used for: **sort.**
- [Insert something in order to file it] Slide the little-finger side of the right *B hand,* palm angled up, between the middle finger and ring finger of the left *B hand* held in front of the chest, palm facing in.

**file²** *v.* See signs for APPLY¹.

**fill in** *v. phrase.*
- [Represents documenting something on paper] Touch the fingertips of the right *flattened O hand,* palm facing down, on the upturned left *open hand* in several places.

**fill up¹** *v. phrase.*
- [Shows rising level of something in a container] Bring the right *B hand,* palm facing down and fingers angled left, upward until level with the index-finger side of the left *C hand,* palm facing right.

**fill up²** *v. phrase.* See sign for REFILL.

**film¹** *n.* Same sign used for: **movie, show.**
- [Flicker of film on a screen] With the heel of the right *5 hand,* palm facing forward, on the heel of the left *open hand,* palm facing in, twist the right hand from side to side with a repeated movement.

**film²** *n.* See sign for MOVIE CAMERA.

**filthy** *adj.* See sign for DIRTY.

**final** *adj.* See sign for LAST[1]. Related form: **finally** *adv.*

**finally** *adv.* Same sign used for: **at last, succeed.**

■ [Moving to higher stages] Beginning with both extended index fingers pointing up near each cheek, palms facing in, twist the wrists forward, ending with the index fingers pointing up in front of each shoulder, palms facing forward.

**find** *v.* Same sign used for: **discover, draw.**

■ [Selecting something held out in the hand] Beginning with the right *curved 5 hand* inserted in palm side of the left *curved 5 hand,* palm facing right in front of the body, bring the right hand upward while closing the thumb and index finger, forming an *F hand.*

**fine**[1] *adj.*

■ [The ruffles on the front of a fine old-fashioned shirt] Beginning with the thumb of the right *5 hand* touching the chest, palm facing left, move the hand forward a short distance.

**fine**[2] *adj*

■ [The fingers feel a fine texture] Beginning with the right *F hand* in front of the right shoulder, palm facing forward, rub the tip of the index finger and thumb together with a quick small movement.

**fine**[3] *n.* See sign for COST[1].

**finest** *adj.* Same sign used for: **awesome, excellent, terrific, whew.**

■ [The ruffles on the front of the fanciest of old-fashioned shirts] With the thumb of the right *5 hand* touching the chest, palm facing left and fingers pointing up, wiggle the fingers with a repeated movement.

# finger

## finger *n.*

- [Location of finger] Rub the fingertip of the extended right index finger back and forth along the length of the index finger of the left *5 hand* with a repeated movement.

## fingerspell *v.* Related form: **fingerspelling** *n.*

- [Represents action of fingers when fingerspelling] Move the right *5 hand,* palm facing down, from in front of the chest to the right while wiggling the fingers.

## finish[1] *v.* Same sign used for: **already, complete, done, over, then.**

- [Something shaken off the hands when finished with it] Beginning with both *5 hands* in front of the chest, palms facing in and fingers pointing up, flip the hands over with a sudden movement, ending with both palms facing down and fingers pointing forward.

## finish[2] *v.* See signs for BEEN THERE, END[1].

## fire[1] *n.* Same sign used for: **burn.**

- [Represents flames] Move both *5 hands,* palms facing up, from in front of the waist upward in front of the chest while wiggling the fingers.

## fire[2] *v.* Same sign used for: **terminate.**

- [Indicates cutting a job short] Swing the back of the right *open hand,* palm facing up, across the index-finger side of the left *B hand,* palm facing in.

## firefighter *n.*

- [Represents the raised front of a firefighter's helmet] Bring the back of the right *B hand,* fingers pointing up and palm facing forward, against the center of the forehead.

**fireworks** *n.*

■ [Represents the bursting of fireworks] Beginning with both *S hands* in front of each side of the body, palms facing forward, bring the hands upward and together in front of the chest and then upward and outward to each side near the head while opening into *5 hands.*

**firm** *adj.* See sign for STRICT.

**first** *adj., n., adv.* Same sign used for: **one dollar.**

■ [**one** formed with a twisting movement used for ordinal numbers] Beginning with the extended right index finger pointing up in front of the right side of the chest, palm facing forward, twist the hand, ending with the palm facing in.

**fish**[1] *n.*

■ [The movement of a fish in water] While touching the wrist of the right *open hand,* palm facing left, with the extended left index finger, swing the right hand back and forth with a double movement.

**fish**[2] *v.* Related form: **fishing** *n.*

■ [Mime fishing with a fishing pole] Beginning with both *modified X hands* in front of the body, right hand forward of the left hand and palms facing in opposite directions, move the hands upward by bending the wrists with a double movement.

**fit**[1] *v.* Same sign used for: **suit.** *n.*

■ [Initialized sign showing that two things fit together] Beginning with the right *F hand* in front of the right shoulder, palm angled down, and the left *F hand* in front of the left side of the body, palm angled up, bring the fingertips together in front of the chest.

# fit

**fit**[2] *v., n.* See sign for MATCH[1].

---

**five cents** *pl. n.* See sign for NICKEL.

---

**fix** *v.* Same sign used for: **maintain, mend, repair.**

■ [The fingers seem to put things together] Brush the fingertips of both *flattened O hands* across each other repeatedly as the hands move up and down in opposite directions in a double movement.

---

**flabbergast** *v.* Same sign used for: **astound, awesome, startle.**

■ [Represents a person's mouth opening in amazement] Beginning with the right *S hand* near the right side of the chin, palm facing forward, open the fingers into a *bent 3 hand* while opening the mouth.

---

**flabby** *adj.* See sign for LOOSE[1].

---

**flag** *n.*

■ [Represents a waving flag] While holding the elbow of the raised right arm in the left palm, wave the right *open hand* back and forth with a repeated movement in front of the right shoulder.

---

**flame** *n.* See sign for CANDLE.

---

**flare up** *v. phrase.* See sign for BOILING MAD.

---

**flash** *n.*

■ [Shows a flash of light] Beginning with the heel of the right *flattened O hand*, palm facing down, on the index-finger side of the left *B hand*, palm facing in, flick the right fingers quickly to form a *curved 5 hand* and back again to form a *flattened O hand*.

---

**flashlight** *n.*

■ [Light from a flashlight] While holding the wrist of the right *flattened O hand* with the left hand, flick the right fingers open into a *5 hand*, palm facing down.

---

**flat** *adj.*

- [Shows flat surface] Beginning with the index-finger side of the right *bent hand* against the little-finger side of the left *bent hand,* both palms facing down, move the right hand forward a short distance.

**flat tire** *n.*

- [Represents air going out of a tire] Beginning with the thumb of the right *open hand,* palm facing down, on the palm of the upturned left *open hand,* close the right fingers to the thumb, forming a *flattened O hand.*

**flatter** *v.* Related form: **flattery** *n.* Same sign used for: **bluff.**

- [Being swayed by flattery coming from different directions] Swing the right *open hand* back and forth with a repeated movement, brushing the fingers against the extended left index finger held in front of the chest, palm facing right, each time it passes.

**flavor** *n.* See sign for FAVORITE[1].

**flesh** *n.* See sign for SKIN.

**flexible**[1] *adj.* Same sign used for: **floppy.**

- [Shows something easily bent] With both *flattened O hands* in front of each side of the chest, palms facing in, bend the wrists to move the hands forward and back with an alternating repeated movement.

**flexible**[2] *adj.* See sign for PLIABLE.

**flip** *v.* See sign for COOK.

**flirt** *v.*

- [Represents batting one's eyelashes] Beginning with the thumbs of both *5 hands* touching in front of the chest, palms facing down and fingers pointing forward, wiggle the fingers up and down with an alternating movement.

# flood

### flood *n., v.*

■ [**water** + showing level of water rising] Tap the index finger of the right *W hand*, palm facing left, against the chin. Then, beginning with both *5 hands* in front of the waist, palms facing down and fingers pointing forward, raise the hands to in front of the chest.

### floor *n.*

■ [Shows flatness of a floor's surface] Beginning with the index-finger side of both *B hands* touching in front of the waist, palms facing down and fingers pointing forward, move the hands apart to each side.

### floppy *adj.* See sign for FLEXIBLE[1].

### flow *v.* See sign for STREAM.

### flower *n.*

■ [Holding a flower to the nose to smell it] Touch the fingertips of the right *flattened O hand*, palm facing in, first to the right side of the nose and then to the left side.

### fluent *adj.* See signs for SMOOTH[2], SMOOTHLY. Related form: **fluently** *adv.*

### flunk *v. Informal.* Same sign used for: **fail.**

■ [Initialized sign] Strike the index-finger side of the right *F hand*, palm facing forward, against the palm of the left *open hand*, palm facing right and fingers pointing up.

### flush *v.* See sign for BLUSH.

### flute *n.*

■ [Mime playing a flute] Move both *curved 4 hands*, palms facing in, with a repeated movement from side to side in front of the mouth while wiggling the fingers.

**fly** *v.* Same sign used for: **wings.**

■ [Mime flapping wings to fly] Beginning with both *open hands* near each shoulder, and fingers angled outward in opposite directions, bend the wrists repeatedly, causing the hands to wave.

**focus**[1] *v., n.*

■ [Mime adjusting the focus on a lens] Beginning with both *C hands* near each other in front of the chest, palms facing each other and left hand nearer the chest than the right hand, twist the right hand downward to the left.

**focus**[2] *v., n.*

■ [Directing one's attention] Beginning with both *B hands* near each side of the face, palms facing each other and fingers pointing up, bring the hands down while tipping the fingers downward and toward each other.

**focus on** *v. phrase.* See signs for ATTENTION, NARROW DOWN.

**foe** *n.* See sign for ENEMY.

**fold** *v.*

■ [Mime folding paper in half] Beginning with both *open hands* near each other in front of the chest, palms facing up, flip the right hand over in an arc, ending with the right palm on the left palm.

**folder** *n.*

■ [Represents inserting papers into a folder] Slide the little-finger side of the right *open hand,* palm facing up, with a double movement into the opening formed by the left *flattened C hand,* palm facing up.

**folk** *n.* See sign for PEOPLE.

# follow

**follow** *v.* Same sign used for: **trail.**

- [One hand follows the other hand] With the knuckles of the right *10 hand,* palm facing left, near the wrist of the left *10 hand,* palm facing right, move both hands forward a short distance.

**food** *n.*

- [Putting food in one's mouth] Bring the fingertips of the right *flattened O hand,* palm facing in, to the lips with a double movement.

**fool** *v.* See signs for BETRAY[1], BLOW[1], TRICK.

**fool around** *v. phrase.* See sign for RUN AROUND.

**foot** *n.*

- [Shows the length of a foot] Move the bent middle finger of the right *5 hand,* palm facing down, up and down the length of the left *open hand,* palm facing down, with a repeated movement.

**football** *n.*

- [Represents scrimmage between two teams] Beginning with both *5 hands* in front of each side of the chest, palms facing in and fingers pointing toward each other, bring the hands together with a short double movement, interlocking the fingers of both hands each time.

**for** *prep.*

- [Knowledge is directed for another's use] Beginning with the extended right index finger touching the right side of the forehead, palm facing down, twist the hand forward, ending with the index finger pointing forward.

**forbid** *v.* Same sign used for: **ban, illegal, prohibit.**

- [Similar to sign for **sue** to show an opposition to something] Bring the palm side of the right *L hand*, palm facing left, sharply against the palm of the left *open hand*, palm facing right and fingers pointing up.

**forecast** *v.* See sign for PREDICT.

**fore** *adj., n.* See sign for FRONT.

**foreign** *adj.*

- [Initialized sign similar to sign for **country**[1,2]] Move the thumb side of the right *F hand*, palm facing left, in a double circular movement near the bent left elbow.

**foresee** *v.* See sign for PREDICT.

**forest** *n.* Same sign used for: **orchard, woods.**

- [**tree** is repeated] Beginning with the bent right elbow resting on the back of the left hand held across the body, palm facing down, twist the right *5 hand* forward with a double movement, moving the arms to the right each time.

**forever** *adv.* Same sign used for: **eternal, everlasting.**

- [**always** + **still**[1]] Move the right *1 hand*, palm facing up, in a circle in front of the right side of the body. Then move the right *Y hand* from in front of the right side of the body, palm facing down, forward and upward in an arc.

**forget** *v.*

- [Wipes thoughts from one's memory] Wipe the fingers of the right *open hand*, fingers pointing left, across the forehead from left to right while closing into a *10 hand* near the right side of the forehead.

# forgive

**forgive** *v.* Same sign used for: **excuse**[1], **pardon**.
- [Wipes away mistake] Brush the fingertips of the right *open hand*, palm facing down, across the palm of the upturned left *open hand* from the heel off the fingertips with a double movement.

**fork** *n.*
- [Tines of a fork] Touch the fingertips of the right *V hand*, palm facing down, on the palm of upturned left *open hand*. Then quickly turn the right hand so the palm faces the body and touch the left palm again.

**form**[1] *n.* Same sign used for: **format**.
- [Initialized sign showing the shape of a form] Beginning with the fingertips of both *F hands* touching in front of the chest, palms facing each other, bring the hands away from each other to about shoulder width and then straight down a short distance, ending with the palms facing forward.

**form**[2] *n., v.* See sign for SHAPE[1].

**formal** *adj.* See sign for FANCY.

**former** *adj.* Same sign used for: **previous**.
- [Hand moves back into the past] Move the right *5 hand*, palm facing left and fingers pointing up, back toward the right shoulder in a double circular movement.

**forsake**[1] *v.* See also sign for ABANDON. Same sign used for: **depart, withdraw**.
- [Represents picking things up to leave] Beginning with both *open hands* in front of the body, palms facing down and fingers pointing forward, bring the hands back toward each side of the chest with a quick movement while closing into *A hands*.

**forsake**[2] *v.* See sign for IGNORE.

**fortunate** *adj.* See sign for LUCK.

**forward** *adv.* See signs for AHEAD, GO ON.

**founded** *adj.* See signs for ESTABLISH, RECOVER, SET UP.

**fountain** *n.*

■ [**water** + spray of water coming up in a fountain] Tap the index-finger side of the right *W hand,* palm facing left, against the chin. Then, beginning with the fingers of both *flattened O hands* touching in front of the body,  palms facing down, bring the hands upward and forward in large arcs while opening into *5 hands* in front of each shoulder, palms facing forward.

**fowl** *n.* See sign for BIRD.

**fox** *n.*

■ [Initialized sign showing the shape of a fox's nose] With the index finger and thumb of the right *F hand* encircling the nose, palm facing left, twist the hand with a repeated movement, ending with the palm facing down.

**fraction** *n.*

■ [Initialized sign showing that a fraction is expressed above and below a dividing line] Move the right *F hand,* palm facing forward, downward in front of the chest, past the index-finger side of the left *open hand* held in front of the chest, palm facing down.

**fragrance** *n.* See sign for SMELL.

**frame** *n., v.*

■ [Shape of a frame] Beginning with the extended fingers of both *G hands* touching in front of the chest, palms facing each other, move the hands apart to in front of each shoulder, then straight down, and finally back together in front of the lower chest.

**frank** *adj.* See sign for HONEST. Related form: **frankly** *adv.*

**fraternity** *n.* See sign for ASSOCIATE.

**fraud** *n.* See signs for CHEAT, DECEIVE[1].

**freak** *n., adj.* See sign for STRANGE.

**free**[1] *adj.* Related form: **freedom** *n.*

■ [Initialized sign similar to sign for **save**[1]] Beginning with both *F hands* crossed at the wrists in front of the chest, palms facing in opposite directions, twist the wrists to move the hands apart to in front of each shoulder, ending with the palms facing forward.

**free**[2] *adj.* See sign for SAVE[1]. Related form: **freedom** *n.*

**freeway** *n.* See sign for HIGHWAY.

**freeze** *v.* Same sign used for: **frost, frozen, ice, rigid, solidify.**

■ [Shows things hardening when frozen] Beginning with both *5 hands* in front of each side of the body, palms facing down and fingers pointing forward, pull the hands back toward the body while constricting the fingers.

**french fries** *pl. n.*

■ [Initialized sign **f-f**] Form an *F* with the right hand, palm facing forward, in front of the right side of the body and then again slightly to the right.

**frequently** *adv.* See sign for OFTEN.

**Friday** *n.*

■ [Initialized sign] Move the right *F hand*, palm facing in, in a repeated circle in front of the right shoulder.

**friend** *n.* Same sign used for: **comrade, pal.**

■ [Indicates the entwined lives of friends who have a close relationship] Hook the bent right index finger, palm facing down, over the bent left index finger, palm facing up. Then repeat, reversing the position of the hands.

**friendly** *adj.* Same sign used for: **cheerful, pleasant.**

■ [The face crinkling with smiles] With both *5 hands* near the cheeks, palms facing back, wiggle the fingers.

**fright** *n.* See sign for AFRAID. Related form: **frightened** *adj.*

**frightened** *adj.* See sign for FEAR.

**frigid** *adj.* See signs for ARCTIC, COLD².

**frog** *n.*

■ Beginning with the index-finger side of the right *S hand* against the chin, palm facing left, flick the index and middle fingers outward to the left with a double movement.

**from** *prep.*

■ [Moving from another location] Beginning with the knuckle of the right *X hand*, palm facing in, touching the extended left index finger, palm facing right and finger pointing up, pull the right hand back toward the chest.

**from now on** See sign for AFTER¹.

**front** *n., adj.* Same sign used for: **fore.**

■ [Location in front of the person] Move the right *open hand*, palm facing in and fingers pointing left, straight down from in front of the face to in front of the chest.

# frost

**frost** *v.* See sign for FREEZE.

**frown** *v., n.*

- [Eyebrows turning down when frowning] Beginning with both extended index fingers near each side of the forehead, palms facing each other and fingers pointing up, bend the fingers downward to form *X hands* near the side of each eye.

**frozen** *adj.* See sign for FREEZE.

**fruit** *n.*

- [Initialized sign] Beginning with the fingertips of the right *F hand* on the right side of the chin, palm facing left, twist the hand forward with a double movement, ending with the palm facing in.

**frustrate** *v.* Related form: **frustration** *n.*

- [Facing a wall of opposition] Bring the back of the right *B hand,* palm facing forward, back against the mouth with a double movement or, sometimes, a single movement.

**fry** *v.* See sign for COOK.

**fuel** *n.* See sign for GAS.

**full**[1] *adj.* Same sign used for: **fed up, stuffed.**

- [Represents feeling full] Move the right *B hand,* palm facing down, from the center of the chest upward with a deliberate movement, ending with back of the right fingers under the chin.

**full**[2] *adj.* Same sign used for: **complete.**

- [Leveling off something that is full] Slide the palm of the right *open hand,* palm facing down, from right to left across the index-finger side of the left *S hand,* palm facing right.

**fume** *n., v.* See signs for BOILING MAD, SMELL[1].

---

**fun** *n.*

- [The nose wrinkles when laughing] Bring the fingers of the right *H hand* from near the nose downward, ending with the fingers of the right *H hand* across the fingers of the left *H hand* in front the chest, both palms facing down.

---

**function** *n., v.*

- [Initialized sign similar to sign for **practice**] Move the fingertips of the right *F hand,* palm facing forward, back and forth across the length of the left *open hand,* palm facing down, with a double movement.

---

**fund** *n.* See signs for MONEY, SUPPORT.

---

**funeral** *n.*

- [Represents a procession following a casket] Beginning with both *V hands* in front of the chest, right hand closer to the chest than the left hand and both palms facing forward, move the hands forward simultaneously in a double arc.

---

**funny** *adj.* Same sign used for: **amuse, humor.**

- [The sign for **fun** moving toward something funny] With a double movement, brush the nose with the fingertips of the ight *U hand,* palm facing in and thumb extended, bending the fingers of the *U hand* back toward the palm each time.

---

**furious** *adj.* See sign for BOILING MAD.

---

**furniture** *n.*

- [Initialized sign] Move the right *F hand,* palm facing forward, from side to side in front of the right side of the chest with a repeated movement.

---

## further

**further** *adv.* See sign for AHEAD.

**fury** *adj.* See sign for ANGER.

**future** *n.*

- [Hand moves forward into the future] Move the right *open hand,* palm facing left and fingers pointing up, from near the right cheek forward in a double arc.

**gab** *v., n. Informal.* See sign for BLAB.

**gain** *v., n.* See sign for INCREASE.

**gala** *adj., n.* See signs for CELEBRATE, DANCE.

**galoshes** *pl. n.* See sign for BOOTS.

**gamble**[1] *v., n.* Same sign used for: **dice.**
- [Mime tossing dice] Beginning with the right *A hand* in front of the right side of the body, palm facing up, thrust the hand forward to the left while opening into a *5 hand.*

**gamble**[2] *n., v.* See sign for BET.

**game** *n.*
- [Represents opposing teams sparring] Bring the knuckles of both *10 hands,* palms facing in, against each other with a double movement in front of the chest.

**gang** *n.* Related form: **gangster** *n.* Same sign used for: **dare, tough.**
- [Rubbing the leather jacket traditionally worn by gang members] Move the right *S hand,* palm facing in, downward on the right side of the chest with a double movement.

**gap** *n.* See sign for BETWEEN.

**garage** *n.*
[Represents a car moving into a garage] Move the right *3 hand,* palm facing left, forward with a short repeated movement under the palm of the left *open hand,* palm facing down and fingers pointing right.

# garbage

**garbage** *n.* Same sign used for: **gross, junk, trash.**

- [Natural gesture of holding one's nose when something smells bad] Beginning with the fingertips of the right *F hand* touching the nose, palm facing in, bring the right hand forward a short distance while opening the index finger and thumb in front of the face.

**garbled** *adj.* See sign for MESSY.

**garden** *n.*

- [Initialized sign encircling an area of land] Move the right *G hand,* palm facing left, in a large circular movement over the bent left arm, beginning near the elbow and ending near the left fingers.

**gas** *n.* Alternate form: **gasoline.** Same sign used for: **fuel.**

- [Mime pouring gas into the gas tank of a vehicle] Tap the extended thumb of the right *10 hand,* palm facing forward, downward with a repeated small movement into the thumb-side opening of the left *S hand.*

**gasp** *v.* See sign for GULP.

**gate** *n.*

- [Shows a gate swinging open] Beginning with both *open hands* in front of the body, palms facing in and the fingers touching, swing the fingers of the right hand forward and back with a double movement.

**gather**[1] *v.* Same sign used for: **assemble, get together.**

- [Represents people coming together] Beginning with both *curved 5 hands* in front of each side of the body, palms facing each other, bring the fingers together in front of the body.

**gather**[2] *v.* See also sign for ATTEND. Same sign used for: **assemble, get together, go to.**

■ [Represents people coming together] Beginning with both *5 hands* in front of each shoulder, palms angled forward, bring the hands forward toward each other, ending with the palms facing down.

**gather**[3] *v.* See sign for COLLECT.

**gay**[1] *adj., n.* Same sign used for: **homosexual, queer** (*slang:* disparaging and offensive).

■ [Initialized sign] Bring the fingertips of the right *G hand,* palm facing in, back to touch the chin with a double movement.

**gay**[2] *adj.* See sign for HAPPY.

**gelatin** *n.* Same sign used for: **Jell-O.**

■ [Shows the shaking movement of gelatin] Shake the right *curved 5 hand,* palm facing down, with a repeated back and forth movement over the left *open hand,* palm facing up.

**general**[1] *adj.* Same sign used for: **broad.**

■ [Hands open up broadly] Beginning with both *open hands* in front of the chest, fingers angled toward each other, swing the fingers away from each other, ending with the fingers angled outward in front of each side of the body.

**general**[2] *adj.* See sign for WIDE.

**general**[3] *n.* See sign for CAPTAIN.

**generous** *adj.* See sign for KIND[1].

**genius** *n.* See sign for SCHOLARLY[1].

**gentle** *adj.* See signs for KIND[1], POLITE, SOFT, SWEET.

**genuine** *adj.* See sign for REAL.

**geography** *n.* See sign for EARTH.

**gesture** *n.*

■ [Mime gesturing with the hands; similar to sign for **sign**[1]] Beginning with both *curved 5 hands* in front of the chest, left hand higher than the right hand and palms facing in opposite directions, move both hands in alternating forward circles.

**get** *v.* Same sign used for: **acquire, attain, obtain, receive, retrieve.**

■ [Reaching for something and bringing it to oneself] Beginning with both *curved 5 hands* in front of the chest, right hand above the left and palms facing in opposite directions, bring the hands back toward the chest while closing into *S hands,* ending with the little-finger side of the right hand on the index-finger side of the left hand.

**get along** *v. phrase.* See sign for GO ON.

**get away** *v. phrase.* See signs for AVOID, AWAY, ESCAPE, RUN AWAY.

**get even** See signs for EQUAL, REVENGE.

**get together** See signs for GATHER[1,2].

**get up** *v. phrase.* See sign for RAISE[1].

**ghost** *n.* See sign for SPIRIT.

**gift** *n.* Same sign used for: **award, charity, contribution, donation, grant, present, reward, tribute.**

■ [Presenting something to another] Move both *X hands* from in front of the body, palms facing each other, forward in simultaneous arcs.

**giggle** *n., v.*

■ [Represents the stomach of a jolly person heaving when laughing] Beginning with the right *bent hand* in front of the chest under the left *bent hand,* both palms facing down, curve the right hand toward the chest with a double movement by bending the wrist.

### giraffe *n.*

- [Shows shape of giraffe's neck] Beginning with the little-finger side of the right *C hand* on the index-finger side of the left *C hand*, both palms facing in at the neck, move the right hand upward in front of the face.

### girl *n.*

- [Formed in the female area of the head] Move the thumb of the right *A hand*, palm facing left, downward on the right cheek to the right side of the chin.

### give *v.* Same sign used for: **contribute, donate, grant, present, provide.**

- [Presenting something to another] Move the right *X hand* from in front of the right side of the chest, palm facing left, forward in a large arc.

### give blood See sign for DRAW BLOOD.

### give up *v. phrase.* Same sign used for: **relinquish, surrender, yield.**

- [Natural gesture used when surrendering] Beginning with both *curved hands* in front of the body, palms facing down, flip the hands upward in large arcs while opening into *5 hands*, ending in front of each shoulder, palms facing forward.

### glad *adj.* See sign for HAPPY.

### glance *v., n.*

- [Represents the eyes moving quickly around] Beginning with the right *V hand* in front of the right side of the face, palm facing down and fingers pointing to the right eye, move the hand forward and outward to the right by twisting the wrist outward with a quick movement, following the fingers with the eyes.

# glare

**glare** *n., v.*

- [Represents light shining down and reflecting off the face] Move the right *flattened O hand,* palm facing left, downward from near the right side of the head toward the face with a double movement, opening into a *curved 5 hand* each time.

**glass**[1] *n.*

- [Shows porcelain on teeth] Tap the fingertip of the right bent index finger against the front teeth with a repeated movement.

**glass**[2] *n.* See sign for BOTTLE.

**glasses** *pl. n.* Same sign used for: **eyeglasses.**

- [Shape and location of eyeglasses] Tap the thumbs of both *modified C hands,* palms facing each other, near the outside corner of each eye with a repeated movement.

**glitter** *v., n.* See sign for SHINY.

**glory** *n.*

- [Shows light and splendor rising from something glorified] Beginning with the palm of the right *open hand* on the up-turned left *open hand,* bring the right hand upward in front of the chest while opening the fingers and wiggling them.

**glossy** *adj.* See sign for SHINY.

**glove** *n.*

- [Represents pulling on a glove] Pull the right *5 hand,* palm facing down, from the fingers up the length of the back of the left *5 hand,* palm facing down. To indicate the plural, repeat with the other hand.

**glow** *v., n.* See signs for CANDLE, SHINY.

**glue** *n., v.*

- [Initialized sign seeming to squeeze glue on paper] Move the fingertips of the right *G hand,* palm and fingers facing down, in a circular movement over the upturned left *open hand.*

**go**[1] *v.* Same sign used for: **depart, go away, leave.**

- [Represents something getting smaller as it disappears into the distance] Beginning with the *flattened C hand* in front of the right shoulder, fingers pointing left, move the hand quickly to the right while closing the fingers into a *flattened O hand.*

**go**[2] *v.* See sign for AWAY.

**go ahead** *v. phrase.* See sign for GO ON.

**goal** *n.* Same sign used for: **aim, ambitious, objective, target.**

- [Indicates directing something toward something else] Move the extended right index finger from touching the right side of the forehead, palm facing down, forward to point toward the extended left index finger held in front of the face, palm facing forward and finger angled up.

**goat** *n.*

- [Represents a goat's beard and horns] Move the right *S hand* from the chin, palm facing in and the heel of the hand pointing down, forward a short distance while flicking up the index and middle fingers. Then repeat the same movement from the forehead.

**go by train** See sign for TRAIN.

**God** *n.*

- [Indicates the spirit of God moving down from above] Move the right *B hand,* palm facing left and fingers angled upward, from above the head downward in front of the face in an inward arc.

# gold

**gold** *n., adj.* Same sign used for: **golden.**

- [Shows a gold earring + **yellow**] With the thumb, index finger, and little finger of the right hand extended, palm facing in, touch the index finger near the right ear. Then bring the right hand downward and forward with a shaking movement while turning the wrist forward and changing into a *Y hand.*

**golden** *adj.* See sign for GOLD. Shared idea of yellow color.

**golf** *n.*

- [Mime swinging a golf club] Beginning with the right *modified X hand* near the right hip, palm facing left, and the left *modified X hand* in front of the right side of the body, palm facing in, swing the right hand upward and to the left.

**gone**[1] *v., adj.* See signs for ABSENT, AWAY.

**gone**[2] *v., adj.* See sign for NOTHING[3].

**good** *adj.* Same sign used for: **well.**

- [Presents something good for inspection] Beginning with the fingertips of the right *open hand* near the mouth, palm facing in and fingers pointing up, bring the hand downward, ending with the back of the right hand across the palm of the left *open hand,* both palms facing up.

**good at** Same sign used for: **expert, proficient.**

- [Similar to sign for **adroit**] Bring the fingertips of the right *F hand,* palm facing in, back against the chin.

**good-bye** *interj., n.* Same sign used for: **bye, farewell.**

- [Natural gesture for waving good-bye] Beginning with the right *open hand* in front of the right shoulder, palm facing forward and fingers pointing up, bend the fingers up and down with a repeated movement.

**good enough** See sign for MAKESHIFT.

**good-looking** *adj.* See sign for LOOKS.

**good luck** *interj.*
- [**good** + a natural "thumbs up" gesture for wishing luck] Beginning with the fingertips of the right *open hand* near the mouth, palm facing in and fingers pointing up, bring the hand downward and forward while changing into a *10 hand,* ending with the thumb pointing up, palm facing left, in front of the right shoulder.

**go on** *v. phrase.* Same sign used for: **all along, continue, forward, get along, go ahead, onward, proceed.**
- [Shows shoving something along ahead of oneself] Beginning with both *open hands* in front of the body, palms facing in and fingers pointing toward each other, move the hands forward a short distance simultaneously.

**goose** *n.*
- [Shows long neck of a goose and the movement of a goose's bill] With the left *open hand* held across the chest, palm facing down, rest the right forearm on the back of the left wrist while closing the extended right index and middle fingers to the right thumb, palm facing forward, with a repeated movement.

**go out** *v. phrase.* See sign for OUT.

**gorilla** *n.* Same sign used for: **ape.**
- [**monkey** + miming a gorilla beating its chest] Beginning with the fingertips of both *curved 5 hands* against each side of the body near the waist, palms facing in, brush the fingertips upward with a double movement. Then pound the palm side of both *S hands* against the chest with an alternating double movement.

**go smoothly** See signs for SMOOTH[2], SMOOTHLY.

# gossip

**gossip**[1] *n., v.* Same sign used for: **rumor.**

■ [Represents mouths opening and closing repeatedly] Move both *G hands,* palms facing each other, in a flat circular movement in front of the chest while pinching the index finger and thumb of each hand together with a repeated movement.

**gossip**[2] *n., v.* See sign for BLAB.

**go steady** See sign for STEADY[1].

**go to** *v. phrase.* See signs for ATTEND, GATHER[2].

## go to bed

■ [Indicates a person's legs getting under a blanket] Insert the fingers of the right *U hand,* palm facing down, into the hole formed by the left *O hand,* palm facing down.

**got you!** or **gottcha!** See sign for ZAP.

**govern** *v.* See sign for MANAGE.

## government *n.* Same sign for: **federal.**

■ [Indicates the head, one in authority] Beginning with the extended right index finger pointing upward near the right side of the head, palm facing forward, twist the wrist to touch the finger to the right temple.

**go with** *v. phrase.* Same sign used for: **accompany.**

■ [Similar to sign for **with** but moving toward a destination] With the palm sides of both *A hands* together in front of the chest, move the hands forward and downward with a deliberate movement.

**grab** *v.* Same sign used for: **take a chance.**

■ [Hand seems to snatch something from the other hand] Bring the right *curved 5 hand* from in front of the right side of the body, palm facing left and fingers pointing forward, in toward the body in a downward arc while changing into an *S hand,* brushing the little-finger side of the right *S hand* across the palm of the left *open hand,* palm facing up in front of the chest.

**gracious** *adj.* See sign for KIND[1].

**grade** *n.* Same sign used for: **incline, slope.**

■ [Demonstrates the shape of an incline] Beginning with the right *open hand* on top of the left *open hand* in front of the chest, both palms facing down and fingers pointing forward, move the right hand upward and forward at an angle.

**graduate** *v.* Related form: **graduation** *n.*

■ [Initialized sign similar to sign for **college**] Beginning with the right *G hand* in front of the right side of the chest, palm facing left and fingers angled forward, move the hand in a small circular movement and then straight down, ending with the little-finger side of the right hand on the left upturned open palm.

**grammar** *n.*

■ [Initialized sign similar to sign for **sentence**] Beginning with both *G hands* in front of the chest, fingers pointing toward each other, bring the hands apart with a wavy movement to in front of each side of the body.

**grand** *adj.* See signs for FANCY, LARGE.

**grandfather** *n.* Alternate form: **grandpa** *(informal).*

■ [man + moving forward one generation] Beginning with the thumb of the right *A hand* touching the forehead, palm facing left, bring the hand downward while opening into a *curved 5 hand* in front of the face, palm angled up.

# grandma

**grandma** *n. Informal.* See signs for GRANDMOTHER.

**grandmother** *n.* Alternate form: **grandma** (*informal*).

■ [**girl** + moving forward one generation] Beginning with the thumb of the right *A hand* touching the chin, palm facing left, bring the hand downward while opening into a *curved 5 hand* in front of the chest, palm facing up.

**grandpa** *n. Informal.* See signs for GRANDFATHER.

**grant** *n., v.* See signs for GIFT, GIVE, LET.

**grapes** *pl. n.*

■ [Shows bumpy shape of a bunch of grapes] Tap the fingertips of the right *curved 5 hand*, palm facing down, down the back of the left *open hand*, palm facing down, from the wrist to the fingers with a bouncing movement.

**graph** *n.* See sign for SCHEDULE[1].

**grass** *n.*

■ [Blades of grass] Push the heel of the right *curved 5 hand*, palm facing up, upward a short distance on the chin.

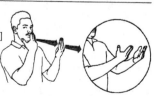

**grateful** *adj.* Same sign used for:
**appreciative, thankful.**

■ [**thank** moving forward toward another] Beginning with the right *open hand* near the mouth and the left *open hand* somewhat forward, palms facing in and fingers pointing up, move both hands forward.

**grave** *n., adj.* See signs for BURY, SAD.

**graveyard** *n.* See sign for CEMETERY.

### gravity *n.*

- **[earth** + a movement showing being pulled downward] Grasping the top of the left hand, palm facing down, with the bent thumb and middle finger of the right *5 hand,* palm facing down, rock the right hand from side to side with a double movement. Then bring the back of the right *S hand,* palm facing in near the neck, downward, ending with the back of the right wrist on the thumb side of the left *open hand,* palm facing down, angled across the chest.

### gravy *n.* Same sign used for: **grease, syrup.**

- [Represents dripping gravy] Beginning with the extended thumb and index finger of the right *G hand* grasping the little-finger side of the left *open hand,* both palms facing in, bring the right hand downward with a double movement while closing the index finger to the thumb each time.

### gray *adj.*

- [Suggests the blending of black and white] Beginning with both *5 hands* in front of the chest, fingers pointing toward each other and palms facing in, move the hands forward and back in opposite directions, lightly brushing fingertips as the hands pass each other.

**grease** *n.* See signs for GRAVY, OIL. Related form: **greasy** *adj.*

**great** *adj.* See signs for LARGE, WONDERFUL.

### greedy[1] *adj.* Same sign used for: **covetous, niggardly, possess, selfish, thrifty, tight.**

- [Clutching a prized possession] Beginning with the right *curved 5 hand* in front of the chin, palm facing in, bring the hand downward with either a single or double movement while closing the hand into an *S hand.*

**greedy[2]** *adj.* See sign for STINGY[2].

### green *adj.*

- [Initialized sign] Twist the right *G hand,* palm facing left, back and forward with a small repeated movement in front of the right shoulder.

# greet

**greet** *v.* See signs for INVITE, MEET.

**grievance** *n.* See sign for PROTEST[1].

**grimace** *n., v.*
- [Shows shape of face when grimacing] Place the right 5 *hand*, palm facing in, near the right side of the face. Then constrict the fingers into a *curved 5 hand*.

**grin** *v., n.* See sign for SMILE.

**grind**[1] *v.*
- [Represents teeth grinding together] Beginning with the palm sides of both *A hands* together in front of the chest, right hand over the left hand, move the hands in opposite directions in double circles while rubbing on each other.

**grind**[2] *v.* See sign for CHEW.

**grind out** *v. phrase.* Same sign used for: **monotonous.**
- [Represents keeping one's nose to the grindstone] Beginning with the extended right index finger touching the nose, palm facing in, move the hand forward while changing into an *S hand*. Then rub the index-finger side of the right *S hand*, palm facing forward, on the palm of the left *open hand*, palm facing right and fingers pointing up, with a double movement.

**grip** *n., v.* See sign for HOLD[1].

**gripe** *v.* See sign for COMPLAIN.

**grocery store** *n.*
- [**food** + **store**[1]] Bring the fingertips of the right *flattened O hand*, palm facing in, to the lips with a repeated movement. Then, beginning with both *flattened O hands* in front of the body, fingers pointing down, swing the fingertips upward and downward from the wrists with a repeated movement.

**gross** *adj.* See signs for GARBAGE, PROFIT.

**ground** *n.* See sign for DIRT.

**group**¹ *n.*
- [Initialized sign similar to sign for **class**] Beginning with both *G hands* in front of the chest, palms facing each other, bring the hands away from each other in outward arcs while turning the palms in, ending with the little fingers near each other.

**group**² *n.* See sign for CLASS.

**grow** *v.* Same sign used for: **sprout.**
- [Represents a plant coming up through the soil] Bring the right *flattened O hand*, palm facing in, up through the left *C hand*, palm facing in and fingers pointing right, while spreading the right fingers into a *5 hand*.

**grow up** *v. phrase.* Same sign used for: **raise, rear.**
- [Shows height as one grows] Bring the right *open hand*, palm facing down and fingers pointing left, from in front of the chest upward.

**grumble** *v.* See sign for COMPLAIN.

**guarantee** *n., v.* See sign for STAMP².

**guess** *v., n.* Same sign used for: **assume, estimate.**
- [Hand seems to snatch at an idea as it passes the face] Move the right *C hand*, palm facing left, from near the right side of the forehead in a quick downward arc in front of the face while closing into an *S hand*, ending with the palm facing down by the left side of the head.

**guide** *v.* See sign for LEAD.

**guilt** *n.* Related form: **guilty** *adj.*

- [Initialized sign formed near the heart] Bring the thumb side of the right *G hand*, palm facing left, back against the left side of the chest.

**guitar** *n.*

- [Mime playing a guitar with a pick] With the left *curved 5 hand* in front of the left shoulder, palm facing right, and the right *F hand* in front of the right side of the body, palm facing in, twist the right hand downward with a double movement.

**gullible** *adj.* See sign for CONSUME.

**gulp**[1] *v.* Same sign used for: **gasp.**

- [Represents the throat constricting as one swallows] Beginning with the right *C hand* near the throat, palm facing in, close the fingers to change into an *S hand*.

**gulp**[2] *v.* See sign for SWALLOW.

**gum** *n.* See sign for CHEWING GUM.

**gun** *n.* Same sign used for: **pistol.**

- [Demonstrates pulling back the hammer on a pointed gun] With the index finger of the right *L hand* pointing forward in front of the right side of the body, palm facing left, wiggle the thumb up and down with a repeated movement.

**gym** *n.* Related form: **gymnasium** *n.*

- [Exercising in gym class] Beginning with the *modified X hands* in front of each shoulder, palms facing each other, move the hands forward in small double circles by moving the arms and the wrists.

## ha ha *interj.*

- [Spell **h-a, h-a**] Beginning with the right *H hand* in front of the right shoulder, palm facing in and the thumb extended up, close the fingers with a double movement, forming an *A hand* each time.

## habit *n.* Same sign used for: **accustomed to.**

- [Symbolizes being bound by tradition] With the heel of the right *S hand* across the wrist of the left *S hand*, both palms facing down, move the hands down simultaneously in front of the chest.

## hack *v.* Same sign used for: **karate.**

- [Mime hacking something down] Beginning with the right *B hand* in front of the left shoulder, palm facing down, bring the hand deliberately down across the body to in front of the right side of the body. Then, beginning with the right *B hand* near the right shoulder, palm facing left, bring the hand down across the body, ending in front of the left side of the body.

## had *v.* See sign for HAVE.

## hail[1] *n., v.t.*

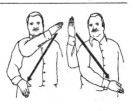

- [Shapes and movement of hail] Beginning with the right *F hand* above the right shoulder and the left *F hand* in front of the left side of the body, both palms facing down, lower the right hand and raise the left hand in a repeated alternating movement.

# hail

**hail²** *v.* Same sign used for: **bow, worship.**

■ [Mime bowing before someone] Beginning with both *open hands* in front of the face, left hand somewhat higher than the right hand, both palms facing forward and fingers pointing up, move the hands downward with a double movement, ending with the palms facing down and the fingers pointing forward.

**hair** *n.*

■ [Location of hair] Hold a strand of hair with the thumb and forefinger of the right *F hand,* palm facing left, and shake it with a repeated movement.

**haircut¹** *n.*

■ [Mime cutting one's hair] Move the right *V hand,* palm facing left and fingers pointing up, from near the right cheek back to near the right ear while opening and closing the index and middle fingers with a double movement.

**haircut²** *n.* See sign for CUT¹.

**hair spray** *n.*

■ [**spray** formed near one's hair] Repeatedly bend the extended right index finger while moving the hand back and forth near the right side of the head.

**half** *adj.* See sign for ONE HALF.

**half-hour** *n.*

■ [Shows thirty-minute movement of minute hand on a clock] With the right index finger extended, palm facing forward, move the thumb side of the right hand in a half circle on the palm of the left *open hand,* palm facing right and fingers pointing upward, ending with the right index finger pointing straight down and palm facing in.

**halftime** *n.* Same sign used for: **intermission**.

- [Indicates a time in the middle] Insert the little-finger side of the right *open hand*, palm angled up and fingers pointing forward, between the middle finger and ring finger of the left *4 hand*, palm facing in.

**hall** *n.* Alternate form: **hallway**. Same sign used for: **corridor**.

- [Shape of a hallway] Move both *open hands*, palms facing each other and fingers pointing up, from in front of each shoulder straight forward.

**hallowed** *adj.* See sign for HOLY.

**Halloween** *n.* Same sign used for: **mask, masquerade**.

- [Represents a Halloween mask] Move both *curved hands* from in front of each eye, palms facing in and fingers pointing up, around to each side of the head, ending with the palms angled forward.

**halt** *v.* See signs for HOLD[2], STOP[1].

**hamburger** *n.*

- [Mime making a hamburger patty] Clasp the right *curved hand*, palm facing down, across the upturned left *curved hand*. Then flip the hands over and repeat with the left hand on top.

**hammer** *n., v.*

- [Mime hitting something with a hammer] Move the right *A hand*, palm facing left, up and down with a repeated movement in front of the right side of the body.

### handkerchief n.

■ [Mime blowing the nose with a handkerchief] Grasp the nose with the index finger and thumb of the right *G hand,* palm facing in. Then move the hand forward a short distance with a double movement, closing the index finger and thumb each time.

---

**handle** *v.* See signs for MANAGE, PIPE².

---

### hands *pl. n.*

■ [Location of one's hands] Beginning with the little-finger side of the right *B hand* at an angle on the thumb side of the left *B hand,* palms facing in opposite directions, bring the right hand down and under the left hand in order to exchange positions. Repeat the movement with the left hand.

---

### handshake *n.* Same sign used for: **shake hands.**

■ [Mime shaking one's own hand] Grasp the left *open hand* with the right *curved hand,* both palms facing in, and shake the hands up and down with a double movement.

---

**hands off** See sign for NOT RESPONSIBLE.

---

### handsome¹ *adj.*

■ [**face + clean**] Move the right extended index finger in a circle in front of the face, palm facing in. Then slide the palm of the right *open hand* from the heel to the fingers of the upturned left *open hand.*

---

**handsome²** *adj.* See sign for LOOKS.

---

**handy** *adj.* See sign for SKILL.

---

### hang *v.*

■ [Represents placing hangers on a rod] With the index finger of the right *X hand,* palm facing left, over the left extended index finger, palm facing down, move both hands downward a short distance.

---

**Hanukkah** or **Chanukah** *n.*

■ [Represents the shape of a Hanukkah menorah] Beginning with the little fingers of both *4 hands* touching in front of the chest, palms facing in and fingers pointing up, move the hands apart in an arc, ending with the hands in front of each shoulder.

**happen** *v.* Same sign used for: **accident, coincidence, event, incident, occur, occurrence.**

■ Beginning with both extended index fingers in front of the body, palms facing up and fingers pointing forward, flip the hands over toward each other, ending with the palms facing down.

**happy** *adj.* Same sign used for: **cheer, cheerful, delighted, gay, glad, jolly, joy, merry.**

■ [Represents joy rising in the body] Brush the fingers of the right *open hand,* palm facing in and fingers pointing left, upward in a repeated circular movement on the chest.

**harassment** *n.* See sign for DANGER.

**hard**[1] *adj.* Same sign used for: **solid.**

■ [Indicates a hard surface] Strike the little-finger side of the right *bent V hand* sharply against the index-finger side of the left *bent V hand,* palms facing in opposite directions.

**hard**[2] *adj.* See sign for DIFFICULT.

**hardly** *adv.* See sign for ANYWAY.

**hare** *n.* See sign for RABBIT.

**harm** *v.* See signs for DANGER, HURT[1].

**harvest** *n., v.* Same sign used for: **chop, cut down.**

■ [Represents cutting down a plant close to the ground] Move the fingers of the right *open hand,* palm facing up and fingers pointing forward, with a double movement under the elbow of the bent left arm, hand pointing up.

## has

**has** *v.* See sign for HAVE.

**hassle** *v.* See sign for HURRY.

**haste** *n.* See sign for HURRY.

**hat** *n.*
- [Location of a hat on one's head] Pat the top of the head with the fingers of the right *open hand,* palm facing down, with a double movement.

**hate** *v.* Same sign used for: **despise, detest.**
- [The fingers flick away something distasteful] Beginning with both *8 hands* in front of the chest, palms facing each other, flick the middle fingers forward, changing into *5 hands.*

**haul**[1] *v.* Same sign used for: **pull, tow.**
- [Shows action of pulling another with a hitch] With the index fingers of both *X hands* around each other, right palm facing in and left palm facing down, move both hands from left to right in front of the chest.

**haul**[2] *v.* See sign for DRAG.

**haunt** *v.* See sign for MONSTER. Related form: **haunted** *adj.*

**have** *v.* Same sign used for: **had, has.**
- [Brings something toward oneself] Bring the fingertips of both *bent hands,* palms facing in, back to touch each side of the chest.

**have to** *auxiliary.* See sign for MUST.

**hawk** *n.*
- [Shows a hawk's claws] Beginning with the back of the right *bent V hand* in front of the mouth, palm facing forward and fingers bent, bring the hand back against the mouth with a double movement while constricting the fingers each time.

**hazard** *n.* See sign for DANGER.

**haze** *v.* See sign for TORTURE.

**hazy** *adj.* See sign for VAGUE.

**he** *pron.* Same sign used for: **her, him, it, she.**
- [Directional sign toward another] Point the extended right index finger, palm facing down, outward to the right or in the direction of the referent.

**head**[1] *n.*
- [Location of the head] Touch the fingertips of the right *bent hand,* palm facing down, first to the right side of the forehead and then to the right side of the chin.

**head**[2] *v.* See sign for LEAD.

**headache** *n.*
- [**hurt**[1] formed near the forehead] With both extended index fingers pointing toward each other in front of the forehead, palms facing down, jab them toward each other with a short double movement.

**headlight** *n.*
- [Shows headlight beams] Beginning with both *flattened O hands* in front of the chest, palms facing down and fingers pointing forward, open the hands into *5 hands.*

**heal** *v.* See sign for WELL[1].

**healthy** *adj.* See sign for WELL[1].

**heap** *n.* See sign for AMOUNT.

**hear** *v.* Related form: **hearing** *n.* Same sign used for: **sound.**
- [Location of the organ of hearing] Bring the extended right index finger to the right ear.

# hearing

### hearing *adj.* Same sign used for: **public.**

- [Indicates a person who talks] Move the extended right index finger, pointing left, in a small double circular movement upward and forward in front of the lips.

### hearing aid *n.*

- [Shape of a hearing aid showing the location behind the ear where it is worn] Tap the index-finger side of the *modified C hand,* palm facing forward, against the head near the right ear.

### heart *n.*

- [Location and action of a heartbeat] Tap the bent middle finger of the right *5 hand,* palm facing in, with a repeated movement on the left side of the chest.

### heart attack *n.*

- [**heart** + **beat**[3]] Beginning with the bent middle finger of the right *5 hand* on the left side of the chest, palm facing in, bring the back of the right hand forward to touch the palm of the left *open hand,* palm facing in and fingers pointing right.

### heat[1] *n., v.*

- [Movement of a flame heating something on the stove] Move the right *curved 5 hand,* palm facing up, in a double circular movement under the upturned left *open hand.*

### heat[2] *adj.* See sign for HOT.

### heaven *n.*

- [Location of heaven] Beginning with both *open hands* in front of each shoulder, palms facing each other and fingers angled up, bring the hands upward toward each other, passing the right hand forward under the left *open hand,* both palms facing down, as the hands meet above the head.

### heavy *adj.*

■ [The hands seem to be weighted down with something heavy] Beginning with both *curved 5 hands* in front of each side of the chest, palms facing up, move the hands downward a short distance.

### hectic *adj.*

■ [Natural gesture used when someone describes rushing around] Beginning with both *5 hands* in front of each side of the chest, palms facing in and fingers pointing toward each other, twist the wrists forward with a repeated movement.

### height *n.*

■ [Indicates the top of oneself] Tap the extended right index finger, palm facing up, on the top of the head with a double movement.

### helicopter *n.*

■ [Represents a helicopter's propeller] With extended thumb of the left *10 hand,* palm facing right, pointing up into the palm of the right *5 hand,* palm facing down, wiggle the right fingers while moving both hands forward a short distance.

### hell *n.*

■ [Initialized sign moving downward to the traditional location of hell] Move the right *H hand* from in front of the left shoulder, palm facing in and fingers angled up, downward with a deliberate movement to the right, ending with the hand in front of the right side of the body, fingers pointing forward and palm facing left.

### hello *interj., n.*

■ [Natural gesture for a salute to greet someone] Beginning with the fingertips of the right *B hand* near the right side of the forehead, palm angled forward, bring the hand forward with a deliberate movement.

205

# helmet

**helmet** *n.*

- [Shape and location of a helmet on the head] Beginning with both *curved 5 hands* near each other at the top of the head, palms facing each other and fingers angled up, move the hands downward along the shape of the head, stopping abruptly near each side of the head.

**help** *v., n.* Same sign used for: **aid, assist.**

- [The lower hand seems to give assistance to the other hand] With the little-finger side of the left *A hand* in the upturned right *open hand,* move both hands upward in front of the chest.

**hen** *n.* See sign for CHICKEN[1].

**henpeck** *v.* See sign for PICK ON.

**her** or **hers** *pron.* See signs for HE, HIS.

**here** *adv., n.* Same sign used for: **present.**

- [Indicates a location near oneself] Beginning with both *curved hands* in front of each side of the body, palms facing up, move the hands toward each other in repeated flat circles.

**hermit** *n.* Same sign used for: **isolated.**

- [Emphasizes a person alone] Beginning with both *I hands* in front of the face, palms facing in, bring the little fingers together with a double movement.

**herself** *pron.* See signs for HIMSELF, ITSELF.

**hesitate** *v.*

- [Natural gesture used to balk at something] With both *open hands* in front of each side of the chest, palms facing forward and fingers pointing up, pull the head and body backward with a short repeated movement.

**hi** *interj.*

■ [Natural gesture for waving in greeting] Move the right *open hand,* palm facing forward and fingers pointing up, from in front of the chest to the right in a smooth arc.

**hiccup** *n., v.*

■ [Shows action of hiccupping] Beginning with the bent index finger of the right hand tucked under the right thumb, palm facing in, flick the index finger upward with a double movement in front of the chest.

**hide** *v.* Same sign used for: **conceal, mystery.**

■ [**secret** + a gesture putting something under the other hand as if to hide it] Move the thumb of the right *A hand,* palm facing left, from near the mouth downward in an arc to under the left *curved hand* held in front of the chest, palm facing down.

**high** *adj., adv.* Same sign used for: **altitude.**

■ [Initialized sign showing a location at a higher elevation] Move the right *H hand,* palm facing left and fingers pointing forward, from in front of the right side of the chest upward to near the right side of the head.

**higher** *adj.* See sign for ADVANCED.

**high school** *n.*

■ [Abbreviation **h-s**] Form the fingerspelled letters H and S in front of the right side of the chest, palm facing in.

# highway

### highway *n.* Same sign used for: **freeway.**

- [Initialized sign representing two streams of traffic going in opposite directions] Beginning with both *H hands* held in front of each side of the chest, palms facing down and fingers pointing toward each other, move the hands past each other toward the opposite sides of the chest with a repeated movement.

### hill *n.*

- [Shows shape of a hillside] Beginning with both *open hands* in front of each side of the waist, palms angled forward and fingers angled up, move the hands forward and upward with a large wavy movement.

### him *pron.* See sign for HE.

### himself *pron.* See also sign for ITSELF. Same sign used for: **herself.**

- [Directional sign toward the person you are referring to] Push the extended thumb of the right *10 hand,* palm facing left, forward with a short double movement in front of the right side of the body.

### hinder *v.* See sign for PREVENT.

### hindsight *n.* Same sign used for: **look back, recollect, recollection, retrospect.**

- [Represents the eyes looking back into the past] Beginning with the fingertips of the right *V hand* pointing toward the right eye, palm facing down, move the hand around to the right side of the head, ending with the fingers pointing back.

### hinge *n.*

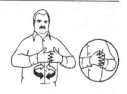

- [Shows action of a door opening on hinges] Beginning with the fingers of both *curved 5 hands* meshed together in front of the chest, palms facing in, bend the fingers forward and back with a double movement by twisting the wrists.

### hire *v.* See sign for INVITE.

**his** *pron.* Same sign used for: **her, hers, its.**

- [Directional sign toward the person referred to] Push the right *open hand,* palm facing forward, at an angle forward in front of the right side of the body.

**history** *n.* Related form: **historical** *adj.*

- [Initialized sign] Move the right *H hand,* palm facing left, downward with a double movement in front of the right side of the body.

**hit**[1] *v.* Same sign used for: **attack, impact, strike.**

- [Demonstrates action of hitting] Strike the knuckles of the right *A hand,* palm facing in, against the extended left index finger held up in front of the chest, palm facing right.

**hit**[2] *v.* See signs for BEAT[3], BEAT UP, PUNCH.

**hitchhike** *v.* Related form: **hitch** *v.*

- [Natural gesture for hitchhiking] Move the thumb of the right *10 hand,* palm facing in, from the front of the right shoulder to the right with a double movement.

**hockey** *n.*

- [Shape and action of a hockey stick] Brush the index finger of the right *X hand* against the upturned palm of the left *open hand* as the right hand moves in a double circular movement.

**hoe** *n.* See sign for RAKE.

# hold

**hold**[1] *v.* Same sign used for: **grip.**

- [The hands seem to hold something securely] Beginning with the little-finger side of the right *C hand* on the index-finger side of the left *C hand*, both palms facing in, move the hands in toward the chest while closing the fingers of both hands into *S hands.*

**hold**[2] or **hold on** *v.* or *v. phrase.* Same sign used for: **halt, pause, stall, suspend.**

- [One hand seems to suspend the other] With the index fingers of both *X hands* hooked together, palms facing down, pull both hands upward.

**hold up** *v. phrase.* See sign for ROB.

**hole** *n.*

- [Shape of a hole] Move the extended right index finger, palm facing back and fingers pointing down, in a large circle around the index-finger side of the left *C hand*, palm facing down.

**holiday** *n.*

- [Gesture often used when one is carefree] Tap the thumbs of both *5 hands* near each armpit, palms facing each other and fingers pointing forward, with a double movement.

**holler** *v.* See sign for CALL[2].

**holy** *adj.* Related form: **holiness** *n.* Same sign used for: **hallowed.**

- [Initialized sign similar to sign for **clean**] Move the right *H hand* in a circular movement over the upturned left *open hand.* Then slide the little-finger side of the right *H hand* from the base to the fingertips of the left hand.

210

**home** *n., adv.*

- [A modification of the signs **eat** and **sleep** indicating that a home is a place where you eat and sleep] Touch the fingertips of the right *flattened O hand* first to the right side of the chin, palm facing down, and then to the right cheek.

**homework** *n.*

- [**home** + **work**] Touch the fingertips of the right *flattened O hand* to the right cheek, palm facing down. Then move the right hand down while changing into an *S hand* and tap the base of the right *S hand* on the back of the left *S hand* held in front of the chest, palm facing down.

**homosexual** *adj., n.* See sign for GAY[1].

**honest** *adj.* Related forms: **honestly** *adv.*, **honesty** *n.* Same sign used for: **frank, frankly, sure.**

- [Initialized sign similar to sign for **clean**] Slide the extended fingers of the right *H hand,* palm facing left, forward from the heel to the fingers of the upturned left *open hand.*

**honey** *n.*

- [Initialized sign similar to sign for **sweet**] Beginning with the fingers of the right *H hand* near the right side of the mouth, palm facing back and fingers pointing left, move the fingers to the right with a double movement, bending the fingers back into the palm to change into an *A hand* each time.

**honeymoon** *n.*

- [Formed with the finger used for feeling, with a movement similar to **bachelor**] Touch the bent middle finger of the right *5 hand,* palm facing in, first to the left side of the chin and then to the right side of the chin.

# honor

**honor** *n., v.* Related form: **honorary** *adj.*

- [Initialized sign similar to sign for **respect**] Beginning with both *H hands* in front of the face, right hand higher than the left hand and palms facing in opposite directions, bring both hands downward and forward in a slight arc.

**hood** *n.* See sign for PONCHO.

**hooked** *adj.* See sign for ADDICTED.

**hook up** *v. phrase.* See sign for BELONG[1].

**hop** *v.*

- [Shows action of hopping] Beginning with the knuckles of the right *bent V hand,* palm facing back, on the heel of the left *open hand* held in front of the chest, palm facing up, raise the right hand while straightening the fingers into a *V hand,* and then bend the fingers again to touch down on the left palm. Repeat, touching farther toward the left fingers each time.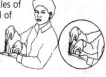

**hope** *v., n.* Same sign used for: **expect, expectation.**

- [The hands seem to compare a thought with the anticipated future] Beginning with the right *open hand* near the right side of the head, palm angled left and fingers pointed up, and the left *open hand* in front of the chest, palm facing right and fingers pointing up, bend the fingers toward each other with a double movement.

**horde** *n.* See also sign for AUDIENCE. Same sign used for: **crowd, mass.**

- [Indicates large crowds of people] Move both *curved 5 hands,* palms facing down, from in front of each side of the upper chest forward with a simultaneous movement.

**horn** *n.*

- [Mime holding a horn and blowing into it] Hold the left *S hand* in front of the mouth, palm facing right, and the right *C hand* in front of the face, palm facing left.

### horns[1] *pl. n.*

- [Shape and location of horns on the head] Beginning with the thumb side of both *O hands* on each side of the head, palms facing forward, bring the hands upward and outward in small arcs while closing into *S hands*.

### horns[2] *pl. n.* See sign for PRESIDENT.

### horrible *adj.* See sign for AWFUL.

### horse *n.*

- [Represents a horse's ears] With the extended thumb of the right *U hand* against the right side of the forehead, palm facing forward, bend the fingers of the *U hand* up and down with a double movement.

### hose[1] *n.*

- [**water** + mime holding a hose to water something] Tap the index-finger side of the right *W hand,* palm facing left, against the chin with a double movement. Then, with the little-finger side of the right *modified X hand* touching the index–finger side of the left *S hand,* palms facing in opposite directions, swing the hands from side to side with a double movement in front of the body.

### hose[2] *n.* See sign for STOCKING.

### hospital *n.*

- [Initialized sign following the shape of a cross, symbolic of the American Red Cross, a health-care organization] Bring the fingertips of the right *H hand,* palm facing right, first downward a short distance on the upper left arm and then across from back to front.

### host *v.* See signs for LEAD, SERVE.

### hostage *n.*

- [Initialized sign similar to sign for **jail**] Beginning with both *H hands* in front of the chest, palms facing in and fingers pointing upward at angles in opposite directions, bring the right *H fingers* in against the left fingers.

# hot

**hot** *adj.* Same sign used for: **heat.**

- [Hand seems to take something hot from the mouth and throw it away] Beginning with the right *curved 5 hand* in front of the mouth, palm facing in, twist the wrist forward with a deliberate movement while moving the hand downward a short distance.

**hot dog** *n.*

- [**hot** + **sausage**] Beginning with the right *curved 5 hand* in front of the mouth, palm facing in, twist the wrist forward with a deliberate movement while moving the hand downward a short distance. Then, beginning with the index-finger sides of both *C hands* touching in front of the body, palms facing forward, bring the hands outward to each side while squeezing them open and closed from *C* to *S hands* repeatedly as the hands move.

**hotel** *n.*

- [Initialized sign] Place the fingers of the right *H hand*, palm facing in and fingers pointing left, on the back of the extended left index finger, palm facing in and index finger pointing up in front of the chest.

**hour** *n.* Same sign used for: **one hour.**

- [Shows minute hand moving 60 minutes around a clock] With the right index finger extended, palm facing left, move the palm side of the right hand in a circle on the palm of the left *open hand*, palm facing right, while twisting the wrist, ending with the right palm facing in.

**hourly** *adj.* Same sign as for HOUR but made with a double movement.

**house** *n.*

- [Shape of house's roof and walls] Beginning with the fingertips of both *open hands* touching in front of the neck, palms angled toward each other, bring the hands at a downward angle outward to in front of each shoulder and then straight down, ending with the fingers pointing up and the palms facing each other.

**how** *adv., conj.*

- [Similar to gesture used with a shrug to indicate not knowing something] Beginning with the knuckles of both *curved hands* touching in front of the chest, palms facing down, twist the hands upward and forward, ending with the fingers together pointing up and the palms facing up.

---

**however** *adv.* See signs for ANYWAY, BUT.

**how many** See sign for HOW MUCH.

**how much** Same sign used for: **how many.**

- [An abbreviated form] Beginning with the right *S hand* in front of the right side of the chest, palm facing up, flick the fingers open quickly into a *5 hand.*

---

**hug** *v.* Same sign used for: **affection, affectionate, embrace.**

- [Mime hugging someone] With the arms of both *S hands* crossed at the wrists, palms facing in, pull the arms back against the chest with a double movement.

---

**hulk** *n.* Same sign used for: **husky.**

- [Shows shape of a hulk's shoulders] Beginning with both *modified C hands* near each side of the neck, move the hands forward from each shoulder, ending with the palms facing in.

---

**hum** *v., n.*

- [Initialized sign using **m** indicating the sound that is made when humming] Beginning with the index-finger side of the right *M hand* near the right side of the face, palm facing left, bring the hand forward with a wavy movement.

---

# humble

**humble** *adj.* Same sign used for: **meek, modest, modesty.**

- [Shows moving oneself under another when humbled] Bring the right *B hand,* palm facing left and fingers pointing up, from in front of the mouth downward and forward under the left *open hand* held in front of the chest, palm facing down.

**humid**[1] *adj.*

- [**hot** + the hands seem to be feeling something wet] Beginning with the right *curved 5 hand* in front of the mouth, palm facing in, twist the wrist forward with a deliberate movement. Then, beginning with the fingers of both *5 hands* near the chin, palms facing in, move the hands downward and forward slightly, changing into *flattened O hands* in front of each shoulder and rubbing the thumbs and fingers together.

**humid**[2] *adj.* See sign for WET.

**humor** *n.* See sign for FUNNY.

**humorous** *adj.* Same sign used for: **comical.**

- [Similar to sign for **silly** except more exaggerated and formed with both hands] With the thumb of the right *Y hand* near the nose and the left *Y hand* somewhat lower and forward, palms facing each other, move both hands downward with a repeated circular movement.

**hundred** *n.*

- [Abbreviation **c** representing the Roman numeral for **hundred**] Move the right *C hand,* palm facing left, from in front of the chest a short distance to the right.

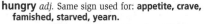

**hungry** *adj.* Same sign used for: **appetite, crave, famished, starved, yearn.**

- [Shows passage to an empty stomach] Beginning with the fingertips of the right *C hand* touching the center of the chest, palm facing in, move the hand downward a short distance.

**hunt** *v.* Related form: **hunting** *n., adj.*

- [Mime aiming a rifle or shotgun] With both *L hands* in front of the chest, right hand closer to the chest than the left, palms facing in opposite directions, and index fingers angled up, move the hands downward with a double movement.

**hunt for** *v. phrase.* See sign for LOOK FOR.

**hurrah** *n.* See sign for RALLY.

**hurry** *v., n.* Same sign used for: **hassle, haste, hustle, rush, urgent.**

- [Initialized sign showing hurried movement] Beginning with both *H hands* in front of each side of the body, palms facing each other, move the hands up and down with a quick short repeated movement, moving the hands slightly forward each time.

**hurt**[1] *v., n.* See also signs for PAIN.
Same sign used for: **ache, harm, wound.**

- [Fingers indicate a stabbing pain] Beginning with both extended index fingers pointing toward each other in front of the chest, palms facing in, jab the fingers toward each other with a short repeated movement.

**hurt**[2] *adj.* See also signs for PAIN. Same sign used for: **bear, sore, wound.**

- [Symbolizes patience when having pain] Beginning with the thumb of the right *A hand* touching the chin, palm facing left, twist the wrist back, ending with the palm facing in.

**husband** *n.*

- [Hand moves from the male area of the head + **marry**] Move the right *C hand* from the right side of the forehead, palm facing left, down to clasp the left *curved hand* held in front of the chest, palm facing up.

**husky** *adj.* See sign for HULK.

**hustle** *v.* See sign for HURRY[1].

# hyena

**hyena** *n.*

■ [**dog** + **hysterical**] Snap the right thumb gently off the right middle finger, palm facing up, in front of the right side of the chest. Then, with the right *curved 5 hand* over the left *curved 5 hand* in front of the chest, move the hands forward and back with a repeated alternating movement.

**hypnotize** *v.* Related form: **hypnosis** *n.*

■ [The fingers seem to put a spell on someone] Beginning with both *5 hands* in front of each side of the chest, palms facing down and fingers pointing forward, wiggle the fingers slowly.

**hypocrite** *n.* Same sign used for: **fake, impostor.**

■ [Hands indicate someone covering the truth.] With the palm of the right *open hand* on the back of the left *open hand*, the fingers of both hands pointing forward and palms facing down, push the fingers of the left hand down with the right fingers.

**hypodermic**[1] *adj., n.*

■ [Mime giving a shot in the arm with a hypodermic] Move the index finger of the right *3 hand* from in front of the right shoulder, palm facing right, back against the right upper arm while closing the middle finger to the thumb.

**hypodermic**[2] *n.* See sign for SHOT.

**hysterical** *adj.* Same sign used for: **laugh, laughter.**

■ [The stomach shaking while one is laughing] Beginning with both *curved 5 hands* in front of the chest, palms facing each other and the right hand above the left hand, move the hands forward and back to the chest with a repeated movement and in opposite directions.

**I**[1] *pron.*
- [Initialized sign formed toward oneself] Bring the thumb side of the right *I hand,* palm facing left, back against the chest.

**I**[2] *pron.* See sign for ME.

**ice** *n.* See sign for FREEZE.

**ice cream** *n.*
- [Mime eating from an ice cream cone] Bring the index-finger side of the right *S hand,* palm facing left, back in an arc toward the mouth with a double movement.

**ice skate** *n., v.* See sign for SKATE[2].

**idea** *n.*
- [Initialized sign representing an idea coming from the head] Move the extended right little finger from near the right temple, palm facing down, upward in an arc.

**ideal** *n., adj.* See sign for PERFECT.

**identical** *adj.* See sign for ALIKE[1].

**identify** *v.*
- [Initialized sign similar to sign for **show**[1]] Tap the thumb side of the right *I hand,* palm facing left, with a double movement against the left open palm held in front of the chest, palm facing forward and fingers pointing up.

# idiom

**idiom** *n.*

- [Initialized sign similar to sign for **quotation**[1]] While holding both *I hands* near each side of the head, palms angled forward, bending the little fingers.

**idiot** *n.*

- [Initialized sign similar to sign for **ignorant**] Bring the thumb side of the right *I hand,* palm facing left, against the forehead.

**if** *conj.* See sign for SUPPOSE.

**ignorant** *adj.* Related form: **ignorance** *n.*

- [The *V hand* indicates a void of knowledge] Bring the back of the right *V hand,* palm facing forward, against the forehead with a deliberate movement.

**ignore** *v.* Same sign used for: **forsake, neglect.**

- [Indicates attention moving away from object or person in view] While looking forward, place the index finger of the right *4 hand,* palm facing forward and fingers pointing up, near the right side of the face. Then move the hand outward to the right with a quick deliberate movement.

**ill** *adj.* See sign for SICK. Related form: **illness** *n.*

**illegal** *adj.* See sign for FORBID.

**illegible** *adj.* See sign for VAGUE.

**illustrate** *v.* See sign for DRAW[1].

**illustration** *n.* See signs for ART, SKETCH[1].

**I love you** (A special handshape in American Sign Language).

- [Abbreviation **i-l-y** formed simultaneously in a single handshape] Hold up the right hand with the thumb, index finger, and little finger extended, palm facing forward, in front of the right shoulder.

**image**[1] *n.* Same sign used for: **indicate, indicator.**

- [Initialized sign similar to sign for **show**[1]] Beginning with the index-finger side of the right *I hand* against the palm of the left *open hand,* palm facing right and fingers pointing up, move both hands forward simultaneously.

**image**[2] *n.* See sign for SHAPE[1].

**imagination** *n.* Same sign used for: **superstition, superstitious.**

- [Initialized sign showing ideas coming from the head] Move the extended little fingers of both *I hands,* palms facing back, in double alternating circles near each side of the head.

**imagine** *v.* Same sign used for: **make believe.**

- [Initialized sign similar to sign for **dream**] Move the extended right little finger from near the right temple, palm facing down, upward in a double circular movement.

**imitate** *v.* See signs for COPY[1,2].

**immigrate** *v.* See sign for ENTER.

**immune** *adj.* See sign for RESIST.

**impact** *n.* See sign for HIT[1].

**impair** *v.* See sign for PREVENT.

**impeach** *v.* See sign for FEEDBACK.

# implore

**implore** *v.* See sign for BEG[1].

**important** *adj.* Same sign used for: **essential, main, significance, significant, value, worth.**
- [The hands bring what is important to the top] Beginning with the little-finger sides of both *F hands* touching, palms facing up, bring the hands upward in a circular movement while turning the hands over, ending with the index-finger sides of the *F hands* touching in front of the chest.

**impose** *v.* See signs for COPY[1,2].

**impossible** *adj.*
- [The hand strikes an unyielding surface] Strike the palm side of the right *Y hand* against the upturned open left palm with a double movement.

**imposter** *n.* See sign for HYPOCRITE.

**impression** *n.* Same sign used for: **emphasis, stress.**
- [Movement seems to press something in order to make an impression] With the extended thumb of the right *10 hand,* palm facing down, pressed into the palm of the left *open hand,* palm facing right, twist the right hand downward while keeping the thumb in place.

**imprisoned** *adj.* See sign for JAIL.

**improve**[1] *v.* Related form: **improvement** *n.*
- [Hands seems to measure out an amount of improvement] Touch the little-finger side of the right *open hand,* palm facing back, first to the wrist and then near the crook of the extended left arm.

**improve**[2] *v.* Related form: **improvement** *n.* Same sign used for: **remodel, renovate.**
- [**improve**[1] formed with a movement that indicates continued improvements] Brush the little-finger side of the right *open hand,* palm facing in and fingers pointing left, upward with a circular movement on the forearm of the bent left arm.

**impulse** *n.*
- [Shows spontaneity] Beginning with both *A hands* near the chest, palms facing in, move the hands suddenly forward while extending the index fingers, palms facing down and index fingers pointing forward.

---

**in** *prep.* Related form: **inner** *adj.*
- [Shows location in something] Insert the fingertips of the right *flattened O hand,* palm facing down, into the center of the thumb side of the left *O hand,* palm facing right in front of the chest.

---

**in accord** See sign for AGREE[1].

**in agreement** See sign for AGREE[1].

**inauguration** *n.* See sign for OATH. Related form: **inaugural** *n.*

**in behalf of** See sign for SUPPORT.

**inch** *n.*
- [Measures out a small length] Place the fingertips of the right *modified C hand,* palm facing left, against the extended thumb of the left *10 hand* held up in front of the chest, palm facing right.

---

**incident** *n.* See signs for HAPPEN, SHOW UP.

**in case of** See sign for SUPPOSE.

**in charge of** See sign for MANAGE.

**incline** *n.* See sign for GRADE.

**include** *v.* Same sign used for: **contained in, everything, involve, within.**
- [The hand seems to encompass everything to gather it into one space] Swing the right *5 hand,* palm facing down, in a circular movement over the left *S hand,* palm facing in, while changing into a *flattened O hand,* ending with the fingertips of the right hand inserted in the center of the thumb side of the left hand.

---

# income

**income**[1] *n.* Same sign used for: **revenue, salary, wages.**

- [**money + earn**] Tap the back of the right *flattened O hand*, palm facing up, with a double movement against the left *open hand*, palm facing up. Then bring the little-finger side of the right *C hand*, palm facing left, with a double movement across the palm of the left *open hand*, closing the right hand into an *S hand* each time.

**income**[2] *n.* See sign for EARN.

**incorrect** *adj.* See sign for WRONG.

**increase** *n., v.* Same sign used for: **gain, raise.**

- [Shows more and more things adding to a pile to increase it] Beginning with the right *U hand*, palm facing up, slightly lower than the left *U hand*, palm facing down, flip the right hand over, ending with the right fingers across the left fingers.

**incredible**[1] *adj.* Same sign used for: **amazed, stunned.**

- [Represents one's mouth dropping open when amazed] Beginning with the back of the right *S hand* against the open mouth, palm facing forward, deliberately open the hand into a *bent 3 hand*.

**incredible**[2] *adj.* See sign for WONDERFUL.

**indecision** *n.* Same sign used for: **doubt, juggle, uncertain, undecided.**

- [Represents "sitting on the fence" when one is undecided] Beginning with the fingers of the right *V hand*, palm facing back and fingers pointing down, straddling the index-finger side of the left *B hand*, palm facing right and fingers pointing forward, rock the right hand back and forth with a double movement.

**independent** *adj.*

- [Initialized sign similar to sign for **save**[1]] Beginning with the wrists of both *I hands* crossed in front of the chest, palms facing in, swing the arms apart, ending with the *I hands* in front of each shoulder, palms facing forward.

**indicate** *v.* See signs for IMAGE, SHOW[1]. Related forms: **indicator** *n.*, **indication** *n.*

**indifferent** *adj.* See sign for DON'T CARE.

**individual** *n., adj.*
■ [Initialized sign similar to sign for **person**] Bring both
*I hands,* palms facing each other, from the chest down
along the sides of the body.

**indoctrinate** *v.* See sign for TEACH. Related form: **indoctrination** *n.*

**induce** *v.*
■ [Similar to sign for **hypnotize** moving toward oneself]
Beginning with both *curved 5 hands* in front of the
face, palms facing each other, wiggle the fingers
while moving the hands in toward the eyes,
closing into *S hands.*

**industry** *n.* See sign for MACHINE.

**inexperienced** *adj.* See signs for CLUMSY[1], UNSKILLED.

**infant** *n.* See sign for BABY.

**in favor of** See sign for SUPPORT.

**infection** *n.* See sign for INSURANCE.

**inferior** *adj.*
■ [Initialized sign similar to sign for **base**] Move the extended
finger of the right *I hand,* palm angled forward, in a double
circular movement under the left *open hand,*
palm facing down.

**infirmary** *n.*
■ [Initialized sign similar to sign for **hospital**]
Move the extended fingertip of the right
*I hand,* palm facing in, first down and
then across on the upper left arm
from back to front.

225

# influence

**influence** *v., n.* Same sign used for: **affect, effect.**

■ [Similar to sign for **advice** except spread outward to others] Beginning with the fingertips of the right *flattened O hand* on the back of the left *open hand,* palm facing down, move the right hand forward while opening into a *5 hand* and bringing the hand in a sweeping arc to in front of the right side of the body.

**inform** *v.* Same sign used for: **issue, let know, notice, notify.**

■ [Indicates taking information from one's head and giving it to others] Beginning with the fingertips of the right *flattened O hand* near the forehead and the left *flattened O hand* in front of the chest, move both hands forward while opening into *5 hands,* palms facing up.

**information** *n.* Similar to sign for **inform** except formed with a double movement.

**infuse** *v.* See signs for INTERFACE, MESH.

**in front of** Same sign used for: **face to face, facing.**

■ [Shows two things facing each other] Beginning with both *open hands* in front of the chest, palms facing each other and fingers pointing up, move both hands forward simultaneously.

**inhale** *v.* See sign for BREATH.

**injury** *n.* See sign for PAIN.

**innocent** *adj.* Same sign used for: **naive.**

■ [Signifies that nothing wrong has been said] Beginning with the fingers of both *U hands* touching the mouth, palms facing in, move the hands forward and outward to in front of each shoulder.

**in order** See sign for PREPARE.

**inquire** *v.* See sign for TEST.

**insect** *n.* See sign for BUG.

**inside** *prep., adv., n., adj.* Same sign used for: **internal.**
■ [Shows location inside] Insert the fingertips of the right *flattened O hand,* palm facing down, into the center of the thumb side of the left *O hand,* palm facing right in front of the chest, with a repeated movement.

**insist** *v.* See sign for DEMAND.

**insomnia** *n.* Same sign used for: **alert, awake.**
■ [Represents the eyes being wide open when one can't sleep] Place both *C hands* around the wide-open eyes with the thumbs near each side of the nose, palms facing forward.

**inspect** *v.* See signs for CHECK[1], INVESTIGATE. Related form: **inspection** *n.*

**inspire** *v.* Related form: **inspiration** *n.* Same sign used for: **pep, revive.**
■ [Represents inspiration moving up in one's body] Beginning with both *flattened O hands* in front of each side of the chest, palms facing in and fingers pointing up, move the hands upward while opening into *5 hands* in front of each shoulder.

**install** *v.* See signs for APPLY[1], PUT.

**installment plan** *n.* Same sign used for: **layaway.**
■ [Pushing money away for payments] Slide the little-finger side of the right bent hand, palm facing in and fingers pointing left, with a short double movement from the wrist to off the fingertips of the left open hand held in front of the chest, palm facing up and fingers angled forward.

**instead** *adv.*
■ [Represents substituting one thing for another] Move the fingertips of the right *F hand* forward in a circle around the fingertips of the left *F hand,* ending with the fingertips touching, palms facing each other.

# institute

**institute** *n.*

- [Initialized sign showing setting something up] Beginning with the right *I hand* in front of the right side of the body, palm facing in, and the left *open hand* held across the chest, palm facing down and fingers pointing right, bring the right hand back toward the chest in a large upward arc and then down, ending with the little-finger side of the right *I hand* on the back of the left hand.

**instruct**[1] *v.* Related form: **instruction** *n.*

- [Initialized sign similar to sign for **teach**] Move both *I hands* forward a short distance with a double movement from in front of each side of the chest, palms facing each other.

**instruct**[2] *v.* See signs for DESCRIBE, TEACH. Related form: **instruction** *n.*

**insult** *v., n.* Related form: **insulting** *adj.*
Same sign used for: **affront.**

- [Finger seems to direct an insult at another] Move the extended right index finger from in front of the right side of the body, palm facing left and finger pointing forward, forward and upward sharply in an arc.

**insurance** *n.* Related form: **insure** *v.*
Same sign used for: **infection.**

- [Initialized sign] Move the right *I hand*, palm facing forward, from side to side with a repeated movement near the right shoulder.

**integrate** *v.* See sign for MESH.

**intelligent** *adj.* See sign for SMART. Related form: **intelligence** *n.*

**intend** *v.* See sign for MEAN[2].

**interact** *v.* See sign for ASSOCIATE.

**intercept** *v.* Same sign used for: **cut off.**

- [The hand moves forward to stop or intercept the other hand] Move the right *V hand*, palm facing left, forward while closing the index and middle fingers together near the end of the extended left index finger held in front of the chest, palm facing down and finger pointing right.

### intercourse *n.*

- [Two bodies coming together] Bring the right *V hand* downward in front of the chest to tap against the heel of the left *V hand* with a double movement, palms facing each other.

### interest[1] *n.* Related form: **interested** *adj.* Same sign used for: **fascinating.**

- [The hands bring thoughts and feelings to the surface] Beginning with the right *modified C hand* in front of the face and the left *modified C hand* in front of the chest, both palms facing in, move the hands forward simultaneously while closing into *A hands.*

### interest[2] *n.*

- [Initialized sign] Rub the little-finger side of the right *I hand,* palm facing the chest, in a repeated circle on the back of left *open hand,* palm facing down.

### interface *n.* Same sign used for: **infuse, merge.**

- [The hands represent things interfacing with each other] Beginning with both *5 hands* in front of each side of the chest, palms facing in and fingers angled toward each other, push the hands toward each other, causing the fingers to mesh together.

### interfere *v.* See signs for ANNOY, MEDDLE[1].

### intermediate *adj.*

- [Shows a location in the middle] Slide the little-finger side of the right *open hand,* palm facing up, with a double movement between the middle and ring fingers of the left *5 hand,* palm facing right.

# intermission

**intermission** *n*. Same sign used for: **halftime**.

- [Shows something being inserted halfway through something] Slide the index-finger side of the right *open hand*, palm facing down, between the index and middle fingers of the left *5 hand*, palm facing in.

**internal** *adj*. See sign for INSIDE.

**international** *adj*.

- [Initialized sign similar to sign for **world**] Move both *I hands* in circles around each other, palms facing each other, ending with the little-finger side of the right hand on the index-finger side of the left hand in front of the chest.

**internship** *n*. Related form: **intern** *n*.

- [Initialized sign similar to sign for **practice**] Slide the little-finger side of the right *I hand*, palm facing left, back and forth with a double movement on the back of the left *open hand*, palm facing down and fingers pointing right.

**interpret** *v*.

- [Uses the same movement as **change**[1]] With the fingertips of both *F hands* touching in front of the chest, palms facing each other, twist the hands in opposite directions to reverse positions.

**interrupt** *v*. See signs for ANNOY, MEDDLE[1].

**intersection** *n*. Same sign used for: **crossing.**

- [Represents two roads crossing each other] Bring the side of the extended right index finger, palm facing left, with a double movement across the extended left index finger, palm facing down.

**interview** *v., n.*

- [Initialized sign similar to sign for **com-munication**] Move both *I hands*, palms facing each other, forward and back toward the mouth with an alternating movement.

---

**into** *prep.* See sign for ENTER.

---

**in touch with** See sign for CONTACT.

---

**intoxicated** *adj.* See sign for DRUNK.

---

**introduce** *v.* Related form: **introduction** *n.*

- [The hands seem to bring two people together] Bring both *bent hands* from in front of each side of the body, palms facing up and fingers pointing toward each other, toward each other in front of the waist.

---

**invent** *v.* Same sign used for: **create, make up, originate.**

- [The hand seems to take ideas from the head] Move the index-finger side of the right *4 hand*, palm facing left, from the forehead upward in an outward arc.

---

**invest** *v.* Related form: **investment** *n.* Same sign used for: **deposit, stocks.**

- [Represents depositing money in a bank] Insert the fingertips of the right *flattened O hand*, palm facing left, into the center of the thumb side of the left *O hand*, palm angled forward.

---

**investigate** *v.* Related form: **investigation** *n.* Same sign used for: **examination, examine, inspect, inspection.**

- [The finger seems to be paging through pages of documents] Brush the extended right index finger with a repeated movement from the heel to the fingertips of the upturned palm of the left *open hand*.

---

# invite

**invite** *v.* Related form: **invitation** *n.* Same sign used for: **employ, greet, hire, welcome.**

- [The hand brings another to oneself] Bring the upturned right *curved hand* from in front of the right side of the body in toward the center of the waist.

**involve** *v.* See sign for INCLUDE.

**iron¹** *n., adj.*

- [Initialized sign] Slide the base of the extended little finger of the right *I hand*, palm facing in, with a double movement across the extended left index finger, palm facing down and finger pointing right in front of the chest.

**iron²** *n., v.*

- [Mime using an iron] Rub the knuckle side of the right *S hand*, palm facing in, back and forth along the length of the upturned left *open hand* with a repeated movement.

**irony** *n.* Related form: **ironic** *adj.* Same sign used for: **sarcastic.**

- [A jabbing movement] With the little finger and index finger of the right hand extended, palm facing left near the nose, and the little finger and index finger of the left hand extended in front of the chest, palm facing down, move the right hand forward and

the left hand back until the hands are facing each other in front of the chest. Then push the hands past each other, ending with the wrists crossed in front of the chest.

**irritate** *v.* See signs for ANNOY, ITCH.

**I should have thought of it before** See sign for DISGUSTED².

**island** *n.*

- [Initialized sign] Rub the side of the extended little finger of the right *I hand,* palm facing left, with a double movement in a circle on the back of the left *S hand,* palm facing down.

**isolated** *adj.* See signs for ALONE[1], HERMIT.

**issue** *v.* See signs for INFORM, NEWSPAPER.

**it** or **its** *pron.* See signs for HE, HIS.

**itch** *n., v.* Related form: **itchy** *adj.* Same sign used for: **irritate.**

- [Mime scratching an itchy place] Move the fingertips of the right *curved 5 hand,* palm facing in, back and forth with a double movement on the back of the left *open hand,* palm facing in and fingers pointing right.

**itself** *pron.* See also sign for HIMSELF. Same sign used for: **herself.**

- [Uses the handshape used for reflexive pronouns to emphasize the location of another thing] Bring the knuckles of the right *10 hand,* palm facing left, firmly against the side of the extended left index finger, palm facing right and finger pointing up in front of the chest.

---

**jab** *v., n.*

- [Mime jabbing someone in the ribs] Poke the extended right index finger, palm facing back, against the right side with a double movement.

---

**jabber** *v.* Same sign used for: **chatter.**

- [**talk**¹ formed with a fast repeated movement] Beginning with the right *5 hand* in front of the mouth, palm facing left and fingers pointing up, and the left *5 hand* near the little finger of the right hand, palm facing right and fingers pointing up, wiggle the fingers repeatedly.

---

**jacket** *n.* See sign for COAT.

---

**jagged** *adj.* See sign for RAGGED.

---

**jail** *n.* Same sign used for: **imprisoned, prison.**

- [Represents jail bars] Bring the back of the right *4 hand* from near the chest forward with a double movement while bringing the left *4 hand* in to meet the right hand, ending with the fingers crossed at an angle, both palms facing in.

---

**jam**¹ *v., n.* Same sign used for: **crowded.**

- [People meshed together + **stuck**] Beginning with both *curved 5 hands* in front of each shoulder, palms facing each other, bring the hands together while bending the fingers and meshing them with each other in front of the chest. Then push the fingers of the right *V hand* against the neck, palm facing down.

---

**jam**² *n.* See sign for JELLY.

---

**jaws** *pl. n.* See sign for ALLIGATOR.

**jealous** *adj.*

- [Initialized sign] Beginning with the extended little finger of the right *J hand* touching the right corner of the mouth, palm facing forward, twist the hand down and forward, ending with the palm facing back.

**jeans** *pl. n.* See sign for PANTS.

**jeer** *v.* See sign for MOCK.

**Jell-O** *Trademark.* See sign for GELATIN.

**jelly** *n.* Same sign used for: **jam.**

- [Initialized sign miming spreading jelly on bread] Strike the extended little finger of the right *J hand* on the upturned left *open hand* as it moves upward in an arc with a double movement.

**jest** *v.* See sign for TEASE.

**jet** *n.* See sign for AIRPLANE.

**jewelry** *n.*

- [Location of necklace and bracelet] Beginning with the fingers of both *5 hands* in front of the chest, palms facing in, bring the hands upward to on top of each shoulder. Then grasp the left wrist with the bent middle finger and thumb of the right hand.

**job** *n.* See sign for WORK.

**jog** *v.* Related form: **jogging** *n.*

- [Mime how the hands are thought to move when jogging] Move both *S hands,* palms facing each other, in repeated alternating outward circles in front of each side of the chest.

# join

**join**[1] *v.* Same sign used for: **participate.**

■ [Represents a person's legs entering a place where there are other people with whom one can have social exchanges] Beginning with the right *H hand* in front of the chest, palm facing left and fingers pointing forward, and the left *C hand* in front of the lower left side of the chest, palm facing right, bring the right hand down in an arc into the palm side of the left hand while closing the left fingers around the fingers of the right *H hand.*

**join**[2] *v.* See sign for BELONG[1].

**joint** *n.* See sign for BELONG[1].

**jolly** *adj.* See sign for HAPPY.

**journal** *n.* See signs for ARTICLE, MAGAZINE.

**journey** *n.* See sign for TRIP.

**joy** *n.* See sign for HAPPY.

**judge** *v.* Same sign used for: **court, justice, trial.**

■ [The hands move up and down indicating weighing a decision] Move both *F hands,* palms facing each other, up and down in front of each side of the chest with a repeated alternating movement.

**juggle** *v.* See sign for INDECISION.

**juice** *n.*

■ [**drink**[1] + initialized sign] Beginning with the thumb of the right *C hand* near the chin, palm facing left, tip the hand up toward the face. Then form a *J* near the right side of the face with the right hand.

**jump** *v., n.*

■ [Demonstrates the action of jumping] Beginning with the extended fingers of the right *V hand,* palm facing in, pointing down and touching the open left palm, move the right hand up and down in front of the chest with a double movement.

**jump rope** *n.*

■ [Mime using a jump rope, with one end of the rope in each hand] Move both *A hands,* palms facing up, in simultaneous outward circles in front of each side of the body.

**junk** *n.* See sign for GARBAGE.

**just** *adv.* Same sign used for: **recently, while ago, a.**

■ [Indicates something in the recent past] Wiggle the index finger of the right *X hand,* palm facing back, up and down with a repeated movement on the lower right cheek.

**justice** *n.* See sign for JUDGE.

**justify** *v.* See sign for CHANGE[1].

**juvenile** *n., adj.*

■ [**young + little**[2]] Beginning with the fingertips of both *bent hands* on each side of the chest, palms facing in and fingers pointing toward each other, brush the fingers upward in a double arc. Then move the right *bent hand* downward with a double movement in front of the right side of the body, palm facing down.

## kangaroo[1] n.
■ [Shows posture of a kangaroo] Move both *bent hands* from in front of each side of the body, palms facing in, forward in small upward arcs.

## karate n. See sign for HACK.

## keen adj. See sign for SHARP.

## keep v. Same sign used for: **maintain.**
■ [Eyes looking in different directions] Tap the little-finger side of the right *K hand* across the index-finger side of the left *K hand* palms facing in opposite directions.

## keep quiet See signs for SEAL ONE'S LIPS[1], SHUT UP[1] (*informal*).

## keep secret See sign for SEAL ONE'S LIPS[1].

## ketchup or catsup n.
■ [Initialized sign] Shake the right *K hand,* palm facing left, up and down with a short repeated movement in front of the right side of the body.

## key n.
■ [Mime turning a key in a lock] Twist the knuckle of the right *X hand,* palm facing down, in the palm of the left *open hand,* palm facing right and fingers pointing forward, with a repeated movement.

**kick** *v.* Same sign used for: **kick off.**

- [Demonstrates the action of kicking something] Bring the right *B hand* in front of the right side of the body, palm facing left and fingers angled down, upward to strike the index-finger side of the right hand against the little-finger side of the left *B hand* held in front of the body, palm facing in and fingers pointing right.

**kick off** *n.* See sign for KICK.

**kid**[1] *n.*

- [Suggests a child's runny nose] With the right index finger and little finger extended, palm facing down, put the extended index finger under the nose, and twist the hand up and down with a small repeated movement.

**kid**[2] *v.* See sign for TEASE. Related form: **kidding** *n.*

**kill** *v.* Same sign used for: **murder, slaughter.**

- [Represents a knife being inserted] Push the side of the extended right index finger, palm facing down, across the palm of the left *open hand,* palm facing right, with a deliberate movement.

**kind**[1] *adj.* Same sign used for: **generous, gentle, gracious.**

- [A comforting movement] Bring the right *open hand,* palm facing in near the middle of the chest, in a forward circle around the back of the left *open hand,* palm facing in, as it moves in a circle around the right hand.

**kind**[2] *n.* Same sign used for: **sort, type.**

- [Initialized sign similar to sign for **world**] Move the right *K hand,* palm facing left, in a forward circle around the left *K hand,* palm facing right, as it moves in a circle around the right hand, ending with the little-finger side of the right hand landing on the index-finger side of the left hand.

# kind

**kind³** *adj.* See sign for SOFT-HEARTED.

## kindergarten *n.*

- [Initialized sign similar to sign for **base**] Move the right *K hand*, palm facing left, with a repeated back and forth movement under the left *open hand*, palm facing down.

## king *n.*

- [Initialized sign following the location of a royal sash] Move the right *K hand*, palm facing in, from touching the left side of the chest near the shoulder downward to touch again near the right side of the waist.

**kink** *n.* See sign for KNOT.

## kiss *v., n.*

- [The hand takes a kiss from the mouth and puts it on the cheek] Touch the fingertips of the right *flattened O hand*, palm facing in, to the right side of the mouth, and then open the right hand and lay the palm of the right *open hand* against the right side of the face.

## kitchen *n.*

- [Initialized sign similar to sign for **cook**] Beginning with the palm side of the right *K hand* on the upturned left *open hand,* flip the right hand over, ending with the back of the right hand in the left palm.

**Kleenex** *Trademark.* See sign for TISSUE.

## kneel *v.*

- [Represents a person's bent knees] Bring the knuckles of the right *bent V fingers,* palm facing in, down on the upturned left *open hand.*

## knife *n.*

■ [Represents the slicing movement done with a knife] Slide the bottom side of the extended right index finger, palm facing in, with a double movement at an angle across the length of the extended left index finger, palm facing right, turning the right palm down each time as it moves off the end of the left index finger.

## knob *n.*

■ [Mime turning a knob] Beginning with the right *curved 5 hand* in front of the right side of the body, palm facing forward, twist the hand, ending with the palm facing left.

## knock *v.*

■ [Mime knocking on something] Hit the palm side of the right *A hand*, palm facing left, with a double movement on the palm of the left *open hand*, palm facing right and fingers pointing up.

## knot *n., v.* Same sign used for: **kink.**

■ [Represents a knotted rope] Beginning with the index finger of the right *X hand*, palm facing down, hooked over the bent left index finger, palm facing up, twist the hands in opposite directions, reversing positions.

## know *v.*

■ [Location of knowledge in the brain] Tap the fingertips of the right *bent hand*, palm facing down, on the right side of the forehead.

## knowledge *n.* See sign for AWARE[1].

## know nothing

■ [**know** + showing zero amount] Bring the fingers of the right *bent hand*, palm facing down, from the forehead downward while changing into an *O hand*, touching the little-finger side of the right *O hand*, palm facing left, against the upturned palm of the left *open hand*.

**label** *n.*, *v.* Same sign used for: **apply, brand, decal, tag.**

- [Demonstrates applying a label] Wipe the extended fingers of the right *H hand*, palm facing left, from the fingers to the heel of the left *open hand*, palm facing right and fingers pointing forward.

**labor** *v.* See signs for ACTIVE[1], WORK.

**lack** *n.* See sign for SKIP[1].

**ladder** *n.* See sign for CLIMB.

**lady** *n.* Same sign used for: **female.**

- [girl + polite] Bring the thumb of the right *A hand*, palm facing left, downward from the right side of the chin while opening, ending by tapping side of the thumb of the right *open hand* in the center of the chest.

**laid up** *adj. phrase.*

- [The legs are pulled back into a resting position] Bring both *bent V hands*, palms facing each other, from in front of each side of the body back toward each side of the chest.

**lake** *n.*

- [water + shape of a lake] Tap the index finger of the right *W hand*, palm facing left, against the chin with a double movement. Then with the *modified C hands*, palms facing each other, in front of each side of the body, move the hands downward a short distance.

## lamp *n.*

■ [Represents light coming out of a table lamp] With the elbow of the raised right arm resting on the palm of the left *open hand* in front of the right side of the chest, open the right *flattened O hand,* forming a *curved 5 hand,* palm facing down and fingers pointing forward.

## land[1] *n.*

■ [**dirt + district**] Beginning with both *flattened O hands* in front of each side of the body, palms facing up, move the thumb of both hands smoothly with a double movement across each fingertip, starting with the little fingers and ending as *A hands* each time. Then move the right *open hand,* palm facing down and fingers pointing forward, from in front of the right side of the body in a large arc forward and in front of the chest over the back of the left *open hand,* held in front of the left side of the body, palm facing down and fingers pointing forward.

## land[2] *n.* See sign for DIRT.

## language *n.*

■ [Initialized sign] Beginning with the thumbs of both *L hands* near each other in front of the chest, palms angled down, bring the hands outward with a wavy movement to in front of each side of the chest.

## lapse *n.* See sign for BETWEEN.

## large *adj.* See also sign for BIG. Same sign used for: **grand, great, massive.**

■ [Initialized sign showing a large size] Move both *L hands* from in front of each side of the chest, palms facing each other, in large arcs beyond each side of the body.

## last[1] *adj., adv., n.* Same sign used for: **end, final, finally.**

■ [Indicates the last thing] Move the extended little finger of the right *I hand,* palm facing left, downward in front of the chest, striking the extended little finger of the left *I hand,* palm facing in, as it passes.

# last

**last**[2] *adj., adv.* See signs for AGO, BEFORE[1], CONTINUE[1].

## last week

- [**week** formed with a movement into the past] Beginning with the back of the right *one hand,* palm facing in, in the palm of the left *open hand,* palm facing in, bring the right hand across the palm and then back with a sweeping movement over the right shoulder.

## last year

- [An abbreviated form of **year** moving into the past] With the back of the right *one hand,* palm facing up, on the index-finger side of the left *S hand,* palm facing down, bend the right extended index finger down toward the chest with a double movement.

## late *adj., adv.* Same sign used for: **delay, tardy.**

- [Hand moves into the past] Bend the wrist of the right *open hand,* palm facing back and fingers pointing down, back near the right side of the waist with a double movement.

## lately *adv.* See sign for SINCE[1].

## later *adv.* Alternate form: **later on.** Same sign used for: **after a while, afterward.**

- [Initialized sign representing the minute hand on a clock moving to indicate the passing of time] With the thumb of the right *L hand,* palm facing forward, on the palm of the left *open hand,* palm facing right and fingers pointing forward, twist the right hand forward, keeping the thumb in place and ending with the right palm facing down.

## laugh[1] *v.*

- [Initialized sign showing the shape of the mouth when one laughs] Beginning with the extended index fingers of both *L hands* at each corner of the mouth, palms facing back, pull the hands outward to each side of the head with a double movement while closing the hands into *10 hands* each time.

**laugh²** *v.* See sign for HYSTERICAL. Related form: **laughter** *n.*

**laugh at** *v. phrase.* See sign for MOCK.

**lavatory** *n.* See sign for TOILET.

**law** *n.* Same sign used for: **legal.**

- [Initialized sign representing recording laws on the books] Place the palm side of the right *L hand,* palm facing left, first on the fingers and then the heel of the left *open hand,* palm facing right and fingers pointing up.

**layaway** *n.* See sign for INSTALLMENT PLAN.

**lay off** *v. phrase. Informal.* See sign for DISMISS.

**layer** *n.* Same sign used for: **plush.**

- [Shows the shape of a layer on top of something] Slide the thumb of the right *modified C hand,* palm facing left, from the heel to off the fingers of the upturned palm of the left *open hand* held in front of the chest.

**lazy** *adj.* Same sign used for: **slothful.**

- [Initialized sign] Tap the palm side of the right *L hand* against the left side of the chest with a double movement.

**lead** *v.* Same sign used for: **conduct, guide, head, host, steer.**

- [One hand leads the other by pulling it] With the fingers of the left *open hand,* palm facing right, being held by the fingers and thumb of the right hand, palm facing in, pull the left hand forward a short distance.

**leaf** *n.*

- [Represents a leaf blowing in the wind on a branch] With the extended left index finger on the wrist of the right *5 hand,* angled down and bent at the wrist, swing the right hand forward and back with a double movement.

# leak

**leak**[1] *v., n.* Same sign used for: **drain, run.**

- [Represents the flow of a leaking liquid] Beginning with the index-finger side of the right *4 hand,* palm facing in and fingers pointing left, touching the palm of the left *open hand,* palm facing down and fingers pointing right, move the right hand down with a double movement.

---

**leak**[2] *n.,v.* See sign for DRIP.

**lean** *adj.* See signs for DIET, THIN.

**learn** *v.* Same sign used for: **acquire, educate, education.**

- [Represents taking information from paper and putting it in one's head] Beginning with the fingertips of the right *curved 5 hand,* palm facing down, on the palm of the upturned left *open hand,* bring the right hand up while closing the fingers and thumb into a *flattened O hand* near the forehead.

---

**least** *adj.*

- [**less**[1] **+ most**] Move the right *bent hand,* palm facing down and fingers pointing left, from in front of the chest downward a few inches above the left *open hand,* palm facing up and fingers pointing right. Then, beginning with the palm sides of both *10 hands* together in front of the chest, bring the right hand upward, ending with the right hand in front of the right shoulder, palm facing left.

---

**leave**[1] *v.* Same sign used for: **depart, desert, withdraw.**

- [The hands move from one location to another] Beginning with both *curved 5 hands* in front of each side of the chest, palms facing down, pull the hands back toward the right shoulder while closing the fingers and thumbs into *flattened O hands.*

---

**leave**[2] *v.* Same sign used for: **leftover, rest.**

- [The hands seem to leave something by thrusting it down] Beginning with both *5 hands* in front of each side of the body, palms facing each other and fingers angled up, thrust the fingers downward with a deliberate movement.

---

**leave**[3] *v.* See sign for GO[1].

**lecture** *v., n.* See sign for SPEAK[2].

**leech** *n.* Same sign used for: **mooch** *(slang),*
**take advantage of.**

- [One hand seems to "put the bite on" the other hand] Tap the fingers of the right *U hand* and extended thumb of the right hand, palm facing left, with a double movement on the fingertips of the left *U hand,* palm facing down and fingers pointing right.

**left** *adj., adv., n.*

- [Initialized sign indicating a direction to the left] Beginning with the right *L hand* in front of the right side of the chest, palm facing forward and index finger pointing up, move the hand deliberately to the left.

**leftover** *n., adj.* See sign for LEAVE[2].

**left turn** *n.*

- [Initialized sign demonstrating a left direction] Move the left *L hand,* palm facing in and index finger pointing right, to the left while twisting the wrist, ending with the palm facing forward and the index finger pointing left.

**leg** *n.*

- [Location of the leg] Pat the palm of the right *open hand,* palm facing left, against the side of the right thigh with a double movement.

**legal** *adj.* See sign for LAW.

**leisure** *n.* See sign for ENJOY.

**lemon** *n.*

- [Initialized sign similar to sign for **sour**] Tap the thumb of the right *L hand,* palm facing left, against the chin with a double movement.

# lend

**lend** *v.* Same sign used for: **loan**.
- [Directional sign toward the person to whom something is lent] With the little-finger side of the right *V hand* across the index-finger side of the left *V hand*, move the hands from near the chest forward and down a short distance.

**lend me** See sign for BORROW.

**length** *n.* See also sign for LONG.
- [The finger measures off a designated distance] Beginning with the extended right index finger, palm facing in and finger pointing down, touching the extended left index finger, palm facing in and finger pointing right, move the right finger outward to the right.

**lesbian** *n., adj.* Related form: **lesbianism** *n.*
- [Initialized sign] Bring the palm side of the right *L hand*, palm facing in and index finger pointing left, back against the chin with a double movement, ending with the chin within the crook between the right index finger and thumb.

**less**[1] *adj., adv.* Same sign used for: **reduce**.
- [The hands demonstrate a decreasing amount] Move the right *open hand*, palm facing down and fingers pointing left, from in front of the chest downward a few inches above the left *open hand*, palm facing up and fingers pointing right.

**less**[2] *adj.* See sign for MINIMUM.

**lessen** *v.* See signs for DECREASE[1,3].

**lesson**[1] *n.*
- [The movement represents breaking up information on a page into lessons] Move the little-finger side of the right *bent hand*, palm facing in, from the fingers to the heel of the left *open hand*, palm facing up.

**lesson**[2] *n.* See sign for COURSE.

---

**let** *v.* Same sign used for: **allow, grant, permit.**

- [The hands outline a path for a person to pass] Beginning with both *open hands* in front of the waist, palms facing each other and fingers pointing down, bring the fingers forward and upward by bending the wrists.

---

**let know** See sign for INFORM.

---

**let's see** Same sign used for: **speculate, speculation.**

- [The fingers represent one's eyes] Tap the fingertips of the right *V hand*, palm facing left and fingers pointing up, with a double movement near the right eye.

---

**letter**[1] *n.* Same sign used for: **literal.**

- [Initialized sign similar to sign for **word**] Tap the thumb of the right *L hand*, palm facing forward, with a double movement against the extended left index finger, palm facing right.

---

**letter**[2] *n.* Same sign used for: **mail.**

- [Shows licking a stamp and placing it on an envelope] Touch the extended thumb of the right *10 hand* to the lips, palm facing in, and then move the thumb downward to touch the fingertips of the left *open hand* held in front of the body, palm facing up.

---

**lettuce** *n.*

- [Initialized sign similar to sign for **cabbage**] Touch the thumb of the right *L hand*, palm facing forward and index finger pointing up, to the right side of the forehead.

---

**level** *adj.* See sign for EVEN[1].

# lever

**lever** *n.* See sign for PIPE[2].

**liability** *n.* See sign for BURDEN.

**liberal** *adj.* See signs for BROAD-MINDED, LIBERTY.

**liberate** *v.* See sign for SAVE[1].

**liberty**[1] *n.* Same sign used for: **liberal.**

- [Initialized sign similar to sign for save[1]] Beginning with the wrists of both *L hands* crossed in front of the chest, palms facing in, twist the wrists to move the hands outward, ending with the hands in front of each shoulder, palms facing forward.

**liberty**[2] *n.* See sign for SAVE[1].

**library** *n.*

- [Initialized sign] Move the right *L hand*, palm facing forward, in a circle in front of the right shoulder.

**license** *n.*

- [Initialized sign similar to sign for **certificate**] Tap the thumbs of both *L hands* with a double movement in front of the chest, palms facing forward.

**lick** *v.*

- [The fingers represent the tongue licking something] Brush the fingertips of the right *U hand*, palm facing back and fingers pointing down, forward with a double movement along the length of the palm of the upturned left *open hand*, held in front of the chest.

**lid** *n.* Same sign used for: **cover.**

- [Mime putting a lid on a jar] Bring the fingers of the right *open hand* from in front of the right shoulder, palm facing left and fingers pointing forward, in an arc down on top of the index-finger side of the left *C hand*, palm facing right in front of the left side of the chest.

**lie**[1] *v., n.* Same sign used for: **fib.**

- [The hand movement indicates that a person is speaking out of the side of the mouth when telling a lie] Slide the index-finger side of the right *bent hand,* palm facing down, with a double movement across the chin from right to left.

**lie**[2] or **lie down** *v.* or *v. phrase.* Same sign used for: **recline.**

- [The fingers represent a person's legs in a reclining position] Beginning with the back of the right *V hand,* palm facing up, on the palm of the left *open hand,* palm facing up, pull the right hand in toward the body.

**lift** *v.* See sign for RAISE[1].

**light**[1] *adj.*

- [The snap of a light being turned on] Beginning with the fingertips of the right *8 hand* near the chin, palm facing in, flick the middle finger upward and forward with a double movement while opening into a *5 hand* each time.

**light**[2] *n.* Same sign used for: **shine.**

- [The hand shows the rays of light beaming from a lamp] Beginning with the right *flattened O hand* held above the right shoulder, palm facing down, open the fingers into a *5 hand.*

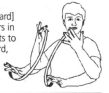

**light**[3] *adj.*

- [The gesture represents something light floating upward] Beginning with both *5 hands* with bent middle fingers in front of the waist, palms facing down, twist the wrists to raise the hands quickly toward each other and upward, ending with the hands in front of each side of the chest, bent middle fingers pointing in.

**light**[4] *adj.* See sign for BRIGHT.

# lighter

## lighter *n.*

- [Mime starting a lighter] Bend the extended thumb of the right *10 hand*, palm facing in, up and down with a double movement in front of the right side of the chest.

## lightning *n.* Same sign used for: **bolt, thunderbolt.**

- [Shows shape of lightning bolt] Beginning with the extended index fingers of both hands touching above the left shoulder, move the right hand downward with a jagged movement in front of the chest, ending in front of the waist, finger pointing forward and palm facing down.

## like[1] *v.*

- [Pulling out feelings] Beginning with the bent thumb and middle finger of the right *5 hand* touching the chest, palm facing in, bring the hand forward while closing the fingers to form an *8 hand*.

## like[2] *v.* (alternate sign)

- [Mime kissing the back of one's hand to show fondness] Bring the back of the right *S hand*, palm facing forward, back to the lips and then forward again.

## like[3] *prep.* See also signs for ALIKE[1,2], SAME.

- [A directional sign in which the hand moves back and forth between the two objects being compared] Move the right *Y hand*, palm facing forward, from side to side with a double movement in front of the right side of the body.

## like[4] *v.* See sign for ENJOY.

## lime *n.*

- [Initialized sign showing slicing a lime] Slide the thumb of the right *L hand*, palm facing left and index finger pointing up, down the back of the left *S hand*, palm facing in, in front of the chest.

**limit** *v.* See sign for RESTRICT.

**line** *n.* Same sign used for: **string, thread.**
■ [Shows shape of a line] Beginning with the extended little fingers of both *l hands* touching in front of the chest, palms facing in, move both hands outward.

**line up** *v. phrase.* Same sign used for: **align, queue, row.**
■ [Represents people lined up in a row] Beginning with the little finger of the right *4 hand,* palm facing left, touching the index finger of the right *4 hand,* palm facing right, move the right hand back toward the chest and the left hand forward.

**link** *v.* See signs for BELONG[1], RELATIONSHIP.

**lion** *n.*
■ [Shows shape and location of lion's mane] Beginning with the fingers of the right *curved 5 hand* pointing down over the forehead, palm facing down, move the hand back over the top of the head.

**lip** *n.*
■ [Location of one's lips] Draw a rectangle around the edge of the mouth with the extended right index finger, palm facing in.

**lipstick** *n.*
■ [Mime putting on lipstick] Move the fingers of the right *modified X hand* back and forth in front of the mouth with a double movement.

**liquor** *n.* See sign for WHISKEY.

# list

**list** *n., v.* Same sign used for: **record, score.**

- [The finger points out items on a list] Touch the bent middle finger of the right *5 hand,* palm facing left, several times on the palm of the left *open hand,* palm facing right and fingers pointing up, as it moves from the fingers downward to the heel.

**listen** *v.* Same sign used for: **eavesdrop.**

- [The fingers bring sound to the ear] With the thumb of the right *curved 3 hand,* palm facing left, touching the right ear, bend the extended index and middle fingers down with a short double movement.

**literal** *adj.* See sign for LETTER[1].

**little**[1] *adj.* See also signs for SMALL[1,2].

- [Shows a small size] Move both *open hands,* palms facing each other, toward each other with a short double movement in front of body.

**little**[2] *adj.* See also signs for SMALL[1,2]. Same sign used for: **short.**

- [Shows someone or something short in size] Move the right *bent hand,* palm facing down, with a short double movement in front of the right side of the body.

**little bit** *n.* See sign for TINY.

**live** *v.* Same sign used for: **alive, dwell, survival, survive.**

- [Outlines life within one's body] Move both *A hands,* palms facing in, upward on each side of the chest.

**living room** *n.*

- [**fancy + box**] Brush the thumb of the right *5 hand,* palm facing left, upward on the chest with a double movement. Then, beginning with both *open hands* in front of each side of the body, palms facing each other, turn the hands sharply in opposite directions, ending with both palms facing in.

**load** *n.* See sign for PILE[1].

**loaf** *n.*
- [Shows shape of a loaf] Beginning with the index fingers of both *C hands* touching in front of the body, palms facing down, bring the hands outward to in front of each side of the body.

**loan** *v.* See sign for LEND.

**loathe** *v.* See sign for DETEST[1].

**lobster** *n.*
- [Represents a lobster's claws] Beginning with both *V hands* in front of each shoulder, palms facing forward, close the index and middle fingers with a double movement.

**local** *adj.* See sign for LOCATION.

**location** *n.* Same sign used for: **local**.
- [Initialized sign similar to sign for **area**[1]] Beginning with the thumbs of both *L hands* touching in front of the body, palms facing down, move the hands apart and back in a circular movement until they touch again near the chest.

**lock** *n., v.*
- [Represents the wrists locked together] Beginning with both *S hands* in front of the body, right hand above left and both palms facing down, turn the right hand over by twisting the wrist, ending with the back of the right *S hand,* palm facing up, on the back of the left *S hand,* palm facing down.

**locked into** See sign for BIND.

**locker** *n.* See sign for CLOSET[1].

# loiter

### loiter v.

■ [**lazy** + dangling the hands lazily] Tap the palm side of the right *L hand* against the left side of the chest. Then drop both *5 hands,* palms facing down, downward in front of each side of the chest.

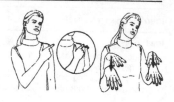

### lollipop n. Same sign used for: **Popsicle** (*trademark*).

■ [Mime holding and licking a lollipop] Bring the thumb side of the right *X hand,* palm facing left, in a double circular movement back toward the mouth.

### lone adj. See sign for ALONE[1]. Related form: **lonely** adj.

### lonely adj. Alternate form: **lonesome.**

■ [Suggests that someone living alone is silent] Bring the side of the extended right index finger, palm facing left, from near the nose slowly downward in front of the mouth.

### long adj. See also sign for LENGTH.

■ [The finger measures out a long length] Move the extended right index finger from the wrist up the length of the extended left arm to near the shoulder.

### long time ago, a Same sign used for: **ancient.**

■ [The hand indicates a time far in the past] Beginning with the right *5 hand* in front of the right shoulder, palm facing left, bring the hand back to behind the right shoulder.

### look alike v. phrase See sign for ALIKE[1].

**look at** *v. phrase.*

- [Represents the eyes directed toward something] Move the right *V hand,* palm facing down and extended fingers pointing forward, forward a short distance in the direction of the referent.

**look back**[1] *v. phrase.* Same sign used for: **memorial, memory.**

- [**look at** directed toward the past] Move the fingers of the right *V hand,* palm facing down and fingers pointing back, back beside the right side of head.

**look back**[2] *v.* See sign for HINDSIGHT.

**look down at** or **on** *v. phrase.* See sign for CONTEMPT.

**look for** *v. phrase.* Same sign used for: **check for, examine, hunt for, search for.**

- [Shows repeated searching for something] Move the right *C hand,* palm facing left, with a double movement in a circle in front of the face.

**look like** See sign for SEEM.

**look out** *v. phrase.* Same sign used for: **watch out, yield.**

- [Represents the eyes moving quickly to observe something] Beginning with the right *V hand* near the right side of the nose, palm facing left and fingers pointing up, bring the hand forward and outward to the right and then downward in front of the chest, ending with the palm facing down and the fingers angled to the left.

**look over** *v. phrase.* Same sign used for: **browse, observe, view.**

- [Represents the eyes surveying something] Beginning with both *V hands* in front of each side of the chest, right hand higher than the left hand, both palms facing down, and fingers pointing forward, move the hands in double alternating circles.

# looks

**looks** *n.* Same sign used for: **good-looking, handsome.**

■ [The location of a person's face] Move the right extended index finger in a circle in front of the face, palm facing in.

**look up** *v.*

■ [The fingers seem to page through a book to look up something] Brush the extended thumb of the right *10 hand,* palm facing down, with a double movement in an arc across the palm of the left *open hand,* palm facing up.

**loop** *n.*

■ [Shape of a loop] Move the extended right index finger, palm facing down and finger pointing left, in a large circle with a double movement around the extended left index finger, palm facing in and finger pointing right.

**loose**[1] *adj.* Same sign used for: **flabby.**

■ [Demonstrates something that is loose and moves easily] With the extended left index finger, palm facing down and finger pointing right, grasped between the thumb and bent middle finger of the right *5 hand,* palm facing left, move the right hand up and down with a double movement.

**loose**[2] *adj.* See sign for DISCONNECT.

**lopsided** *adj.*

■ [Position of a lopsided object] Beginning with both *open hands* in front of each side of the chest, palms facing down and fingers pointing forward, and hands angled downward to the right, drop the right hand while tipping the right side of the body downward at the same time.

**lose**[1] *v.*

■ [The hands seem to drop something as if to lose it] Beginning with the fingertips of both *flattened O hands* touching in front of the body, palms facing up, drop the fingers quickly downward and away from each other while opening into *5 hands,* ending with both palms and fingers angled downward.

### lose[2] *v.*

- Bring the palm side of the right *V hand* from in front of the right shoulder, palm facing forward, downward to land on the upturned palm of the left *open hand* in front of the body.

### lose[3] *v.* See sign for DECREASE[1].

### lot *n.* See sign for MUCH.

### lotion *n.*

- [Shows pouring lotion from a bottle into one's hand] Bring the thumb of the right *Y hand* from in front of the right shoulder, palm facing right, downward to touch the left *open hand* held in front of the chest, palm facing up and fingers pointing right.

### lots to do *n. phrase.* See sign for BUSY[2].

### loud[1] *adj.*

- [**hear** formed with both hands + **noise**] Move both extended index fingers from pointing to each ear forward while changing into *S hands,* and shake them with a repeated movement.

### loud[2] *adj.* See sign for NOISE.

### lousy *adj. Slang.* Related form: **louse** *n.*

- [Suggests that someone with a runny nose feels lousy] Beginning with the thumb of the right *3 hand* touching the nose, palm facing left, bring the hand downward in front of the chest.

### love *v., n.*

- [The hands bring something that is loved close to oneself] With the wrists of both *S hands* crossed in front of the chest, palms facing in, bring the arms back against the chest.

# lovely

**lovely** *adj.* See signs for BEAUTIFUL, PRETTY.

---

**lover** *n.* See sign for SWEETHEART.

---

**low** *adj.* Related form: **lower** *adj.* Same sign used for: **demote.**

■ [Indicates a location lower than another location] Beginning with both *bent hands* in front of each shoulder, palms facing each other, move them downward in front of each side of the chest.

---

**loyal** *adj.*

■ [Initialized sign formed similarly to the sign for **respect**] Beginning with the thumb of the right *L hand,* palm facing left, touching the forehead, move the right hand forward in an arc.

---

**luck** *n.* Related form: **lucky** *adj.* Same sign used for: **fortunate.**

■ [Similar to sign for **favorite**[1] but directed toward another] Beginning with the bent middle finger of the right *5 hand,* palm facing in, touching the chin, twist the wrist to swing the hand forward with a quick movement, ending with the palm angled forward.

---

**luggage** *n.* See sign for BAGGAGE.

---

**lump**[1] *n.* See also sign for BUMP.

■ [Shows the size of a small amount or swelling] Beginning with the side of the extended right index finger, palm facing left and finger pointing forward, on the back of the left *open hand,* palm facing down and fingers pointing right, bring the right finger upward in a small arc, ending farther back on the back of the left hand.

---

**lump**[2] *n.* See sign for AMOUNT.

---

**lunch** *n.*

■ [eat + noon] Bring the fingers of the right *flattened O hand* to the lips, palm facing in. Then place the elbow of the bent right arm, arm extended up and open right palm facing forward, on the back of the left *open hand* held in front of the body, palm facing down.

---

**lung** *n.*
- [Shows location of one's lungs] Rub the fingertips of both *bent hands,* palms facing in, up and down near the center of the chest with a repeated movement.

**luxury** *adj.* See sign for FANCY.

---

**machine** *n.* Same sign used for: **factory, industry, manufacture, mechanism, motor, run.**

- [Represents movement of gears meshing together] With the fingers of both *curved 5 hands* loosely meshed together, palms facing in, move the hands up and down in front of the chest with a repeated movement.

---

**mad** *adj.* See signs for ANGER, CROSS[2].

---

**magazine** *n.* Same sign used for: **brochure, journal, pamphlet.**

- [Shows the spine of a magazine] Grasp the little-finger side of the left *open hand,* palm angled up, with the index finger and thumb of the right *A hand,* and slide the right hand from heel to finger-tips of the left hand with a double movement.

---

**magic** *n., adj.*

- [The hands seem to cast a spell] Beginning with both *S hands* in front of each side of the body, palms facing forward, drop the hands downward and forward with a quick movement while opening into *5 hands.*

---

**magnet** *n.* Related form: **magnetic** *adj.*

- [Demonstrates action of a magnet pulling something to itself] Beginning with the right *flattened C hand,* palm angled forward, near the palm of the left *open hand,* palm facing right and fingers pointing up, bring the index-finger side of the right hand against the left palm while closing the right fingers into a *flattened O hand.*

---

**magnetic** *adj.* See sign for ABSORB[1].

---

**mail**[1] *n., v.* Alternate form: **mail out.** Same sign used for: **send, send out.**

- [Shows sending something forward] Flick the fingertips of the right *bent hand* forward across the back of the left *open hand*, both palms facing down, with a quick movement, straightening the right fingers as the right hand moves forward.

**mail**[2] *n.* See sign for LETTER[2].

**main** *adj.* See sign for IMPORTANT.

**mainstream** *n., adj., v.* Same sign used for: **blend, emerge, merge.**

- [Represents things coming together to merge] Beginning with both *5 hands* in front of each side of the chest, palms facing down and fingers pointing toward each other, move the hands downward and forward toward each other, ending with the right hand on the back of the left hand in front of the chest.

**maintain** *v.* See signs for FIX, KEEP.

**maintenance** *n.* See sign for WRENCH.

**major** *v.* See sign for SPECIALIZE.

**majority** *n.*

- [specialize + class] Slide the little-finger side of the right *B hand,* palm facing left and fingers pointing forward, along the length of the index finger of the left *B hand,* palm facing right and fingers pointing forward. Then, beginning with both *C hands* in front of each side of the chest, palms facing each other, bring the hands away from each other in outward arcs while turning the palms in.

**make** *v.* Same sign used for: **create, manufacture, produce.**

- [The hands seem to be molding something] Beginning with the little-finger side of the right *S hand* on the index-finger side of the left *S hand,* twist the wrists in opposite directions with a small, quick, grinding movement.

# make believe

**make believe** See sign for IMAGINE.

**make love** See sign for PET².

**makeshift** *adj.* Same sign used for: **good enough.**
- [The sign for **favorite¹** is discarded] Beginning with the bent middle finger of the right *5 hand* touching the chin, palm facing in, move the hand forward while twisting the wrist, ending with the palm facing down.

**make-up¹** or **makeup** *n.* Same sign used for: **cosmetics.**
- [Mime dabbing make-up on one's face] Move the fingertips of both *flattened O hands,* palms facing each other, in double alternating circles near each cheek.

**make up²** *v. phrase.* See sign for INVENT.

**make up your mind** See sign for DECIDE.

**malady** *n.* See sign for SICK.

**male** *n.* See signs for BOY, MAN.

**maltreatment** *n.* See sign for TORTURE.

**mama** *n.* See sign for MOTHER.

**man** *n.* Same sign used for: **male.**
- [A combination of **boy** and a gesture indicating the height of a man] Beginning with the thumb side of the right *flattened C hand* in front of the right side of the forehead, palm facing left, bring the hand straight forward while closing the fingers to the thumb.

**manage** *v.* Same sign used for: **administer, control, direct, govern, handle, in charge of, operate, preside over, reign, rule.**
- [Mime holding a horse's reigns indicating being in a position of management] Beginning with both *modified X hands* in front of each side of the body, right hand forward of the left hand and palms facing each other, move the hands forward and back with a repeated alternating movement.

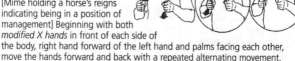

**manners** *n*. See sign for POLITE.

**manufacture** *v*. See signs for MACHINE, MAKE.

**many** *adj., pron.* Same sign used for: **a lot, multiple, numerous.**

- [Natural gesture for indicating many things] Beginning with both *S hands* in front of each side of the chest, palms facing up, flick the fingers open quickly with a double movement into *5 hands*.

**march** *v*. Same sign used for: **parade.**

- [The hands represent people moving forward in a procession] Beginning with both *4 hands* in front of the body, the right hand somewhat forward of the left hand, both palms facing in, and fingers pointing down, flip the fingers forward and back with a double movement by bending the wrist.

**marble** *n*.

- [Mime shooting a marble] Beginning with right the *modified X hand* in front of the right shoulder, palm facing left, flick the thumb upward with a double movement.

**margarine** *n*. See sign for BUTTER.

**marijuana** *n*. Same sign used for: **cannabis, pot** (*slang*).

- [Mime holding and smoking a marijuana cigarette] Move the right *F hand*, palm facing left, from near the pursed mouth forward with a short double movement.

**marionette** *n*. See sign for PUPPET.

**market** *n*. See sign for STORE¹.

**marry** *v*.

- [Symbolizes joining hands in marriage] Bring the right *curved hand*, palm facing down, downward in front of the chest to clasp the left *curved hand*, palm facing up.

# marshall

**marshall** *n.* See sign for POLICE.

**mart** *n.* See sign for STORE[1].

**marvel** *n.* See sign for WONDERFUL. Related form: **marvelous** *adj.*

**mash** *v.* Same sign used for: **smash.**
- [Mime mashing something with the heel of the hand] Bring the heel of the right *open hand* downward on the heel of the left *open hand,* palms facing each other, while twisting the right wrist and grinding the heel on the left palm.

**mask**[1] *n.*
- [Initialized sign showing the location of a mask] Beginning with both *M hands* in front of the face, palms facing in and fingers pointing up, move the hands to each side of the face while turning the palms toward each other.

**mask**[2] *n.* See sign for HALLOWEEN.

**masquerade** *n.* See sign for HALLOWEEN.

**mass** *n.* See signs for CLASS, HORDE.

**massive** *adj.* See signs for EXCESS, LARGE.

**mass-produce** *v.* See sign for ASSEMBLY LINE.

**match**[1] *v., n.* Same sign used for: **combine, fit, merge, suit.**
- [The fingers move together to match with each other] Beginning with both *5 hands* in front of each side of the chest, palms facing in, bring the hands together, ending with the bent fingers of both hands meshed together in front of the chest.

**match**[2] *n.*
- [Mime striking a match] Flick the fingertips of the *modified X hand,* palm facing left, upward with a double movement on the palm of the left *open hand,* palm facing right and fingers pointing forward.

### material *n.*

■ [The hands seem to feel material with the fingers]
Rub the thumbs of both *flattened O hands*
against the fingers of each hand in front of
each side of the chest, palms facing up.

---

### materialize *v.* See sign for SHOW UP.

---

### materials *pl. n.* Same sign used for: **media.**

■ [Initialized sign similar to sign for **thing**] Beginning with the
right *M hand* in front of the body, palm facing up, move the
hand in a double arc to the right.

---

### mathematics *n.* Alternate form: **math.**
Same sign used for: **multiplication.**

■ [Initialized sign similar to sign for **arithmetic**]
Brush the back of the right *M hand* across the
index-finger side of the left *M hand,* both palms
facing in, as the hands cross with a double
movement in front of the chest.

---

### matinee *n.* See sign for AFTERNOON.

---

### maximum *n., adj.* Same sign used for: **up to.**

■ [Shows reaching the top] Beginning with the right
*B hand,* palm facing down and fingers pointing left,
a few inches under the left *open hand,* palm facing
down and fingers pointing right, bring the back of
the right hand up against the left palm.

---

### may *v.* See signs for CAN[1], MAYBE.

---

### maybe *adv.* Same sign used for: **may,
might, perhaps, probability,
probable, probably.**

■ [Indicates weighing possibilities]
Beginning with both *open hands*
in front of each side of the chest,
palms facing up and fingers pointing
forward, alternately move the hands
up and down with a double movement.

**mayonnaise** *n.*

- [Initialized sign miming spreading mayonnaise on bread] Move the fingers of the right *M hand,* palm facing down, in a double circular movement on the palm of the left *open hand,* palm facing up.

**me** *pron.* Same sign used for: **I.**

- [Directional sign toward self] Point the extended right index finger to the center of the chest.

**meager** *adj.* See sign for SMALL².

**mean**¹ *adj.* Related form: **meanness** *n.* Same sign used for: **bust, cruel, rude.**

- [Shows a rough movement against another] Beginning with both *5 hands* in front of the body, palms facing in opposite directions and the right hand above the left hand, close the hands into *A hands* while quickly moving the right hand down brushing the knuckles against the left knuckles as it passes.

**mean**² *v.* Related form: **meaning** *n.* Same sign used for: **intend, purpose, stand for.**

- [Exchanging things to look at their relative standing] Touch the fingertips of the right *V hand,* palm facing down, in the palm of the left *open hand,* palm facing up and fingers pointing forward, and then twist the right wrist and touch the fingertips down again.

**meanness** *n.* Same sign used for: **cruel, rude.**

- [Shows an unpleasant contact] Bring the knuckles of the right *bent V hand,* palm facing in, downward, brushing the knuckles of the left *bent V hand,* palm facing in, as the right hand passes.

**meanwhile** *n.* See sign for DURING.

### measles *n.*

- [Shows location of measles spots] Beginning with the fingers of both *curved 5 hands,* palms facing each other, on each side of the chin, move the hands upward, touching the fingertips to the cheeks and then to each side of the forehead.

### measure *v.* Related form: **measurement** *n.*
Same sign used for: **size.**

- [The fingers seem to measure something] Tap the thumbs of both *Y hands,* palms facing down, together in front of the chest with a double movement.

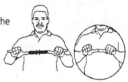

### measure up *v. phrase.* See sign for MEET.

### measuring *n., adj.* See sign for ENGINEER.

### meat *n.*

- [Indicates the meaty part of the hand] With the bent index finger and thumb of the right *5 hand,* palm facing down, grasp the fleshy part of left *open hand* near the thumb, palm facing right and fingers pointing forward, and shake the hands forward and back with a double movement.

### mechanism *n.* See sign for MACHINE.

### medal *n.* Same sign used for: **prize, ribbon.**

- [Symbolizes pinning on a medal] Bring the index-finger side of the right *H hand,* palm facing down and fingers pointing down, back against the left side of the chest with a deliberate movement.

### meddle[1] *v.* Same sign used for: **interfere, interrupt.**

- [Hand seems to interrupt in the middle of something] Bring the little-finger side of the right *open hand,* palm facing left, downward sharply between the middle finger and ring finger of the left *5 hand* held in front of the chest, palm facing in and fingers pointing up.

# meddle

**meddle**[2] *v.* See sign for NOSY[2].

**media** *pl. n.* See sign for MATERIALS.

**medical** *adj.* See sign for DOCTOR[1].

**medicine** *n.* Related forms: **medical** *adj.*, **medication** *n.*
- [Represents mixing a prescription with a mortar and pestle] With the bent middle finger of the right *5 hand*, palm facing down, in the palm of the left *open hand*, rock the right hand from side to side with a double movement while keeping the middle finger in place.

**meditate** *v.* See sign for WONDER. Related form: **meditation**.

**meek** *adj.* See sign for HUMBLE.

**meet** *v.* Same sign used for: **greet, measure up.**
- [Represents two people approaching each other when meeting] Beginning with the extended index fingers of both hands pointing up in front of each shoulder, palms facing each other, bring the hands together in front of the chest.

**meeting** *n.* Related form: **meet** *v.* Same sign used for: **assembly, conference, convention, convocation, council.**
- [Represents many people coming together for a meeting] Beginning with both open hands in front of the chest, palms facing each other and fingers pointing up, close the fingers with a double movement into *flattened O hands* while moving the hands together.

**mellow** *adj.* See sign for SOFT.

**melody** *n.* See sign for MUSIC.

**melon** *n.* See sign for PUMPKIN.

**melt** *v.* See sign for DISSOLVE.

**member** *n.*

■ [Similar to sign for **committee**] Touch the fingertips of the right *bent hand*, first to the left side of the chest and then to the right side of the chest.

---

**memorial** *n.* See sign for LOOK BACK[1]. Shared idea of preserving the memory of a person or event.

---

**memorize** *v.* Related form: **memory** *n.*

■ [The hand seems to take information from the brain and then hold on to it tightly, as if to keep it in the memory] Beginning with the fingertips of the right *curved hand* touching the right side of the forehead, palm facing in, bring the hand forward and down while closing the fingers into an *S hand*, palm facing in.

---

**memory** *n.* See sign for LOOK BACK[1].

---

**mend** *v.* See sign for FIX.

---

**Mennonite** *n.* See sign for SCARF.

---

**menstruation** *n.* Same sign used for: **period.**

■ [With the mouth representing the uterus, the hand hits it to loosen the menses] Tap the palm side of the right *A hand* against the right side of the chin with a double movement.

---

**mention** *v.*

■ [**say + call**[3]] Beginning with the extended right index finger near the mouth, palm facing in and finger pointing up, bring the right hand downward while changing into an *H hand*, ending with the middle-finger side of the right *H hand* across the index-finger side of the left *H hand* in front of the chest.

---

**menu** *n.*

■ [**food + list**] Bring the fingertips of the right *flattened O hand*, palm facing down, to the lips with a repeated movement. Then touch the little-finger side of the right *bent hand*, palm facing left, several times on the palm of the left *open hand*, palm facing in and fingers angled upward, as it moves from the fingertips downward to the heel of the left palm.

# merchandise

**merchandise** *n*. See sign for SELL.

**mercy** *n*. Related form: **merciful** *adj*. Same sign used for: **poor thing**.

- [The finger used to show feeling is directed toward another] Beginning with the bent middle finger of the right *5 hand* pointing forward in front of the right shoulder, move the hand forward in a repeated circular movement.

**merge** *v*. See signs for CIRCULATE, INTERFACE, MAINSTREAM, MATCH¹, MESH.

**merry** *adj*. See sign for HAPPY.

**mesh** *v*. Same sign used for: **blend, combine, infuse, integrate, merge.**

- [Shows the fingers coming together to merge] Beginning with both *curved 5 hands* in front of each side of the chest, palms facing in, drop the hands down while meshing the fingers together, and then drop them apart in front of each side of the body.

**messy** *adj*. Same sign used for: **chaos, disorder, garbled, riot, stir, storm.**

- [Represents something turned upside down, causing a mess] Beginning with both *curved 5 hands* in front of the body, right hand over the left hand, twist the hands with a deliberate movement, reversing the positions.

**metal** *n*., *adj*. Same sign used for: **rock, steel.**

- [Striking the chin which represents a hard substance] Bring the top of the bent index finger of the right *X hand,* palm facing left, forward from under the chin with a double movement.

**method** *n*.

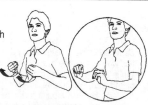

- [Initialized sign similar to sign for **road**] Move both *M hands* from in front of each side of the body, palms facing in and fingers angled up, downward and forward simultaneously in an arc, ending with the palms facing forward and the fingers pointing down.

milk

**microwave** *n.* Alternate form: **microwave oven.**, *v.*

- [Abbreviation **m-w**] Beginning with both *M hands* in front of each side of the chest, palms facing in, move the hands toward each other while extending the fingers toward each other with a double movement, changing into *W hands* each time.

**midday** *n.* See sign for NOON.

**middle** *adj., n.* See also sign for CENTER.

- [Indicates the middle of something] Move the bent middle finger of the right *5 hand*, palm facing down, in a circular movement and then down into the palm of the left *open hand* held in front of the chest, palm facing up.

**middle of the night** See sign for MIDNIGHT.

**midnight** *n.* Same sign used for: **middle of the night.**

- [Represents the sun being on the other side of the world at midnight] With the fingertips of the left *open hand*, palm facing in, touching the crook of the extended right arm, fingers pointing down and palm facing left, move the right *open hand,* to the left with a short double movement.

**midst** *prep.* See sign for AMONG.

**might** *v.* See sign for MAYBE.

**mighty** *adj.* See sign for POWER[1].

**military** *n.* See sign for ARMY.

**milk** *n.*

- [Mime squeezing a cow's udder to get milk] Beginning with the right *C hand*, palm facing left, in front of the right side of the body, squeeze the fingers together with a double movement, forming an *S hand* each time.

# million

### million *adj.*

- [Initialized sign similar to sign for **thousand** except repeated] Touch the fingertips of the right *M hand*, palm facing down, first on the heel, then in the middle, and then on the fingers of the upturned left *open hand*.

### mimic *v.*

- [Represents copying another repeatedly] Move the right *5 hand* from in front of the chest, palm angled forward, down with a repeated movement to touch the upturned palm of the left *open hand* while closing the right fingers and thumb into a *flattened O hand* each time.

### mind *n.* Same sign used for: **brain, sense.**

- [Location of the mind] Tap the bent extended right index finger, palm facing in, against the right side of the forehead with a double movement.

### mine *pron.* See sign for MY.

### mingle *v.* See sign for ASSOCIATE.

### mini *adj.* See signs for SMALL[1,2].

### minimum *n., adj.* Same sign used for: **below, less.**

- [Indicates that something exceeds the base or minimum] Beginning with the back of the right *B hand*, palm facing down and fingers pointing left, touching the palm of the left *open hand*, palm facing down and fingers pointing right, bring the right hand downward a few inches.

### minor *adj.*

- [Shows something taking a lesser position under another] Slide the index-finger side of the right *B hand*, palm facing left and fingers pointing forward, forward under the little-finger side of the left *B hand*, palm facing right and fingers pointing forward.

### minority *n.*

■ [**minor + class**] Slide the index-finger side of the right *B hand*, palm facing left and fingers pointing forward, forward under the little-finger side of the left *B hand*, palm facing right and fingers pointing forward.

Then, beginning with both *C hands* in front of the chest, palms facing each other, bring the hands away from each other in outward arcs while turning the palms in toward each other.

---

### minus *prep.*

■ [Shape of a minus sign] Touch the thumb side of the extended right index finger, palm facing down and finger pointing forward, against the palm of the left *open hand*, palm facing right.

---

### minute *n.* Same sign used for: **moment, momentarily, one minute.**

■ [The finger represents the movement of the minute hand on a clock] Move the extended right index finger, palm facing left, forward a short distance, pivoting the closed fingers of the right hand on the palm of the left *open hand*, palm facing right and fingers pointing up.

---

### mirror *n.*

■ [The hand represents a mirror] Beginning with the right *open hand* held up near the right shoulder, palm facing left, twist the wrist to turn the palm in and back with a double movement.

---

**mischief** *n.* See sign for DEVIL. Related form: **mischievous** *adj.*

---

**misconception** *n.* See sign for MISUNDERSTAND.

---

**miser** *n.* See sign for STINGY[2].

---

### miserable *adj.*

■ [The sign for **disappointed** is repeated] With a repeated alternating movement, touch the chin with the extended right index finger and then the left, palms facing in.

---

# miss

**miss¹** *v.*

- [The hand seems to snatch at something as it passes] Move the right *C hand,* palm facing left, from near the right side of the forehead in a quick downward arc in front of the face while closing into an *S hand,* ending with the palm facing down in front of the left shoulder.

**miss²** *Slang.* Same sign used for: **You're too late.**

- [**train + zoom¹**] Rub the extended fingers of the right *H hand* across the back of the extended fingers of the left *H hand,* both palms facing down. Then beginning with the thumb of the right *L hand,* palm facing forward, on the base of the extended left index finger, palm facing down, move the right hand quickly to the right while closing the index finger to the thumb.

**miss³** *v.* See signs for ABSENT, DISAPPOINTED, SKIP¹. Related form: **missing** *adj.*

**missile** *n.*

- [Shows movement of a missile ejecting] Beginning with the heel of the right *one hand,* palm facing forward, on the back of the left *open hand,* palm facing down, raise the right hand upward in front of the face.

**mistake** *n.* Related form: **mistaken** *adj.*
Same sign used for: **accident.**

- [Similar to sign for **wrong** but made with a double movement] Tap the middle fingers of the right *Y hand,* palm facing in, against the chin with a double movement.

**misty** *adj.* See sign for WET.

**misunderstand** *v.* Related form: **misunderstanding** *n.*
Same sign used for: **misconception.**

- [The fingers indicate something turned around in the mind] Touch the index finger of the right *V hand* to the right side of the forehead, palm facing forward, and then twist the wrist and touch the middle finger to the forehead, ending with the palm facing back.

**mitten** *n.* Alternate form: **mitt** *n.*

■ [Shape of a mitten] With the extended right index finger, palm facing down and finger pointing forward, trace the shape of the left *open hand*, palm facing in and fingers pointing up, beginning at the base of the thumb and ending at the base of the little finger.

**mix**[1] *v.* Same sign used for: **blend, complex, confuse, disorder, scramble, stir.**

■ [Mime mixing things up] Beginning with the right *curved 5 hand* over the left *curved 5 hand*, palms facing each other, move the hands in repeated circles in opposite directions in front of the chest.

**mix**[2] *v.* See signs for BEAT[1], CIRCULATE.

**mixed up** *v. phrase.* See sign for CONFUSE[1].

**mobile** *adj.* Same sign used for: **movable.**

■ [Sign similar to sign for **move** except indicates moving in different directions] Beginning with both *flattened O hands* in front of the right side of the body, palms facing down, move the hands forward with a wavy movement.

**mobilize** *v.* See sign for TRIP.

**mock** *v.* Same sign used for: **jeer, laugh at.**

■ [The fingers seem to jeer at another] Move both *Y hands*, palms facing down, forward a short distance with a double movement from in front of each side of the chest.

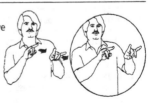

**modest** *adj.* See sign for HUMBLE. Related form: **modesty** *n.*

**modify**[1] *v.* Related form: **modification** *n.*

■ [Initialized sign similar to sign for **change**[1]] Beginning with the palm sides of both *M hands* facing each other in front of the chest, twist the hands in opposite directions with a double movement.

# modify

**modify²** *v.* See sign for CHANGE¹.

---

**moist** *adj.* See sign for WET. Related forms: **moisten** *v.*, **moisture** *n.*

---

**mole¹** *n.*

- [Represents the action of mole burrowing through dirt] Beginning with the back of both *open hands* together in front of the chest, palms facing in opposite directions, bend the fingers of each hand downward toward each palm with a double movement.

---

**mole²** *n.*

- [**brown** + shape and location of a mole on the face] Slide the index-finger side of the right *B hand*, palm facing left, down the right cheek with a repeated movement. Then bring the thumb side of the right *F hand*, palm facing forward, against the right side of the chin.

---

**molest** *v.*

- [One finger abuses another finger] With the index finger of the left hand extended in front of the chest, palm facing right, rub the knuckles of the extended right index finger hand, palm facing forward, back and forth with a double movement against the thumb side of the left hand.

---

**mom** *n.* See sign for MOTHER. Alternate form: **mommy** *n.*

---

**moment** *n.* See sign for MINUTE. Related form: **momentarily** *adv.*

---

**momentum** *n.* See sign for CONSTANT¹.

---

**Monday** *n.*

- [Initialized sign] Move the right *M hand*, palm facing in, in a double circle in front of the right shoulder.

---

**money** *n.* Same sign used for: **fund.**

- [Represents putting money in one's hand] Tap the back of the right *flattened O hand*, palm facing up, with a double movement against the palm of the left *open hand*, palm facing up.

---

**monitor** *v.* See sign for CARE[1].

**monkey** *n.* Same sign used for: **ape, chimpanzee.**

- [Mime the scratching motion done by monkeys] Beginning at the waist, scratch the fingertips of both *curved 5 hands,* palms facing in, upward on each side of the body with a double movement.

**monotone** *adj.* See sign for MONOTONOUS[1].

**monotonous**[1] *adj.* Related form: **monotony** *n.* Same sign used for: **monotone.**

- [Shows repetitive activity] Rub the index-finger side of the right *S hand,* palm facing down, in a repeated circular movement on the palm of the left *open hand* held in front of the chest, palm facing right.

**monotonous**[2] *adj.* See sign for GRIND OUT.

**monster** *n.* Same sign used for: **haunt, haunted, spooky.**

- [Mime the action and facial expression of a monster] Beginning with both *curved 5 hands* held near each side of the head, palms facing down, move the hands up and down with a double movement accompanied by a menacing facial expression.

**month** *n.* Same sign used for: **one month.**

- [The finger moves down the weeks on a calendar] Move the extended right index finger, palm facing in and finger pointing left, from the tip to the base of the extended left index finger, palm facing right and finger pointing up in front of the chest.

**monument** *n.*

- [Shows the shape of the top of a monument] Beginning with both *B hands* in front of each shoulder, palms angled down, bring the hands upward toward each other, ending with the fingertips touching in front of the head.

# mooch

**mooch** *v. slang.* See sign for LEECH.

## moon *n.*

- [The shape of the crescent moon] Tap the thumb of the right *modified C hand,* palm facing left, against the right side of the forehead with a double movement.

## mop *n., v.*

- [Mime using a mop] Beginning with both *modified X hands* in front of the body, the left hand lower than the right hand, right palm angled left and left palm angled up, move the hands forward and downward with a double movement.

## more *adj., adv.*

- [The hands seem to add more and more things together] Tap the fingertips of both *flattened O hands,* palms facing each other, together in front of the chest with a double movement.

**more than** See sign for EXCESS.

## morning *n.*

- [Represents the sun coming up over the horizon] With the left *open hand* in the crook of the bent right arm, bring the right *open hand* upward, palm facing in.

## mortgage *n.*

- [Initialized sign similar to sign for **lend**] With the little finger of the right *M hand* on the index finger of the left *M hand,* fingers pointing in opposite directions and palms facing in, tip the hands forward.

**mosquito**[1] *n.*

- [Represents a mosquito biting one's cheek, causing one to hit it in order to kill it] Touch the fingertips of the right *F hand,* palm facing left, on the right cheek. Then place the palm of the right *open hand* against the same place on the right cheek.

**mosquito**[2] *n.* See sign for BEE.

**most** *adj., adv., n.*

- [The hand rises to a higher level] Beginning with the palm sides of both *10 hands* together in front of the chest, bring the right hand upward, ending with the right hand in front of the right shoulder, palm facing left.

**mother** *n.* Same sign used for: **mama, mom, mommy.**

- [Formed in the female area of the head] Tap the thumb of the right *5 hand,* palm facing left, against the chin with a double movement.

**mother-in-law** *n.*

- [**mother + law**] Tap the thumb of the right *5 hand,* palm facing left against the chin with a double movement. Then place the palm side of the right *L hand* first on the fingers and then on the heel of the upturned left *open hand* held in front of the body.

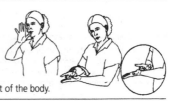

**motion** *v.* See sign for SUGGEST.

**motive** *n.* See signs for FEEL, ZEAL. Related form: **motivation.**

**motor** *n.* See sign for MACHINE.

**motorcycle** *n.*

- [Mime the action of one's hands on a motorcycle's handlebars] Beginning with both *S hands* held near each side of the waist, palms facing back, twist the wrists to move the hands up and down with a repeated movement.

# mount

**mount** *v.* See sign for PUT.

## mountain *n.*

■ [**rock**[1] + the shape of a mountainside] Tap the palm side of the right *S hand* on the back of the left *S hand,* both palms facing down in front of the body. Then, beginning with both *open hands* in front of each side of the waist, palms facing down and fingers angled up, move the hands upward and forward at an angle with a large wavy movement.

## mouse *n.*

■ [Represents the twitching of a mouse's nose] Flick the extended right index finger, palm facing left, across the tip of the nose with a double movement.

## mouth *n.*

■ [Location of the mouth] Draw a circle around the mouth with the extended right index finger, palm facing in.

**move** *v.* Related form: **movement** *n.* Same sign used for: **relocate.**

■ [The hands seem to move something from one place to another] Beginning with both *flattened O hands* in front of the body, palms facing down, move the hands in large arcs to the right.

**movable** *adj.* See sign for MOBILE.

**movie** *n.* See sign for FILM[1].

## movie camera *n.* Same sign used for: **camera, film, shoot, video camera, videotape.**

■ [Shows the action of movie film going through the camera] Move the right *modified X hand,* palm facing down, in a forward circular movement near the palm of the left *open hand,* palm facing right and fingers pointing up, in front of the upper chest.

**much** *n., adj., adv.* Same sign used for: **a lot, lot.**

■ [The hands expand to encompass something large] Beginning with the fingertips of both *curved 5 hands* touching each other in front of the body, palms facing each other, bring the hands outward to in front of each side of the chest.

**muffle** *v.*

■ [Natural gesture] Place the palm side of the right *C hand* over the mouth.

**mule** *n.* See sign for DONKEY.

**mull** or **mull over** *v.* Same sign used for: **cogitate, deliberate, ponder.**

■ [Represents the brain as it cogitates] Wiggle the fingers of the right *4 hand* in a small repeated circle near the forehead, palm facing in.

**mumps** *n.*

■ [Shows the shape of one's swollen jaws from mumps] Beginning with both *curved 5 hands* in front of each shoulder, palms facing each other, bring the hands in to touch each side of the neck.

**multiplication** *n.* See signs for ARITHMETIC, MATHEMATICS.

**multiply** *v.* Same sign used for: **estimate, figure, figure out.**

■ [The movement suggests combining things] Brush the back of the right *V hand* across the palm side of the left *V hand*, both palms facing up, as the hands cross in front of the chest.

**murder** *v.* See sign for KILL.

# muscle

### muscle *n.*

■ [Location of a muscle in the arm] Tap the extended right index finger against the upper part of the bent left arm with a double movement.

### museum *n.*

■ [Initialized sign showing the shape of museum shelves] Beginning with both *M hands* in front of chest, palms facing forward, bring the hands outward to in front of each shoulder and then straight down.

### music *n.* Same sign used for: **chant, melody, sing, song.**

■ [Demonstrates the rhythm of music] Swing the little-finger side of the right *open hand,* palm facing left, back and forth with a double movement across the length of the bent left forearm held in front of the chest.

### must *auxiliary v.* Same sign used for: **have to, necessary, ought to.**

■ [Suggests standing firm on a position] Move the bent index finger of the right *X hand,* palm facing forward, downward with a deliberate movement in front of the right side of the body by bending the wrist down.

### mustache *n.*

■ [Location of a mustache] Beginning with the index finger and thumb of each hand pinched together under the nose, palms facing each other, bring the hands straight apart to near each side of the mouth.

**mute** *adj.* See sign for SILENT.

**mutilate** *v.* See sign for TORTURE.

**my** *pron.* Same sign used for: **mine, own.**
- [Pulling something to oneself] Place the palm of the right *open hand* on the chest, fingers pointing left.

**myself** *pron.*
- [Sign moves toward oneself] Tap the thumb side of the right *A hand,* palm facing left, against the chest with a double movement.

**mystery** *n.* See sign for HIDE.

---

**nab**[1] *v.* Same sign used for: **capture, catch, corner, caught in the act.**

■ [The fingers seem to nab a suspect] Bring the right *bent V fingers*, palm facing down, sharply forward on each side of the extended left index finger held up in front of the chest, palm facing right.

---

**nab**[2] *v.* See signs for CATCH[2], SOLICIT.

---

**nag** *v.* See sign for PICK ON, PREACH.

---

**nail file** *n.* See sign for PUMICE.

---

**naive** *adj.* See sign for INNOCENT.

---

**naked** *n.* See sign for NUDE.

---

**name**[1] *n., v.*

■ [The hands form an "X," which is used by illiterate people to sign their names] Tap the middle-finger side of the right *H hand* across the index-finger side of the left *H hand*.

---

**name**[2] *v.* See sign for CALL[3].

---

**napkin** *n.*

■ [Mime wiping one's mouth with a napkin] Wipe fingertips of the right *open hand* from side to side over the lips with a double movement, palm facing in.

---

**narrow** *adj.*

■ [The hands demonstrate something getting narrower] Bring both *open hands* from in front of each side of the body, palms facing each other, toward each other in front of the waist.

---

286

**narrow down** *v. phrase*. Same sign used for: **convey, focus on.**

- [The hands move downward from wider to narrower] Beginning with both *open hands* in front of each shoulder, palms facing each other and fingers pointing forward, bring the hands downward toward each other in front of the body.

**nasty** *adj*. See signs for BAD, DIRTY.

**nation** *n*. Same sign used for: **native, natural, nature, normal, of course.**

- [Initialized sign] Beginning with the right *N hand*, palm facing down, over the left *open hand*, palm facing down, move the right hand in a small circle and then straight down to land on the back of the left *open hand*.

**native** *n*. See sign for NATION.

**natural** *n*. See sign for NATION.

**nature** *n*. See sign for NATION.

**naughty** *adj*. See sign for BAD.

**nausea** *n*. See sign for DISGUSTED[1].

**nay** *adv*. *Archaic*. See sign for NEVER MIND.

**near** *adv*. See signs for APPROACH[1], CLOSE[1,2].

**near future, in the** See sign for SOON[1].

**nearly** *adv*. See sign for ALMOST.

**neat** *adj*.

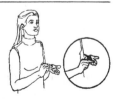

- [Initialized sign similar to sign for **clean**] Slide the extended fingers of the right *N hand*, palm facing down, from the heel to the fingers of the upturned left *open hand*, fingers pointing forward.

**necessary** *adj*. See sign for MUST, NEED.

# neck

**neck¹** *n.*

- [Location of the neck] Tap the fingertips of the right *bent hand,* palm facing down, against the neck with a double movement.

**neck²** *v.* See sign for PET².

**necklace¹** *n.*

- [Location of a necklace] Beginning with both extended index fingers touching near each side of the neck, bring the hands downward to touch near the middle of the chest.

**necklace²** *n.* See sign for BEADS.

**necktie** *n.* Same sign used for: **tie.**

- [Initialized sign showing the location of a necktie] Touch the fingertips of the right *N hand* first to near the neck and then to the lower chest, palm facing in.

**need** *v., n.* Same signs used for: **necessary, should.**

- [A forceful movement to emphasize need] Tap the bent index finger of the right *X hand,* palm facing down, with a short, repeated downward movement in front of the right side of the body, by bending the wrist down.

**needle** *n.*

- [Represents threading a needle] Move the index finger of the right *modified C hand,* palm facing left, downward with a double movement to brush the index finger of the left *L hand,* palm facing right.

**needlework** *n.* Same sign used for: **sew.**

- [Mime sewing] Beginning with the right *F hand*, palm facing down, above the left *F hand*, palm facing up, move the right hand upward with a short repeated movement.

**negative** *adj.*

- [Shape of a minus sign] Tap the thumb side of the extended right index finger, palm facing down and finger pointing forward, against the palm of the left *open hand*, palm facing right and fingers pointing up, with a double movement.

**neglect** *v.* See sign for IGNORE. Related forms: **negligence** *n.*, **negligent** *adj.*

**negotiate** *v.* Related form: **negotiation** *n.*

- [Initialized sign similar to sign for **communication**] Move both *N hands*, palms facing each other, forward and back from the chin with an alternating movement.

**neighbor** *n.*

- [**next door** + **person marker**] Beginning with the palm of the right *bent hand*, palm facing in and fingers pointing left, touching the back of the left *bent hand*, palm facing in and fingers pointing right, move the right hand forward in a small arc. Then move both *open hands*, palms facing each other, downward along each side of the body.

**neighborhood** *n.*

- [**next door** + **district**] Beginning with the palm of the right *bent hand*, palm facing in and fingers pointing left, touching the back of the left *bent hand*, palm facing in and fingers pointing right, move the right hand forward in a small arc.

## nephew *n.*

- [Initialized sign formed near the male area of the head] Beginning with the extended fingers of the right *N hand* pointing toward the right side of the forehead, palm facing left, twist the wrist to point the fingers forward with a double movement.

## nervous *adj.* Related form: **nervously** *adv.* Same sign used for: **anxiety, anxious.**

- [Natural gesture of shaking when nervous] Shake both *5 hands* with a loose, repeated movement in front of each side of the body, palms facing each other and fingers pointing forward.

## nervy *adj. Informal.* Related form: **nerve** *n.*

- [Indicates the cheekiness of a nervy person] Beginning with the bent fingers of the right *V hand* against the right cheek, palm facing forward, twist the wrist, ending with the palm facing back.

## net *n.* Same sign used for: **screen.**

- [Shows the mesh of a net] Beginning with the fingers of the right *4 hand* across the back of the fingers of the left *4 hand*, both palms facing forward, move the fingers of both hands slightly upward with a double movement.

## network *n., v.*

- [Similar to the sign for **contact** to indicate many contacts in a network] Beginning with the bent middle fingers of both *5 hands* touching in front of the right side of the chest, right palm angled forward and left palm facing in, twist both wrists and touch again in front of the left side of the chest, ending with the right palm facing in and left palm angled forward.

**neutral** *adj.*

- [Initialized sign] Move the right *N hand,* palm facing forward, from side to side with a small double movement in front of the right shoulder.

**never** *adv.*

- [Natural gesture used to wave an unwanted thing away] Move the right *open hand* from near the right side of the face, palm facing left, downward with a large wavy movement to in front of the right side of the body, ending with the palm facing down.

**never mind** *Slang.* Same sign used for: **blah** (*slang*), **nay** (*archaic*).

- [Natural gesture] Beginning with the right *open hand* in front of the right shoulder, palm facing forward and fingers pointing up, bend the wrist to bring the hand downward to the right side of the body, ending with the fingers pointing down and the palm facing back.

**nevertheless** *adv.* See sign for ANYWAY.

**new** *adj.*

- [One hand presents the other hand with something new] Slide the back of the right *curved hand,* palm facing up, from the fingertips to the heel of the upturned left *open hand.*

**newspaper** *n.* Same sign used for: **issue, press, print, publication.**

- [Represents putting movable type into place to set up a newspaper] Beginning with the right *G hand,* palm facing forward, above the left *open hand,* palm facing up, pull the right hand down toward the heel of the left hand with a double movement, closing the right thumb and index finger together each time.

# next

**next**[1] *adj., adv., prep.* See sign for BESIDE.

- [Demonstrates one hand overcoming an obstacle to move on to the next thing] Beginning with the right *bent hand,* palm facing in and fingers pointing left, closer to the chest than the left *open hand,* palm facing in and fingers pointing right, move the right hand up and over the left hand, ending with the right palm on the back of the left hand.

**next**[2] *adj.* See sign for TURN.

**next door** or **next-door** *adv.*

- [Shows a location next to another thing] Beginning with the palm of the right *bent hand,* palm facing in and fingers pointing left, touching the back of the left *curved hand,* palm facing in and fingers pointing right, move the right hand forward in a small arc.

**next to** *prep.* See sign for BESIDE.

**nickel** *n.* Same sign used for: **five cents.**

- [The sign **cent** is formed with a *5 hand*] Beginning with the bent index finger of the right *5 hand,* palm facing left, touching the right side of the forehead, bring the hand forward with a double movement.

**nickname** *n.*

- [**short**[1] + **name**[1]] Rub the middle-finger side of the right *H hand,* palm angled left, back and forth with a repeated movement on the index-finger side of the left *H hand,* palm angled right. Then place the middle-finger side of the right *H hand* across the index-finger side of the left *H hand.*

**niece** *n.*

- [Initialized sign formed near the female area of the head] Beginning with the extended fingers of the right *N hand* pointing toward the right cheek, palm facing left, twist the wrist to point the fingers forward with a double movement.

**niggardly** *adj.* See sign for GREEDY[1].

**night** *n.* Same sign used for: **tonight.**

■ [Represents the sun going down over the horizon] Tap the heel of the right *bent hand,* palm facing down, with a double movement on the back of the left *open hand* held across the chest, palm facing down.

**nightgown** *n.*

■ [Initialized sign] Beginning with the extended fingers of both *N hands* touching each side of the forehead, palms facing each other, bring the hands downward with a long wavy movement, ending with the *N hands* in front of each side of the body, fingers pointing toward each other and palms facing in.

**nipple** *n.*

■ [Indicates position of nipples] Beginning with both *S hands* in front of the chest, palms facing down, flick each index finger forward with a double movement.

**no**[1] *adv.*

■ [Fingerspell **n-o** quickly] Snap the extended right index and middle fingers closed to the extended right thumb, palm facing down, while moving the hand down slightly.

**no**[2] *adv.* See sign for NONE[1].

**nobody** *pron.* Same sign used for: **no one.**

■ [Similar to sign for **none**[1] but formed with one hand] Move the right *O hand,* palm facing forward, from side to side with a double movement in front of the right shoulder.

**nod** *v.* See sign for BOW[1].

# no good

**no good** *adj.*

- [Abbreviation **n-g**] Beginning with the right *N hand* in front of the right side of the chest, palm facing down, quickly twist the wrist to form a *G hand*, palm facing left.

**noise** *n.* Same sign used for: **aloud, loud, sound.**

- [Indicates the vibration of a loud sound coming from the ears] Beginning with the bent index fingers of both *5 hands* touching each ear, palms facing in, move the hands forward with a deliberate movement while shaking the hands.

**nominate** *v.* See signs for APPLY², SUGGEST.

**nonchalant** *adj.* See sign for DON'T CARE.

**none¹** *pron.* Same sign used for: **no.**

- [Indicates zero amount of something in the hand] Move both *flattened O hands,* palms facing forward, from side to side with a repeated movement in front of each side of the chest.

**none²** *pron.* (alternate sign) Same sign used for: **zero.**

- [Indicates zero amount of something] Move the right *O hand,* palm facing left, from in front of the chest forward, ending with the little-finger side of the right hand on the palm of the left *open hand.*

**none³** *pron.* See sign for NOTHING³.

**noodle** *n.*

- [The shape of a thin noodle] Beginning with the fingertips of both *I hands* touching in front of the chest, palms facing in, bring the hands apart with a double movement, bending the little fingers back toward the palms each time.

**noon** *n*. Alternate form: **noontime.**
Same sign used for: **midday.**

- [Represents the sun straight overhead at noon] Place the right elbow, arm extended up and right *open hand* facing forward, on the back of the left *open hand* held across the body, palm facing down.

**no one** *pron*. See sign for NOBODY.

**normal** *n., adj*. See sign for NATION.

**north** *n., adj., adv*.

- [Initialized sign moving in the direction of north on a map] Move the right *N hand*, palm facing forward, upward in front of the right shoulder.

**nose** *n*.

- [Location of the nose] Touch the extended right index finger to the right side of the nose, palm facing down.

**nosebleed** *n*. See sign for RUN[4].

**nosy**[1] *adj. Informal*.

- [Shape of a large nose] Beginning with the extended right index finger touching the nose, palm facing down, twist the wrist to bring the finger around the end of the nose, ending with the finger under the nose, palm facing in.

**nosy**[2] *adj. Informal*. (alternate sign) Same sign used for: **butt in, meddle, peek, pry, snoop.**

- [Represents one's nose extending to insert it into another's business] Beginning with the bent index finger of the right *X hand* beside the nose, palm facing left, bring the right hand downward and insert the bent index finger in the thumb-side opening of the left *O hand*, palm facing right.

# not

**not**[1] *adv.* Same sign used for: **don't.**

- [Flicking away something distasteful] Bring the extended thumb of the right *10 hand* from under the chin, palm facing left, forward with a deliberate movement.

**not**[2] *adv.* (alternate sign) Same sign used for: **don't.**

- [Natural gesture forbidding something] Beginning with the right *open hand* crossed over the left *open hand* in front of the body, palms facing down, swing the hands outward to in front of each side of the body.

## nothing[1] *n.*

- [The hand opens to reveal nothing in it] Beginning with the index-finger side of the right *O hand* under the chin, palm facing forward, bring the hand downward and forward while opening into a *5 hand*, palm facing down.

**nothing**[2] *n.* (alternate sign)

- [The hand opens to reveal nothing in it] Beginning with the index-finger side of the right *S hand* under the chin, palm facing left, bring the hand downward and forward while opening into a *5 hand*, palm facing down.

**nothing**[3] *n.* (alternate sign) Same sign used for: **all gone, gone, none.**

- [Natural gesture for showing nothing in one's hand] With the right *curved hand* in front of the upper chest, palm facing up, blow across the palm.

**notice**[1] *v.* Same sign used for: **aware, recognize.**

- [Brings the eye down to look at something in the hand] Bring the extended curved right index finger from touching the cheek near the right eye, palm facing left, downward to touch the palm of the left *open hand*, palm facing right in front of the chest.

**notice**[2] *v.* See sign for INFORM.

**notify** *v.* See sign for INFORM.

**notorious** *adj.* See sign for FAMOUS.

**not my fault** See sign for NOT RESPONSIBLE.

**not responsible** *adj.* Same sign used for: **hands off, not my fault.**

- [Natural gesture for flicking away responsibility] Beginning with the fingertips of both *8 hands* touching each shoulder, palms facing each other, flick the hands quickly forward while opening into *5 hands.*

**now** *adv.* Same sign used for: **current, present, prevailing, urgent.**

- [Indicates a presence right before you] Bring both *bent hands,* palms facing up, downward in front of each side of the body.

**Now I remember** See sign for DISGUSTED[2]. Shared idea of disgust with oneself for having forgotten.

**nude** *adj.* Same sign used for: **bare, naked.**

- [The sign **empty** formed downward on the hand representing a person's body] Move the bent middle finger of the right *5 hand,* palm facing in, downward on the back of the left *open hand,* palm facing in and fingers pointing down, from the wrist to off the fingertips.

**nuisance** *n.* Same sign used for: **pest.**

- [The finger used for feeling is jabbed at another] Move the bent middle finger of the right *5 hand* forward and back with a short, quick movement in front of the chest, palm facing forward.

# number

**number** *n.* Alternate form: **numeral.**
Related form: **numeric** *adj.*

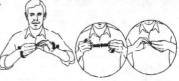

■ [Adding two quantities together]
Beginning with the fingertips of
both *flattened O hands* touching,
left palm angled forward and
right palm facing in, bring
the hands apart while twisting
the wrists in opposite directions and touch the fingertips again, ending with
the left palm facing in and the right palm angled forward.

**numerous** *adj.* See signs for MANY, MULTIPLE.

**nurse** *n.*

■ [Initialized sign similar to sign for **doctor**] Tap the
extended fingers of the right *N hand,* palm facing
down, with a double movement on the wrist of
the left *open hand* held in front of the body,
palm facing up.

**nut** *n.* See sign for PEANUT.

**oath** *n*. Same sign used for: **inaugural, inauguration, pledge.**

- [Natural gesture for putting one's hand on the Bible and taking an oath] Hold the left *open hand* in front of the left side of the body, palm facing down and fingers pointing forward, and the right *open hand* in front of the right shoulder, palm facing forward and fingers pointing up.

**obey** *v*. Related forms: **obedience, obedient.**

- [Represents placing one's own ideas in a position subservient to another's] Beginning with the right *O hand* in front of the forehead and the left *O hand* in front of the left shoulder, both palms facing in, bring the hands downward simultaneously while opening the fingers, ending with both *open hands* in front of the body, palms facing up and fingers pointing forward.

**object** *v*. See signs for COMPLAIN, DISAGREE.

**objection** *n*. See sign for PROTEST¹.

**objective**¹ *n*.

- [Initialized sign similar to sign for **goal**] Move the extended right index finger from in front of the right side of the forehead, palm facing left and finger pointing up, forward toward the thumb side opening of the left *O hand* held in front of the left shoulder, palm facing right.

**objective**² *n*. See sign for GOAL.

**obligate** *v*. See sign for VOW.

**obligation** *n*. See sign for BURDEN.

**observe** *v*. See sign for LOOK OVER.

# observe

**observe**[1] *v.* Related form: **observant** *adj.*

- [Represents one's eyes surveying the surroundings] Beginning with both *V hands* in front of the chest, palms facing down and fingers pointing forward, swing the hands to the left, following the fingers with the eyes.

**observe**[2] *v.* See sign for LOOK OVER.

**obsession** *n.* Related forms: **obsess** *v.*, **obsessive** *n., adj.* Same sign for: **persevere, persistent.**

- [The finger used for feeling remains on the other hand during a movement that signifies duration] With the bent middle finger of the right *5 hand* on the back of the left *open hand*, both palms facing down, move the hands forward in a repeated circular movement in front of the body.

**obstruct** *v.* See sign for PREVENT.

**obtain** *v.* See sign for GET.

**occasional**[1] *adj.* Related form: **occasionally** *adv.* Same sign used for: **once in a while, periodically.**

- [**next-next-next**] Beginning with the right *bent hand* in front of the right side of the chest, palm facing left and fingers pointing left, move the hand forward in a deliberate double arc.

**occasional**[2] *adj.* See sign for SOMETIMES.

**occupation** *n.* See sign for WORK.

**occupy** *v.* See sign for CAPTURE.

**occur** *v.* See signs for HAPPEN, SHOW UP. Related form: **occurrence** *n.*

# ocean *n.*

- [**water** + the shape of an ocean wave] Tap the index-finger side of the right *W hand,* palm facing left, against the chin with a double movement. Then, beginning with both *5 hands* in front of the body, palms facing down and fingers pointing forward, move the hands upward and forward in a large wavy movement.

**odd** *adj.* See sign for STRANGE.

**odor** *n.* See sign for SMELL[1].

**of course** See sign for NATION.

**off** *prep., adv.*
- [Shows moving one hand off the other hand] Beginning with the palm of the right *open hand* across the back of the left *open hand* at an angle, both palms facing down in front of the body, raise the right hand upward in front of the chest.

**offer** *v.* See sign for SUGGEST.

**office** *n.*
- [Initialized sign similar to sign for **box**] Beginning with both *O hands* in front of each side of the body, palms facing each other, move the hands deliberately in opposite directions, ending with the left hand near the chest and the right hand several inches forward of the left hand, both palms facing in.

**officer** *n.* See signs for CAPTAIN, CHIEF.

**officially** *adv.* See sign for DECIDE.

**offshoot** *n.* See sign for ASTRAY.

**off the point** See signs for ASTRAY, DIGRESS.

**off the subject** See sign for DIGRESS.

**off track** See signs for ASTRAY, DIGRESS.

**often** *adv.* Same sign used for: **frequently.**
- [The sign **again** formed with a repeated movement to indicate frequency of occurrence] Touch the fingertips of the right *bent hand*, palm facing left, first on the heel and then on the fingers of the left *open hand*, palm angled up.

# Oh

**Oh** *interj.*

■ [Symbolizes nodding one's head in agreement] Tap the right *Y hand,* palm angled down, with a double movement in front of the right side of the body.

**oil** *n.* Related form: **oily** *adj.* Same sign used for: **grease, greasy.**

■ [Shows oil dripping off something] Beginning with the bent thumb and middle finger of the right *5 hand,* palm facing up, on each side of the little-finger side of the left *open hand,* palm facing right and fingers pointing forward, bring the right hand downward with a double movement, pinching the thumb and middle finger together each time.

**ointment** *n.*

■ [**medicine** + mime rubbing ointment on the hand] With the bent middle finger of the right *5 hand,* palm facing down, in the upturned palm of the left *open hand,* rock the right hand from side to side with a double movement while keeping the middle finger in place. Then rub the fingers of the right *open hand* with a double movement on the back of the left *open hand* held in front of the chest, both palms facing down.

**okay**[1] or **OK** or **O.K.** *interj., adj.*

■ [Spell **o-k**] Form an *O* and a *K* quickly in front of the right side of the chest, palm facing forward.

**okay**[2] *adj.* See sign for SUPERB.

**old** *adj.*

■ [Shows the shape of a beard on an old man] Move the right *C hand* from near the chin, palm facing left, downward a short distance while closing into an *S hand.*

**old-fashioned** *adj.*

- [**old** + **fashion**] Move the right *C hand* from near the chin, palm facing left, downward a short distance while closing into an *S hand.* Then move the right *F hand,* palm facing down and fingers pointing forward, from in front of the right side of the body to the right a short distance in a small arc.

**Olympics** or **Olympic Games** *pl. n.* See sign for CHAIN.

**omit** *v.* See sign for ELIMINATE[1].

**on** *prep.*

- [Shows moving one hand on the other] Bring the palm of the right *open hand* downward on the back of the left *open hand* held in front of the body, both palms facing down.

**once** *adv.*

- Beginning with the extended right index finger touching the left *open hand* held in front of the body, palm facing right and fingers pointing forward, bring the right finger upward with a quick movement while twisting the right wrist in, ending with the palm facing in and finger pointing up in front of the right side of the chest.

**once in a while** See sign for OCCASIONAL[1].

**one another** *pron.* See sign for ASSOCIATE.

**one dollar** *n. phrase.* See sign for FIRST.

**one fourth** *n.* Related form: **one-fourth** *adj.*
Same sign used for: **quarter.**

- [**one** + **four** formed over each other as in a fraction] Beginning with the extended right index finger pointing up in front of the right side of the chest, palm facing in, drop the hand while opening into a *4 hand.*

**one half** *n.* Related form: **one-half** *adj.* Same sign used for: **half.**

- [**one** + **two** formed over each other as in a fraction] Beginning with the extended right index finger pointing up in front of the right side of the chest, palm facing in, drop the hand while opening into a *2 hand.*

# one minute

**one minute** *n.* See sign for MINUTE.

**one month** *n.* See sign for MONTH.

**one third** *n.* Related form: **one-third** *adj.* Same sign used for: **third.**

- [one + three formed over each other as in a fraction] Beginning with the extended right index finger pointing up in front of the right side of the chest, palm facing in, drop the hand while opening into a *3 hand*.

**one week** *n.* See sign for WEEK.

**onion** *n.*

- [As if wiping a tear away from onion fumes] Twist the knuckle of the bent index finger of the right *X hand*, palm facing forward, with a double movement near the outside corner of the right eye.

**only**[1] *adj., adv.*

- [Emphasizes one alone] Beginning with the extended right index finger pointing up in front of the right shoulder, palm facing forward, twist the wrist in, ending with the palm facing in near the right side of the chest.

**only**[2] *adj., adv.* See sign for ALONE[1].

**onward** *adv.* See sign for GO ON.

**open** *adj., v.*

- [Represents doors opening] Beginning with the index-finger sides of both *B hands* touching in front of the chest, palms facing forward, twist both wrists while bringing the hands apart to in front of each side of the chest, ending with the palms facing each other and the fingers pointing forward.

**open-minded** *adj.* See sign for BROAD-MINDED.

**operate**[1] *v.* Related form: **operation** *n.*
Same sign used for: **surgery.**

- [Represents the action of cutting during surgery] Move the thumb of the right *A hand*, palm facing down, from the fingers to the heel of the left *open hand*, palm facing right and fingers pointing forward.

**operate**[2] *v.* See signs for MANAGE, RUN[3].

**opinion** *n.*

- [Initialized sign] Move the right *O hand*, palm facing left in front of the forehead, toward the head with a double movement.

**opponent** *n.* See sign for ENEMY.

**opportunity** *n.*

- [Abbreviation **o-p** formed in a way that is similar to the sign for **permit**[1]] Beginning with both *O hands* in front of the chest, palms facing down, move the hands forward and upward in an arc while changing into *P hands*.

**opposed to** See sign for AGAINST.

**opposite** *adj.* Related form: **oppose** *v.* Same sign used for: **contrary, contrast, counter.**

- [Shows two things repelled by each other] Beginning with the fingertips of both extended index fingers touching in front of the chest, palms facing in, bring the hands straight apart to in front of each side of the chest.

**opposition** *n.* See sign for STRUGGLE.

**oppress** *v.* Related form: **oppression** *n.*

- [Demonstrates pushing an oppressed thing down] Push the palm of the left *5 hand* downward on the extended right index finger, palm facing left and finger pointing up, forcing the right hand downward with a double movement.

# optimistic

**optimistic** *adj.*

- [**feel + plus**[1]] Move the bent middle finger of the right *5 hand,* palm facing in, upward on the chest with a double movement. Then bring the side of the extended right index finger, palm facing left and finger pointing up, with a double movement against the extended left index finger, palm facing down and finger pointing right in front of the chest.

**or**[1] *conj.* Same sign used for: **then.**

- [Touches two choices] Tap the extended right index finger, palm facing in, first to the thumb tip and then to the end of the index finger of the left *L hand,* palm facing right and index finger pointing forward.

**or**[2] *conj.* See sign for EITHER.

**orange** *n., adj.*

- [The hand seems to squeeze an orange] Beginning with the right *C hand* in front of the mouth, palm facing left, squeeze the fingers open and closed with a repeated movement, forming an *S hand* each time.

**orbit**[1] *n., v.*

- [Shows movement of one thing around another] Move the extended right index finger, palm facing down, in a circle around the fingers of the left *flattened O hand,* palm facing down in front of the chest.

**orbit**[2] *n.* See sign for YEAR-ROUND.

**orchard** *n.* See sign for FOREST.

**ordeal** *n.* See sign for EXPERIENCE.

**order** *n., v.* Same sign used for: **command, direct.**

- [Represents taking words from the mouth and directing them at another] Move the extended right index finger, palm facing left and finger pointing up, from in front of the mouth straight forward while turning the palm down, ending with the finger pointing forward.

**ordinary**[1] *adj.*

■ [**daily** + **same**[1]] Move the palm side of the
right *10 hand* forward on the right side
of the chin with a double movement.
Then, beginning with both index
fingers pointing forward in front
of the each side of the body, palms facing
down, bring the hands together, ending
with the index fingers side by side in front of the body.

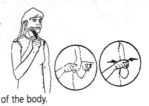

**ordinary**[2] *adj.* See sign for DAILY.

**organ** *n.* See sign for PIANO.

**organization** *n.* Related form: **organize** *v.*

■ [Initialized sign similar to sign for **class**] Beginning
with the fingertips of both *O hands* touching in
front of the chest, palms angled forward, bring
the hands away from each other in outward
arcs while turning the palms in, ending with
the little fingers touching.

**organize** *v.* See sign for PLAN, PREPARE.

**orientation** *n.*

■ [Initialized sign similar to sign for **situation**] Move
the palm side of the right *O hand* in a circle around
the extended left index finger held in front of the
chest, palm facing in and finger pointing up.

**origin** *n.* See sign for START[1]. Related form: **origination** *n.*

**originate** *v.* See sign for INVENT.

**orthodox** *adj.*

■ [Initialized sign similar to sign for **clean**] Slide
the little-finger side of the right *O hand*, palm
facing in, from the heel to the fingertips of
the left *open hand* held in front of the chest,
palm facing up and fingers angled forward.

# other

**other**[1] *adj., n.* Same sign used for: **else.**

- ■ [The thumb points over to another person, object, etc.] Beginning with the right *10 hand* in front of the chest, palm facing down, twist the hand upward to the right, ending with the palm facing up and the extended thumb pointing right.

**other**[2] *adj.* See sign for ANOTHER.

**ought to** See sign for MUST.

**our** *adj.* Related form: **ours** *pron.*

- ■ [The hand seems to draw a possession to oneself] Beginning with the thumb side of the right *C hand* on the right side of the chest, palm facing left, bring the hand forward in an arc across the chest, ending with the little-finger side of the left hand on the left side of the chest, palm facing right.

**ourselves** *pl. pron.*

- ■ [Uses the handshape used for reflexive pronouns] Beginning with the thumb of the right *A hand* touching the right side of the chest, palm facing left, bring the hand in an arc across the chest and touch again on the left side of the chest.

**out** *adv.* Same sign used for: **go out.**

- ■ [Demonstrates a movement out of something] Beginning with the right *5 hand,* palm facing down, inserted in the thumb side opening of the left *C hand,* palm facing right, bring the right hand upward, closing the fingers and thumb together into a *flattened O hand.*

**outbreak** *n.* See sign for SPREAD.

**outdoors** *adv.* See sign for OUTSIDE.

**out of the way** See sign for ASTRAY.

**outrage** *n.* See sign for ANGER.

**outreach** *n., adj.*

■ [**out** + **touch**] Beginning with the fingertips of the right *flattened O hand,* palm facing down, inserted in the thumb side opening of the left *C hand,* palm facing right, bring the right hand upward to the right, then touch the bent middle finger of the right *5 hand,* palm facing down, to the back of the left *open hand* held across the chest, palm facing down.

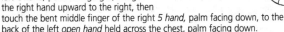

---

**outside** *n., adj., adv., prep.* Same sign used for: **external, outdoors.**

■ [An exaggerated form of the sign for **out**] Beginning with the right *5 hand,* palm facing down, inserted in the thumb side opening of the left *C hand,* palm facing right, bring the right hand upward and forward in an arc while closing the fingers and thumb together into a *flattened O hand* in front of the chest, fingers pointing in.

---

**oven** *n.*

■ [The hand seems to put something in the oven] Move the fingers of the right *open hand,* palm facing up and fingers pointing forward, forward with a double movement under the left *open hand* held in front of the chest, palm facing down and fingers pointing right.

---

**over**[1] *prep.* Same sign used for: **exceed, too much.**

■ [Shows a location higher than another] Beginning with the fingertips of the right *bent hand* on the fingertips of the left *bent hand,* palms facing each other and fingers pointing in opposite directions, bring the right hand upward a short distance in a small arc.

---

**over**[2] *prep., adv.* See signs for ABOVE, ACROSS, END[1], FINISH[1].

---

**overall** *adj., adv.* See sign for ALL OVER.

---

**overcome** *v.* See sign for DEFEAT.

---

**overflow** *v.* Same sign used for: **plenty, run over.**

■ [Demonstrates a substance flowing over the sides of a container] Slide the fingers of the right *open hand,* palm facing forward, over the index-finger side of the left *open hand,* palm facing in, while opening into a *5 hand* as it goes over to the back of the left hand.

# overlook

**overlook** *v.* Same sign used for: **oversight.**

■ [Represents something passing in front of the eyes without notice] Beginning with the right *open hand* near the right side of the head, palm facing left and fingers pointing up, move the hand in an arc in front of the face to the left while turning the fingers down, ending with the fingers pointing left and the palm facing in, in front of the left side of the chest.

**overnight** *adj., adv.* See sign for ALL NIGHT.

**oversight** *n.* See sign for OVERLOOK.

**oversleep** *v.*

■ [**sleep + sunrise**] Beginning with the right *curved 5 hand* in front of the forehead, palm facing in, bring the hand downward while closing the fingers and thumb together, forming a *flattened O hand* in front of the nose. Then, beginning with the right *F hand* in front of the body, palm facing

forward, bring the hands straight upward in front of the little-finger side of the left *open hand* held across the chest, palm facing down and fingers pointing right, ending with the right *F hand* in front of the face.

**overwhelm** *v.*

■ [Represents everything coming at one at once, as if to overwhelm] Beginning with both *A hands* in front of each side of the face, palms facing in, bring the hands back along each side of the head while opening into *5 hands*.

**owe** *v.* See sign for AFFORD.

**own**[1] *adj., pron.* Same sign used for: **self.**

■ [The hand moves back toward oneself] Bring the knuckles of the right *10 hand,* palm facing right, back against the center of the chest.

**own**[2] *adj., pron.* See sign for MY.

**pace** *n.* See signs for PROCEDURE, STEP. Shared idea of taking orderly steps.

**pack** *v.*

- [Mime putting things into a suitcase] Beginning with both *flattened O hands* in front of each side of the chest, palms facing down, move the hands downward with an alternating double movement.

**package** *n.* See signs for BOX, ROOM.

**page** *n.* Same sign used for: **dictionary.**

- [The thumb seems to flip through the pages of a book] Strike the extended thumb of the right *A hand,* palm facing down, against the left open palm with a double circular upward movement.

**pail** *n.* See sign for BUCKET.

**pain** *n.* See also signs for HURT[1,2]. Same sign used for: **ache, injury.**

- [Similar to sign for **hurt**[1] except with a twisting movement] Beginning with both extended index fingers pointing toward each other in front of the chest, right palm facing down and left palm facing up, twist the wrist in opposite directions, ending with right palm facing up and the left palm facing down.

**paint** *n., v.* Same sign used for: **brush.**

- [Mime the action of a paintbrush's bristles moving when painting] Bring the fingertips of the right *open hand* down the length of the left palm from the fingertips to the base with a double movement, pulling the back of the right fingers up the left palm to the fingertips each time.

# pair

**pair** *n.* See signs for BOTH, COUPLE.

**pajamas** *n.*

- [Abbreviation **p-j**] Form a *P* and then a *J* with the right hand in front of the right side of the chest.

**pal** *n.* See sign for FRIEND.

**pale** *adj.* Same sign used for: **Caucasian.**

- [**white** + a gesture indicating that a person's face is white] Beginning with the fingertips of the right *5 hand* on the chest, pull the hand forward while closing into a *flattened O hand*. Then place the right *5 hand* in front of the face.

**pamphlet** *n.* See sign for MAGAZINE.

**pancake** *n.*

- [Indicates turning a pancake over while cooking] Beginning with the back of the right *open hand* across the palm of the left *open hand,* both palms facing up, flip the right hand over, ending the right palm facing down across the left palm.

**panel** *n.*

- [**discuss** + represents the legs of people sitting in a circle] Tap the side of the extended right index finger, palm facing in, on the upturned open left palm with a double movement. Then, beginning with the knuckles of both *bent V hands* together in front of the body, palms facing down, bring the hands away from each other in outward arcs while turning the palms out, ending in front of each side of the body.

**panic** *n.,v.* See sign for AFRAID.

**pant** *v.* See sign for BREATH.

**panties** *n.*

- [Mime pulling up panties] Beginning with the fingertips of both *F hands,* palms facing in, touching each hip, move the hands up to touch the fingertips again at the waist.

**pants** *n.* Same sign used for: **jeans, slacks, trousers.**

- [Shows location of pants on both legs] Beginning with the fingertips of both *open hands* touching each hip, palms facing in, move the hands upward toward the waist with a double movement.

**pantyhose** *n.* See sign for STOCKING.

**papa** *n.* See sign for FATHER.

**paper** *n., adj.*

- [The pressing of pulp to make paper] Brush the heel of the right *open hand,* palm facing down, on the heel of the left *open hand,* palm facing up, in front of the body with a double movement.

**paper clip** *n.*

- [Demonstrates clipping a paper clip on the edge of paper] Beginning with the extended thumb of the right *U hand* against the palm side of the left *B hand,* palm facing down, close the extended right middle and index fingers down against the back of the left hand.

**parable** *n.* See sign for STORY.

**parachute** *n., v.*

- [Represents the shape of a parachute circling around] Beginning with the right *curved 5 hand,* palm facing down, over the extended right index finger, palm facing right and finger pointing up, in front of the right side of the body, move the hands to the left side of the chest and then outward in an arc back to the right side of the chest.

# parade

**parade** *n*. See sign for MARCH.

**paradox** *n*. See sign for PUZZLED.

**paragraph** *n*.
■ [Marks off the size of a paragraph] Tap the fingertips of the right *C hand*, palm facing left, against the palm of the left *open hand*, palm facing right and fingers pointing up, with a double movement.

**paralysis** *n*. Related form: **paralyze** *v*.
■ [Mime the rigid body of a person with paralysis] Beginning with both *5 hands* held limply in front of each side of the body, fingers pointing down and palms facing back, jerk the right hand upward in front of the right side of the chest while dropping the left hand downward, bending the hand awkwardly at the wrist near the left hip.

**parallel** *adj*.
■ [Shows two things that are parallel to each other] Beginning with the index fingers of both hands in front of each side of the chest, palms facing down and index fingers pointing forward, move the hands forward simultaneously.

**paranoid** *adj*.
■ [Initialized sign] Beginning with the extended middle finger of the right *P hand* touching the right side of the forehead, palm facing left, move the right hand quickly forward with a double movement while bending the middle finger down.

**parched** *adj*. See sign for THIRSTY.

**pardon** *v*. See signs for DISMISS, FORGIVE.

**pare** *v*. See sign for PEEL[1].

**parentheses** *pl. n*.
■ [Draw a pair of parentheses in the air] Beginning with both extended index fingers angled upward in front of each shoulder, palms facing forward, move both hands in outward and downward arcs while turning the wrists in.

**parents** *n.*

■ [**mother + father**] Touch the thumb of the right *5 hand*, palm facing left, first to the chin, then to the forehead.

**park** *v.*

■ [The handshape represents a vehicle that is set on the other hand as if to park] Tap the little-finger side of the right *3 hand*, palm facing left and fingers pointing forward, on the palm of the left *open hand*, palm facing up, with a repeated movement.

**parole** *n.,v.* See sign for DISMISS.

**parrot** *n.* Same sign used for **parakeet**.

■ [Shows the action of a parrot's beak closing] Pinch the bent index and middle fingers and thumb of the right hand together near the right side of the mouth with a double movement, palm facing forward.

**part**[1] *n.* Related form: **partial** *adj.* Same sign used for: **piece, section, segment**.

■ [The hand seems to divide what is in the other hand into parts] Slide the little-finger side of the right *open hand*, palm facing left, across the palm of left *open hand*, palm facing up, with a curved movement.

**part**[2] *v.* Same sign used for: **apart, separate**.

■ [The hands separate two things] Beginning with the fingers of both *10 hands* together in front of the chest, palms facing in, bring the hands apart in front of each side of the chest.

**part**[3] *n., adj.* See sign for SOME.

**part from** *v. phrase.* See sign for DISCONNECT.

# partial to

**partial to** *adj.* Same sign used for: **favorite.**

- [Pointing out a favorite] Tap the fingertips of the right *B hand*, palm facing left, with a double movement against the index finger of the left *B hand* held up in front of the chest, palm facing right.

**participate** *v.* See sign for JOIN[1].

**particular** *adj.* See sign for POINT[2].

**parting** *n.* Same sign used for: **depart, departure.**

- [Represents two people moving apart when parting] Beginning with both extended index fingers pointing up in front of the chest, palms facing forward, bring the hands apart to in front of each shoulder.

**party** *n.*

- [Initialized sign] Beginning with both *P hands* in front of the right side of the body, palms facing down, swing the hands from side to side in front of the body with a large double arc.

**partying** *n.*

- [Waving the hands in glee] Beginning with both *5 hands* near each side of the head, palms facing each other and fingers pointing up, flip the hands forward with a double movement, turning the palms forward each time.

**pass** *v.* Same sign used for: **by, past.**

- [One hand moves past the other hand] Beginning with both *A hands* in front of the body, palms facing in opposite directions and left somewhat forward of the right hand, move the right hand forward, striking the knuckles of the left hand as it passes.

**pass around** *v. phrase*. Same sign used for: **deal, pass out.**

■ [Mime passing something around] Beginning with the fingers of both *flattened O hands* together in front of the body, palms facing up, move the right hand forward and then twist it around to the right, ending with the palm facing left.

**passion** *n*. See sign for WANT.

**passionate** *adj*. Related form: **passion** *n*.

■ [Shows the location of deep feelings] Move the fingertips of the right *C hand* down the center of the chest with a deliberate double movement.

**passive** *adj*. See sign for QUIET.

**pass out**[1] *v. phrase*.

■ [Abbreviation **p-o**] Place the thumb side of the right *P hand* and, then, the right *O hand* against the forehead, palm facing left.

**pass out**[2] *v. phrase* See sign for PASS AROUND.

**past** *adv*. See signs for AGO, BEFORE[1], PASS, WAS[1].

**path** *n*. See sign for ROAD. Related form: **pathway** *n*.

**patient**[1] *adj*. Related form: **patience** *n*.
Same sign used for: **bear, tolerant, tolerate.**

■ [The thumb seems to seal the lips as a person tolerates something] Move the right *A hand*, palm facing left, downward in front of the chin.

**patient**[2] *n*.

■ [Initialized sign similar to sign for **hospital**] Move the extended middle finger of the right *P hand*, palm facing in, first down and then forward on the left upper arm.

## patrol

**patrol** *v.* See sign for CARE[1].

**pattern** *n.*

- [same-same-same indicating a repetition as in a pattern] Beginning with both *Y hands* in front of the left side of the body, palms facing down, move the hands in simultaneous repeated arcs to in front of the right side of the body.

**pauper** *n.* See sign for POOR.

**pause** *v.* See sign for HOLD[2].

**pave** *v.*

- [Demonstrates the action of moving dirt in order to pave] Slide the little-finger side of the right *bent hand,* palm facing in, from the wrist to off the fingertips of the left *open hand,* palm facing down and fingers pointing forward.

**pay** *v.*

- [Represents directing money from the hand to pay another person] Beginning with the extended right index finger touching the palm of the left *open hand,* palms facing each other, move the right finger forward and off the left fingertips.

**pay attention** See sign for ATTENTION.

**pay for** *v. phrase.* Same sign used for: **pay in full, pay off.**

- [Represents directing money from the hand to pay another person + **clean**] Touch the bent middle finger of the right *5 hand* to the palm of the left *open hand,* palms facing each other and fingers pointing forward. Then wipe the right *open hand* across the left *open hand* from the heel to off the fingertips with a deliberate movement.

**pay in full** *v. phrase.* See sign for PAY FOR.

**pay off** *v. phrase.* See sign for PAY FOR.

**peace** *n.* Related form: **peaceful** *adj.*

■ [**become + settle**] Beginning with the palms of both *open hands* together in front of the chest, right palm facing forward and left palm facing in, twist the wrist to reverse positions. Then move the hands downward, ending with both *open hands* in front of each side of the waist, palms facing down and fingers pointing forward.

**peach** *n.*

■ [The fingers seem to feel peach fuzz] Beginning with the fingertips of the right *curved 5 hand* on the right cheek, palm facing left, bring the fingers down with a double movement, forming a *flattened O hand* near the right side of the chin.

**peacock** *n.*

■ [**bird** + a gesture indicating a peacock's tail feathers] Close the index finger and thumb of the right *G hand,* palm facing forward, with a repeated movement in front of the mouth. Then, beginning with the right *O hand,* palm facing in, near the crook of the bent left arm held across the chest, raise the right hand upward in an arc while opening into a *4 hand* as it passes in front of the face.

**peak** *n.*

■ [The shape of a peak] Move both extended index fingers from in front of each shoulder upward toward each other until they meet in front of the head.

**peanut** *n.* Same sign used for: **nut.**

■ [Represents peanut butter sticking to the back of one's teeth] Flick the extended right thumb, palm facing left, forward off the edge of the top front teeth with an upward double movement.

# peanut butter

### peanut butter *n.*

- [**peanut + butter**] Flick the extended right thumb, palm facing left, forward off the edge of the top front teeth with an upward double movement. Then wipe the extended middle and index fingers of the right hand, palm facing left, on the palm of the left *open hand,* palm facing right, toward the heel with a double movement, drawing the fingers back into the right palm each time.

### pear *n.*

- [Shows the shape of a pear] Beginning with the fingertips of right *curved 5 hand* cupped around the fingertips of the left *flattened O hand,* both palms facing in, bring the right hand outward to the right while closing the fingers to the thumb, forming a *flattened O hand.*

### peas *pl. n.*

- [The finger points to peas in a pod] Touch the fingertips of the right *modified X hand,* palm facing down, on the extended left index finger, palm facing in and finger pointing right, moving from the base to the tip and touching down in several places.

### peck *v.* See sign for PICK ON.

### peculiar *adj.* See sign for STRANGE.

### peddle *v.* See sign for SELL.

### pee *n. Slang (sometimes vulgar).* See sign for PENIS.

### peek[1] *v., n.*

- [Mime peeking around a partition] Beginning with the index-finger side of the right *B hand* in front of the nose, palm facing left, move the head to the right to look around the hand.

### peek[2] *v.* See sign for NOSY[2].

### peel[1] *v.* Same sign used for: **pare.**

- [Mime peeling with a small knife] Beginning with the knuckles of the right *10 hand* against the extended left index finger, both palms facing down, move the right thumb open and closed with a double movement.

**peel**[2] *v.*

- [Demonstrates the action of peeling something with the fingers] Beginning with the fingertips of the right *9 hand* touching the back of the left *S hand*, both palms facing down, move the right hand upward and forward while twisting the palm back.

**pee wee** *n.* See sign for SMALL[1].

**penalty** *n.* See sign for PUNISH. Related form: **penalize** *v.*

**pencil** *n.*

- [Indicates wetting the tip of a pencil and then writing with it] Touch the fingertips of the right *modified X hand*, palm facing in, near the mouth. Then move the right hand smoothly down and across the upturned left *open hand* from the heel to off the fingertips.

**penetrate** *v.* Same sign used for: **pierce, pierced.**

- [Demonstrates something penetrating something else] Insert the extended right index finger, palm facing left and finger pointing forward, with a deliberate movement between the middle and ring fingers of the left *open hand* held in front of the chest, palm facing in and fingers angled right.

**penis** *n.* Same sign used for: **pee** (*slang, sometimes vulgar*), **urine.**

- [Initialized sign] Tap the middle finger of the right *P hand*, palm facing in, against the nose with a double movement.

**penitent** *adj.* See sign for SORRY. Related form: **pentitence** *n.*

**pennant** *n.*

- [The shape of a pennant] Beginning with the extended thumb and index finger of the right *L hand*, palm facing forward, touching the thumb and extended index finger of the left hand, palm facing forward, move the right hand to the right while closing the index finger to the thumb in front of the right side of the body.

**penniless** *adj.* Same sign used for: **broke** (*informal*).

■ [Gesture indicates a broken neck to signify being broke] Bring the little-finger side of the right *bent hand,* palm facing down and fingers pointing back, against the right side of the neck with a deliberate movement while bending the head down to the left.

**penny** *n.* See sign for CENT.

**pension** *n.* Same sign used for: **allowance, royalty, subscribe, welfare.**

■ [Collecting money out of nowhere] With right *curved hand* in front of the right shoulder, palm facing back, bring the hand downward and inward toward the right side of the chest with a double movement, closing the fingers to form an *A hand* each time.

**people** *n.* Same sign used for: **folk, public.**

■ [Initialized sign] Move both *P hands,* palms facing down, in alternating forward circles in front of each side of the body.

**pep** *n.* See sign for INSPIRE.

**pepper** *n.*

■ [The hand seems to drop pepper on food] Shake the right *F hand,* palm facing down, up and down in front of the right side of the body with a repeated movement.

**per** *prep.* See sign for EACH.

**per annum** See sign for ANNUAL.

**perceive** *v.* See signs for PREDICT, UNDERSTAND. Related form: **perception** *n.*

**percent** *n.* Related form: **percentage** *n.*

■ [Draw the shape of a percent sign in the air] Move the right *O hand* from near the right side of the face, palm facing forward, a short distance to the right, then down at an angle to in front of the right side of the chest.

**perennial** *adj.*

■ [**continue**[1] + **annual**] Beginning with the thumb of the right *10 hand* on the thumbnail of the left *10 hand,* both palms facing down in front of the chest, move the hands downward and forward in an arc. Then, beginning with the little-finger side of the right *S hand* on the index-finger side of the left *S hand,* palms facing in opposite directions, move the right hand upward and forward in an arc while extending the right index finger.

**perfect** *adj.* Related form: **perfection** *n.*
Same sign used for: **accurate, ideal.**

■ [Initialized sign showing things matching perfectly] Move the right *P hand,* palm facing left, in a small circle above the left *P hand,* palm facing up. Then move the right hand downward to touch both middle fingers together in front of the chest.

**perform** *n.* See signs for ACT[2], DO. Related form: **performance** *n.*

**perfume** *n.*

■ [Represents applying perfume to the neck] Touch the thumb of the right *Y hand,* palm facing left, to the throat. Then twist the hand slightly to the left and touch the thumb to the throat again.

**perhaps** *adv.* See sign for MAYBE.

**period**[1] *n.*

■ [Draw a period in the air] With the right index finger and thumb pinched together, palm facing forward in front of the right side of the chest, push the right hand forward a short distance.

**period**[2] *n.*

■ [Initialized sign similar to sign for **time**[1]] Move the right *P hand,* palm facing left, in a small circle near the palm of the left *open hand,* palm angled forward, ending with the right palm against the left palm.

# period

**period**[3] *n.* See signs for MENSTRUATION, TIME[1].

**periodically** *adv.* See sign for OCCASIONAL[1].

**perish** *v.* See signs for DIE, DISSOLVE.

**permanent wave** *n.* Alternate form: **permanent.**

- [Represents the action of rollers crimping the hair] Beginning with both *C hands* near each side of the head, palms facing forward, bring the hands back toward the sides of the head while closing into *S hands.* Then move the hands downward and repeat the movement.

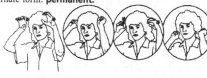

**permeate** *v.* Same sign used for: **soak through.**

- [Demonstrates something penetrating through something else] Beginning with both *5 hands* in front of each side of the chest, palms facing in and fingers pointing toward each other, bring the right hand forward, interlocking the left fingers. Then bring the right fingers back toward the chest, ending with the right palm facing right.

**permit**[1] *v.* Related form: **permission** *n.* Same sign used for: **privilege.**

- [Initialized sign similar to sign for **try**] Beginning with both *P hands* in front of the body, palms facing down, swing the wrist to move both hands forward and upward in small arcs.

**permit**[2] *v.* See sign for LET.

**perpendicular** *adj.*

- [Demonstrates the angle created when one thing is perpendicular to another thing] Tap the extended right index finger, palm facing in and finger pointing down, with a double movement on the extended left index finger held across the chest, palm facing in and finger pointing right.

324

**perpetual** *adj.*

■ [**continue**[1] + **forever**] Beginning with the thumb of the right *10 hand* on the thumb-nail of the left *10 hand*, both palms facing down in front of the chest, move the hands downward and forward in an arc. Then, beginning with the extended right index finger touching the right side of the fore-head, palm angled in, move the hand downward and form a large circle in front of the right side of the body, palm facing in and finger pointing up.

**perplexed** *adj.* See sign for PUZZLED.

**persecute** *v.* See sign for TORTURE. Related form: **persecution** *n.*

**persevere**[1] *v.* Related form: **perseverance** *n.* Same sign used for: **persistence, persistent.**

■ [**stubborn** + **continue**[1]] With the extended thumb of the right *open hand* touching the right side of the forehead, palm facing forward, bend the fingers forward and downward with a double movement. Then, beginning with the thumb of the right *10 hand* on the thumbnail of the left *10 hand*, both palms facing down in front of the chest, move the hands downward and forward in an arc.

**perservere**[2] *v.* See sign for OBSESSION.

**persistent** *adj.* See signs for OBSESSION, PERSEVERE[1], STUBBORN. Related form: **persistence** *n.*

**person** *n.*

■ [Initialized sign following the shape of a person] Bring both *P hands*, palms facing each other, downward along the sides of the body with a parallel movement.

**personal** *adj.* Same sign used for: **personnel.**

■ [Initialized sign] Move the right *P hand*, palm facing down, in a small double circle on the left side of the chest with a double movement.

# personality

### personality *n.*

■ [Initialized sign similar to sign for **character**[1]] Move the right *P hand*, palm facing down, in a small circle in front of the left side of the chest. Then bring the thumb side of the right *P hand* back against the left side of the chest.

### person marker *n.*

■ [The hands follow the shape of a person] Move both *open hands*, palms facing each other, downward along each side of the body.

### personnel *n.* See sign for PERSONAL.

### perspective *n.* Same sign used for: **point of view, viewpoint.**

■ [Represents eyes looking at something from different directions] Beginning with the index fingers of both *V hands* near each side of the face, palms facing down and fingers pointing toward each other, bring the hands outward in an arc and then forward toward each other in front of the chest.

### perspire *v.* See sign for SWEAT. Related form: **perspiration** *n.*

### persuade *v.* See sign for URGE.

### pessimistic *adj.*

■ [none[2] + hope] Beginning with both *O hands* in front of each side of the chest, palms facing each other, move the hands forward and downward in an arc. Then, beginning with the right *open hand* near the right side of the head, palm angled forward and fingers pointing up, and the left *open hand* in front of the chest, palm facing right and fingers pointing up, bend the fingers toward each other with a double movement.

### pest *n.* See signs for NUISANCE, PICK ON.

**pet**[1] *v.* Same sign used for: **favor, spoil, tame.**

■ [Demonstrates the action of petting something]
Pull the fingertips of the right *open hand,* palm
facing down, back toward the chest from the
fingers to the wrist of the left *open hand,* palm
facing down, with a long movement while bending
the finger back into the palm.

**pet**[2] *v.* Slang. Same sign used for: **make love, neck.**

■ [The fists represent two head close together] Beginning
with both *S hands* crossed at the wrists in front of the
chest, palms facing in opposite directions, bend the
hands downward with a short double movement.

**petition**[1] *n.*

■ [**sign**[2] **+ paper**] Place the extended fingers of the right *H
hand,* palm facing down, on the
upturned palm of the left *open
hand,* fingers pointing forward.
Then brush the heel of the right
*open hand,* palm facing down,
on the heel of the left *open hand,*
palm facing up, in front of the body with a double movement.

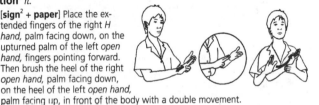

**petition**[2] *n.* See sign for SUGGEST.

**pew** *n.* See sign for COUCH.

**pharmacy** *n.*

■ [**medicine + store**[1]] With the bent middle
finger of the right *5 hand,* palm facing
down, in the upturned palm of the left
*open hand,* rock the right hand from side
to side with a double movement while
keeping the middle finger in place. Then,
beginning with both *flattened O hands*
held in front of each side of the chest,
palms facing down and fingers pointing
down, swing the fingertips upward and
back by twisting the wrists.

**phew** *interj.* See sign for STINK.

# philosophy

**philosophy** *n.*

- [Initialized sign similar to sign for **theory**] Bring the right *P hand,* palm facing left, downward with a short double movement in front of the right side of the forehead.

**phone** *n., v.* See sign for TELEPHONE.

**photo** *n.* See sign for PICTURE. Alternate form: **photograph.**

**photocopy** *v.* See sign for COPY².

**photograph** *v.* See sign for TAKE PICTURES.

**phrase** *n.* See sign for STORY.

**physical** *adj.*

- [Initialized sign similar to sign for **body**] Touch the palm sides of both *P hands,* palms facing in and fingers pointing toward each other, first on each side of the chest and then on each side of the waist.

**physician** *n.* See sign for DOCTOR.

**physics** *n.*

- [The coming together of electrons] Tap the knuckles of both *bend V hands,* palms facing in, against each other in front of the chest with a double movement.

**physique** *n.*

- [Shows the shape of one's figure + **hulk**] Beginning with both *curved hands* near each side of the chest, palms facing each other, move the hands downward along the sides of the body with a wiggly movement, twisting the wrists up and down as the hands move. Then, beginning with both *modified C hands* in front of each shoulder, palms facing each other, move the hands outward to each side with a large movement.

**piano** *n.* Same sign used for: **organ.**

■ [Mime playing a piano] Beginning with both *curved 5 hands* in front of the right side of the body, palms facing down, move the hands to the left and then back to the right again while wiggling the fingers.

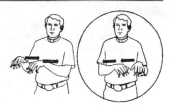

**pick¹** *v.*

■ [A directional sign demonstrating picking something] Beginning with the bent thumb and index finger of the right *5 hand* pointing forward in front of the right shoulder, palm facing forward, bring the right hand back toward the right shoulder while pinching the thumb and index finger together.

**pick²** *v.* See signs for CHOOSE¹, SELECT.

**picket** *v., n.* Same sign used for: **protest.**

■ [Mime holding a picket sign] With the little-finger side of the right *S hand* on top of the index-finger side of the left *S hand,* both palms facing in, move the hands forward in a short double movement.

**pickle** *n.*

■ [Similar to sign for **sour**] Twist the tip of the extended right index finger near the right corner of the mouth with a short double movement.

**pick on** *v.* Same sign used for: **henpeck, nag, peck, pest.**

■ [Indicates picking on someone] Tap the fingertips of the right *modified X hand,* palm facing left, against the extended left index finger, palm facing right and finger pointing up, in front of the chest with a double movement.

# picnic

### picnic *n.*
- [Represents eating a sandwich at a picnic] With the left *bent hand* over the back of the right *bent hand*, both palms facing down and fingers pointing toward the mouth, move the hands toward the mouth with a repeated movement.

### picture *n.* Same sign used for: **photo, photograph.**
- [The hand seems to focus the eyes on an image and then record it on paper] Move the right *C hand*, palm facing forward, from near the right side of the face downward, ending with the index-finger side of the right *C hand* against the palm of the left *open hand*, palm facing right.

### pie *n.*
- [Demonstrates cutting a pie into slices] Slide the fingertips of the right *open hand*, palm facing left, from the fingers to the heel of the upturned left hand, fingers pointing forward, and then perpendicularly across the left palm.

### piece *n.* See sign for PART[1].

### pierce *v.* See sign for PENETRATE. Related form: **pierced** *adj.*

### pierced ears *pl. n.*
- [Shows where holes are pierced into ears] Move the extended index fingers of both hands, palms facing down, toward each ear.

### pig *n.*
- [Similar to sign for **dirty**] With the back of the right *open hand* under the chin, palm facing down, bend the right fingers down and up again with a double movement.

**pigeon** *n.*

■ [Shows the pigeon's puffed out neck] With the extended right index finger touching the right side of the neck, palm facing forward, twist the hand forward, ending with the palm facing back.

**pile**[1] *n.* Same sign used for: **batch, bulk, load.**

■ [The shape and size of a pile] Move the right *5 hand* from in front of the left side of the chest, palm facing right and fingers pointing forward, upward in an arc in front of the right shoulder, ending near the right side of the body, palm facing left.

**pile**[2] *n.* See signs for AMOUNT, STACK.

**pill** *n.*

■ [Represents flicking a pill into the mouth] Beginning with the index finger of the right *A hand* tucked under the thumb, palm facing in, flick the right index finger open toward the mouth with a double movement.

**pillage** *v.* See sign for STEAL[1].

**pillar** *n.* Same sign used for: **column.**

■ [The shape of a pillar] Rest the elbow of the bent right arm on the back of the left hand held across the chest, palm facing down. Then slide the left *C hand* from the elbow upward to the wrist of the bent right arm.

**pillow** *n.*

■ [The hands seem to squeeze a soft pillow] With the fingers of both *flattened C hands* pointing toward each other near the right ear, palms facing each other, close the fingers to the thumbs of each hand with a repeated movement.

# pimples

### pimples *pl. n.*

- [Represents a pimple popping out] Beginning with the right *S hand* against the right cheek, palm facing left, flick the right index finger upward with a double movement.

### pin *n.*

- [Represents clipping on a pin] Beginning with the thumb of the right *modified C hand* against the left side of the chest, palm facing left, pinch the right index finger to the thumb.

### pinball machine *n.*

- [Mime pushing buttons to play a pinball machine] Beginning with both *curved 5 hands* in front of each side of the body, angled toward each other and finger pointing forward, move the hands downward with a double movement toward each other while bending the middle finger of each hand.

### pinch *v.*

- [Mime pinching] Move the curved index finger and thumb of the right hand downward in front of the chest, palm facing down, to pinch the back of the left *open hand*, palm facing down.

### pineapple *n.*

- [Initialized sign] Beginning with the middle finger of the right *P hand* touching the right cheek, palm facing left, twist the hand forward with a repeated movement, turning the palm back.

### Ping-Pong *Trademark.* Same sign used for: **table tennis.**

- [Mime swinging a Ping-Pong paddle] Beginning with the right *flattened O hand* in front of the right shoulder, palm facing down and fingers pointing down, swing the fingertips forward. Then move the right hand in front of the left side of the chest and swing the fingers forward again.

**pink** *adj.*

- [Initialized sign similar to sign for **red**] Brush the middle finger of the right *P hand,* palm facing in, downward across the lips with a short repeated movement.

**pinpoint** *n.* See sign for POINT².

**pipe¹** *n.*

- [Represents smoking a pipe] Pat the thumb of the right *Y hand,* palm facing left, against the right side of the chin with a repeated movement.

**pipe²** *n.* Same sign used for: **handle, lever, pole, rod.**

- [The shape of a pipe] Beginning with the index-finger sides of both *O hands* touching in front of the chest, palms facing forward, move the hands apart to in front of each side of the chest.

**pipe³** *n.* See sign for STICK².

**pistol** *n.* See sign for GUN.

**pit** *n.*

- [**hole** + shape of a pit] Move the extended right index finger, palm facing in and finger pointing down, in a large circle near the palm side of the left *C hand,* palm facing right. Then move the right *B hand,* palm facing in and fingers pointing left, from the thumb of the left *C hand* in a downward arc while twisting the right wrist, ending with the right fingers, palm facing forward, near the little finger of the left hand.

**pitch¹** *v.*

- [Mime pitching a ball] Beginning with the right *curved 3 hand* near the right shoulder, palm facing left, bring the right hand downward and forward to the left with a quick double movement, ending with the palm facing up.

# pitch

**pitch**[2] *v.* See sign for THROW.

**pitcher** *n.*

- [Represents pouring from a pitcher into another container] Beginning with the left *C hand* in front of the left side of the body, palm facing right, and the right *S hand* in front of the right side of the body, palm facing in, bring the right hand upward in an arc while turning the palm down, and then back down again in the original position.

**pizza** *n.*

- [**z** formed with *P hand*] Form a Z with the right *P hand*, palm facing left, in front of the right side of the chest.

**place**[1] *n.* Same sign used for: **position.**

- [Initialized sign outlining an area] Beginning with the middle fingers of both *P hands* touching in front of the body, palms facing each other, move the hands apart in a circular movement back until they touch again near the chest.

**place**[2] *v.* See sign for PUT.

**place**[3] *n.* See sign for AREA[1].

**plain** *adj.*

- [The hand seems to clean off something to make it plain] Beginning with the index-finger side of the right *open hand* against the chin, palm facing left, move the right hand down across the palm of the left *open hand* from the heel to the fingertips, palm facing up.

**plan** *n., v.* See also sign for PREPARE. Same sign used for: **arrange, schedule.**

- [The hands show a smooth and orderly flow of events] Move both *open hands* from in front of the left side of the body, palms facing each other and fingers pointing forward, in a long smooth movement to in front of the right side of the body.

**plane** *n.* See sign for AIRPLANE.

**plant¹** *n.*

- [Represents a seed sprouting and growing as it emerges from the ground] Bring the right *flattened O hand,* palm facing in, with a repeated movement upward through the left *C hand,* palm facing in and fingers pointing right, while spreading the right fingers into a *5 hand* each time.

**plant²** *v.* Same sign used for: **sow.**

- [Mime dropping seeds in a garden to plant them] Beginning with the right *flattened O hand* in front of the right side of the body, palm facing down, quickly close the fingers into an *A hand.* Repeat again somewhat forward from the body.

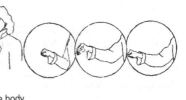

**plaster** *n., v.*

- [Mime spreading plaster on a wall] Beginning with the palm side of the right *S hand* on the open left palm, palms facing each other, move the right hand upward in an arc to the left.

**plate** *n.*

- [The shape of a plate] Move both *modified C hands* downward with a short repeated movement in front of each side of the body, palms facing each other.

**play¹** *v., n.* Same sign used for: **romp.**

- [The movement is loose and playful] Swing both *Y hands* up and down by twisting the wrists in front of each side of the body with a repeated movement.

# play

**play**[2] *n.* See sign for ACT[2]

**play cards** See sign for CARDS.

**plead** *v.* See sign for BEG[1].

**pleasant** *adj.* See signs for COOL, FRIENDLY.

**please**[1] *adv.*

- [Rubbing the heart, indicating a feeling of well-being] Rub the palm of the right *open hand* in a large circle on the chest.

**please**[2] *v.* See sign for ENJOY. Related form: **pleasure** *n.*

**please**[3] *adv.* See sign for WORSHIP[1]. Used in the context of pleading only.

**pledge** *n.* See signs for OATH, VOW.

**plenty** *n.* See signs for ENOUGH, OVERFLOW.

**pliable** *adj.* Same sign used for: **flexible.**

- [easy + bend[1]] Brush the fingertips of the right *curved hand* upward on the back of the fingertips of the left *curved hand* with a double movement, both palms facing up. Then, with the fingers of the right *flattened O hand* grasping the fingers of the left *open hand,* both palms facing in, bend the left fingers forward and back with a double movement.

**pliers** *pl. n.*

- [Demonstrates the squeezing action used with pliers] Open and close the finger of the right *C hand* in front of the right side of the chest with a double movement, palm facing in.

**plod** *v.* Same sign used for: **trudge.**

- [Represents the movement of a horse's hoofs when walking slowly] Beginning with both *S hands* in front of each side of the chest, right hand higher than the left hand, move the hands up and down with an alternating double movement by bending the wrists.

**plop** *v., n.* Same sign used for: **splat.**

- [Demonstrates something falling and spreading out as it lands] Beginning with the palm side of the right *S hand* on the index-finger side of the left *S hand,* bring the right hand forward and downward in a large arc while opening into a *5 hand* in front of the body.

**plow**[1] *n., v.*

- [Represents pushing dirt forward with a plow] Slide the little-finger side of the right *bent hand,* palm facing in and fingers pointing left, with a double movement from the wrist to off the fingertips of the left *open hand* held in front of the chest, palm facing down and fingers pointing forward.

**plow**[2] *v.* See sign for RAKE.

**plug** *n., v.*

- [Represents inserting a plug into a socket] Move the right *V hand,* palm facing down, forward from in front of the right shoulder, ending with the fingers of the right *V hand* on either side of the extended left index finger held pointing up in front of the chest, palm facing right.

**plus**[1] *prep.* Same sign used for: **addition.**

- [Shows the shape of a plus sign] Place the side the extended right index finger, palm facing down and finger pointing left, against the extended left index finger, palm facing right and finger pointing up in front of the chest.

**plus**[2] *prep.* See sign for ADD[1].

**plush** *adj.* See sign for LAYER.

**pneumonia** *n.*

■ [Initialized sign similar to sign for **lung**] Rub the middle fingers of both *P hands*, palms facing in and fingers pointing toward each other, up and down on each side of the chest with a double movement.

**pocket** *n., v.*

■ [Mime putting the hand in one's pocket] Slide the fingertips of the right *open hand*, palm facing in, up and down a short distance on the right side of the body with a repeated movement.

**pocketbook** *n.* See sign for PURSE.

**pod** *n.*

■ [Shows the shape of a pod opening] Beginning with the heels and fingers of both *curved hands* together in front of the chest, open the fingers with a small double movement while keeping the heels together.

**poem** *n.* Same sign used for: **poetry, Psalms.**

■ [Initialized sign similar to sign for **music**] Swing the middle finger of the right *P hand*, palm facing in, back and forth across the length of the bent left forearm, palm facing right.

**poetry** *n.* See sign for POEM.

**point**[1] *n.* Same sign used for: **tip.**

■ [Indicates the top point of something] Tap the extended right index finger, palm facing down and finger pointing left, down on the tip of the extended left index finger, palm facing right and finger pointing up, with a double movement.

**point**[2] *n.* Same sign used for: **particular, pinpoint, specific, target.**

■ [Demonstrates pointing at a specific thing] Bring the right extended index finger from in front of the right shoulder, palm facing left and finger pointing up, downward to touch the left extended index finger held in front of the left side of the chest, palm facing right and finger pointing up.

**point**[3] *v.* See sign for THERE.

**point of view** *n.* See sign for PERSPECTIVE.

**poison** *n., v.*

■ [Represents the crossbones from the skull and crossbones symbol on labels for poison] Cross the wrists of both *bent V hands,* palms facing the body, in front of the chest.

**pole** *n.* See signs for PIPE[2], POST[1], STICK[2].

**police** *n.* Same sign used for: **badge, cop, marshall, security, sheriff.**

■ [Shows the location of a police badge] Tap the thumb side of the right *modified C hand,* palm facing left, against the left side of the chest with a double movement.

**policy** *n.* See sign for PRINCIPLE.

**polish** *v.* Same sign used for: **rub.**

■ [Demonstrates action of polishing something] Rub the knuckles of the right *A hand,* palm facing down, with a repeated movement on the back of the left *B hand,* palm facing down.

**polite** *adj.* Same sign used for: **courteous, courtesy, gentle, manners, prim.**

■ [The ruffles on an old-fashioned shirt worn in polite society] Tap the thumb of the right *5 hand,* palm facing left, with a double movement against the center of the chest.

# politics

**politics** *n.* Related form: **political** *adj.*

■ [Initialized sign similar to sign for **government**] Beginning with the right *P hand* near the right side of the head, palm facing forward, twist the wrist to turn the palm back and touch the middle finger of the right *P hand* against the right side of the forehead.

**pollution** *n.* See sign for DIRTY.

**poncho** *n.* Same sign used for: **hood.**

■ [Mime pulling up the hood of a poncho] Beginning with both *modified X hands* near each shoulder, palms facing down, bring the hands upward and forward in an arc, ending with the palms facing up near each side of the head.

**pond** *n.* See sign for PUDDLE.

**ponder** *v.* See signs for MULL, WONDER.

**pool**[1] *n.* Same sign used for: **billiards.**

■ [Mime holding a pool cue] With the right elbow bent and extended back, move the right *A hand* forward a short distance near the right side of the body while holding the left *F hand* extended in front of the left side of the body.

**pool**[2] *v.* See sign for CHIP IN.

**poor** *adj.* Same sign used for: **pauper, poverty.**

■ [Represents the tattered sleeves on the elbows of poor people] Beginning with the fingertips of the right *curved 5 hand*, palm facing up, touching the elbow of the bent left arm, pull the right hand downward while closing the fingers to the thumb with a double movement, forming a *flattened O hand* each time.

**poor thing** See sign for MERCY.

### popcorn *n.*
- [Shows action of popcorn popping] Beginning with both *S hands* in front of each side of the body, palms facing up, alternately move each hand upward while flicking out each index finger with a repeated movement.

### Popsicle *Trademark.* See sign for LOLLIPOP.

### popular *adj.*
- [Represents many people surrounding a popular person] With the extended left index finger against the palm of the right *5 hand,* palm facing forward, twist the right hand around the index finger with a double movement, ending with the palm facing in.

### population *n.*
- [Initialized sign similar to sign for **among**] Move the extended middle finger of the right *P hand,* palm facing in, in and out between the fingers of the left *5 hand,* palm facing in.

### pop up *v. phrase.* See sign for SHOW UP.

### porch *n.*
- [Suggests places to hang a swing on a porch] Strike the index-finger side of the right *S hand,* palm facing in, first near the elbow then on the forearm of the bent left arm held across the chest, palm of the left *open hand* facing down.

### porpoise *n.* Same sign used for: **dolphin.**
- [fish[1] + diving movement] With the extended left index finger, palm facing in, touching the right wrist, move the right *B hand* from right to left with a double movement by bending the wrist. Then move the right *B hand,* palm facing left and fingers pointing up, in a large upward arc over the left arm held across the chest, ending with the right fingers pointing down in front of the left arm.

## portray

**portray** v. See sign for SHOW[1].

**position** n. See sign for PLACE.

**possess**[1] v. Related form: **possession** n.

■ [my + capture] Pat the palm side of the right *open hand*, palm facing in and fingers pointing left, against the center of the chest. Then, beginning with both *curved 5 hands* in front of each side of the chest, palms facing down and fingers pointing forward, move the hands downward with a quick movement while changing into *S hands*.

**possess**[2] v. See signs for CAPTURE, GREEDY[1].

**possible** adj. Same sign used for: **potential.**

■ [Similar to sign for **can** but made with a double movement] Move both *S hands*, palms angled forward, downward simultaneously in front of each side of the body with a double movement by bending the wrists.

**post**[1] n. Same sign used for: **pole.**

■ [The shape of a post] Beginning with the little-finger side of the right *C hand* on the index-finger side of the left *C hand*, palms facing in opposite directions, raise the right hand upward in front of the chest.

**post**[2] v. See signs for APPLY[1], BULLETIN BOARD.

**postage** n. See sign for STAMP[1].

**postage stamp** n. See sign for STAMP[1].

**post a notice** See sign for BULLETIN BOARD.

**poster** n. See sign for BULLETIN BOARD.

**postpone** v. Same sign used for: **defer, delay, put off.**

■ [Represents taking something and putting it off until the future] Beginning with both *F hands* in front of the body, palms facing each other and the left hand nearer to the body than the right hand, move both hands forward in small arcs.

**pot**[1] *n. Slang.* See sign for MARIJUANA.

**pot**[2] *n.* See signs for BOWL, BUCKET.

### potato *n.*

- [Represents putting fork tines into a baked potato to see if it is done] Tap the fingertips of the right *bent V hand,* palm facing down, with a double movement on the back of the left *open hand,* palm facing down.

**potent** *adj.* See sign for POWER[1].

**potential** *adj.* See sign for POSSIBLE.

### poultry *n.*

- [**bird + meat**] Open and close the extended fingers of the right *G hand,* palm facing forward, with a double movement in front of the mouth. Then, with the bent index finger and thumb of the right *5 hand,* palm facing down, grasp the fleshy part of the left *open hand,* palm facing down and fingers pointing right, and shake the hands forward and back with a double movement.

### pound[1] *v.*

- [Mime pounding something] Strike the little-finger side of the right *S hand,* palm facing in, with a repeated movement on the upturned palm of the left *open hand* held in front of the waist, fingers pointing forward.

**pound**[2] *n.* See sign for WEIGH.

### pour *v.*

- [Mime holding a large container and pouring from it] Beginning with both *C hands* in front of the body, palms facing each other, tip the hands so that the right hand is above the left hand, palm facing down, and the left hand is in front of the body, palm facing up.

**poverty** *n.* See sign for POOR.

---

**power**[1] *n.* Related form: **powerful** *adj.* Same sign used for: **mighty, potent, strength, sturdy.**

■ [Demonstrate power in one's arms] Move both S hands, palms facing in, forward with a short deliberate movement from in front of each shoulder.

---

**power**[2] *n.* See sign for STRONG[1].

---

**powerful** *adj.* Same sign used for: **strong.**

■ [Shows the large muscles in the arms of a powerful person] Bring the fingertips and thumb of the right *C hand* down against the biceps of the bent left arm.

---

**practice** *n., v.* Same sign used for: **exercise, rehearse, training.**

■ [The repetitive action symbolizes doing something again and again] Rub the knuckles of the right *A hand*, palm facing down, back and forth on the extended left index finger held in front of the chest, palm facing down and finger pointing right, with a repeated movement.

---

**praise** *v., n.* Same sign used for: **acclamation, compliment.**

■ [real + applaud] Bring the extended right index finger, palm facing left and finger pointing up, from in front of the mouth forward while changing into an *open hand*. Then clap the palms of both *open hands* together with a double movement in front of the body.

---

**pray**[1] *v.* Related form: **prayer** *n.*

■ [Natural gesture for praying] With the palms of both *open hands* together in front of the chest, fingers angled upward, move the hands forward with a double circular movement.

---

**pray**[2] *v.* See signs for AMEN, ASK, WORSHIP[1]. Related form: **prayer** *n.*

---

**pre-**¹ *prefix.* Same sign used for: **previous.**

■ [Initialized sign similar to sign for **before**²] Beginning with the back of the right *P hand,* palm facing in, touching the palm of the left *open hand,* palm facing in and fingers pointing right in front of the chest, move the right hand in toward the chest a short distance.

**pre-**² *prefix.* See sign for BEFORE².

**preach** *v.* Same sign used for: **nag.**

■ [Information is directed emphatically toward another] Move the right *F hand,* palm facing forward, with a short double movement forward in front of the right shoulder.

**preceding** *adj.* See sign for BEFORE².

**precious** *adj.* Same sign used for: **cherish.**

■ [Holding something of value tightly in the hand] Beginning with the right *curved 5 hand* in front of the mouth, palm facing back, slowly close the fingers into an *S hand.*

**precise** *adj.* Same sign used for: **concise, exact.**

■ [Demonstrates something coming together precisely] Beginning with the right *modified X hand* near the left *modified X hand,* move the right hand in a small circle and then forward to touch the hands together in front of the chest.

**predict** *v.* Same sign used for: **forecast, foresee, perceive, perception, prophecy.**

■ [Represents the eyes looking forward into the future] Beginning with the fingers of the right *V hand* pointing to each eye, move the right hand forward under the palm of the left *open hand.*

# prefer

**prefer**[1] *v.* Same sign used for: **rather.**

■ [**favorite**[1] + **better**] Beginning with the bent middle finger of the right *5 hand* touching the chin, palm facing in, bring the hand forward to the right while closing into a *10 hand.*

**prefer**[2] *v.* See sign for FAVORITE[1]. Related form: **preference** *n.*

**pregnant**[1] *adj.* Same sign used for: **breed, conceive.**

■ [The shape of a pregnant woman's stomach] Bring both *5 hands* from in front of each side of the body, palms facing in, toward each other, entwining the fingers in front of the stomach.

**pregnant**[2] *adj.* See sign for STUCK. This sign is used only when referring to an unwanted pregnancy.

**prejudice** *n.* See sign for AGAINST.

**premeditate** *v.*

■ [**concern**[1] + **plan**] Move both extended index fingers in large alternating circles in front of each side of the forehead. Then move both *open hands* from in front of the left side

of the body, palms facing each other and fingers pointing forward, in a long smooth movement to in front of the right side of the body.

**prepare** *v.* See also sign for PLAN. Same sign used for: **arrange, in order, organize, sequence, sort.**

■ [Putting things in order] Beginning with both *open hands* in front of the left side of the body, palms facing each other and finger pointing forward, move the hands in double downward arcs to in front of the right side of the body.

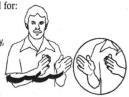

**prepay** *v.*

- **[finish¹ + pay]** Beginning with both *5 hands* in front of each side of the chest, palms facing in and fingers pointing up, flip the hands over with a sudden movement, ending with both palms facing down  and fingers pointing forward. Then, beginning with the extended right index finger touching the palm of the left *open hand* held in front of the body, palm facing up and fingers pointing right, move the right finger forward off the left fingertips while turning the right palm down, ending with the finger pointing forward.

**preschool** *adj., n.*

- **[pre-¹ + school]** Beginning with the left *open hand* in front of the chest, palm facing in and fingers pointing right, and the right *P hand* somewhat closer to the chest, palm facing in, bring the right *P hand* toward the chest. Then clap the palms of both *open hands* together with a double movement in front of the chest.

**present¹** *n.* See signs for BOX, GIFT, ROOM.

**present²** *adv.* See signs for HERE, NOW.

**present³** *v.* See sign for GIVE.

**presentation** *n.* See sign for SPEAK².

**preserve** *v.* See sign for SAVE². Related form: **preservation** *n.*

**preside over** *v. phrase.* See sign for MANAGE.

**president** *n.* Same sign used for:
**horns, superintendent.**

- [The horns of authority, as on a stag] Beginning with the index-finger sides of both *C hands* near each side of the forehead, palms facing forward, move the hands outward to above each shoulder while closing into *S hands*.

**press** *n.* See sign for NEWSPAPER.

## pressure

**pressure** *n.* Same sign used for: **repress, repression, stress, suppress, suppression.**

- [Demonstrates the action of applying pressure] Push the palm of the right *5 hand,* palm facing down, on the index-finger side of the left *S hand,* palm facing in, forcing the left hand downward.

**pretty** *adj.* See also sign for BEAUTIFUL. Same sign used for: **lovely.**

- [The hand encircles the beauty of the face] Beginning with the right *5 hand* in front of the face, palm facing in, move it in a circular movement, closing the fingers to the thumb in front of the chin, forming a *flattened O hand.*

**prevailing** *adj.* See sign for NOW.

**prevent** *v.* Same sign used for: **ban, barrier, block, blockage, hinder, impair, obstruct.**

- [The hands seem to shield the body with a barrier] With the little-finger side of the right *B hand,* palm facing down, against the index-finger side of the left *B hand,* palm facing right, move the hands forward a short distance.

**preview** *v., n.*

- [**see + before²**] Bring the fingers of the right *V hand* from pointing at the eyes, palm facing in, forward a short distance. Then, beginning with the back of the right *open hand,* palm facing in and fingers pointing left, touching the palm of the left *open hand,* palm facing in and fingers pointing right, move the right hand back toward the right shoulder.

**previous¹** *adj.*

- [The hand indicates a time in the past] Tap the fingertips of the right *bent hand* on the right shoulder with a double movement.

**previous²** *adj.* See signs for BEFORE¹, FORMER, PRE-¹.

**price** *n*. See signs for COST[1,2].

**prim** *adj*. See signs for POLITE, SOPHISTICATED.

**prime** *n*.
■ [**my** + **top**] Bring the palm of the right *open hand* against the chest, palm facing in and fingers pointing left. Then bring the palm of the right *open hand* from near the right side of the head downward to touch the fingertips of the left *open hand* held in front of the chest, palm facing right and fingers pointing up.

**principal** *n*.
■ [Initialized sign] Move the right *P hand*, palm facing down, in a small circle above the left *open hand*, palm facing down, ending with the middle finger of the right hand on the back of the left hand.

**principle** *n*. Same sign used for: **policy.**
■ [Initialized sign similar to sign for **law**] Touch the index-finger side of the right *P hand*, palm facing down, first against the fingers and then against the heel of the left *open hand*, palm facing forward and fingers pointing up.

**print** *v*., *n*. See sign for NEWSPAPER.

**prior** *adj*. See signs for BEFORE[1,2].

**priority** *n*. Related form: **prioritize** *v*.
■ [Initialized sign touching each item on a list showing the order of priorities] Touch the middle finger of the right *P hand*, palm facing in, first to the thumb, then the index finger, and then the middle finger of the left *5 hand* held in front of the body, palm facing right and fingers pointing forward.

**prison** *n*. See sign for JAIL.

**private** *adj*. See sign for SECRET. Related form: **privacy** *n*.

**private eye** *n. Informal.* See sign for DETECTIVE.

**privilege** *v.* See signs for PERMIT[1], RIGHT[2].

**prize** *n.* See sign for MEDAL.

**probably** *adv.* See sign for MAYBE. Related forms: **probability** *n.*, **probable** *adj.*

**probation** *n.* See sign for TORTURE.

### problem[1] *n.*

- [The knuckles rub together with friction] Beginning with the knuckles of both *bent V hands* touching in front of the chest, twist the hands in opposite directions with a deliberate movement, rubbing the knuckles against each other.

**problem[2]** *n.* See sign for DIFFICULT.

### procedure *n.* Related form: **procedural** *adj.* Same sign used for: **pace, process, progress, take steps.**

- [Represents the progression of activities in a procedure] Beginning with both *open hands* in front of the body, palms facing in, left fingers pointing right and right fingers pointing left, and the right hand closer to the chest than the left hand, move the right hand over the left hand and then the left hand over the right hand in an alternating movement.

**proceed** *v.* See sign for GO ON.

**process** *n.* See sign for PROCEDURE.

### procession *n.*

- [Represents people marching in a procession] Beginning with both *4 hands* in front of the chest, left hand somewhat forward of the right hand, palms facing forward, and fingers pointing up, move the hands smoothly forward.

**proclaim** *v.* See sign for ANNOUNCE. Related form: **proclamation** *n.*

**procrastinate**[1] *v.* See signs for DEFER[1], POSTPONE.

- [The hand seems to put something off time and time again] Beginning with the fingertips of the right F hand touching the fingertip of the left F hand, palms facing each other, move the right hand forward in a series of small arcs.

**produce**[1] *v.*

- [Initialized sign similar to sign for **make**] Beginning with the little-finger side of the right P hand on the index-finger side of the left P hand, palms facing in, twist the hands so that the fingers point forward, ending with the palms facing in opposite directions.

**produce**[2] *v.* See sign for MAKE.

**profession** *n.* Related form: **professional** *n.*, *adj.*

- [Initialized sign similar to sign for **specialize**] Move the middle finger of the right P hand, palm facing down, from the base of the index finger of the left B hand, palm facing right and fingers pointing forward, to its tip.

**proficient** *adj.* See signs for GOOD AT, SKILL.

**profit** *n.* Same sign used for: **gross.**

- [The hand seems to put a profit into one's pocket] Move the right F hand, palm facing down, downward with a double movement near the right side of the chest.

**program** *n.*

- [Initialized sign] Move the middle finger of the right P hand, palm facing left, from the fingertips to the base of the left open hand, palm facing right and fingers pointing up. Repeat the movement on the back side of the left hand.

# progress

**progress** *n.* See sign for PROCEDURE.

---

**prohibit** *v.* See sign for FORBID.

---

**project** *n.*

- [Abbreviation **p-j** similar to sign for **program**] Move the middle finger of the right *P hand*, palm facing left, from the fingertips to the base of the palm of the left *open hand*, palm facing right and fingers pointing up. Then move the right extended little finger from the fingertips to the base of the back of the left hand.

---

**prolong** *v.* See sign for EXAGGERATE.

---

**prominent** *adj.* See signs for ADVANCED, CHIEF[1].

---

**promise** *n., v.* See also sign for VOW. Same sign used for: **commit.**

- [**true** + a gesture seeming to seal a promise in the hand] Bring the extended right index finger, palm facing left and finger pointing up, from in front of the lips downward, changing into an *open hand* and placing the palm of the right hand on the index-finger side of the left *S hand* held in front of the body, palm facing right.

---

**promiscuous** *adj.*

- [Represents jumping from bed to bed] Move the right *bent V hand* from in front of the right side of the body, palm facing down, in an arc to in front of the body, and then to in front of the left side of the body.

---

**promote**[1] *v.* Related form: **promotion** *n.* Same sign used for: **rank.**

- [**advanced** formed with a repeated movement to indicate levels of promotion] Move both *bent hands*, palms facing each other, from near each side of the head upward in a series of deliberate arcs.

---

**promote**[2] *v.* See sign for ADVANCED. Related form: **promotion** *n.*

**prompt** *adj.* Same sign used for: **punctual.**

- [**fast** + **on** + **time**[2]] Beginning with the thumbs of both *A hands* tucked under the index fingers, palms facing each other in front of the body, flick the thumbs out while twisting the wrists quickly forward. Next bring the palm of the right *open hand* downward across the back of the left *open hand* held in front of the body, both palms facing down. Then tap the index finger of the right *X hand*, palm facing down, with a double movement on the wrist of the left *open hand* held across the body, palm facing down.

**promptly** *adv.* See sign for REGULAR[1].

**prone** *v.* See signs for CATCH[3], TEND.

**pronounce** *v.*

- [Initialized sign similar to sign for **tell**[1]] Move the middle finger of the right *P hand*, palm facing in, upward in front of the lips in an upward double arc in front of the lips.

**proof** *n.* Related form: **prove** *v.* Same sign used for: **evidence.**

- [The hand seems to bring something forward to present to another as proof] Move the fingertips of the right *open hand*, palm facing in, from in front of the mouth downward, ending with the back of the right hand on the palm of the left *open hand*, both palms facing up in front of the chest.

**propaganda** *n.* See sign for ADVERTISE.

**proper** *adj.* See sign for REGULAR[1]. Related form: **properly** *adv.*

**prophecy** *n.* See sign for PREDICT.

**proportion** *n.* See sign for ACCORDING TO.

**proposal**[1] *n.* Related form: **propose** *v.*

- [Initialized sign similar to sign for **suggest**] Beginning with both *P hands* in front of each side of the body, palms facing each other, move the hands upward and forward in simultaneous arcs.

# proposal

**proposal**[2] *n.* See sign for SUGGEST. Related form: **propose** *v.*

**prose** *n.* See sign for STORY.

**prosper** *v.* Related form: **prosperity** *n.*

- [grow + big] Bring the right *flattened O hand*, palm facing in and fingers pointing up, upward through the left *C hand*, palm facing right, while spreading the right fingers into a *curved 5 hand* in front of the chest. Then, beginning with both *modified C hands* together in front of the chest, palms facing each other, bring the hands apart, ending in front of each shoulder.

**prosecute** *v.* See sign for TORTURE. Related form: **prosecution** *n.*

**prosper** *v.* See sign for SUCCESSFUL.

**prostitute** *n.* Same sign used for: **whore.**

- [Similar to sign for **ashamed**] Twist the back of the fingers of the right *bent hand*, palm facing back, forward on the right side of the chin with a double movement, changing into an *open hand* each time.

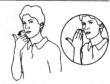

**protect** *v.* See sign for DEFEND.

**protest**[1] *n.* Same sign used for: **complaint, grievance, objection.**

- [Similar to sign for **complain** but formed with a single movement] Strike the fingertips of the right *curved 5 hand* against the center of the chest with a double movement.

**protest**[2] *n., v.* Same sign used for: **rebel, rebellion, strike.**

- [Natural gesture indicating that a person is on strike] Beginning with the right *S hand* in front of the right shoulder, palm facing back, twist the hand sharply forward.

**protest**[3] *v.* See signs for COMPLAIN, PICKET.

**proud** *adj.* Related form: **pride** *n.* Same sign used for: **arrogant.**

- [Feelings of self-worth welling up in the body] Move the thumb of the right *10 hand,* palm facing down, from the center of the lower chest upward with a smooth movement.

**provide** *v.* See signs for GIVE, SUGGEST.

**prune** *v.* Same sign used for: **trim.**

- [The left hand represents a tree and the right hand shows trimming it] With the bent left arm held up in front of the left side of the body, palm facing right, move the fingers of the right *V hand,* palm facing left, up the left arm while closing the fingers together with a repeated movement.

**pry** *v.* See sign for NOSY².

**Psalms** *n.* See sign for POEM.

**pseudo** *adj.* See sign for FAKE².

**psychiatry** *n.*

- [Initialized sign similar to sign for **psychology**] Tap the middle finger of the right *P hand,* palm facing left, in the crook between the thumb and index finger of the left *open hand,* palm facing forward, with a double movement.

**psychology** *n.*

- [Suggests the mind is split open for analysis] Tap the little-finger side of the right *open hand,* palm angled left, in the crook between the thumb and the index finger of the left *open hand,* palm facing forward, with a double movement.

**public** *n.* See signs for HEARING, PEOPLE.

**publication** *v.* See sign for NEWSPAPER.

# publicize

**publicize**[1] *v.* Related form: **publicity** *n.*

- [**newspaper + spread**] Bring the thumb side of the right *G hand*, palm facing down, against the left *open hand*, palm facing up, while pinching the right index finger and thumb together with a double movement. Then, beginning with the fingers of both *flattened O hands* touching in front of the body, palms facing down, move the hands outward to each side while opening into *5 hands* in front of each side of the body.

**publicize**[2] *v.* See sign for ADVERTISE. Related form: **publicity** *n.*

**puddle** *n.* Same sign used for: **pond.**

- [**water** + indicating the size of a puddle] Tap the index-finger side of the right *W hand*, palm facing left, against the chin with a double movement. Then move both *modified C hands*, palms facing each other, downward in front of the chest a short distance.

**pull** *v.* See signs for DRAG, HAUL[1].

**pumice** *n.* Same sign used for: **emery board, nail file.**

- [Represents filing one's nails on pumice] Move the fingertips of the left *curved hand* downward with a repeated movement on the knuckles of the right *curved hand*, both palms facing in.

**pump** *n.*

- [Mime using a water pump] With the right elbow extended, move the right *A hand*, palm facing in, up and down in front of the right side of the body with a double movement.

**pumpkin** *n.* Same sign used for: **melon.**

- [Represents testing a pumpkin's ripeness by thumping it] With a double movement, flick the middle finger of the right *8 hand*, palm facing down, off the back of the left *S hand*, palm facing down, bouncing the right hand up slightly each time.

**punch** *n., v.* Same sign used for: **hit.**

- [Mime giving a punch] Beginning with the right *S hand* in front of the right shoulder, palm facing forward, move the hand upward and forward in a large arc.

**punctual** *adj.* See sign for PROMPT.

**punish** *v.* Same sign used for: **penalize, penalty.**

- [The arm is struck] Strike the extended right index finger, palm facing left, downward across the elbow of the left bent arm.

**puny** *adj.* See sign for TINY¹.

**pupil**¹ *n.* Same sign used for: **student.**

- [**learn + person marker**] Beginning with the fingertips of the right *flattened C hand,* palm facing down, on the upturned palm of the left open hand, bring the right hand up while closing the fingers and thumb into a *flattened O hand* near the forehead. Then move both open hands, palms facing each other, downward along each side of the body.

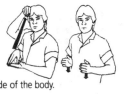

**pupil**² *n.*

- [**eye**¹ + the shape of one's pupil in the eye] Point the extended right index finger to the right eye, palm facing in. Then place the thumb side of the right *F hand,* palm facing left, in front of the right eye.

**puppet** *n.* Same sign used for: **marionette.**

- [Mime the action of moving a puppet's strings] With the bent middle fingers of both *5 hands* pointing down in front of each side of the chest, palms facing down, move the hands up and down with an alternating movement in front of each side of the chest.

# purchase

**purchase** *v.* See sign for BUY.

**pure** *adj.* Related forms: **purification** *n.*, **purify** *v.*

- [Initialized sign similar to sign for **clean**] Move the middle finger of the right *P hand* from the heel to off the fingertips of the up-turned left *open hand*.

**purge** *v.* Same sign used for: **remove**.

- [Similar to sign for **remove** except mime throwing whatever is removed over the shoulder] Bring the fingertips of the right *curved 5 hand*, palm facing down, downward to the palm of the left *open hand* held in front of the body, palm facing up, while closing the right hand into an *A hand* as it  lands on the left palm. Then bring the right hand upward in a large arc while twisting the palm backward and opening the fingers into a *5 hand* as it goes over the right shoulder.

**purple** *n.*, *adj.*

- [Initialized sign] Shake the right *P hand*, palm facing down, back and forth in front of the right side of the body with a double movement.

**purpose** *n.* See sign for MEAN[2].

**purse** *n.* Same sign used for: **luggage, pocketbook, suitcase**.

- [Mime holding a purse] Shake the right *S hand*, palm facing left, up and down near the right side of the waist with the elbow bent.

**pursue** *v.* See sign for CHASE.

**push**[1] *v.*

- [Mime pushing something] Move the palms of both *open hands*, palms facing forward, with a deliberate movement forward in front of the chest.

**push**[2] *v.* See sign for SHOVE.

**pushpin** *n.* See sign for THUMBTACK.

**put** *v.* Same sign used for: **install, mount, place, set.**
■ [The hands seem to take an object and put it in another location]
Beginning with both *flattened O hands* in front of the body,
palms facing down, move the hands upward and forward in a
small arc.

**put aside** *v. phrase.* See sign for ASIDE.

**put away** *v. phrase.* See sign for ASIDE.

**put down**[1] *v. phrase.* Same sign used for:
**document, record.**
■ [The hand seems to put something on a list]
Touch the fingertips of the right *flattened O*
*hand,* palm facing down, to the palm of the
left *open hand,* palm facing up. Then slap
the palm of the right *open hand* against the
left palm.

**put down**[2] *v. phrase.*
■ [Represents putting a stack of money down as a deposit] Move
the right *curved 3 hand,* palm facing forward, from in front of
the chest in an arc over the back of the left *open hand,* palm
facing down and fingers pointing right.

**put off** *v. phrase.* See signs for DEFER[1], POSTPONE.

**put together** *v. phrase.* See sign for ASSEMBLE[1].

**putrid** *adj.* See sign for STINK.

**putty** *n.*
■ [Mime pushing putty into a hole in the wall] With
the thumb of the right *A hand* against the palm
of the left *open hand,* palm facing right and
fingers pointing up, twist the right hand
forward and downward with a double
movement.

# puzzle

## puzzle *n.*

- [Represents fitting the pieces of a puzzle together] Beginning with the extended fingertips of both *H hands* touching in front of the chest, right palm facing forward and left palm facing in, twist the hands in opposite directions to reverse positions with a double movement.

**puzzled** *adj.* Same sign used for: **bewildered, paradox, perplexed.**

- [Indicates a question in the mind] Beginning with the extended right index finger in front of the forehead, palm facing forward and finger angled up, bring the back of the right hand against the forehead while bending the finger into an *X hand*.

---

**qualification** *n.* Related form: **qualify.**

■ [Initialized sign similar to sign for **character**[1]] Move the right *Q hand* in a small circle and then back against the right side of the chest, palm facing down.

---

**quarrel** *v.* See sign for ARGUE.

---

**quarter**[1] *n.*

■ [Initialized sign] Move the right *Q hand*, palm facing down, in a small circle in front of the right side of the body with a double movement.

---

**quarter**[2] *n.* Same sign used for: **twenty-five cents.**

■ [**cent** + **twenty-five**] Beginning with the extended right index finger touching the right side of the forehead, palm facing left and finger pointing up, twist the hand forward while changing into a *5 hand* with a wiggling bent middle finger, palm facing forward.

---

**quarter**[3] *n.* See sign for ONE FOURTH.

---

**quarterly** *adj., adv.* Same sign used for: **every three months.**

■ [**three** + **month** are signed simultaneously] Move the right *3 hand*, palm facing in, with a double movement down the thumb side of the extended left index finger pointing up in front of the chest, palm facing right.

---

# queen

**queen** *n.*

■ [Initialized sign similar to sign for **king**] Move the right *Q hand*, palm facing left, from touching the left side of the chest near the shoulder, downward to touch again near the right side of the waist.

---

**queer**[1] *adj.* See sign for STRANGE.

---

**queer**[2] *n.* See sign for GAY[1].

---

**query** *v.* See also sign for QUESTION.

■ [Form a question mark with each hand] Beginning with both extended index fingers pointing up in front of each side of the chest, palms facing forward, move the right hand down while bending into an *X hand* and then the left hand down while bending into an *X hand,* ending with both *X hands* in front of the chest.

---

**question** *n., v.* See also sign for QUERY.

■ [Draw a question mark in the air] Move the extended right index finger from pointing forward in front of the right shoulder, palm facing down, downward with a curving movement while retracting the index finger and then pointing it straight forward again at the bottom of the curve.

---

**queue** *v.* See sign for LINE UP.

---

**quick** *adj., adv.* See signs for ABRUPT, FAST. Related form: **quickly** *adv.*

---

**quiet** *adj.* Same sign used for: **calm, calm down, passive, silence, silent, still, tranquil.**

■ [Natural gesture requesting others to be quiet] Beginning with both *B hands* crossed in front of the upper chest, palms angled outward in either direction, bring the hands downward and outward, ending with both *B hands* in front of each side of the waist, palms facing down.

---

**quick-witted** *adj.* See sign for SMART.

---

**quiet down** *v. phrase.* See sign for SETTLE.

**quit**[1] *v.*
■ [Formed with the opposite movement as **join**[1] and indicates with-drawing involvement with others] Beginning with the extended fingers of the right *H hand* inside the opening of the left *O hand* held in front of the body, palm facing right, bring the right hand upward, ending in front of the right shoulder, palm facing left and fingers pointing up.

**quit**[2] *v.* See signs for RESIGN, STOP[1].

**quiver** *v.* See sign for SHIVER.

**quiz** *n., v.* See sign for TEST.

**quota** *n.* See sign for RESTRICT.

**quotation**[1] *n.* Related form: **quote** *n., v.* Same sign used for: **theme.**
■ [Natural gesture forming quota-tion marks in the air] Beginning with both *V hands* held near each side of the head, palms angled forward and fingers pointing up, bend the fingers downward with a double movement.

**quotation**[2] *n.* See sign for EXCERPT. Related form: **quote** *n., v.*

**quotes** *pl. n.* See sign for TITLE.

---

**rabbit** *n.* Same sign used for: **hare.**

- [Represents a rabbit's ears] With the *U hands* crossed above the wrists, palms facing in and thumbs extended, bend the fingers of both hands forward and back toward the chest with a double movement.

---

**raccoon** *n.*

- [Indicates the distinctive coloring around the eyes of a raccoon] Beginning with the fingers of both *V hands* pointing toward each other around each eye, palms facing back, bring the hands outward to each side of the head while closing the index and middle fingers of each hand.

---

**race** *v.*

- [The hands move back and forth as if in contention with each other in a race] With an alternating movement, move both *A hands* forward and back past each other quickly, palms facing each other in front of the body.

---

**radar** *n.*

- [Represents the screening action of a radar dish] With the extended left index finger touching the wrist of the right *C hand,* palm facing forward, twist the right wrist to move the hand outward and around.

---

**radiant** *adj.* See sign for BRIGHT.

---

**radio** *n.*

- [Represents radio headphones on the ears] With the fingers of the right *curved 5 hand* near the right ear, twist the hand forward with a double movement.

---

**rage** *n.* See sign for ANGER.

**ragged** *adj.* Same sign used for: **crack, cracked, jagged.**

■ [Shows the shape of a ragged crack] Beginning with the right *B hand* near the right side of the head, palm facing forward and fingers pointing up, move the hand in a large jagged movement down to in front of the right side of the body, ending with the palm facing left and the fingers pointing forward.

**rah** *inject.* See sign for RALLY.

**raid** *v.* See sign for ROB.

**railroad** *n.* See sign for TRAIN.

**rain** *n., v.*

■ [Represents raindrops falling] Bring both *curved 5 hands,* palms facing down, from near each side of the head downward to in front of each shoulder with a double movement.

**rainbow** *n.*

■ [The shape of a rainbow] Beginning with the right *4 hand* in front of the left shoulder, palm facing in and fingers pointing left, bring the hand upward in front of the face, ending in front of the right shoulder, palm facing in and fingers pointing up.

**raise**[1] *v.* Same sign used for: **get up, lift, rise.**

■ [Natural gesture of raising something] Beginning with both *open hands* in front of each side of the body, palms facing up, lift the hands upward to in front of each shoulder.

**raise**[2] *v.* See sign for GROW UP.

**raise**[3] *n.* See sign for INCREASE.

# rake

**rake** *n.* Same sign used for: **hoe, plow, scratch.**

- [Demonstrate the action of raking] Move the fingertips of the right *curved 5 hand,* palm facing down, from the fingers to the heel of the upturned left *open hand* with a double movement.

**rally** *n.* Same sign used for: **hurrah, rah.**

- [Natural gesture used in leading a rally] Beginning with both *S hands* in front of each shoulder, palms facing each other, move the hands energetically forward with a double movement.

**ranch** *n.* See sign for FARM.

**random** *adj.* See signs for CIRCULATE, VARIETY.

**range** *n.* See sign for VARIETY.

**rank** *n.* See sign for PROMOTE.

**rape** *v.* See sign for STUCK.

**rapture** *n.* Same sign used for: **absorb, evaporate, take up, vapor.**

- [Indicates something being absorbed] Beginning with both *5 hands* dangling down in front of each side of the body, palms facing in, bring the hands upward to in front of each shoulder while closing the fingers, forming *flattened O hands.*

**rascal** *n.* See sign for DEVIL.

**rat¹** *n.*

- [Initialized sign similar to sign for **mouse**] Brush the index finger side of the right *R hand,* palm facing left, back and forth across the tip of the nose with a double movement.

**rat²** *v. Slang.* See sign for TATTLE.

**rather** *adv.* See signs for FAVORITE, PREFER¹.

**ratio** *n.* See sign for ACCORDING TO.

**rational** *adj.* See sign for REASON.

**rationale** *n.* See sign for REASON.

**rattle** *v., n.*

- [**hear** + mime shaking a rattle] Point the extended right index finger to the right ear. Then shake the right *modified X hand* with a short repeated movement in front of the right side of the body, palm facing left.

**rave** *v.* Same sign used for: **wild.**

- [Indicates that the head is all mixed up] Move both *5 hands* from in front of each side of the head in large repeated forward circles.

**razor** *n.* See signs for SHAVE¹,².

**reach¹** *v.*

- [Demonstrates reaching for something] Move the right *curved 5 hand,* palm facing down, from in front of the right side of the body forward while changing into an *S hand.*

**reach²** *v.* See sign for ARRIVE.

**react** *v.* See signs for ANSWER, REPORT. Related form: **reaction** *n.*

**reaction** *n.* Related form: **react** *v.*

- [Initialized sign formed similar to the sign for **opposite**] Beginning with the fingertips of both *R hands* touching in front of the chest, palms facing in, bring the hands apart to in front of each side of the chest.

**read** *v.*

- [Represents the movement of the eyes down a page to read it] Move the fingertips of the right *V hand,* palm facing down, from the fingertips to the heel of the left *open hand,* palm facing right.

**ready** *adj.* Related form: **readiness.**

- [Initialized sign] Move both *R hands* from in front of the left side of the body, palms facing each other and fingers pointing forward, in a smooth movement to in front of the right side of the body.

---

**real** *adj.* Same sign used for: **actual, genuine.**

- [Movement emphasizes validity of one's statement] Move the side of the extended right index finger from in front of the mouth, palm facing left and finger pointing up, upward and forward in an arc.

---

**realize** *v.* See sign for REASON. Related form: **realization** *n.*

**really** *adj.* See sign for TRUTH.

**rear**[1] *v.* See sign for GROW UP.

**rear**[2] *n.* See sign for BACK.

**reason** *n.* Related form: **reasonable** *adj.* Same sign used for: **rational, rationale, realization, realize.**

- [Initialized sign similar to sign for **think**[1]] Move the fingertips of the right *R hand,* palm facing in, in a double circular movement in front of the right side of the forehead.

---

**rebuke** *v.* See sign for WARN.

**rebel** *v.* See sign for PROTEST[2]. Related form: **rebellion.**

**recall** *v.* Same sign used for: **recollect, remember, remind.**

- [Represents finding something way back in one's head] Bring the extended right index finger, palm facing in, deliberately against the right side of the forehead.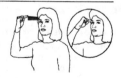

---

**receive** *v.* See sign for GET.

**recently**[1] *adv.* Related form: **recent** *adj.* Same sign used for: **a while ago.**

- [Represents the minute hand on a clock moving a short distance into the past] With the little-finger side of the right *1 hand,* palm facing in and finger pointing up, against the palm of the left *open hand,* palm facing right and fingers pointing up, bend the extended right index finger back toward the chest with a double movement.

---

**recently**[2] *adv.* See sign for JUST.

**reception** *n.* See sign for BANQUET.

**recess** *n.* See sign for REST[1].

**reckless** *adj.* See sign for CARELESS.

**recline** *v.* See sign for LIE[2].

**recognize** *v.* See sign for NOTICE.

**recollect** *v.* See signs for HINDSIGHT, RECALL. Related form: **recollection** *n.*

**recommend** *v.* Related form: **recommendation** *n.*
- [Initialized sign similar to sign for **suggest**] Bring both *R hands* from in front of the chest, palms facing up, forward in an upward arc.

**record**[1] *n.*
- [Initialized sign] With the heel of the right *R hand,* palm facing forward and fingers pointing up, on the index-finger side of the left *4 hand,* palm facing in and fingers pointing right, rock the right hand from side to side with a double movement.

**record**[2] *n., v.* See sign for LIST.

**record**[3] *v.* See sign for PUT DOWN[1].

**recover**[1] *v.*
- [**again + well**[1]] Beginning with the bent right hand beside the left *curved hand,* both palms facing up, bring the right hand up while turning it over, ending with the fingertips of the right hand touching the palm of the left hand. Then, beginning with the fingertips of both *curved 5 hands* touching each shoulder, palms facing in, bring the hands forward with a deliberate movement while closing into *S hands.*

**recover**[2] *v.* See sign for SET UP.

# recruit

**recruit**[1] *v.*

- [Natural gesture for beckoning someone] Beginning with the right *X hand* in front of the right shoulder, palm facing in, swing the hand in front of the chest with a double movement, bending the index finger repeatedly as the hand moves.

**recruit**[2] *v.* See sign for BECKON.

**rectangle** *n.*

- [Draw the shape of a rectangle in the air] Beginning with both extended index fingers side by side in front of the chest, palms angled forward and fingers pointing forward, bring the hands apart to in front of each shoulder, then straight down, and finally back together again in front of the lower chest.

**red** *adj.*

- [Shows the redness of the lips] Bring the extended right index finger, palm facing in, from the lips downward with a short double movement.

**reduce** *v.* See signs for BRIEF, DECREASE[1,2,3], LESS[1]. Related form: **reduction** *n.*

**refer** *v.*

- [Initialized sign] Beginning with the fingers of the right *R hand,* palm facing in, on the back of the left *open hand,* palm facing in, twist the right hand forward, ending with the right palm facing down.

**referee** *n.* Same sign used for: **whistle.**

- [Natural gesture used to whistle between one's teeth] Tap the fingertips of the right *bent V hand,* palm facing in, against the lips with a double movement.

**refill** *n.*, *v.* Same sign used for: **fill up.**

- [Shows the level of something rising to the top] Beginning with the right *open hand* in front of the waist and the left *open hand* in front of the chest, both palms facing down and fingers pointing in opposite directions, move the right hand up against the left palm.

---

**reflect**[1] *v.* Related form: **reflection** *n.*

- [Initialized sign demonstrating something reflecting off another thing] With a bouncing movement, bring the extended fingertips of the right *R hand* against the open left palm and off again.

---

**reflect**[2] *v.* See sign for WONDER.

**refresh** *v.* See sign for COOL.

**refrigerator** *n.*

- [Initialized sign similar to sign for **door**] Beginning with the thumb side of the right *R hand*, palm facing forward and fingers pointing up, against the palm side of the left *open hand*, palm facing right and fingers pointing up, move the right hand to the right in an arc while twisting the palm back in front of the right side of the chest.

---

**refund** *v.*, *n.* Same sign used for: **come back, return.**

- [Shows the direction that something takes in coming back to oneself] Beginning with both extended index fingers pointing up in front of the chest, palms facing in, bring the fingers back to point at each side of the chest, palms facing down.

---

**refuse** *v.* See signs for DECLINE[3], WON'T.

**register**[1] *v.* Related form: **registration** *n.*

- [Initialized sign similar to sign for **sign**[2]] Touch the fingertips of the right *R hand*, palm facing down, first to the heel and then to the fingertips of the palm of the left *open hand*.

---

# register

**register**[2] *v.* See sign for SIGN[2].

**regret** *n.* See sign for SORRY.

**regular**[1] *adj.* Related form: **regularly** *adv.* Same sign used for: **appropriate, appropriately, promptly, proper, properly.**
- [The fingers hit with regularity] With the right index finger extended, brush the little-finger side of the right hand, palm facing in, across the extended left index finger, palm facing in, as the right hand moves toward the chest in a double circular movement.

**regular**[2] *adj.* See sign for CONSISTENT.

**rehabilitation** *n.* Related form: **rehabilitate** *v.*
- [Initialized sign similar to sign for **help**] With the little-finger side of the right *R hand* resting on the open left palm, raise the hands upward in front of the chest.

**rehearse**[1] *v.* Related form: **rehearsal** *n.*
- [Initialized sign similar to sign for **practice**] Rub the heel of the right *R hand,* palm facing forward and fingers pointing up, back and forth on the back of the left *open hand* held in front of the chest, palm facing down and fingers pointing right, with a double movement.

**rehearse**[2] *v.* See sign for PRACTICE.

**reign** *v.* See sign for MANAGE.

**reindeer** *n.* See sign for DEER.

**reinforce** *v.* Same sign used for: **resource.**
- [Initialized sign similar to sign for **help**] With the fingertips of the right *R hand,* palm facing in and fingers pointing up, touching the little-finger side of the left *S hand,* palm facing in, raise both hands upward in front of the chest.

**reiterate** *v.* See sign for AGAIN.

**reject**[1] *v.* Same sign used for: **turn down, veto.**

- [Natural gesture indicating turning down something] Beginning with the right *10 hand* in front of the right shoulder, elbow extended and palm facing down, twist the wrist downward, ending with the thumb pointing down and the palm facing right.

**reject**[2] *v.* See also sign for EXCLUDE.

- [The hand brushes away something that is not desired] Brush the fingertips of the right *open hand*, palm facing in, with a forward movement from the heel to the fingertips of the left *open hand*, palm facing up.

**rejoice** *v.* See sign for CELEBRATE.

**relate** *v.* See sign for COORDINATE.

**relationship** *n.* Related form: **relate** *v.* Same sign used for: **ally, connection, link, tie.**

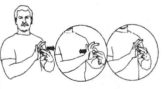

- [Represents a link between two persons or things] With the thumbs and index fingers of both *F hands* intersecting, move the hands forward and back toward the chest with a double movement.

**relative** *n.*

- [Initialized sign similar to sign for **friend**] Beginning with the extended fingers of the right *R hand*, palm facing down, across the extended fingers of the left *R hand*, palm facing up, twist the wrists in opposite directions to reverse positions.

**relax** *v.* See signs for REST[1], SETTLE.

**relief** *n.* Related form: **relieved** *v.*

- [Shows feeling being calmed in the body] With the index-finger sides of both *B hands* against the chest, left hand above the right hand, move the hands downward simultaneously.

# relinquish

**relinquish** *v.* See sign for GIVE UP.

**relocate** *v.* See sign for MOVE.

**rely** *v.* See sign for DEPEND.

**remain** *v.* See signs for CONTINUE[1], STAY.

**remark** *v.* See sign for SAY.

**remarkable** *adj.* See sign for WONDERFUL.

**remarks** *pl. n.* See sign for SAY, STORY.

## remember[1] *v.*
- [Bringing a thought from the mind forward to examine it] Move the thumb of the right *10 hand* from the right side of the forehead, palm facing left, smoothly down to touch the thumb of the left *10 hand* held in front of the body, palm facing down.

**remember**[2] *v.* See sign for RECALL.

## remind[1] *v.*
- [Natural gesture to tap someone to remind them of something] Tap the fingertips of the right *bent hand* with a double movement on the right shoulder, palm facing down.

## remind[2] *v.*
- [Tapping someone as a reminder] Tap the fingertips of the right *bent hand*, palm facing down, with a double movement against the extended left index finger held up in front of the chest.

**remind**[3] See sign for RECALL.

**remodel** *v.* See signs for IMPROVE[2], RENOVATE.

## remorse *n.*
- [**feel + sorry**] Move the bent middle finger of the right *5 hand,* palm facing in, upward on the chest with a repeated movement. Then rub the palm side of the right *10 hand* in a repeated circle on the left side of the chest.

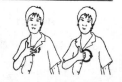

**remote** *adj.* See sign for FAR.

**remote control** *n.*

- [Mime operating a remote control with one's thumb] Bend the extended thumb of the right *10 hand,* palm facing in, up and down with a repeated movement in front of the right shoulder.

**remove**[1] *v.* Related form: **removal** *n.*
Same sign used for: **abolish, abort, abortion.**

- [Demonstrates picking something up and tossing it away to remove it] Bring the fingertips of the right *curved hand* against the palm of the left *open hand* while changing into an *A hand,* palms facing each other. Then move the right hand downward off the left fingertips while opening into a *curved 5 hand* in front of the right side of the body.

**remove**[2] *v.* See signs for ELIMINATE[1], PURGE, TAKE OFF.

**renovate** *v.* Same sign used for: **remodel, restore.**

- [Sign similar to **improve**[2] but made with a repeated movement] Slide the little finger side of the right *open hand,* palm facing in, in a forward circular movement on the back of the left bent arm held in front of the body with a double movement.

**rent** *v., n.*

- [Initialized sign similar to sign for **month**] Move the middle finger side of the right *R hand,* palm facing down and fingers pointing left, downward with a double movement from the tip to the base of the extended left index finger, palm facing right and finger pointing up in front of the chest.

**repair** *v.* See sign for FIX.

**repeat** *v.* See sign for AGAIN.

**repel** *v.* See sign for ELIMINATE[1].

# repent

**repent** *v.* See sign for SORRY.

**replace** *v.* See sign for TRADE.

**reply** *n., v.* See signs for ANSWER, REPORT.

**report** *n., v.* Same sign used for: **react, reaction, reply, respond, response.**
- [Initialized sign similar to sign for **answer**] Beginning with fingers of both *R hands* pointing up, right hand closer to the mouth than the left hand and the palms facing in opposite directions, move the hands forward and downward with a deliberate movement, ending with the palms facing down and fingers pointing forward.

**repossess** *v.* See sign for CAPTURE.

**represent** *v.*
- [Initialized sign similar to sign for **show**[1]] With the fingertips of the right *R hand*, palm facing down, against the left *open hand*, palm facing right and fingers pointing forward, move the hands forward together a short distance.

**repress** *v.* See sign for PRESSURE. Related form: **repression.**

**reprimand** *v.* See sign for SCOLD.

**reptile** *n.* See sign for SNAKE.

**republic** *n.* See sign for REPUBLICAN.

**Republican** *n.* Same sign used for: **republic** *n.*
- [Initialized sign] Shake the right *R hand,* palm facing forward, from side to side in front of the right shoulder with a double movement.

**reputation** *n.*
- [Initialized sign similar to sign for **character**[1]] Beginning with the right *R hand* in front of the chest, palm facing down, twist the wrist to bring the fingertips of the right *R hand* back against the left side of the chest.

**request** *v.* See sign for ASK.

**require** *v.* See sign for DEMAND.

**research** *n., v.*

■ [Initialized sign similar to sign for **investigate**] Move the fingertips of the right *R hand*, palm facing down, across the open left palm from the heel to the fingertips with a double movement.

**reservation** *n.* See sign for APPOINTMENT.

**residue**[1] *n.*

■ [**leave**[2] + **layer**] Beginning with both *5 hands* in front of each side of the body, palms facing each other and fingers pointing down, thrust the fingers downward with a deliberate movement. Then slide the thumb of the right *G hand*, palm facing left, from the heel to off the fingers of the palm of the upturned left *open hand* held in front of the chest.

**residue**[2] *n.* See sign for SEDIMENT.

**resign** *v.* Same sign used for: **back out, draw back, drop out, quit.**

■ [Represents pulling one's legs out of a situation] Beginning with the fingers of the right *bent U hand*, palm facing down, in the opening of the left *O hand*, palm facing right, pull the right fingers out to the right.

**resist** *v.* Same sign used for: **anti-, defensive, immune, uncertain.**

■ [Natural gesture for resisting something] Move the right *S hand*, palm facing down, from in front of the right side of the body outward to the right with a deliberate movement.

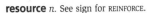

**resource** *n.* See sign for REINFORCE.

**respect** *v., n.* Related form: **respectful** *adj.*

■ [Initialized sign similar to sign for **loyal**] Beginning with the index-finger side of the right *R hand*, palm facing left, near the right side of the forehead, bring the hand downward and forward.

# respiration

**respiration** *n.* See sign for BREATH.

**respond** *v.* See sign for REPORT. Related form: **response** *n.*

**response** *n.* See sign for ANSWER.

**responsibility** *n.* Related form: **responsible** *adj.*

■ [Initialized sign indicating burden on one's shoulders] Tap the fingers of both *R hands,* palms facing in, on the right shoulder with a double movement.

**responsibility** *n.* See sign for BURDEN. Related form: **responsible** *adj.*

**rest**[1] *v., n.* Same sign used for: **recess, relax.**

■ [Shows laying one's hands on one's chest as if in repose] With the arms crossed at the wrists, lay the palm of each *open hand* on the chest near the opposite shoulder.

**rest**[2] See sign for LEAVE[2].

**restaurant** *n.*

■ [Initialized sign similar to sign for **cafeteria**] Touch the fingers of the right *R hand,* palm facing in, first to the right and then to the left side of the chin.

**restless** *adj.*

■ [Represents one's legs turning over restlessly during a sleepless night] With the back of the right *bent V hand* laying across the open left palm, both palms facing up, turn the right hand over and back with a double movement.

**rest of** See sign for AFTER[1].

**restore** *v.* See signs for RENOVATE, SAVE[2].

**restrain** *v.* See sign for CONTROL[1]. Related form: **restraint** *n.*

**restrict** *v.* Same sign used for: **limit, quota.**

- [Shows the level of limit] Beginning with both *bent hands* in front of the chest, right hand above the left hand and both palms facing down, move both hands forward simultaneously.

**rest room**[1] *n.*

- [Abbreviation **r-r**] Tap the right *R hand,* palm facing down and the fingers pointing forward, downward first in front of the right side of body and then again slightly to the right.

**rest room**[2] *n.* See sign for TOILET.

**result** *n.*

- [Initialized sign similar to sign for **end**[1]] Move the fingertips of the right *R hand,* palm facing down, along the length of the index finger of the left *B hand,* palm facing in, and then down off the fingertips.

**résumé** or **resume** *n.*

- [Initialized sign showing the shape of a typed resume] Beginning with the fingertips of both *R hands* touching in front of the chest, palms angled forward, bring the hands apart to in front of each shoulder, then straight down, and finally back together in front of the lower chest.

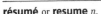

**retail** *v.* See sign for SELL.

**retain** *v.* See sign for SAVE[2].

**retaliate** *v.* See sign for REVENGE.

**retire** *v.*

- [Initialized sign similar to sign for **holiday**] Touch the extended thumbs of both *R hands,* palms facing each other, against each side of the chest.

**retirement** *n.* Similar to sign for RETIRE but made with a double movement.

**retreat** *n.*

■ [Initialized sign similar to sign for **run away**] Beginning with the extended fingers of the right *R hand*, palm facing forward, pointing up between the index finger and middle finger of the left *5 hand*, palm facing down, move the right hand outward to the right.

**retrieve** *v.* See sign for GET.

**retrospect** *n.* See sign for HINDSIGHT.

**return** *v.* See sign for BRING, REFUND.

**reveal** *v.* See signs for ANNOUNCE, TELL[1].

**revenge** *n.* Same sign used for: **avenge, get even, retaliate, vengance.**

■ [Suggests two people striking each other] Beginning with both *modified X hands* in front of the chest, left hand above the right hand and palms facing each other, bring the right hand upward until the knuckles of both the hands touch.

**revenue** *n.* See sign for INCOME[1].

**reverberate** *v.* See sign for BELL. Related form: **reverberation** *n.*

**reverse** *n., adj., v.* Same sign used for: **revert, swap, switch.**

■ [The fingers seem to reverse positions] Beginning with both *V hands* in front of the chest, right palm facing in and fingers pointing left, and left palm facing out and fingers pointing right, twist the hands in opposite directions to turn the palms the opposite way.

**revert** *n.* See sign for REVERSE.

**review** *v.*

■ [Initialized sign] With the little-finger side of the right *R hand*, palm facing left, on the open left palm, twist the right fingers back toward the chest.

**revive** *v.* See sign for INSPIRE.

**revoke** *v.* See sign for TEAR.

**revolve** *v.* See sign for AROUND[1].

**reward** *n.,v.* See sign for GIFT.

**ribbon** *n.* See signs for BOW[2], MEDAL.

**rice** *n.*

- [Initialized sign similar to sign for **soup**] Move the right *R hand* from touching the open left palm held in front of the body, upward to the mouth.

**rich** *adj.* Same sign used for: **wealth.**

- [Represents a pile of money in one's hand] Beginning with the little-finger side of the right *S hand,* palm facing left, in the open left palm held in front of the body, raise the right hand a short distance while opening into a *curved 5 hand,* palm facing down.

**rid** *v.* See sign for ELIMINATE[1].

**ride in a car, truck, etc.**

- [Represents a person sitting in a vehicle] With the fingers of the right *bent U hand,* palm facing down, hooked over the thumb of the left *C hand,* palm facing right, move the hands forward from in front of the body.

**ridiculous** *adj.* See sign for SILLY.

**rifle** *n.*

- [Mime pulling a trigger on a rifle] With the index fingers of both *L hands* pointing forward in front of the body, palms facing in opposite directions and right hand nearer the chest than the left hand, wiggle the thumb of the right hand up and down with a repeated movement.

# right

**right¹** *n., adj., adv.*

- [Initialized sign showing a right direction] Move the right *R hand,* palm facing forward, from in front of the right side of the body to the right a short distance.

**right²** *n.* Same sign used for: **all right, privilege.**

- [Shows the approved path] Slide the little-finger side of the right *open hand,* palm facing left, in an upward arc across the upturned left palm held in front of the body.

**right³** *adj.* Same sign used for: **accurate, correct.**

- With the index fingers of both hands extended forward at right angles, palms angled in and right hand above left, bring the little-finger side of the right hand sharply down across the thumb side of the left hand.

**right turn** *n.*

- [Shows direction of a right turn] Move the right *open hand,* palm facing in and fingers pointing up, to the right by twisting the wrist, ending with the palm facing forward.

**rigid** *adj.* See sign for FREEZE.

**ring¹** *n.*

- [The location of a ring on the ring finger] Move the bent thumb and index finger of the right *5 hand,* palm facing down, back and forth the length of the ring finger of the left *5 hand,* palm facing down, with a repeated movement.

**ring²** *v., n.*

- [Initialized sign similar to sign for **bell**] Quickly tap the index-finger side of the right *R hand,* palm facing forward, against the open left palm with a repeated movement.

**ring**³ *v., n.* See sign for BELL.

**rinse** *n., v.* See sign for DYE.

**riot** *v., n.* See signs for COMPLAIN, MESSY.

**rip** *v.* See sign for TEAR.

**rise** *v., n.* See sign for RAISE.

**risk**¹ *n., v.* Same sign used for: **cutthroat.**
- [Shows the throat being cut] Move the extended right index finger from left to right across the throat, palm facing down and finger pointing left.

**risk**² *n.* See sign for DANGER.

**rival** *n.* See sign for ENEMY.

**river** *n.*
- [**water** + a gesture showing the movement of waves] Tap the index-finger side of the right *W hand,* palm facing left, against the chin with a double movement. Then move both *5 hands,* palms facing down, forward from in front of the chest with an up-and-down wavy movement.

**road** *n.* Same sign used for: **path, route, street, way.**
- [Indicates the shape of a road] Move both *open hands* from in front of each side of the body, palms facing each other, forward with a parallel movement.

**roam** *v.* Same sign used for: **adrift, wander.**
- [Represents the aimless movement of a roaming person] Beginning with the extended right index finger pointing up in front of the right shoulder, palm facing forward, move the hand to in front of the chest and then outward again in a large arc.

**roar** *v., n.* See sign for SCREAM.

# rob

**rob** *v.* Related form: **robbery.** Same sign used for:
**burglary, hold up, raid.**

- [Represents pulling out one's guns for a robbery] Beginning
  with both *H hands* in front of each side of the waist,
  palms facing each other and fingers pointing down,
  twist the wrists upward, bringing the hands up in
  front of each side of the body, palms facing each
  other and fingers pointing forward.

**robe** *n.*

- [Shows location of a robe on one's torso and then
  the way a robe overlaps] Touch the fingers of both
  *bent hands,* palms facing in and fingers pointing
  toward each other, first to the upper chest and
  then near the waist. Then bring both *open
  hands,* palms facing in and fingers pointing
  down, across each other in front of the waist.

**robot** *n.*

- [Mime the traditional arm movements of a
  robot] Beginning with the right *open hand* in
  front of the right side of the body, palm
  facing left and fingers pointing forward,
  and the left *open hand* near the left hip,
  palm facing in and fingers pointing down,
  move the hands up and down with a
  deliberate alternating double movement.

**rock**[1] *n.* Same sign used for: **stone.**

- [Indicates the hardness of a rock] Tap the back of the
  right *S hand,* palm facing up, on the back of the left
  *S hand* held in front of the chest, palm facing down,
  with a repeated movement.

**rock**[2] *v.*

- [Shows movement of a rocking chair] Beginning with the
  thumbs of both *L hands* on each side of the chest, palms
  facing each other and index fingers pointing up, bring the
  hands forward and down to in front of each side of the
  waist, index fingers pointing forward, and then back up
  again with a double movement.

**rock**[3] *n.* See sign for METAL.

### rocket *n.*

■ [Initialized sign showing the movement of a rocket being launched] Beginning with the heel of the right *R hand*, palm facing forward and fingers pointing up, on the back of the left *S hand* held in front of the chest, palm facing down, move the right hand upward in front of the face.

---

### rod *n.* See signs for PIPE², STICK².

### role *n.*

■ [Initialized sign similar to sign for **character**²] Move the fingers of the right *R hand* in a small circle near the open left palm, ending with the right fingertips touching the left palm.

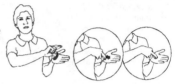

---

### roller skate *n., v.* See sign for SKATE¹.

### romance *n.*

■ [Initialized sign] Bring the extended fingers of the right *R hand,* palm facing back, from touching the shoulder forward in a double arc.

---

### romp *v., n.* See sign for PLAY¹.

### roof *n.*

■ [Initialized sign showing the shape of a roof] Beginning with the fingertips of both *R hands* touching in front of the forehead, palms angled down, bring the hands downward and outward at an angle to about shoulder width.

---

### room *n.* See sign for BOX. Same sign used for:
**package, present.**

■ [Shows the four walls of a room] Beginning with both *open hands* in front of each side of the chest, palms facing each other and fingers pointing forward, move the hands in opposite directions by bending the wrists, ending with the left hand near the chest and the right hand several inches forward of the left hand, both palms facing in.

---

**root** *n.*

■ [Initialized sign representing roots growing beneath the soil] Push the fingers of the right *R hand*, palm facing in, down through the opening of the left *C hand*, palm facing right, while opening the fingers into a *5 hand* as it emerges.

**rope** *n.*

■ [Initialized sign showing the shape of a rope] Beginning with the fingertips of both *R hands* pointing toward each other and touching in front of the chest, bring the hands outward to in front of each shoulder while twisting the wrists as the hands move.

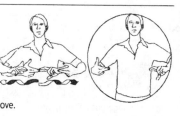

**rose** *n.*

■ [Initialized sign similar to sign for **flower**] Touch the extended fingertips of the right *R hand*, palm facing in, first to the right side of the nose and then to the left side.

**rot** *v.*, *n.* See sign for WEAR OUT. Related form: **rotten** *adj.*

**rotary** *adj.* See sign for AROUND¹.

**rotate** *v.* Related form: **rotation** *n.*

■ [Initialized sign showing the movement of something rotating around something else] Move the extended fingers of the right *R hand*, palm facing in and fingers pointing down, in a circle around the fingertips of the left *R hand*, palm facing in and fingers pointing up.

**rough** *adj.* Same sign used for: **approximate, coarse, draft, estimate.**

■ [Indicates a rough, scratchy surface] Move the fingertips of the right *curved 5 hand*, palm facing down, from the heel to the fingertips of the upturned left *open hand* held in front of the body.

**round**[1] *n.*

- [Initialized sign similar to sign for **circle**[1]] Move the extended fingers of the right *R hand* from pointing down in front of the body in a large flat circle in front of the body.

---

**round**[2] *adj.* See sign for CIRCLE[1].

---

**route** *n.* See sign for ROAD.

---

**routine** *n.* See sign for DAILY.

---

**row**[1] *n.*

- [Represents legs sitting in a row] Beginning with the index–finger sides of both *bent V hands* touching in front of the body, palms facing down, move the hands apart to in front of each side of the body.

---

**row**[2] *n.* See sign for LINE UP.

---

**royalty** *n.* See sign for PENSION.

---

**rub**[1] *v.*

- [Mime rubbing ointment on something] Rub the fingers of the right *open hand,* palm facing down, back and forth across the palm of the left *open hand,* palm facing up, with a double movement.

---

**rub**[2] *v.* See signs for POLISH, WASH.

---

**rubber** *n., adj.*

- [The movement of the jaw when chewing a rubbery substance] Bring the index-finger side of the right *X hand,* palm facing forward, downward on the right cheek with a double movement.

---

**rubber band** *n.*

- [**rubber** + a sign similar to **stretch**[1]] Bring the index-finger side of the right *X hand,* palm facing forward, downward on the right cheek with a double movement. Then, beginning with the knuckles of both *modified X hands* touching in front of the chest, palms facing in, pull the hands apart to in front of each side of the chest with a double movement.

**rude** *adj.* See sign for MEAN[1].

**ruin**[1] *v.* Same sign used for: **spoil**.

- [A ripping movement] Slide the little-finger side of the right *X hand*, palm facing left, across the index–finger side of the left *X hand*, palm facing right.

**ruin**[2] *v.* See sign for DAMAGE.

**rule**[1] *n.*

- [Initialized sign similar to sign for **law**] Touch the fingertips of the right *R hand* first on the fingers and then on the heel of the left *open hand*, palms facing each other.

**rule**[2] *v.* See sign for MANAGE.

**ruler** *n.*

- [The shape of a ruler + **measure**] Beginning with the index fingers and thumbs of both *G hands* touching in front of the chest, palms angled forward, bring the hands apart to in front of each side of the chest. Then tap the thumbs of both *Y hands*, palms together angled forward in front of the chest with a double movement.

**rumor** *n.* See sign for GOSSIP[1].

**run**[1] *v.*

- [Represents one's legs moving when running] With the index finger of the right *L hand*, palm facing left and index finger pointing forward, hooked on the thumb of the left *L hand*, palm facing right and index finger pointing forward, move both hands forward.

**run**[2] *v.* See sign for LEAK[1].

**run³** *v.* Same sign used for: **operate.**

■ [Represents the smooth operation of an assembly line] Brush the palm of the right *open hand* upward with a double movement across the left *open hand,* palms facing each other and fingers pointing forward.

**run⁴** *v.* (of the nose) Same sign used for: **nosebleed.**

■ [Represents fluid dripping from the nose] Beginning with the index finger of the right *4 hand* touching the nose, palm facing in and fingers pointing left, bring the hand straight down with a double movement.

**run⁵** *v.* See signs for EXECUTE, MACHINE.

**run around** *v. phrase.* Same sign used for: **fool around, tour, travel.**

■ [Shows movement in different directions] With the left extended index finger pointing up in front of the body and the right extended index finger pointing down above it, both palms facing in, move both hands in alternate circles in front of the body.

**run away** *v. phrase.* See also sign for ESCAPE. Same sign used for: **get away, split** (*slang*)**.**

■ [Represents one taking off quickly] Move the extended right index finger, palm facing left and finger pointing up, from between the index and middle fingers of the left *5 hand,* palm facing down in front of the chest, forward with a deliberate movement.

**run out of** *v. phrase.* Same sign used for: **all gone, deplete, use up.**

■ [Indicates grabbing everything so that nothing is left] Beginning with the little-finger side of the right *5 hand,* palm facing in, on the heel of the left *open hand,* palm facing up, bring the right hand forward to the left fingertips while changing into an *S hand.*

**run over** *v. phrase.* See sign for OVERFLOW.

**rush** *v., n.* See sign for HURRY.

**sack** *n.* See sign for BAG.

**sacrifice** *n., v.*

■ [Initialized sign similar to sign for **suggest**] Beginning with both *S hands* in front of each side of the body, move the hands quickly upward while opening into *5 hands*, palms facing in.

**sad** *adj.* Same sign used for: **grave**.

■ [The hands seem to pull the face down to a sad expression] Move both *5 hands* from in front of each side of the face, palms facing in and fingers pointing up, downward a short distance.

**safe**[1] *n.*

■ [The shape of a safe + **knob**] Beginning with the index-finger sides of both *open hands* together in front of the body, palms facing down and fingers pointing forward, bring the hands apart and then straight down while turning the palms toward each other. Then turn the right *curved 5 hand*, palm facing forward, in a double movement in front of the right side of the body.

**safe**[2] *adj.* See sign for SAVE[1].

**sail** *n.* See sign for BOAT. Related form: **sailing** *n.*

**sailboat** *n.*

■ [The right hands represents a boat's sail and the left hand represents a boat] Beginning with the little-finger side of the right *B hand*, palm facing in, against the palm side of the left *3 hand*, palm facing right, move both hands forward a short distance.

**salad** *n.*

■ [Mime tossing a salad] Move both *curved hands,* palms facing up and fingers pointing toward each other, from in front of each side of the body toward each other with a double movement.

**salary** *n.* See signs for EARN, INCOME[1].

**sale** *n.* See sign for SELL.

**salt** *n.*

■ [Represents tapping out salt from a shaker on one's food] Alternately tap the fingers of the right *V hand* across the back of the fingers of the left *V hand,* both palms facing down.

**salute** *v., n.*

■ [Natural gesture for saluting] With a deliberate movement, bring the index-finger side of the right *B hand* against the right side of the forehead, palm angled left.

**salvation** *n.* See sign for SAVE[1].

**same**[1] *adj., pron., adv.* See also signs for ALIKE[1,2], LIKE[3].

■ [The fingers come together to show that they are the same] Beginning with both extended index fingers pointing forward in front of each side of the body, palms facing down, bring the hands together, ending with the index fingers together in front of the body.

**same**[2] *adj.* See sign for STANDARD.

**sample** *n.* See sign for SYMBOL.

# sandal

### sandal *n.*

- [Shows a thong coming between the toes] Beginning with the left *5 hand* in front of the body, palm facing down and fingers pointing forward, pull the extended right index finger back from between the index finger and middle finger of the left hand toward the chest with a double movement.

### sandwich *n.*

- [Represents a sandwich being eaten] With the palms of both *open hands* together, right hand above left, bring the fingers back toward the mouth with a short double movement.

### Santa Claus *n.*

- [Hand follows the shape of Santa Claus's beard] Beginning with the index-finger side of the right *curved hand* held on the chin, palm facing down, bring the hand forward and downward in an arc, ending with the little-finger side against the chest, palm facing up.

**sarcastic** *adj.* See sign for IRONY.

**Satan** *n.* See sign for DEVIL.

### satisfy *v.* Related form: **satisfaction** *n.* Same sign used for: **appease, content, contentment.**

- [A settling down of feelings] Beginning with both *B hands* in front of the chest, right hand above the left hand and both palms facing down, bring the index-finger sides of both hands against the chest.

### Saturday *n.*

- [Initialized sign] Move the right *S hand,* palm facing back, in a small circle in front of the right shoulder.

**sauce** *n.*

- [Represents pouring sauce over food] Move the extended thumb of the right *10 hand,* palm angled down, in a circle over the palm of the left *open hand,* palm facing up in front of the body.

**sausage** *n.* Same sign used for: **wiener.**

- [Shows the shape of sausage] Beginning with the index-finger sides of both *C hands* touching in front of the chest, palms facing forward, bring the hands apart while squeezing them open and closed from *C* to *S hands,* ending with *S hands* outside the sides of the body.

**save**[1] *v.* Same sign used for: **free, freedom, liberate, liberty, safe, salvation, secure, security.**

- [Initialized sign representing breaking the chains of captivity] Beginning with both *S hands* crossed at the wrists in front of the chest, palms facing in opposite directions, twist the wrists and move the hands apart, ending with the hands in front of each shoulder, palms facing forward.

**save**[2] *v.* Related form: **savings** *pl. n.* Same sign used for: **preservation, preserve, restore, retain, storage, store, stuff.**

- [The *S hand* holds one's savings behind the bars of a bank cage] Tap the fingers of the right *V hand* with a double movement on the back of the fingers of the left *V hand,* both palms facing in.

**saw** *n.* See sign for WOOD.

**say** *v.* Same sign used for: **comment, remark, remarks, state.**

- [Points to where words are said] Tap the extended right index finger, palm facing in, on the chin with a double movement.

**scalp** *n.* See sign for BALD.

**scant** *adj.* See sign for TINY.

# scared

**scared** *adj.* See signs for AFRAID, FEAR.

**scarf** *n.* Same sign used for: **Mennonite.**

■ [Mime tying a scarf under the chin] Beginning with both *modified X hands* touching each side of the head, palms facing each other, bring the hands downward around the face, ending near each other under the chin.

**scatter** *v.*

■ [Mime scattering something] Beginning with both *S hands* in front of each side of the chest, palms facing forward, move the hands alternately forward while opening into *5 hands.*

**scent** *n., v.* See sign for SMELL[1].

**schedule**[1] *n.* Same sign used for: **chart, graph.**

■ [Shows the rows and columns on a schedule] Beginning with the left *open hand* held in front of the left shoulder, palm facing right and fingers pointing forward, bring the fingers of the right *4 hand,* palm facing left, down the heel of the left hand, and then drag the back of the right fingers across the length of the left palm from the heel to the fingertips.

**schedule**[2] *n.* See signs for PLAN.

**scholarly** *adj.* See also sign for SMART. Same sign used for: **genius.**

■ [Shows the size of a large brain] Touch the thumb of the right *C hand,* palm facing left, against the forehead.

**school** *n.*

■ [A teacher claps for attention] Tap the fingers of right *open hand,* palm facing down, with a double movement on the upturned palm of left *open hand.*

**science** *n.*
- [Represents mixing chemicals in a scientific experiment] Beginning with the right *10 hand* in front of the right shoulder and the left *10 hand* in front of the left side of the chest, both palms facing forward, move the hands in large alternating circles toward each other.

**scissors** *n.* Same sign used for: **clippers, shears.**
- [Mime cutting with scissors] Open and close the index and middle fingers of the right *V hand,* palm facing in and fingers pointing left, with a repeated movement.

**scold** *v.* Same sign used for: **admonish, reprimand.**
- [Natural gesture for scolding someone] Move the extended right index finger from in front of the right shoulder, palm facing left and finger pointing up, forward with a double movement.

**score** *n., v.* See sign for LIST.

**scorn** *n.* See sign for CONTEMPT.

**scramble** *v.* See sign for MIX[1].

**scratch**[1] *v.*
- [Shows the action of scratching] Pull the curved extended right index finger with a short double movement downward on the palm of the left *open hand,* palm facing right and fingers pointing forward.

**scratch**[2] *v.* See sign for RAKE.

**scream** *v., n.* Same sign used for: **cry, roar, shout, yell.**
- [The hand seems to take a loud sound from the mouth and direct it outward] Beginning with the fingers of the right *C hand* close to the mouth, palm facing in, bring the hand forward and upward in an arc.

# screen

**screen** *n.* See sign for NET.

**screw**[1] *v.* Same sign as for SCREWDRIVER but formed with a single movement.

**screw**[2] *n.* See sign for SCREWDRIVER.

**screwdriver** *n.* Same sign used for: **screw.**
- [Shows the action of using a screwdriver] Twist the fingertips of the right *H hand* in the palm of the left *open hand,* palm facing right, with a double forward movement.

**scribble** *v.* See sign for WRITE.

**scroll** *v.* Related form: **scrolling** *n.*
- [Shows how information moves up a screen when scrolling] Beginning with the little finger of the right *4 hand* on the index finger of the left *4 hand,* both palms facing in and fingers pointing in opposite directions in front of the chest, move the hands upward in front of the chest with a double movement.

**sculpt** *v.* See sign for CARVE.

**sculpture** *n.* Related form: **sculpt** *v.*
- [**carve** + showing the shape of a sculpture] Flick the thumb of the right *10 hand* upward with a double movement off the palm of the left *open hand* held in front of the chest. Then, beginning with both *5 hands* in front of each side of the chest, palms facing each other and fingers pointing forward, move the hands downward with a wavy movement, twisting the wrists up and down as the hands move.

**seal**[1] *n.*
- [Shows a clapping movement often made by seals with their flippers] With the backs of both *open hands* together in front of the chest, palms facing in opposite directions and fingers pointing down, bend the fingers with a repeated movement.

**seal**[2] *v.* See also sign for STAMP[2]. Same sign used for: **airtight.**

- [Represents putting a stopper on a jar] Bring the right *curved 5 hand* from in front of the chest, palm facing down, deliberately downward to land on the index-finger side of the left *S hand* held in front of the body, palm facing in.

**seal one's lips**[1] Same sign used for: **keep quiet, keep secret.**

- [Represents sealing one's mouth] Beginning with the index-finger side of the right *C hand* in front of the mouth, palm facing left, close the fingers together to form an *S hand.*

**seal one's lips**[2] See sign for SHUT UP[1].

**search for** *v. phrase.* See sign for LOOK FOR.

**seasoning** *n.*

- [Mime shaking seasoning on food] Shake the right *curved hand,* palm facing forward and fingers pointing left, downward in front of the chest with a double movement.

**seat** *n.* See sign for CHAIR.

**seat belt**[1] *n.*

- [**sit** + a gesture showing pulling a seat belt across oneself and fastening] Place the fingers of the right *H hand,* palm facing down, across the extended fingers of the left *H hand* held in front of the chest, palm facing down and fingers pointing right. Then move the right *H hand* from near the right shoulder downward toward the left *H hand* held in front of the waist until the fingers overlap, both palms facing in.

**seat belt**[2] *n.* See sign for BUCKLE.

**second**[1] *n.*

- [Shows the movement of the second hand on a clock] With the palm side of the right *1 hand* against the left open palm, fingers pointing up, twist the extended right finger forward a very short distance.

# second

**second**[2] *adj., n., adv.* Same sign used for: **two dollars.**

■ [**two** + a twisting movement used to indicate ordinals] Beginning with the right *2 hand* in front of the right shoulder, palm facing forward and fingers pointing up, twist the wrist, ending with the palm facing in.

**second-hand** *adj.* Same sign used for: **used.**

■ [Two fingers turned over, indicating a second use] Beginning with the right *L hand* in front of the right side of the chest, palm facing down and index finger pointing forward, twist the wrist up and down with a double movement.

## second the motion

■ [Two fingers waving for attention during a parliamentary procedure] Beginning with the right *L hand* in front of the right side of the head, palm facing left and index finger pointing up, move the hand deliberately forward while tipping the hand downward, ending with the index finger pointing forward.

**secret** *adj., n.* Same sign used for: **classified, confidential, privacy, private.**

■ [The movement seems to silence the lips to keep a secret] Tap the thumb side of the right *A hand,* palm facing left, against the mouth with a repeated movement.

**secretary** *n.*

■ [The hand seems to take words from the mouth and write them on paper] Bring the right *modified X hand* from near the right side of the chin downward across the palm of the left *open hand* from the heel to off the fingertips.

**section** *n.* See signs for CLASS, PART[1].

**secure** *v.* See sign for SAVE[1]. Related form: **security** *n.*

**security** *n.* See signs for DEFEND, POLICE, SAVE[1].

**sediment** *n.* Same sign used for: **residue.**

■ [**layer** + **leave**²] Slide the thumb of the
right *G hand,* palm facing forward,
from the wrist to off the fingers of
the index-finger side of the left
*B hand* held in front of the chest,
palm facing in and fingers pointing right.

Then, beginning with both *5 hands* in front of each side of the body, palms
facing each other and fingers angled forward, thrust the fingers downward
with a deliberate movement.

**see** *v.* Same sign used for: **sight, visualize.**

■ [The fingers follow the direction of vision from the eyes]
Bring the fingers of the right *V hand* from pointing at the
eyes, palm facing in, forward a short distance.

**seem** *v.* Same sign used for: **apparently, appear, look like.**

■ [Looking in a mirror] Beginning with the right *open
hand* near the right shoulder, palm facing forward and
fingers pointing up, turn the hand so the palm faces
back.

**seethe** *v., n.* See sign for BOILING MAD.

**segment** *n.* See sign for PART¹.

**seize** *v.* See sign for CAPTURE.

**seldom** *adv.*

■ [**once** formed with a rhythmic repeated movement] Bring the
extended right index finger, palm facing in, downward
against the upturned palm of the left *open hand* and
then swing it upward in a slow upward arc with a
double movement.

**select** *v.* Related forms: **selection** *n.*, **selective** *adj.*
Same sign used for: **pick.** See also signs for APPOINT¹,
CHOOSE.

■ [**pick**¹ formed with a repeated movement]
Beginning with the bent thumb and index
finger of the right *5 hand* pointing forward in
front of the right shoulder, palm facing forward,
bring the right hand back toward the right shoulder while
pinching the thumb and index finger together. Repeat with the left hand in front
of the left shoulder.

# self

**self** *n.* See sign for OWN.

**selfish**[1] *adj.*

- Beginning with both *3 hands* in front of each side of the body, palms facing down, bring the hands back toward the body while bending the fingers in toward the palms.

**selfish**[2] *n.* See sign for GREEDY[1].

**sell** *v.* Same sign used for: **distribute, merchandise, peddle, retail, sale.**

- [The hands seem to hold something out for inspection in order to sell it] Beginning with both *flattened O hands* held in front of each side of the chest, palms facing down and fingers pointing down, swing the fingertips forward and back by twisting the wrists upward with a double movement.

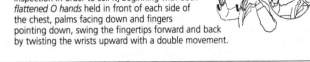

**semester** *n.*

- [Initialized sign] Move the right *S hand* from in front of the right shoulder, palm facing forward, a short distance to the right and then straight down in front of the chest.

**semiannual** *adj.* See sign for BIANNUAL.

**seminary** *n.*

- [Initialized sign similar to sign for **college**] Beginning with the right *S hand,* palm facing down, on the palm of the left *open hand* held in front of the chest, palm facing up, move the right hand upward in an arc.

**senate** *n.* Same sign used for: **staff.**

- [Initialized sign similar to sign for **Congress**] Move the index-finger side of the right *S hand,* palm facing left, from the left side of the chest to the right side of the chest in a small arc.

**send** *v.* See sign for MAIL[1].

**send out** *v. phrase.* See sign for MAIL[1].

**senior** *n., adj.*
- [Shows the top year in school] Place the palm of the right *5 hand,* palm facing down and fingers pointing left, on the thumb of the left *5 hand,* palm facing in and fingers pointing right.

**senior citizen** *n.*
- [Abbreviation **s-c** formed in the same location as the sign for **old**] With the right hand, form an *S* and then a *C* in front of the chin, palm facing left.

**sensation** *n.* See sign for FEEL.

**sense** *v., n.* See signs for FEEL, MIND.

**senseless** *adj.*
- [**think**[1] + **nothing**[3]] Move the extended right index finger from touching the right side of the forehead, palm facing in, forward while opening the fingers into an *open hand* in front of the right shoulder, palm facing up. Then blow across the palm of the right *open hand.*

**sensitive** *adj.*
- [Formed with the finger used for feelings] Beginning with the bent middle finger of the right *5 hand* touching the right side of the chest, flick the wrist forward, ending with the palm facing down.

**sentence** *n.* Same sign used for: **statement.**
- [Represents stretching out words into a sentence] Beginning with the thumbs and index fingers of both *F hands* touching in front of the chest, palms facing each other, pull the hands apart with a wiggly movement, ending in front of each side of the chest.

# separate

**separate** *v.*, *adj.* Related form: **separation** *n.*

- [Things pulled apart] Beginning with the knuckles of both *A hands* touching in front of the chest, palms facing in, bring the hands apart.

**sequel** *n.* See sign for UPDATE.

**sequence** *n.* See signs for PLAN, PREPARE.

**series** *n.* See sign for CLASS.

**serious** *adj.* Same sign used for: **severe.**

- [Drilling a serious point in] With the extended right index finger touching the chin, palm facing left, twist the right hand, ending with the palm facing back.

**serpent** *n.* See sign for SNAKE.

**serve** *v.* Related form: **service** *n.* Same sign used for: **host.**

- [The hands seem to carry something to serve it] Beginning with both *open hands* in front of each side of the body, palms facing up and right hand closer to the body than the left, move the hands forward and back with an alternating movement.

**set**[1] *n.* See sign for SOCIETY. Shared idea of a group of instructions combined to perform certain functions (*as in computer programming*).

**set**[2] *v.* See sign for PUT.

**set off** *v. phrase.* See sign for ZOOM[1].

**settle** or **settle down** *v.* Same sign used for: **calm, calm down, quiet down, relax.**

- [Natural gesture for calming someone down] Beginning with both *5 hands* in front of each side of the chest, palms facing down, move the hands slowly down to in front of each side of the waist.

**set up** *v. phrase*. Same sign used for: **founded, recover**. See also sign for ESTABLISH.

■ [The movement represents setting up something] Beginning with the fingertips of both *curved hands* touching in front of the chest, palms facing down, bend the fingers upward, ending with the fingers angled upward and touching each other.

---

**several** *adj*. See sign for FEW.

---

**severe** *adj*. See sign for SERIOUS.

---

**sew¹** *v*. Related form: **sewing** *n*. Same sign used for: **stitch**.

■ [Mime sewing with a needle] With the thumbs and index fingers of both *F hands* touching in front of the chest, palms facing each other, move the right hand in a double circular movement upward in front of the right shoulder, meeting the fingertip of the left hand each time it passes.

---

**sew²** *v*. Related form: **sewing** *n*. Same sign used for: **sewing machine, stitch**.

■ [Represents the action of a sewing machine needle moving across fabric] Move the bent index finger of the right *X hand*, palm facing down, with a double movement from the base to off the fingertip of the extended left index finger, palm facing down and finger angled to the right.

---

**sew³** *v*. See sign for NEEDLEWORK.

---

**sewing machine** *n*. See sign for SEW².

---

**sex** *n*. Related form: **sexual** *adj*.

■ [Denotes the male and female areas of the head] Touch the index-finger side of the right *X hand*, first to near the right eye and then to the lower chin, palm facing forward.

---

# shake

**shake** *v.*

■*[Mime shaking something] With both *A hands* in front of each side of the body, palms facing down, move the hands from side to side with a repeated movement.

**shake hands** *v. phrase.* See sign for HANDSHAKE.

**sham** *n.* See sign for FAKE².

**shame**¹ *n.* Related form: **shameful** *adj.*

■ [A blush rising in the cheek] Beginning with the backs of the fingers of the right *bent hand* against the right side of the chin, palm facing down, twist the hand upward and forward, ending with the right *bent hand* in front of the right side of the chest, palm facing up.

**shame**² *n.* See sign for ASHAMED. Related form: **shameful** *adj.*

**shampoo** *n., v.* Same sign used for: **wash one's hair.**

■ [Mime shampooing one's hair] Move both *curved 5 hands*, palms facing each other, in and out near each side of the head with a repeated movement.

**shape**¹ *n.* Same sign used for: **form, image.**

■ [The hands outline the image of a shape] Beginning with both *10 hands* in front of each side of the chest, palms facing forward, bring the hands downward with a wavy movement, ending in front of each side of the waist.

**shape**² *n.* See sign for STATUE.

**share** *v.* Same sign used for: **change.**

■ [The hand moves back and forth as if to share a portion of something] Move the little-finger side of the right *open hand*, palm facing in, back and forth with a double movement at the base of the index finger of the left *open hand*, palm facing in.

**sharp** *adj.* Same sign used for: **keen.**

■ [Feeling something sharp] Flick the bent middle finger of the right *5 hand*, palm facing down, forward off the back of the left *open hand* held in front of the body.

**shave**[1] *v.* Same sign used for: **razor.**

■ [Represents holding an electric razor to shave] Move the fingertips of the right *flattened C hand* up and down on the right cheek with a repeated movement.

**shave**[2] *v.* Same sign used for: **razor.**

■ [Represents holding a hand razor to shave] Move the knuckles of the right *Y hand*, palm facing left, downward on the right cheek with a repeated movement.

**she** *pron.* See sign for HE.

**shears** *n.* See sign for SCISSORS.

**shed** *v.* See sign for BLOOD.

**sheep** *n.*

■ [Represents cutting the wool from sheep] Slide the back of the fingers of the right *K hand*, palm facing up, from the wrist up the inside forearm of the left bent arm with a short repeated movement.

**shelf** *n.*

■ [The shape of a shelf] Beginning with the index-finger sides of both *B hands* touching in front of the chest, palms facing down and fingers pointing forward, bring the hands apart to in front of each side of the chest.

**sheriff** *n.* See sign for POLICE.

**shield** *v.* See sign for DEFEND.

**shift** *v.* See sign for CHANGE[1].

**shine** *v.* See sign for LIGHT[2].

# shiny

**shiny** *adj.* Related form: **shine** *n., v.* Same sign used for: **glitter, glossy, glow, sparkle.**

■ [Indicates the glare reflecting off something shiny] Beginning with the bent middle finger of the right *5 hand,* palm facing down, touching the back of the left *open hand,* palm facing down, bring the right hand upward in front of the chest with a wiggly movement.

**ship**[1] *n.* Same sign used for: **cruise.**

■ [The right hand represents a ship moving on waves] With the little-finger side of the right *3 hand,* palm facing left, resting on the palm of the left *open hand,* palm facing up, move both hands forward in a series of small arcs.

**ship**[2] *n.* See sign for BOAT.

**shirk** *v.* See sign for AVOID.

**shirt** *n.*

■ [Indicates the location of a shirt] Pull a small portion of clothing from the upper right chest forward with the fingers of the right *F hand,* palm facing in, with a double movement.

**shiver** *v., n.* See also sign for COLD[2]. Same sign used for: **quiver.**

■ [Represents teeth rattling together when shivering] Beginning with the heels of both *bent V hands* touching in front of the chest, twist the right hand with a double movement.

**shock** *n., v.* Related form: **shocking** *adj.* Same sign used for: **astounded, startled.**

■ [Represents one's eyes bulging open when shocked] Beginning with the index-finger sides of both *S hands* in front of each eye, palms facing each other, open the hands simultaneously into *C hands.*

### shoe *n.*

■ [Represents clicking the heels of shoes together] Tap the index-finger sides of both *S hands* together in front of the chest with a double movement, palms facing down.

---

**shoot**[1] *v.* See signs for MOVIE CAMERA, TAKE PICTURES.

**shoot**[2] *interj.* See sign for ALAS.

### shoot up *v. phrase.* Same sign used for: **become successful, skyrocket, zoom.**

■ [An upward movement] Slide the index-finger side of the right *B hand,* palm angled forward, upward from the heel to off the fingertips of the left *open hand* held in front of the chest, palm facing right and fingers pointing up.

---

### shop[1] *v.* Related form: **shopping** *n.*

■ [The hand takes money and gives it in payment] Beginning with the back of the right *flattened O hand,* palm facing up, across the palm of the left *open hand,* palm facing up, move the right hand forward and slightly upward with a double movement.

---

**shop**[2] *n.* See sign for STORE[1].

### shoplift *v.* See also sign for STEAL. Same sign used for: **burglary, theft.**

■ [The hands spread out to grab things] Beginning with the fingers of both *5 hands* pointing toward each other in front of the body, palms facing down, bring the hands outward and away from each other in arcs, ending with the hands in front of each side of the body. Then close the fingers into *A hands.*

---

### short[1] *adj.* Related form: **shortage** *n.* See also sign for BRIEF. Same sign used for: **soon, temporary.**

■ [The fingers measure off a short distance] Rub the middle-finger side of the right *H hand,* palm angled left, back and forth with a repeated movement on the index-finger side of the left *H hand,* palm angled right.

# short

**short**[2] *adj.* See signs for LITTLE[2], THIN[1].

## shortcut *n.*

■ [**short**[1] + **brief**] Brush the middle-finger side of the right *H hand*, palm angled left, with a sweeping movement across the index-finger side of the left *H hand*, palm angled right. Then, beginning with both *curved 5 hands*
in front of the chest, right hand higher than the left hand and fingers pointing in opposite directions, bring the hand toward each other while squeezing the fingers together, ending with the little-finger side of the right *S hand* on top of the thumb side of the left *S hand*.

## shortly *adv.* See sign for SOON[1].

## shorts *n.*

■ [Shows the length of shorts] Slide the little finger sides of both *bent hands*, palms facing up, with a double movement from in front of each thigh around to each side, ending with the fingertips touching the sides of each thigh.

## shot *n.* Same sign used for: **hypodermic, vaccine.**

■ [Mime pushing the plunger on a hypodermic syringe] With the index finger of the right *L hand* touching the left upper arm, bend the right thumb up and down with a repeated movement.

## should *auxiliary v.* See sign for NEED.

## shoulder *n.*

■ [The location of one's shoulder] Pat the palm of the right *curved hand*, palm facing down, with a single movement on the left shoulder.

## shout *v.* See sign for SCREAM.

## shove *v.* Same sign used for: **push.**

■ [Mime shoving someone or something] Move the right *5 hand*, palm facing forward, from the chest forward with a deliberate movement.

**shovel** *v.* See sign for DIG[1].

**show**[1] *v.* Same sign used for: **demonstrate, example, expose, indicate, indication, portray.**

- [The finger points to something in the hand and moves it to show it to someone else] With the extended right index finger, palm facing in, touching the open left palm, move both hands forward a short distance.

**show**[2] *v.* (*alternate sign, used when something is shown to many people*) Same sign used for: **exhibit.**

- [Represents showing something around to many people] With the extended right index finger, palm facing in, touching the open left palm, move both hands in a flat circle in front of the body.

**show**[3] *n.* See sign for ACT[2], FILM.

**shower** *n., v.*

- [Represents water coming down from a shower head] Beginning with the right *O hand* above the right side of the head, palm facing down, open the fingers into a *5 hand* with a double movement.

**show off** *v. phrase.* See sign for BRAG.

**show up** *v. phrase.* Same sign used for: **appear, come up, incident, materialize, occur, pop up, surface, turn up.**

- [Represents something popping up into sight] Push the extended right index finger, palm angled left, upward between the index finger and middle finger of the left *open hand,* palm facing down.

**shrimp** *n.*

- [Represents a shrimp's tail] Beginning with the extended right index finger pointing left in front of the right side of the chest, palm facing in, bend the finger into an *X hand* with a double movement.

# shrink

**shrink** *v.* See signs for DECREASE[2], DIET.

## shudder *v.*

- [Natural gesture showing a shudder] With both *5 hands* in front of each side of the chest, palms facing forward and fingers pointing up, shake the hands back and forth with a repeated movement.

## shuffle *v.*

- [Mime mixing up a deck of cards] With the little-finger side of the right *C hand* on the index-finger side of the left *C hand* in front of the chest, palms facing in opposite directions, raise the right *C hand* upward a short distance at an angle to the right with a double movement.

## shut out *v. phrase.*

- [Indicates a score of zero] Move the right *O hand*, palm angled forward, from near the right eye forward with a deliberate movement.

## shut up[1] *v. phrase.* Same sign used for: **keep quiet, seal one's lips.**

- [Represents closing one's mouth to shut it up] Beginning with the thumb of the *flattened C hand* touching the chin, palm facing in, close the fingers to the thumb, forming a *flattened O hand*.

## shut up[2] *v. phrase.* (alternate sign) Same sign used for: **didn't say that, didn't mean that.**

- [The finger quiets the mouth] Bring the extended right index finger sharply against the mouth, palm facing left and finger pointing up, while shaking the head negatively.

## shy[1] *adj.*

- [The blush in the cheeks] Beginning with the palm side of the right *A hand* against the lower right cheek, twist the hand forward, ending with the palm facing back.

**shy**² *adj.* See sign for ASHAMED.

**sick** *adj.* Related form: **sickness** *n.* Same sign used for: **ill, illness, malady.**

- [The finger used to indicate feeling touches the forehead to show that a person doesn't feel well] Touch the bent middle finger of the right *5 hand,* palm facing in, to the forehead.

**sick of** *Informal.*

- [**sick** formed with a deliberate twist] With the bent middle finger of the right *5 hand* touching the forehead, twist the hand to the left with a deliberate movement.

**side** *n.*

- [Shows the shape of the side of a wall] Bring the right *open hand,* palm facing left and fingers pointing forward, downward in front of the right side of the body.

**sidestep** *v.*

- [Represents a person's legs moving off to the side] Move the fingers of the right *bent V hand,* palm facing down, from the extended left index finger held in front of the left side of the chest, palm facing right, in a downward arc to the right.

**sidetracked** *adj.* See sign for ASTRAY.

**sight** *n.* See sign for SEE.

**sightseeing** *n.*

- [The fingers represent one's vision as one goes sightseeing] Beginning with the right *V hand* in front of the chest and the left *V hand* in front of the left shoulder, move both hands to the right with a wavy movement, ending with the right *V hand* in front of the right shoulder and the left *V hand* in front of the chest, both palms facing down.

## sign

**sign**[1] *v., n.*

- [Represents one's hands moving when using sign language] Beginning with both extended index fingers pointing up in front of each side of the chest, palms facing forward and the left hand higher than the right hand, move the hands in large alternating circles toward the chest.

**sign**[2] *v.* Same sign used for: **register.**

- [Represents placing one's name on a paper] Place the extended fingers of the right *H hand*, palm facing down, firmly down on the upturned palm of the left *open hand* held in front of the chest.

**sign**[3] *n.* See signs for SQUARE, SYMBOL.

**signature** *n.* Same sign as for SIGN[2] but made with a double movement.

**significant** *adj., n.* See sign for IMPORTANT. Related form: **significance** *n.*

**sign language** *n.*

- [**sign**[1] + **language**] Beginning with both extended index fingers pointing up in front of each side of the chest, palms facing forward and the left hand higher than the right hand, move the hands in large alternating circles toward the chest. Then move both *L hands* from in front of the center of the chest, palms angled down, away from each other to in front of each shoulder with a wavy movement.

**silence** *n.* See sign for QUIET.

**silent** *adj.* Same sign used for: **calm, calm down, mute, quiet, still.**

- [The fingers seem to silence the mouth, and the hands move down as if to show quiet] Beginning with both extended index fingers pointing up in front of the mouth, right hand closer to the face than the left hand and palms facing in opposite directions, bring the hands downward and outward, ending with both *open hands* in front of each side of the chest, palms angled down.

**silky** *adj.* See sign for SMOOTH[2].

**silly** *adj.* Same sign used for: **ridiculous.**

- [Looking past something worthless] Beginning with the right *Y hand* in front of the face, palm facing in, twist the wrist outward with a double movement, brushing the right thumb across the nose with each movement.

**silver** *n., adj.*

- [Initialized sign similar to sign for **gold**] Bring the extended right index finger, palm facing in, from pointing to the right ear downward and forward with a shaking movement while turning the palm forward and changing into an *S hand.*

**similar** *adj.* See signs for ALIKE[1,2].

**simple**[1] *adj.*

- [A simple movement] Beginning with both *F hands* in front of the body, right hand higher than the left hand and palms facing in opposite directions, bring the right hand down, striking the fingertips of the left hand as it passes.

**simple**[2] *adj.* See sign for EASY.

**sin** *n., v.* Same sign used for: **trespass.**

- [The fingers move in opposition to each other as do good and evil] Beginning with both extended index fingers angled upward in front of each side of the chest, palms facing in, move the hands toward each other in double circular movement.

**since**[1] *prep.* Same sign used for: **all along, been, ever since, lately.**

- [Shows passage of time from the past to the present] Move the extended index fingers of both hands from touching the upper right chest, palms facing in, forward in an arc, ending with the index fingers angled forward and the palms angled up.

**since**[2] *conj.* See sign for BECAUSE.

# sing

**sing** *v.* See sign for MUSIC.

**single** *adj.* Same sign used for: **alone.**
- [Shows a person moving around alone] Beginning with the extended right index finger pointing up in front of the right side of chest, palm facing in, move the hand into the middle of the chest and then back to the right again.

**siren** *n.* See sign for AMBULANCE.

**sister** *n.*
- [The female area of the head plus a sign similar to **same** indicating a girl in the same family] Beginning with the thumb of the right *L hand* touching the right side of the chin, palm facing left, move the right hand downward, ending with the little-finger side of the right *L hand* across the thumb side of the left *L hand* held in front of the chest, palms facing right.

**sister-in-law** *n.*
- [A combination similar to the signs for **sister + law**] Beginning with the thumb of the right *L hand* touching the right side of the chin, palm facing left, move the right hand downward, landing on the upturned palm of the left *open hand.* Then move the right *L hand* to touch again near the heel of the left *open hand,* palm facing up and fingers pointing forward.

**sit** *v.*
- [The bent fingers represent one's legs dangling from the edge of a seat] Hook the fingers of the right *curved U hand,* palm facing down, perpendicular to the fingers of the left *U hand* held in front of the chest, palm facing down and fingers pointing right.

**situation** *n.* Same sign used for: **surround.**
- [Initialized sign showing the area around a thing] Move the right *S hand* in a circle around the extended left index finger, palm facing right in front of the chest, by twisting the right wrist.

**six months** *pl. n.* See sign for BIANNUAL.

**size**[1] *n.*

■ [The hands seem to measure out a size] Beginning with the thumbs of both *Y hands* touching in front of the chest, palms facing down, bring the hands apart to in front of each side of the chest.

**size**[2] *n.* See sign for MEASURE.

**skate**[1] *n.. v.* Same sign used for:
**roller skate.**

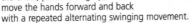

■ [Shows the action of a person roller skating] With both *bent V hands* in front of each side of the chest, palms facing up, move the hands forward and back with a repeated alternating swinging movement.

**skate**[2] *n., v.* Same sign used for:
**ice skate.**

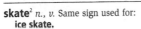

■ [Shows the action of a person who is ice skating] With both *X hands* in front of each side of the chest, palms facing up, move the hands forward and back with a repeated alternating swinging movement.

**skeleton** *n.* Same sign used for: **bone.**

■ [Resembles the skull and crossbones symbol on poisons] With the arms crossed at the wrists, lay the palms of both *V hands* on the chest near the opposite shoulder and bend the fingers up and down with a repeated movement.

**skeptical** *adj.* See also sign for DOUBTFUL.

■ [As if one is blind to what is doubted] Beginning with the right bent V fingers in front of the eyes, palm facing in, constrict the fingers with a short double movement.

# sketch

**sketch**[1] *v., n.* Same sign used for: **draft, drawing, illustration.**

- [The finger moves as if sketching something] Move the right *I hand,* palm facing in, with a repeated movement in front of the left side of the chest while holding the left *open hand* in front of the left shoulder, palm angled right and fingers pointing forward.

**sketch**[2] *n.* See sign for ART.

**sketch**[3] *v.* See sign for DRAW.

**ski** *n., v.* Related form: **skiing** *n.*

- [Represents the movement of skis on snow] Beginning with both *X hands* in front of the chest, palms facing up and right hand closer to the chest than the left hand, move the hands forward.

**skill** *n.* Related form: **skilled** *adj.* Same sign used for: **ability, able, agile, capable, efficient, enable, expert, handy, proficient, talent.**

- [The edge of the hand is honed as are skills] Grasp the little-finger side of the left *open hand* with the curved right fingers. Then pull the right hand forward while closing the fingers into the palm.

**skillful** *adj.* See sign for ADROIT.

**skin** *n.* Same sign used for: **flesh.**

- [The location of skin on one's hand] Pinch and shake the loose skin on the back of the left *open hand,* palm facing down, with the bent thumb and index finger of the right *5 hand.*

**skinny** *adj.* See also sign for THIN[2].

- [Indicates the shape of a skinny person] Move the right *I hand,* palm facing in and finger pointing up, downward in front of the right side of the chest.

**skip**[1] *v.* See also sign for ABSENT. Same sign used for: **lack, miss.**

- [Points out the hiding finger] Beginning with the left *5 hand* held across the chest, middle finger bent downward, move the extended right index finger, palm facing left and finger pointing forward, from right to left in front of the chest, hitting the bent left middle finger as it passes.

**skip**[2] *n., v.*

- [Shows the action of skipping] Touch the middle finger of the right *P hand*, palm facing down, on the palm of the left *open hand*, first near the base and then near the fingertips.

**skip**[3] *v.*

- [The right fingers represent a person's legs skipping on to the next item] Tap the palm side of the right *bent V hand*, palm facing forward, first on the index finger and then the middle finger of the left *5 hand* held in front of the chest, palm facing in.

**skirt** *n.*

- [The location of a skirt] Brush the thumbs of both *5 hands*, palms facing in and fingers pointing down, from the waist downward and outward with a repeated movement.

**sky** *n.*

- [The location of the sky] Bring the right *curved hand* from over the left side of the head, palm facing down, in a large arc to the right, ending above the right shoulder.

**skyrocket** *v.* See sign for SHOOT UP.

**slacks** *pl. n.* See sign for PANTS.

# slaughter

**slaughter** *v.* See sign for KILL.

**slap** *v.*

- [Demonstrates the action of slapping something] Bring the fingers of the right *open hand* from in front of the right side of the chest, palm facing left and fingers pointing forward, with a deliberate movement to in front of the left side of the chest, hitting the extended left index finger held in front of the chest, palm facing forward and finger pointing up, as the right hand moves.

**slavery** *n.* Related form: **slave** *n.*

- [Represents a person's wrists being bound in slavery; formed with a continuing movement] With the wrists of both *S hands* crossed in front of the body, palms facing down, move the arms in a large, flat circle in front of the body with a double movement.

**sled** *n.*

- [Represents the runners on a sled moving across the snow] Beginning with the back of the right *bent V hand,* palm facing up, across the back of the left *open hand,* palm facing down, push the right hand forward.

**sleep** *v., n.* Same sign used for: **doze, slumber.**

- [The hand brings the eyes and face down into a sleeping position] Bring the right *open hand,* palm facing left and fingers point up, in against the right cheek.

**slice** *v., n.*

- [Demonstrates the action of slicing off the end of something] Bring the palm side of the right *open hand,* palm facing left and fingers pointing forward, from in front of the chest straight down near the thumb side of the left *S hand* held in front of the body, palm facing down.

**slide** *v.* See sign for SLIP.

### slides *pl. n.*

■ [Represents a slide moving into position in a projector] Beginning with both *H hands* in front of the chest, palms facing in, left fingers pointing right, and right fingers pointing left, move the right fingers to the left across the back of the left fingers with a double movement.

### slim *adj.* See signs for DIET, THIN².

### slip¹ *v.* Same sign used for: **slide.**

■ [Represents a person's legs slipping] Beginning with the fingertips of the right *V hand* touching the upturned palm of the left *open hand,* push the right fingers forward, ending with the right palm on the left palm.

### slip² *v.* Same sign used for: **put clothes on.**

■ [Represents pulling clothes down over one's body] Move the palm side of the right *C hand* from in front of the right shoulder, palm facing left, downward around the extended left index finger, palm facing right and finger pointing up.

### slipper *n.*

■ [Represents sliding one's foot into a slipper] Slide the right *open hand,* palm facing down, forward across the palm of the left *curved hand,* palm facing up, while closing the left fingers around the right fingers.

### slope *n.* See sign for GRADE.

### sloppy *adj.* See sign for FARM.

### slothful *adj.* See sign for LAZY.

### slow *adj.* Related form: **slowly** *adj.*

■ [Demonstrates a slow movement] Pull the fingertips of the right *5 hand,* palm facing down, from the fingers toward the wrist of the back of the left *open hand,* palm facing down.

# slumber

**slumber** *n.* See sign for SLEEP.

**small**[1] *adj.* See also signs for LITTLE[1,2]. Same sign used for: **mini, pee wee.**

- [Shows a small size] Hold the right *G hand* beside the right side of the face, palm angled forward.

**small**[2] *adj.* (alternate sign) See also signs for LITTLE[1,2], TINY[2]. Same sign used for: **meager, mini.**

- [Shows a small size] Beginning with both *open hands* in front of each side of the chest, palms facing each other and fingers pointing forward, bring the palms close to each other in front of the chest.

**smart** *adj.* See also sign for SCHOLARLY. Same sign used for: **brilliant, clever, intelligence, intelligent, quick-witted.**

- [Indicates brightness coming from the brain] Bring the bent middle finger of the right *5 hand* from touching the forehead, palm facing in, forward with a wavy movement.

**smash** *v.* See sign for MASH.

**smear** *v.*

- [Represents something spreading and smearing] Beginning with the right *A hand* in front of the right side of the chest, palm facing left, and the left *A hand* in front of the left side of the chest, palm facing right, move the right hand to the left in an arc while opening both hands into *5 hands* and rubbing the right hand across the palm of the left.

**smell**[1] *v., n.* Same sign used for: **fragrance, fume, odor, scent.**

- [Represents bringing something in front of the nose to smell it] Brush the fingers of the right *open hand*, palm facing in, upward in front of the nose with a double movement.

**smell**[2] *v.* See sign for SNIFF.

**smile** *v.*, *n.* Same sign used for: **grin**.

- [The shape of the mouth when smiling] Beginning with both *flattened C hands* near each side of the mouth, palms facing each other, pull the fingers back and upward past each cheek in the shape of a smile while pinching the fingers together, forming *flattened O hands* near each side of the head, palms facing down.

**smoke**[1] *v.* Related form: **smoking** *n.*

- [Mime smoking a cigarette] Beginning with the fingers of the right *V hand* touching the right side of the mouth, palm facing in, bring the hand forward with a double movement.

**smoke**[2] *n.*

- [Shows the movement of smoke upward from a fire] Beginning with the right *curved 5 hand* above the left *curved 5 hand*, palms facing each other in front of the chest, move the hands in repeated flat circles in opposite directions.

**smooth**[1] *adj.*

- [Demonstrates a smooth flat surface] Move the fingers of the right *open hand*, palm facing down, from the wrist to the fingertips across the top of the left *open hand* held in front of the body, palm facing down.

**smooth**[2] *adj.* Related form: **smoothly** *adv.* Same sign used for: **fluent, fluently, go smoothly, silky**.

- [The fingertips seem to feel something smooth] Beginning with both *flattened O hands* in front of each side of the chest, palms facing up, slide the thumb of each hand across the fingertips from the little fingers to the index fingers with a smooth movement, ending with *A hands*.

# smother

**smother** *v.*

- [The hand covers the mouth as if to smother a person] Bring the palm side of the right *curved hand* firmly back across the mouth.

**snack** *v., n.*

- [Demonstrates picking up a snack to eat it] Move the fingertips of the right *F hand* from touching the open left palm held in front of the chest, palms facing each other, upward to the mouth with a double movement.

**snake** *n.* Same sign used for: **reptile, serpent.**

- [Represents a snake striking with its fangs] Beginning with the back of the right *bent V hand* in front of the mouth, palm facing forward, move the hand forward in a double spiral movement.

**snap** *n., v., adj.* See sign for ABRUPT.

**sneak** *v.*

- [Represents a person sneaking around] With the right index finger extended, move the right hand, palm facing down and finger pointing forward, in a wavy movement under the left *curved hand,* sliding the left palm up the right forearm as the right hand moves forward.

**sneakers** *pl. n.*

- [**rubber + shoe**] Bring the index-finger side of the right *X hand,* palm facing forward, downward on the right cheek with a double movement. Then tap the index-finger sides of both *S hands* together in front of the chest with a double movement, palms facing down.

**sneeze** *v.*

- [Natural gesture used in trying to stop a sneeze] With the extended right index finger under the nose, palm facing down and finger pointing left, bend the head downward a short distance.

**sniff** *v.* Same sign used for: **smell.**

- [Represents pulling air into the nostrils when sniffing] Bring the back of the *curved 5 hand,* palm facing forward and fingers pointing forward, back against the nose while closing into a *flattened O hand.*

**snob** *n.* Same sign used for: **snub.**

- [Indicates one's nose up in the air] Push the extended right index finger, palm facing left, upward and forward in front of the nose, moving the chin upwards as the finger passes the nose.

**snoop** *v.* See sign for NOSY[2].

**snow** *n.,v.*

- [Represents snow on one's shoulder + the movement of snow falling] Beginning with the fingers of both *5 hands* touching each shoulder, palms facing down, turn the hands forward and bring the hands slowly down to in front of each side of the body while wiggling the fingers as the hands move.

**snub** *v.* See sign for SNOB.

**soak through** *v. phrase.* See sign for PERMEATE.

**soap** *n.*

- [Represents rubbing soap on one's hands] Wipe the fingers of the right *bent hand* on the palm of the left *open hand* from the fingers to the heel with a double movement, bending the right fingers back into the palm each time.

## so-called

**so-called** *adj.* See sign for TITLE.

**so far** *adv.* See sign for SINCE.

**soccer** *n.*
- [Formed similarly to **kick** but with a double movement] Move the right *B* hand upward in front of the body to hit the index-finger side of the right hand against the little-finger side of the left *B* hand with a double movement, both palms angled in.

**socialize** *v.* See sign for ASSOCIATE.

**society** *n.* Related form **social** *n.* Same sign used for: **set** (*computer*), **sorority**.
- [Initialized sign similar to sign for **class**] Beginning with the index finger of both *S* hands touching in front of the chest, palms facing forward, move the hands away from each other and in outward arcs until the little fingers meet again in front of the chest.

**sock** *n.*
- [Suggests needles used for knitting socks] Rub the sides of both extended index fingers back and forth with an alternating movement, palms facing down and fingers pointing forward in front of the body.

**soda pop** *n.* Alternate forms: **soda, pop.** Same sign used for: **soft drink.**
- [Represents recapping a soda pop bottle] Insert the bent middle finger of the right *5 hand,* palm facing down, into the hole formed by the left *O hand,* palm facing right. Then slap the right *open hand,* palm facing down, sharply on the thumb side of the left *O hand.*

**sofa** *n.* See sign for COUCH.

**soft** *adj.* Same sign used for: **gentle, mellow, tender.**
- [The hands seem to feel something soft] Beginning with both *curved 5 hands* in front of each side of the chest, palms facing up, bring the hands down with a double movement while closing the fingers to the thumbs each time.

424

**softball** *n.* See sign for BASEBALL.

**soft drink** *n.* See sign for SODA POP.

**soft-hearted** *adj.* Alternate form: **big-hearted** *adj.*
Same sign used for: **kind, tender.**

- [**soft** formed near the heart] Beginning with the
  right *curved 5 hand* near the left side of the
  chest and the left *curved 5 hand* somewhat
  lower in front of the left side of the body,
  bring the hands downward with a double
  movement while closing the fingers to the thumbs each time.

**soil** *n.* See sign for DIRT.

**soiled** *adj.* See sign for DIRTY.

**solely** *adv.* See sign for ALONE¹.

**solicit** *v.* Same sign used for: **nab.**

- [The fingers seem to nab one who has been
  solicited] Move the fingers of the right *V hand*
  from in front of the right side of the chest in
  an arc forward around to hook on the extended
  left index finger, palm facing forward and finger
  pointing up, pulling the left index finger back
  toward the chest.

**solid** *adj.* See signs for HARD¹, STRONG¹, STURDY¹.

**solidify** *v.* See sign for FREEZE.

**some** *adj.*

- [The hand seems to divide an object] Pull the little-
  finger side of the right *bent hand*, palm facing left,
  across the palm of the left *open hand*, palm facing
  up and fingers pointing forward.

**someone** *pron.* Alternate form: **somebody** *adj.*
Same sign used for: **something.**

- [Indicates one person] With the right extended index finger
  pointing up in front of the right side of the chest, palm
  facing in, move the right hand in a circle with
  a repeated movement.

# something

**something** *n*. See sign for SOMEONE.

**sometimes** *adv*. Same sign used for: **occasional.**
- [Similar to sign for **once** except repeated to indicate reoccurrence] Bring the extended right index finger, palm facing in, downward against the upturned palm of the left *open hand* and up again in a rhythmic repeated circular movement.

**son** *n*.
- [A shortened form of the combination of the signs for **boy** and **baby**] Beginning with the fingertips of the right *B hand* against the forehead, palm facing left, bring the right hand downward, ending with the bent right arm cradled in the bent left arm held across the body, both palms facing up.

**song** *n*. See sign for MUSIC.

**son-in-law** *n*.
- [A combination similiar to the signs for **son + law**] Beginning with the fingertips of the right *open hand* against the forehead, palm facing left, bring the right hand downward, ending with the bent right arm cradled in the bent left arm held across the body, both palms facing up. Then move the right *L hand* from touching first on the palm of the upturned left *open hand* to touching on the left wrist.

**soon**[1] *adv*. Same sign used for: **near future, in the; shortly.**
- [The movement is close, indicating immediacy] Touch the fingertips of the right *F hand*, palm facing in, to the middle of the chin.

**soon**[2] *adv*. See sign for SHORT[1].

**sophisticated** *adj*. Same sign used for: **prim.**
- With the thumb, index finger, and little finger of the right hand extended, push the right index finger upward and forward under the chin, palm facing left.

**sordid** *adj*. See sign for AWFUL.

**sore** *adj.* See sign for HURT[2].

**sorority** *n.* See sign for SOCIETY.

**sorry** *adj.* Related form: **sorrow** *n.* Same sign used for: **apologize, apology, penitence, penitent, regret, repent.**
- [Indicates rubbing the chest in sorrow] Rub the palm side of the right *A hand* in a large circle on the chest with a repeated movement.

**sort**[1] *n.* See sign for KIND[2].

**sort**[2] *v.* See signs for FILE[1], PLAN, PREPARE.

**sort of** See sign for FAIR[2].

**soul** *n.* See sign for SPIRIT.

**so-so** *adj.* See sign for FAIR[2].

**sound**[1] *n.*
- [Initialized sign formed near the ear] Move the right *S hand,* palm facing forward, from near the right ear outward to the right.

**sound**[2] *n.* See signs for HEAR, NOISE.

**soup** *n.*
- [Mime eating soup with a spoon] With the thumb extended, move the fingers of the right *U hand* from touching the palm of the left *open hand* upward to the mouth, both palms facing up.

**sour** *adj.* Same sign used for: **bitter.**
- [Points to puckered lips from eating something sour] With the tip of the extended right index finger on the chin near the mouth, palm facing left, twist the hand, ending with the palm facing back.

**source** *n.* See sign for START[1].

**south** *n.*, *adj.*, *adv.*
- [Initialized sign indicating a southern direction on a map] Move the right *S hand*, palm facing in, downward in front of the right side of the chest.

**sow** *v.* See sign for PLANT[2].

**space** *n.* See sign for AREA[1].

**spacecraft** *n.* See sign for SPACESHIP.

**spaceship** *n.* Same sign used for: **spacecraft.**
- [The hand shape represents a spaceship moving through space] Move the right curved *3 hand*, palm facing in and fingers pointing left, from in front of the head to the right.

**spade** *n.*, *v.* See sign for SPATULA.

**spaghetti** *n.*
- [The shape of spaghetti] Beginning with both extended little fingers touching in front of the chest, palms facing in, bring the hands apart in small arcs, ending in front of each shoulder.

**spank** *v.* Related form: **spanking** *n.* Same sign used for: **whack, whip, whipping.**
- [Demonstrates the action of spanking] Bring the palm of the right *open hand* downward from in front of the right side of the chest to strike against the palm of the left *open hand*, palm facing up, with a repeated movement.

**spark** *n.*
- [Shows the flash of a spark] Beginning with the right *modified X hand* touching the extended left index finger in front of the chest, both palms facing forward, flick the right index finger upward with a double movement.

**sparkle** *v.* See sign for SHINY.

**spatula** *n.* Same sign used for: **dig, spade.**

- [Shows action of turning food over with a spatula] Push the fingertips of the right *open hand,* palm facing up and fingers pointing forward, with a short movement forward on the fingers of the left *open hand* held in front of the chest, palm facing up. Then flip the right hand over in an arc, ending with the palm facing down.

**speak**[1] *v.* Same sign used for: **talk.**

- [Represents words coming from the mouth] Beginning with the index-finger side of the right *4 hand* touching the chin, palm facing left, move the hand forward with a repeated movement.

**speak**[2] *v.* Same sign used for: **address, lecture, presentation, speech.**

- [Waving the hand when making a point] Beginning with the right *open hand* near the right side of the head, palm facing left and fingers pointing up, twist the wrist to move the fingers forward and back with a short repeated movement.

**special** *adj.* Same sign used for: **especially, unique.**

- [Demonstrates pulling one thing out that is special] Grasp the left extended index finger, palm facing in and finger pointing up, with the fingers of the right *G hand* and pull upward in front of the chest.

**specialize** *v.* Related form: **specialty** *n.* Same sign used for: **field, major, straight.**

- [Suggests going in a specific direction] Slide the little-finger side of the right *B hand,* palm facing left and fingers pointing forward, along the index-finger side of the left *B hand* held in front of the chest, palm facing right and fingers pointing forward.

**specific** *adj.* See sign for POINT[2].

## speculate

**speculate** *v.* See sign for LET'S SEE. Related form: **speculation** *n.*

**speech**[1] *n.*
- [Shows the movement of the lips when speaking] Move the bent fingers of the right *V hand,* palm facing in, in a small repeated circle in front of the mouth.

**speech**[2] *n.* See sign for SPEAK[2].

**speed** *n., v.*
- Beginning with both extended index fingers pointing forward in front of each side of the chest, palms facing in opposite directions and right hand forward of the left hand, bend the fingers with a double movement.

**spend**[1] *v.*
- [Represents money slipping through one's hands] Beginning with both *curved hands* in front of each side of the chest, right hand nearer the chest than the left hand and both palms facing up, move the hands forward while moving the thumbs across the fingers, ending with *10 hands.*

**spend**[2] *v.*
- [Flicking away minutes] Beginning with the index fingers and thumbs of both hands pinched together, palms facing up in front of the body, move the hands upward while flicking the index fingers forward.

**spider** *n.*
- [Represents a spider's legs] With the wrists of both *curved 4 hands* crossed in front of the body, palms facing down and right wrist over the left wrist, wiggle the fingers with a repeated movement.

**spill** *v.*

■ [Represents something spreading out when it is spilled] Beginning with both *flattened O hands* touching in front of the body, palms facing down and fingers pointing down, move the hands forward and apart while opening the fingers into *5 hands,* palms facing down.

**spiral** *n., adj.*

■ [The shape of a spiral] With the extended right index finger pointing down in front of the head, and the extended left index finger pointing up in front of the chest, both palms facing in and fingers pointing toward each other, move the hands in repeated circular movements as the hands pull away from each other.

**splrlt** *n.* Related form: **spiritual** *adj.* Same sign used for: **ghost, soul.**

■ [Showing a filmy substance] Beginning with the bent index finger and thumb of the right *5 hand* pointing down above the bent index finger and thumb of the left *5 hand,* palms facing each other, close the index fingers and thumbs of both hands together, touching each other. Then pull the hands apart, moving the right hand upward in front of the chest.

**spit** *v., n.*

■ [Indicates the movement of spitting] Beginning with the thumb holding down the bent index finger of the right hand in front of the mouth, palm facing forward, move the hand forward while flicking the index finger forward.

**splash** *v.* Same sign used for: **splatter.**

■ [Represents the movement of a liquid splashing] Beginning with both *S hands* near each other in front of the chest, palms facing forward, move the hands upward and apart while opening quickly into *5 hands,* ending in front of each shoulder, palms facing forward and fingers pointing up.

**splat** *v.* See sign for PLOP.

# splatter

**splatter** *n.* See sign for SPLASH.

**split**[1] *n., v.* See signs for CRACK[1], DIVIDE.

**split**[2] *Slang.* See sign for RUN AWAY.

**split up** *v. phrase.* See sign for DIVIDE.

**spoil** *v.* See signs for PET[1], RUIN[1].

**sponsor** *v.* See sign for SUPPORT.

**spooky** *adj.* See sign for MONSTER.

**spoon** *n.*

- [The fingers represent a spoon scooping up food] Wipe the backs of the fingers of the right *U hand*, palm facing up and thumb extended, across the upturned palm of the left *open hand* from the fingers to the heel with a double movement.

**spot**[1] *v.*

- [Indicates a person's eyes directed at whatever is spotted] Beginning with the right *S hand* near the right cheek, palm facing forward, move the hand forward while flicking the thumb and index finger open to form a *G hand*.

**spot**[2] *n.* Same sign used for: **stain.**

- [Shape and location of a spot] Touch the thumb side of the right *F hand* to the left side of the chest, palm facing left.

**sprain** *v., n.*

- [Shows a twist causing a sprain] Beginning with both *bent V hands* in front of the chest, right palm facing out and left palm facing in, twist the hands in opposite directions, reversing the direction of the palms.

**spray** *v.*

■ [Mime pushing down on an aerosol can] Beginning with the extended right index finger pointing up in front of the right shoulder, palm facing forward, bend the finger down to form an *X hand* with a double movement while moving the hand from side to side.

**spread** *v.* Same sign used for: **disseminate, distribute, outbreak.**

■ [Demonstrates something spreading outward] Beginning with the fingertips of both *flattened O hands* touching in front of the chest, palms facing down, move the hands forward and away from each other while opening into *5 hands* in front of each side of the body, palms facing down.

**spring** *n.*

■ [Similar to sign for **grow** except with a double movement] Beginning with the right *flattened O hand,* palm facing up, being held by the left *C hand,* palm facing in, move the right hand upward with a double movement, opening into a *5 hand* each time.

**sprinkle** *v.*

■ [Mime sprinkling something] Move the right *curved hand* forward in front of the chest while wiggling the fingers with a repeated movement.

**sprout** *v.* See sign for GROW.

**spy** *n., v.*

■ [Represents eyes peeking around a corner to spy] Bring the right *V hand,* palm facing down, from behind the bent left arm held up in front of the left shoulder, in an arc forward and to the left around the left arm.

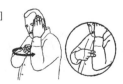

**squabble** *v.* See sign for ARGUE.

# squander

**squander** *v.*

- [Represents throwing money away] Beginning with both *A hands* near each side of the body, palms facing in, thrust the hands upward with a double movement while changing into *5 hands* in front each shoulder, palms facing in.

**square** *n., adj.* Same sign used for: **sign.**

- [Draw a square in the air] Beginning with both extended index fingers touching in front of the upper chest, palms angled forward and fingers pointing upward, bring the hands straight out to in front of each shoulder then straight down, and finally back together in front of the waist.

**squeal** *v. Slang.* See sign for TATTLE.

**squeeze¹** *v.*

- [Mime squeezing a tube with both hands] Beginning with the little-finger side of the right *C hand,* palm facing left, above the index-finger side of the left *C hand,* palm facing right, twist the hands in opposite directions while closing into *S hands.* Repeat if desired.

**squeeze²** *n.* See sign for BRIEF.

**squirrel** *n.*

- [Represents the gnawing action of a squirrel's teeth] With the heels of both hands together in front of the chest, palms facing each other, tap the fingertips of both *bent V hands* together with a double movement.

**stab** *v.*

- [Mime stabbing something with a knife] Bring the right *S hand* in a large arc from in front of the right shoulder forward to hit against the open left palm held in front of the chest, with a deliberate movement.

**stack** *n., v.* Same sign used for: **pile.**

■ [Shows a pile of things stacked on top of other things] With an alternating movement, bring each *open hand* upward over the other hand in a small arc as the hands rise in front of the chest, both palms facing down and fingers angled in opposite directions.

**staff** *n.* See sign for SENATE.

**stage** *n.*

■ [Initialized sign representing the stage floor] Move the right *S hand*, palm facing forward, across the back of the left *open hand*, palm facing down, from the wrist to off the fingers.

**stain**[1] *n., v.*

■ [**eat** + a gesture indicating food spilling on one's clothes + **spot**[2]] Bring the fingertips of the right *flattened O hand*, palm facing in, back to the mouth with a double movement. Next move the palm side of the right *5 hand* against the chest with a sudden movement. Then place the index-finger side of the right *F hand*, palm facing left, against the chest.

**stain**[2] *n.* See sign for SPOT[2].

**staircase** *n.* See sign for STAIRS.

**stairs** *n.* Same signs used for: **staircase, stairway.**

■ [Demonstrates the action of walking up stairs] Move the fingertips of the right *bent V hand*, palm facing forward, in an alternating crawling movement up the extended left index finger, palm facing forward.

**stairway** *n.* See sign for STAIRS.

**stall** *v.* See sign for HOLD[2].

# stamp

**stamp**[1] *n., v.* Same sign used for: **postage, postage stamp.**

- [The fingers seem to lick a stamp and place it on an envelope] Move the fingers of the right *H hand* from the mouth, palm facing in, down to land on the fingers of the left *open hand,* palm facing up, in front of the body.

**stamp**[2] *n., v.* See also sign for SEAL[2]. Same sign used for: **brand, guarantee.**

- [Mime stamping something with a rubber stamp] Move the right *S hand,* palm facing left, from in front of the chest downward, ending with the little-finger side of the right *S hand* on the upturned palm of the left *open hand.*

**stand** *v.*

- [The fingers represent erect legs] Place the fingertips of the right *V hand,* palm facing in and fingers pointing down, on the up-turned palm of the left *open hand* held in front of the body.

**standard** *n., adj.* Related form: **standardized** *adj.* Same sign used for: **common, same.**

- [**same**[1] formed with a large circular movement to indicate everything is the same] Beginning with both *Y hands* in front of the body, palms facing down, move the hands in a large flat circle.

**stand for** *v. phrase.* See sign for MEAN[2].

**staple** *v.* Same sign as for STAPLER but formed with a single movement.

**stapler** *n.*

- [Mime pushing down on a stapler] Press the heel of the right *curved 5 hand,* palm facing down, on the heel of the left *open hand,* palm facing up, with a double movement.

**star** *n.*

■ [Striking flints to create sparks that look like stars] Brush the sides of both extended index fingers against each other, palms facing forward, with an alternating movement as the hands move upward in front of the face.

**stare** *v.*

■ [Directional sign indicating that all eyes turn to look at you] Beginning with both *4 hands* in front of each side of the chest, palms facing down and fingers pointing forward, twist the wrists toward each other to point the fingers back toward the face.

**start**[1] *n.* Same sign used for: **beginning, origin, origination, source.**

■ [Represents turning a key to start ignition] Beginning with the extended right index finger, palm facing in, inserted between the index and middle fingers of the left *open hand,* palm facing right and fingers pointing forward, twist the right hand back, ending with the palm angled forward.

**start**[2] *v.*

■ [Mime turning a key to start an ignition] Beginning with the right *A hand* in front of the right side of the body, palm facing forward, twist the wrist to turn the palm to the left.

**starter** *n.* Same sign as for **start**[2] but formed with a double movement. Same sign used for: **ignition.**

**startle** *v.* See signs for FLABBERGAST, SURPRISE.

**startled** *adj.* See sign for SHOCK.

**starved** *adj.* See sign for HUNGRY.

**state**[1] *n.*

■ [Initialized sign similar to sign for **law**] Move the index-finger side of the right *S hand*, palm facing forward, down from the fingers to the heel of the left *open hand*, palm facing right and fingers pointing up, in front of the chest.

# state

**state**[2] *v.* See sign for SAY.

**statement** *n.* See sign for SENTENCE.

**statistics** *n.*
- [Initialized sign similar to sign for **mathematics**] Beginning with both *S hands* in front of each side of the chest, palms facing in, move the hands past each other with a double movement while rubbing the little-finger side of the right hand over the index-finger side of the left hand.

**statue** *n.* Same sign used for: **shape.**
- [The shape of a statue] Beginning with both *S hands* near each other in front of the face, palms facing forward, bring the hands downward and apart in a wavy movement.

**stay** *v.* Same sign used for: **remain.**
- [Continuity of movement] With the thumb of the right *10 hand* on the thumb-nail of the left *10 hand*, both palms facing down in front of the chest, move the hands forward and down a short distance.

**stay away** *v. phrase.*
- [Movement directs someone to another place] Beginning with the thumb of the right *Y hand* touching the thumb of the left *Y hand* in front of the chest, both palms angled down, move the right hand forward and to the right in a small arc.

**steadfast** *adj.* See sign for CONSTANT[3].

**steady**[1] *Informal., n., adj.* Same sign used for: **companion, go steady.**
- [**with** signed with a repeated movement] Beginning with the palm sides of both *A hands* together in front of the chest, move the hands forward with a repeated movement.

**steady**[2] *adj.* See signs for CONSTANT[2,3].

**steal** *v.* See sign for SHOPLIFT. Same sign used for: **burglary, pillage, theft.**

- [The fingers seem to snatch something] Beginning with the index-finger side of the right *V hand,* palm facing down, on the elbow of the bent left arm, held at an upward angle across the chest, pull the right hand upward toward the left wrist while bending the fingers in tightly.

**steel**[1] *n.*

- [As if sharpening a sharp edge on steel] Move the little-finger side of the right *S hand,* palm facing in, forward from the base to the tip of the extended left index finger, palm facing in and finger pointing right, with a double movement.

**steel**[2] *n.* See sign for METAL.

**steer** *v.* See sign for LEAD.

**stem** *n.*

- [The shape of a long stem] Beginning with the thumb and index finger of the right *G hand,* palm facing left, holding the base of the extended left index finger, palm facing right and finger pointing up, pull the right hand upward along the length of the index finger and off its tip a short distance, while pinching the thumb and index finger together.

**step** *n., v.* Same sign used for: **pace.**

- [Demonstrates the action of stepping forward] Beginning with both *open hands* in front of the body, palms facing down and fingers pointing forward, move the right hand upward and forward in an arc.

**stepbrother** *n.*

- [second-hand + brother] Beginning with the right *L hand* in front of the right side of the chest, palm facing down, twist the wrist forward with a deliberate movement. Then bring the right *L hand,* palm facing left, from the forehead down while closing the thumb to the hand, ending with the index fingers of both *1 hands* together in front of the chest.

# stepdaughter

### stepdaughter *n.*

■ **[second-hand + daughter]** Beginning with the right *L* hand in front of the right side of the chest, palm facing down, twist the wrist forward with a deliberate movement. Then bring the right *B* hand, palm facing left, from the chin downward while opening into an *open hand,* ending with the bent right arm cradled on the bent left arm held across the body, both palms facing up.

### stepfather *n.*

■ **[second-hand + father]** Beginning with the right *L* hand in front of the right side of the chest, palm facing down, twist the wrist forward with a deliberate movement. Then, tap the thumb of the right *5* hand against the forehead, palm facing left and fingers pointing up.

### stepmother *n.*

■ **[second-hand + mother]** Beginning with the right *L* hand in front of the right side of the chest, palm facing down, twist the wrist forward with a deliberate movement. Then, tap the thumb of the right *5* hand against the chin, palm facing left and fingers pointing up.

### stepsister *n.*

■ **[second-hand + sister]** Beginning with the right *L* hand in front of the right side of the chest, palm facing down, twist the wrist forward with a deliberate movement. Then bring the thumb of the right *L* hand, palm facing left, from the chin smoothly down while closing the thumb to the hand, ending with the index fingers of both *1* hands together in front of the chest.

### stepson *n.*

■ **[second-hand + son]** Beginning with the right *L* hand in front of the right side of the chest, palm facing down, twist the wrist forward with a deliberate movement. Then bring the fingers of the right *B* hand from touching the right side of the forehead downward while opening into an *open hand,* ending with the bent right arm cradled on the bent left arm held across the body, both palms facing up.

**sterilization** *n.* Related form: **sterilize** *v.*
Same sign used for: **tubal ligation, vasectomy.**

- [Mime tying to represent tying one's tubes for sterilization] Beginning with both *modified X hands* touching in front of the waist, right palms facing down and left palm facing in, twist the wrists in opposite directions and pull the hands deliberately apart to each side of the waist.

**stern** *adj.* See sign for STRICT.

**stick**[1] *v.* Same sign used for: **adhere, adhesive, expose, fasten.**

- [Demonstrates something sticky causing the finger and thumb to stick together] With the thumb of the right *5 hand,* palm facing down, touching the palm of the left *open hand,* palm facing up, close the right middle finger down to the thumb.

**stick**[2] *n.* Same sign used for: **pipe, pole, rod.**

- [Shape of a stick] Beginning with the thumb sides of both *F hands* touching in front of the chest, palms facing forward, move the hands apart.

**sticky** *adj.* Same sign as for STICK[1] but formed with a double movement.

**still**[1] *adv.* See also sign for YET.

- [Formed with a continuing movement to show passage of time] Move the right *Y hand,* palm facing down, from in front of the right side of the body forward and upward in an arc.

**still**[2] *adj.* See signs for QUIET, SILENT.

**sting** *v., n.*

- [Represents the stinger of an insect penetrating to wound] Beginning with the right *X hand* held in front of the right side of the chest, palm facing left, bring the bent index finger down deliberately against the back of the left *S hand,* palm facing down, and then back upward quickly.

# stingy

**stingy**[1] *adj.* Same sign used for: **thrifty.**

- [Represents scraping] Beginning with the fingertips of the right *curved 5 hand* on the fingers of the left *open hand,* palm facing up, bring the right hand back toward the left heel with a double movement while closing into an *A hand* each time.

**stingy**[2] *adj.* (alternate sign) Same sign used for: **greedy, miser, thrifty, tightwad** (*informal*).

- [Clutching a prized item] Beginning with the fingers of the right *curved 5 hand* in front of the chin, palm facing in, bring the hand downward while closing into an *S hand.*

**stink** *v., n.* Related form: **stinky** *adj.* Same sign used for: **phew, putrid.**

- [Natural gesture for holding the nose when something smells bad] Bring the thumb and index finger of the right *G hand,* palm facing in, back to pinch the nose.

**stir** *v.* See signs for BEAT[1], MESSY, MIX[1].

**stitch** *v.* See signs for SEW[1,2].

**stocking** *n.* Same sign used for: **hose, pantyhose.**

- [Represents pulling on a long stocking] Bring the fingers of the right *5 hand,* palm facing in, from the wrist up the forearm of the extended left arm with a smooth movement.

**stocks** *pl. n.* See sign for INVEST.

**stomach** *n.* See sign used for: **abdomen.**

- [Location of stomach] Tap the fingertips of the right *bent hand,* palm facing up, against the center of the body with a double movement.

**stomachache**[1] *n.*

■ [**hurt**[1] formed near the stomach] Beginning with both extended index fingers pointing toward each other in front of the body, palms facing up, jab the fingers toward each other with a short double movement.

**stomachache**[2] *n.* See sign for DISGUSTED[1].

**stone** *n.* See sign for ROCK[1].

**stop**[1] *v.* Same sign used for: **cease, halt, quit.**

■ [Demonstrates an abrupt stopping movement] Bring the little-finger side of the right *open hand,* palm facing left and fingers pointing up, sharply down on the upturned palm of the left *open hand* held in front of the body.

**stop**[2] *v.* See sign for DESIST.

**storage** *n.* See sign for SAVE[2].

**store**[1] *n.* Same sign used for: **market, mart, shop.**

■ [The hands seem to hold merchandise out for inspection and sale] Beginning with both *flattened O hands* in front of each side of the body, palms facing down and fingers pointing down, swing the fingers forward and back from the wrists with a repeated movement.

**store**[2] *v.* See sign for SAVE[2].

**storm** *n.* See signs for MESSY, WIND.

**story** *n.* Same sign used for: **parable, phrase, prose, remarks, tale.**

■ [The hands seem to pull out sentences to form a story] Beginning with both *flattened C hands* in front of the chest, palms facing each other and the right hand slightly over the left hand, close the fingertips to the thumbs of each hand and then pull the hands straight apart in front of each shoulder with a double movement.

**straight**[1] *adj., adv.* Same sign used for: **direct.**

■ [Indicates a straight direction] Beginning with the index-finger side of the right *B hand* against the right shoulder, palm facing left and fingers pointing up, move the hand straight forward by bending the wrist down.

# straight

**straight**[2] *adj., adv.* See sign for SPECIALIZE.

**stranded** *adj.* See sign for STUCK.

**strange** *adj.* See also sign for WEIRD. Same sign used for:
**bizarre, freak, odd, peculiar, queer, unusual.**

- [Something distorting one's vision] Move the right *C hand* from near the right side of the face, palm facing left, downward in an arc in front of the face, ending near the left side of the chin, palm facing down.

**strategy** *n.*

- [Initialized sign] Beginning with both *S hands* in front of each side of the chest, palms facing forward, move the hands downward with a wavy movement.

**straw** *n.*

- [The right hand represents a straw leading from a liquid to the mouth] Beginning with both *G hands* together in front of the body, palms facing each other and right hand closer to the lips than the left hand, move the right hand upward to touch the mouth with a short double movement.

**strawberry** *n.*

- [Similar to sign for **red** indicating a strawberry's color] Wipe the right extended index finger, palm facing in, downward on the lips. Then wipe the thumb of the right *10 hand*, palm facing in, downward on the lips.

**stray** *v.* See sign for ASTRAY.

**stream** *n., v.* Same sign used for: **flow.**

- [Represents liquid flowing down] Beginning with both *B hands* in front of the right side of the chest, right palm facing up and left palm facing down, move the hands downward to the left with a double movement.

**street**[1] *n.*
- [Initialized sign formed similar to **road**] Move both *S hands* from in front of the body, palms facing each other, forward with a parallel movement.

**street**[2] *n.* See sign for ROAD.

**strength** *n.* See signs for POWER[1], STRONG[1], WELL[1].

**stress** *n.* See signs for IMPRESSION, PRESSURE.

**stretch**[1] *v.* Same sign used for: **elastic.**
- [Mime stretching out some elastic] Beginning with the knuckles of both *S hands* touching in front of the chest, palms facing in, bring the hands apart to in front of each side of the chest with a double movement.

**stretch**[2] *v.* See sign for EXAGGERATE.

**strict** *adj.* Same sign used for: **bold, firm, stern.**
- Strike the index-finger side of the right *bent V hand* against the nose with a deliberate movement, palm facing left.

**strike** *v.* See signs for BEAT[3], BEAT UP, COMPLAIN, HIT[1], PROTEST[2].

**string** *n.* See sign for LINE.

**strip**[1] *n.*
- [The shape of strips of something] Beginning with the thumbs and index fingers of both *G hands* touching, left hand palm facing down, over the right hand palm facing left, move the right hand straight down with a double movement in front of the chest.

**strip**[2] *v.* See sign for TEAR.

**stripe** *n.*
- [Represents the shape of stripes] Beginning with the right *4 hand* in front of the left shoulder, palm facing in and fingers pointing left, pull the hand straight across the chest to in front of the right shoulder.

# strive

**strive** *v.* See sign for TRY.

**stroll** *v.* See sign for WALK.

**strong**[1] *adj.* Same sign used for: **power, solid, strength.**

- [Initialized sign formed similar to **power**[1]] Beginning with the index-finger side of the right *S hand* near the left shoulder, palm facing left, move the right hand down in an arc, ending with the little-finger side of the right *S hand* touching near the crook of the left arm, palm facing up.

**strong**[2] *adj.* See sign for POWERFUL, WELL[1].

**structure** *n.*

- [Initialized sign formed similar to **build**] Beginning with the left *S hand* on the back of the right *S hand*, both palms facing down, move the right hand in a forward and upward arc to reverse positions. Repeat as the hands move upward in front of the chest.

**struggle** *v., n.* Same sign used for: **antagonism, at odds, banter, conflict, controversy, opposition.**

- [Represents opposing forces struggling] Beginning with both extended index fingers pointing toward each other in front of the chest, palms facing in and right hand closer to the body than the left hand, move the hands back and forth simultaneously with a double movement.

**stubborn**[1] *adj.* Same sign used for: **persistence, persistent**

- [Similar to sign for **donkey** signifying a donkey's stubborn nature] Beginning with the extended thumb of the right *open hand* touching the right temple, palm facing forward and fingers pointing up, bend the fingers downward with a deliberate movement.

**stubborn**[2] *adj.* See sign for DONKEY.

**stuck** *adj.* Same sign used for: **confined, pregnant, rape, stranded, trapped.**

- [Indicates where food gets stuck in the throat] Move the fingertips of the right *V hand*, palm facing down, against the throat with a deliberate movement.

**student** *n.* See sign for PUPIL[1].

**study** *v., n.*
- [Eyes scanning information held in the hand in order to learn it] While wiggling the fingers, move the right *5 hand,* palm facing down, with a double movement toward the left *open hand* held in front of the chest, palm facing up.

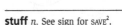

**stuff** *n.* See sign for SAVE[2].

**stuffed** *adj.* See sign for FULL[1].

**stunned** *adj.* See sign for INCREDIBLE.

**stupid** *adj.* See sign for DUMB.

**sturdy**[1] *adj.* Same sign used for: **solid, tough.**
- [Striking something that is sturdy] Move the right *S hand* from in front of the right side of the chest, palm facing in, in a downward arc across the back of the left *S hand* held in front of the chest, palm facing down, and back again.

**sturdy**[2] *adj.* See sign for POWER[1].

**sub-** *prefix.*
- [Initialized sign formed similar to sign for **base**] Move the right *S hand,* palm facing forward, in a double circular movement under the left *open hand* held across the chest, palm facing down and fingers pointing right.

**subdue** *v.* See sign for DEFEAT.

**subject** *n.* See sign for TITLE.

**submit** *v.* See signs for ADMIT[1], SUGGEST. Related form: **submission** *n.*

**subscribe** *v.* See sign for PENSION.

**substance** *n.*
- [Represents feeling a substance] Grasp the left *open hand* with the fingers of the right *flattened C hand,* both palms facing down, and slide the right hand forward and back with a double movement.

# substitute

**substitute** *v.* See sign for TRADE. Related form: **substitution** *n.*

---

**subtract** *v.* Same sign used for: **deduct, discount, eliminate, exempt.**

- [Demonstrates removing something] Beginning with the fingertips of the right *curved 5 hand* touching the palm of the left *open hand* held in front of the left side of the chest, palm facing right and fingers pointing up, bring the right hand down off the base of the left hand while changing into an *S hand.*

---

**subway** *n.*

- [Initialized sign formed under the left hand representing moving under street level] Move the right *S hand,* palm facing left, forward and back under the palm of the left *open hand* held across the chest, palm facing down and fingers pointing right.

---

**succeed** *v.* See sign for FINALLY.

---

**success** *n.* See sign for ACHIEVE.

---

**successful** *adj.* Related forms: **succeed** *v.*, **success** *n.* See also sign for ACHIEVE. Same sign used for: **accomplish, accomplishment, achievement, prosper, triumph.**

- [Moving to higher stages] Beginning with both extended index fingers pointing up in front of each shoulder, palms facing back, move the hands in double arcs upward and back, ending near each side of the head.

---

**suck** *v.*

- [Represents the mouth when sucking] Open and close the fingers of the right *flattened C hand* with a double movement around the fingertips of the left *flattened O hand* held in front of the chest, left palms facing in and right palm facing forward. Then pull the right hand back toward the chest while closing the fingers into a *flattened O hand* and puckering the lips as if sucking.

---

**sudden** *adj., adv.* See sign for FAST.

---

**sue** *v.*

- [Shows an opposition to something] Beginning with the right *B hand* in front of the right shoulder, palm facing left and fingers angled forward, bring the hand down to sharply touch the fingertips against the palm of the left *open hand,* palm facing in and fingers angled to the right.

**suffer** *v.*

- [Similar to **hurt**[2] except formed with a double movement] Beginning with the thumb of the right *A hand* touching the chin, palm facing left, twist the hand to the left with a double movement.

**sufficient** *adj.* See sign for ENOUGH.

**sugar** *n.* See sign for CANDY[1].

**suggest** *v.* Related form: **suggestion** *n.*
Same sign used for: **appeal, bid, motion, offer, nominate, petition, proposal, propose, provide, submit, submission.**

- [The hands seem to put forward a suggestion] Beginning with both *open hands* in front of each side of the chest, palms facing up and fingers pointing forward, move the hands simultaneously upward in an arc.

**suicide** *n.*

- [**kill + myself**] Push the side of the extended right index finger, palm facing down, across the palm of the left *open hand,* palm facing right, with a deliberate movement. Then tap the thumb side of the right *10 hand,* palm facing left, against the chest with a double movement.

**suit**[1] *n.* See signs for AGREE[1], FIT[1], MATCH[1].

**suit**[2] *n.* See sign for CLOTHES.

**suitcase** *n.* See signs for BASKET, PURSE.

**sum** *v.* See sign for ADD[1].

**summarize** *v.* See sign for BRIEF.

## summer

**summer** *n.*

■ [Represents wiping sweat from the brow] Bring the thumb side of the extended right index finger, palm facing down and finger pointing left, across the forehead while bending the index finger into an *X hand*.

**summon** *v.* See sign for CALL[1].

**sun** *n.*

■ [Represents shielding one's eyes from the sun] Tap the thumb and index finger of the right *C hand*, palm facing forward, against the right side of the head with a double movement.

**Sunday** *n.*

■ [The movement of the hands shows reverence and awe] Beginning with both *open hands* in front of each shoulder, palms facing forward and fingers pointing up, move the hands forward and back with a small double movement.

**sundown** *n.* See sign for SUNSET.

**sunrise** *n.* Same sign used for **dawn**.

■ [Represents the sun coming up over the horizon] Bring the index-finger side of the right *F hand*, palm facing left, upward past the little-finger side of the left *open hand*, palm facing down and fingers pointing right, held across the chest, ending with the right *F hand* in front of the face.

**sunset** *n.* Same sign used for: **sundown**.

■ [Represents the sun going down below the horizon] Move the thumb side of the right *F hand*, palm facing left, downward past the little-finger side of the left *open* hand held across the chest, palm facing down and fingers pointing right.

**superb** *adj.* Same sign used for: **excellent, fantastic, okay.**

- [Natural gesture to indicate something is superb] Move the right *F hand*, palm facing left, forward with a short double movement in front of the right shoulder.

**superintendent** *n.* See sign for PRESIDENT.

**superior** *n.* See sign for CHIEF[1].

**superstition** *n.* See sign for IMAGINATION. Related form: **superstitious** *adj.*

**supervise** *v.* See sign for CARE[1].

**supplement** *v.* See sign for ADD[2].

**supply** *v.* See sign for FEED.

**support** *v., n.* Same sign used for: **advocate, allegiance, backup, boost, fund, in behalf of, in favor of, sponsor.**

- [Initialized sign similar to sign for **help**] Push the knuckles of the right *S hand*, palm facing left, upward under the little-finger side of the left *S hand*, palm facing in, pushing the left hand upward a short distance in front of the chest.

**suppose** *v.* Same sign used for: **if, in case of.**

- [Indicates a thought coming from the mind] Move the extended little finger of the right *I hand*, palm facing in, forward from the right side of the forehead with a short double movement.

**suppress** *v.* See signs for CONTROL[1], PRESSURE. Related form: **suppression** *n.*

**supreme** *adj.* See sign for ADVANCED.

**sure**[1] *adj.* Same sign used for: **certain.**

- [Indicates that facts are coming straight from the mouth] Move the extended right index finger from in front of the mouth, palm facing left and finger pointing up, forward with a deliberate movement.

# sure

**sure²** *adj.* See sign for HONEST.

---

**surface¹** *n.*

■ [Indicates the surface of something] Move the palm side of the right *open hand* in a circle on the back of the left *open hand*, both palms facing down in front of the chest.

---

**surface²** *v.* See sign for SHOW UP.

---

**surfboard** *n.* Same sign used for: **surfing**.

■ [Represents a person standing on a surfboard] With the fingertips of the right *H hand*, palm facing down, on the back of the left open hand, palm facing down in front of the chest, move both hands forward.

---

**surgery** *n.* See sign for OPERATE¹.

---

**surprise** *n., v.* Same sign used for: **amaze, amazement, astound, bewilder, startle.**

■ [Represents the eyes widening in surprise] Beginning with the index fingers and thumbs of both hands pinched together near the outside of each eye, palms facing each other, flick the fingers apart, forming *L hands* near each side of the head.

---

**surrender** *v.* See sign for GIVE UP.

---

**surround** *v.* See sign for SITUATION.

---

**surrounding** *adj.* See sign for AROUND¹.

---

**survive** *v.* See sign for LIVE. Related form: **survival** *n.*

---

**suspect** *v.* Related forms: **suspicion** *n.*,
**suspicious** *adj.*

- [Digging into the mind] Beginning with
  the extended right index finger touching
  the right side of the forehead, palm facing
  down, bring the hand forward a short
  distance with a double movement, bending
  the index finger into an *X hand* each time.

**suspend** v. See sign for HOLD².

**swallow** *v.* Same sign used for: **gulp.**

- [Shows the path food follows when swallowed] Move the extended right index finger, palm facing left and finger angled
  upward, in an arc from in front of the chin down the length
  of the neck.

**swap** *v.* See signs for REVERSE, TRADE.

**swap places** *v. phrase.* See sign for TRADE PLACES.

**swear** *v.* See signs for CURSE, VOW.

**sweat** *v., n.* Same sign used for: **perspire,
perspiration, toil.**

- [Represents sweat coming from one's
  brow] Beginning with both *S hands*
  in front of each side of the forehead, move the hands forward
  while opening into *curved hands,*
  palms facing down and fingers pointing
  toward each other.

**sweater** *n.*

- [Demonstrates pulling on a sweater] Beginning with
  the thumb sides of both *A hands* on each side of the
  chest, palms facing in, bring the hands straight
  downward.

# sweep

**sweep** *v.* See sign for BROOM.

**sweet** *adj.* Same sign used for: **gentle.**
- [Licking something sweet from the fingers] Wipe the fingertips of the right *open hand,* palm facing in and fingers pointing up, downward off the chin while bending the fingers.

**sweetheart** *n.* Same sign used for: **beau, lover.**
- [Two people nodding toward each other] With the knuckles of both *10 hands* together in front of the chest, palms facing in and thumbs pointing up, bend the thumbs downward toward each other with a double movement.

**swim** *v.* Related form: **swimming** *n.*
- [Demonstrates the movement of the hands when swimming] Beginning with the fingers of both *open hands* crossed in front of the chest, palms facing down, move the hands apart to each side with a double movement.

**swindle** *v.* See sign for BETRAY[1].

**switch** *v.* See signs for CHANGE[1], REVERSE, TRADE.

**switch places** *v. phrase.* See sign for TRADE PLACES.

**swollen**[1] *adj.*
- [Indicates the shape of a swelling on the wrist] Beginning with the right *curved 5 hand* on the back of the left *open hand* held in front of the chest, both palms facing down, raise the right hand a short distance.

**sworn** *adj.* See sign for VOW.

### syllable *n.*

- [**word** signed in several places to show the small parts of a word] Move the right G hand, palm facing left, in short arcs across the length of the extended left index finger held in front of the chest, palm facing right and finger pointing forward.

### symbol *n.* Same sign used for: **sample, sign, symptom.**

- [Initialized sign similar to sign for **show**[1]] With the index-finger side of the right S hand, palm facing forward, against the palm of the left open hand held in front of the chest, palm facing right and fingers pointing up, move both hands forward a short distance.

### symptom *n.* See sign for SYMBOL.

### synagogue *n.*

- [Initialized sign similar to sign for **church**] Tap the heel of the right S hand, palm facing forward, downward with a double movement on the back of the left open hand held in front of the chest.

### syrup[1] *n.*

- [Wiping sticky lips] Wipe the extended right index finger, palm facing down, from under the nose across the right cheek.

### syrup[2] *n.* See sign for GRAVY.

### system *n.*

- [Initialized sign] Beginning with the index-finger sides of both S hands touching in front of the chest, palms angled down, move the hands outward to in front of each shoulder and then straight down a short distance.

**tabernacle** *n.* See sign for TEMPLE.

**table**¹ *n.*
- [Represents the flat surface of a table top] Beginning with the bent arms of both *open hands* across the chest, right arm above the left arm, move the right arm down with a short double movement.

**table**² *n.* See sign for DESK.

**table tennis** *n.* See sign for PING-PONG (*trademark*).

**tack** *n.* See sign for THUMBTACK.

**tag** *n.* See sign for LABEL.

**take** *v.* Same sign used for: **acquire, adopt, assume, assumption, takeover, take up.**
- [The hands seem to take up something] Beginning with both *curved 5 hands* in front of each side of the body, palms facing down, move the hands upward toward the body while changing into *S hands*.

**take a chance** See sign for GRAB.

**take advantage of** See signs for ADVANTAGE¹, LEECH.

**take care of** See sign for CARE¹.

**take off** *v. phrase.* Same sign for: **remove, undress.**
- [Mime taking off one's clothes] Beginning with the fingers of both *curved hands* on each side of the chest, palms facing in, bring the hands outward to in front of each shoulder while closing into *S hands*, palms facing each other.

**takeover** *n.* See signs for CAPTURE, TAKE.

**take pictures** Same sign used for: **photograph, shoot.**

■ [Represents the shutter on a camera opening and closing] Beginning with both *modified C hands* near the outside of each eye, palms facing each other, bend the right index finger downward.

---

**take steps** See sign for PROCEDURE.

**take up** *v. phrase.* See signs for RAPTURE, TAKE.

**tale** *n.* See sign for STORY.

**talent** *n.* See sign for SKILL.

**talk**[1] *v.*

■ [Shows words coming from the mouth] Beginning with the index-finger side of the right *4 hand* in front of the mouth, palm facing left and fingers pointing up, move the hand forward with a double movement.

---

**talk**[2] *v.* See signs for BLAB, CHAT[1], SPEAK[1]. Related form: **talkative** *adj.*

**tall** *adj.*

■ [Indicates the height of a tall person] Move the extended right index finger, palm facing forward and finger pointing up, from the heel upward to off the fingertips of the left *open hand,* palm facing right and fingers pointing up, ending with the right hand in front of the head.

---

**tame** *v.* See sign for PET[1].

**tan** *adj., n.*

■ [Initialized sign similar to sign for **brown**] Slide the index-finger side of the right *T hand,* palm facing left, downward on the right cheek.

---

**tardy** *adj.* See sign for LATE.

**target** *n.* See signs for GOAL, POINT[2].

**task** *n.* See sign for WORK.

# taste

**taste** *n., v.*
- [The finger used for feeling points toward the sense of taste] Touch the bent middle finger of the right *5 hand*, palm facing in, to the lips.

---

**tasty** *adj.* See sign for DELICIOUS.

---

**tattle** *v.* Same sign used for: **rat** (*slang*), **squeal, tattletale.**
- [Words shooting from the mouth] Beginning with the index-finger side of the right *S hand* in front of the mouth, palm facing left, move the hand forward with a double movement, extending the right index finger each time.

---

**tattletale** *n.* See sign for TATTLE.

---

**tax** *adj.* See sign for COST[1].

---

**taxi** *n.* See sign for CAB.

---

**tea** *n.*
- [Mime dipping a tea bag in hot water] With the fingertips of the right *F hand*, palm facing down, inserted in the hole formed by the left *O hand* held in front of the chest, palm facing in, move the right hand in a small circle.

---

**teach** *v.* Same sign used for: **educate, education, indoctrinate, indoctrination, instruct, instruction.**
- [The hands seem to take information from the head and direct it toward another person] Move both *flattened O hands*, palms facing each other, forward with a small double movement in front of each side of the head.

---

**team** *n.*
- [Initialized sign similar to sign for **class**] Beginning with the index-finger sides of both *T hands* touching in front of the chest, palms angled forward, bring the hands away from each other in outward arcs while turning the palms in, ending with the little fingers touching.

---

**tear** *v.* Same sign used for: **revoke, rip, strip, torn.**

■ [Mime ripping a piece of paper] Beginning with the index-finger sides of both *F hands* touching in front of the chest, palms facing down, move the right hand back toward the body with a deliberate movement while moving the left hand forward.

**tear apart** *v. phrase.* See sign for BREAK.

**tear down** *v. phrase.* See sign for BREAK DOWN.

**teardrop** *n.* See sign for TEARS.

**tears** *pl. n.* Same sign used for: **teardrop.**

■ [Represents tears flowing from the eye] Beginning with the index finger of the right *4 hand* touching the cheek near the right eye, palm facing in and fingers pointing left, bring the hand downward a short distance.

**tease** *v.* Related form: **teasing** *n.* Same sign used for: **jest, kid, kidding.**

[The hand seems to direct jabbing remarks at someone] Push the little-finger side of the right *X hand,* palm facing left, forward with a repeated movement across the index-finger side of the left *X hand,* palm facing right.

**technical** *adj.* Same sign used for: **technology.**

■ Tap the bent middle finger of the right *5 hand,* palm facing up, upward on the little-finger side of the left *open hand,* palm facing right and fingers pointing forward, with a double movement.

**technology** *n.* See sign for TECHNICAL.

**teeny** *adj.* See sign for TINY.

**teeth** *pl. n.*

- [Location of the teeth] Move the curved index finger of the right *X hand* from right to left across the top front teeth, palm facing in.

**telephone** *n., v.* Same sign used for: **call, phone.**

- [Represents holding a telephone receiver to the ear] Tap the knuckles of the right *Y hand,* palm facing in, with a double movement on the lower right cheek, holding the right thumb near the right ear and the little finger in front of the mouth. The same sign is used for the verb, as in *to telephone my sister,* but the sign is made with a single movement.

**tell**[1] *v.* Same sign used for: **reveal.**

- [Represents words coming from the mouth toward another person] Beginning with the extended right index finger near the chin, palm facing in and finger pointing up, move the finger forward in an arc by bending the wrist, ending with the finger angled forward.

**tell**[2] *v.* See sign for ANNOUNCE.

**temperature** *n.*

- [Symbolizes the mercury in a thermometer rising and falling] Slide the back of the extended right index finger, palm facing in and finger pointing left, up and down with a repeated movement on the extended index finger of the left hand, palm facing right and finger pointing up

**temple** *n.* Same sign used for: **tabernacle, tomb.**

- [Initialized sign similar to sign for **church**] Tap the heel of the right *T hand,* palm facing forward, with a double movement on the back of the left *S hand* held in front of the chest, palm facing down.

**temporary** *adj.* See sign for SHORT[1].

# terrific

**tempt** *v.* Related form: **temptation** *n.* Same sign used for: **entice.**

- [Shows tapping someone in order to tempt] Tap the curved right index finger, palm facing up, with a double movement on the elbow of the bent left arm.

**ten cents** *pl. n.* See sign for DIME.

**tend** *v.* Related form: **tendency** *n.* Same sign used for: **prone.**

- [The fingers used for feeling move from the heart] Beginning with the bent middle fingers of both *5 hands* touching each side of the chest, palms facing in, move both hands forward in small arcs.

**tender** *adj.* See signs for SOFT, SOFT-HEARTED.

**tent** *n.* See sign for CAMP.

**terminal**[1] *n.*

- [Initialized sign showing the shape of a terminal] Beginning with the index-finger sides of both *T hands* together in front of the chest, palms facing forward, bring the hands apart to in front of each shoulder and then straight down.

**terminal**[2] *adj.* Related form: **terminate** *n.*

- [Initialized sign similar to sign for **end**[1]] Slide the heel of the right *T hand*, palm facing forward, along the index-finger side of the left *B hand* held in front of the chest, palm facing in and fingers pointing right, and then straight downward in front of the right side of the body.

**terminate** *v.* See signs for ELIMINATE[1], FIRE[2].

**terrible** *adj.* See sign for AWFUL.

**terrific** *adj.* See sign for FINEST.

# test

**test** *n., v.* Same sign used for: **examine, examination, inquire, quiz.**

■ [Draw a question mark in the air + a gesture representing distributing the test to a group] Beginning with both extended index fingers pointing up in front of the head, palms facing forward, bring the hands in arcs to the side and then downward while bending the index fingers into *X hands* and continuing down while throwing the fingers open into *5 hands* in front of the body, palms facing down and fingers pointing forward.

**testimony** *n.* Related form: **testify** *v.*

■ [Sign **talk**[1] while holding the hand up as if giving testimony in court] While holding the left *open hand* in front of the left shoulder, palm facing forward and fingers pointing up, with a double movement, move the fingers of the right *4 hand* forward a short distance in front of the mouth, palm facing left and fingers pointing up.

**text** *n.* See sign for WORD.

**than** *conj.*

■ [The levels of the hands are used for comparison] Move the fingers of the right *open hand,* palm angled left, downward by bending the right wrist, hitting the fingers of the left *bent hand* held in front of the chest, palm and fingers angled forward, as it passes.

**thank** *v.* Same sign used for: **thank you.**

■ [The hand takes gratitude from the mouth and presents it to another] Move the fingertips of the right *open hand,* palm facing in and fingers pointing up, from the mouth forward and down, ending with the palm angled up in front of the chest.

**thankful** *adj.* See sign for GRATEFUL.

**thank you** See sign for THANK.

**Thanksgiving** *n.*

[Represents the shape of a turkey's wattle] Beginning with the right *G hand* in front of the nose, palm facing left, bring the hand downward in an arc with a double movement, bringing the hand forward in front of the chest each time.

**that** *pron., adj.*
- [Points out something in the hand] Bring the palm side of the right *Y hand* with a deliberate movement down to land on the palm of the left *open hand* held in front of the chest, palm facing up.

**theater** *n.* See sign for ACT[2].

**theft** *n.* See signs for SHOPLIFT, STEAL.

**their** *pron.* Related form: **theirs** *pron.*
- [Points toward the referents being discussed] Move the right *open hand*, palm facing forward and fingers pointing up, from in front of the right side of the body outward to the right.

**them** *pron.* Same sign used for: **these, they.**
- [Points toward the referents being discussed] Move the extended right index finger, palm facing down and finger pointing forward, from in front of the right side of the body outward to the right.

**theme** *n.* See signs for QUOTATION, TITLE.

**themselves** *pl. pron.*
- [This hand shape is used for reflexive pronouns and is directed toward the referents being discussed] Move the right *10 hand* from in front of the right side of the body, palm facing left, outward to the right.

**then** *adv.* See signs for FINISH[1], OR.

**theory** *n.*
- [Initialized sign similar to sign for **wonder**] Move the right *T hand*, palm facing forward, in a double circle near the right side of the forehead.

# therapy

**therapy** *n.*

- [Initialized sign similar to sign for **help**] Beginning with the little-finger side of the right *T hand,* palm facing in, on the palm of the left *open hand* held in front of the body, palm facing up, move both hands upward in front of the chest.

**there** *adv.* Same sign used for: **point.**

- [Points to a specific place away from the body] Push the extended right index finger from in front of the right shoulder forward a short distance, palm facing forward and finger pointing forward.

**therefore** *adv.*

- [Sets up a ratio for comparison] Move the right *modified X hand,* palm facing forward in front of the right shoulder, outward to the right and then downward in an angle to the left in front of the body.

**these** *pron.* See sign for THEM.

**they** *pron.* See sign for THEM.

**thick** *adj.*

- [Shows the thickness of a thick layer] Slide the thumb side of the right *modified C hand,* palm facing forward, from the wrist across the back of the left *open hand* held in front of the chest, palm facing down.

**thin**[1] *adj.* Same sign used for: **short.**

- [Shows the thickness of a thin layer] Slide the thumb side of the right *G hand,* palm facing forward, from the wrist to the fingers of the left *open hand* held in front of the chest, palm facing down.

**thin**[2] *adj.* (alternate sign) See also sign for SKINNY. Same sign used for: **lean, slim.**

- [Indicates something or someone that is very thin] Beginning with the extended little fingers of both *I hands* touching in front of the chest, right hand above the left hand and palms facing in, bring the right hand upward and the left hand downward.

**thin**[3] *adj.* See sign for DIET.

**thing** *n.*
- [Something in the hand] Bring the right *open hand,* palm facing up and fingers pointing forward, from in front of the body in a large arc to the right.

**think**[1] *v.*
- [Indicates the location of the mind] Tap the extended right index finger, palm facing in, to the right side of the forehead with a short double movement.

**think**[2] *v.* See signs for CONCERN[1], WONDER.

**think about** *v. phrase.* See sign for WONDER.

**thinking** *n.* See sign for WONDER.

**third** *adj.* See sign for ONE THIRD.

**thirsty** *adj.* Related form: **thirst** *n.* Same sign used for: **parched.**
- [Indicates a dry throat] Move the extended right index finger, palm facing in and finger pointing up, downward on the length of the neck, bending the finger down as it moves.

**this** *pron., adj.*
- [Points to a specific thing held in the hand] Move the extended right index finger, palm facing down and finger pointing down, from in front of the chest in a circular movement and then down to touch the left *open hand* held in front of the body, palm facing up.

**thoughtless** *adj.* Related form:
**thoughtlessly** *adv.*

- [**concern**[1] + a variation of the sign
for **none**[1]] Beginning with both
extended index fingers in front
of each side of the forehead,
palms facing in and fingers angled
up, move the fingers in repeated alternating circular
movements toward each other in front of the face. Then move both *O*
hands, palms facing forward in front of the body, apart to the sides.

**thousand** *n., adj.*

- [An *M* hand representing *mille*, the Latin word for thousand]
Bring the fingertips of the right *bent hand*, palm facing left,
against the palm of the left *open hand* held in front of the
body, palm facing right and fingers pointing forward.

**thread** *n.* See signs for CORD, LINE.

**threat** *n.* See sign for DANGER.

**thrifty** *adj.* See signs for GREEDY[1], STINGY[1,2].

**thrilling** *adj.* See sign for WHAT'S HAPPENING.

**throat** *n.*

- [Location of the throat] Move the extended fingers of
the right *G hand*, palm facing in, downward along
the length of the neck.

**through** *prep.* Same sign used for: **via.**

- [Demonstrates movement through something]
Slide the little-finger side of the right *open
hand*, palm facing in and fingers angled to
the left, between the middle finger and ring
finger of the left *open hand* held in front of
the chest, palm facing right and fingers
pointing up.

**throw** *v.* Same sign used for: **cast, dump, pitch, throw away, toss.**

- [Mime throwing something] Beginning with the right *S hand* in front of the right shoulder, palm facing forward, move the hand forward and downward while opening into a *5 hand*, palm facing down.

**throw away** *v. phrase.* See sign for THROW.

**throw out** *v. phrase.* See sign for ABANDON.

**throw up** *v. phrase.* See sign for VOMIT.

**thumbtack** *n.* Same sign used for: **pushpin, tack.**

- [Mime pushing a thumbtack into a wall] Push the extended thumb of the right *10 hand*, palm angled left, first against the fingers and then the heel of the left *open hand* held in front of the left side of the chest, palm facing right and fingers pointing up.

**thunder** *n., v.*

- [**hear** + a movement that represents the vibration of a loud sound] Touch the extended right index finger to the right ear, palm facing left. Then shake both *S hands* from side to side with a repeated movement in front of each shoulder, palms facing forward.

**thunderbolt** *n.* See sign for LIGHTNING.

**Thursday** *n.*

- [Abbreviation **t-h**] Beginning with the right *T hand* in front of the right shoulder, palm facing left, flick the index and middle fingers forward, forming an *H hand*.

**tie**[1] *v.* Same sign used for: **knot.**

- [Mime tying a bow] Beginning with the fingers of both *F hands* together in front of the chest, move the fingers around each other and then apart, miming tying a bow.

# tie

**tie**[2] *v.* See sign for NECKTIE.

**tight**[1] *adj., adv.*

- [Shows shaking something that is tight] With rigid, bent arms, shake both *S hands*, palms facing in, in front of each side of the chest.

**tight**[2] *adj.* See sign for GREEDY[1].

**tightwad** *n. Informal.* See sign for STINGY[2].

**time**[1] *n.* Same sign used for: **period.**

- [Initialized sign showing the movement of the minute hand around a clock face] Move the right *T hand*, palm facing left, in a circle around the left *open hand* held in front of the chest, palm facing right, ending with the right hand on the left heel.

**time**[2] *n.*

- [Indicates the location of a person's watch] Tap the bent index finger of the right *X hand*, palm facing down, with a double movement on the wrist of the left *wrist* held in front of the chest, palm facing down.

**timeout** *n.*

- [This is the signal used in sports to indicate a timeout] With a double movement, tap the palm of the right *open hand* held in front of the chest, palm facing down, downward on the fingertips of the left *open hand*, palm facing right.

**timepiece** *n.* See sign for WATCH[1].

**timid** *adj.* See sign for AFRAID.

**tint** *n., v.* See sign for DIM[1].

**tiny** *adj.* Same sign used for: **little bit, puny, scant, teeny.** See also sign for SMALL[2].

- [Shows a tiny movement] Beginning with the right *6 hand* in front of the right side of the chest, palm facing up, flick the thumb off the little finger with a quick movement.

**tip** *n*. See sign for POINT[1].

**tiptoe** *v., n*.

■ [Natural gesture to indicate quiet + a movement that represents a person moving on tiptoes] Bring the side of the extended right index finger, palm facing left, to 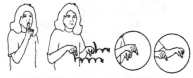 the mouth. Then move both extended index fingers from in front of each side of the body, palms and fingers pointing down, forward in a series of alternating arcs.

**tired** *adj*. Same sign used for: **exhausted, fatigue, weary.**

■ [The hands show that energy has dropped in the body] Beginning with the fingertips of both *bent hands* on each side of the chest, palms facing in, roll the hands downward on the fingertips, ending with the little-finger sides of both hands touching the chest, palms facing outward.

**tissue** *n*. Same sign used for: **Kleenex** (*trademark*).

■ [**cold**[1] + **paper**] Bring the index finger and thumb of the right *G hand,* palm facing in, downward on each side of the nose with a double movement, pinching the fingers together each time. Then brush the heel of the right *open hand,* palm facing down and fingers pointing left, with a double movement on the heel of the left *open hand* held in front of the body, palm facing up and fingers pointing right.

**title** *n*. Same sign used for: **entitle, quotes, so-called, subject, theme, topic.**

■ [Represents quotation marks around a title] Beginning with both *bent V hands* near each side of the head, palms facing forward, twist the hands while bending the fingers down, ending with the palms facing back.

# toast

**toast**[1] *n., v.*

■ [Represents the prongs of a toaster holding the bread in place] Touch the fingertips of the right *bent V hand,* palm facing left, first on the palm and then on the back of the left *open hand* held in front of the chest, palm facing right and fingers pointing up.

**toast**[2] *n., v.*

■ [Represents clicking two glasses together in a toast] Beginning with both *C hands* in front of each side of the chest, palms facing in, bring the hands upward and toward each other in a large arc, ending with the knuckles of both hands touching in front of the face, palms facing in.

**tobacco** *n.* Same sign used for: **chewing tobacco.**

■ [Shows tobacco in the cheek] Rotate the fingertips of the right *curved hand,* palm facing forward, against the right side of the chin while turning the palms down.

**today** *n., adv.*

■ [Sign similar to **now** except with a double movement] Bring both *Y hands,* palms facing up, with a short double movement downward in front of each side of the body.

**together** *adv.*

■ [Sign similar to **with**[1] except with a circular movement indicating duration] With the palm sides of both *A hands* together in front of the body, move the hands in a flat circle.

**toil** *n.* See signs for SWEAT, WORKAHOLIC.

**toilet** *n.* Same sign used for: **bathroom, lavatory, rest room, washroom.**

■ [Initialized sign] Move the right *T hand,* palm facing forward, from side to side in front of the right shoulder with a repeated shaking movement.

**tolerant** *adj.* See signs for BROAD-MINDED, PATIENT[1].

**tolerate** *v.* See signs for CONTROL[1], PATIENT[1]. Related form: **tolerant** *adj.*

**tomato** *n.*

■ [**red** + a gesture that shows slicing] Bring the extended right index finger from the lips, palm facing in, downward with a deliberate movement across the thumb side of the left *O hand* held in front of the chest, palm facing down, ending with the right palm facing down in front of the body.

**tomb** *n.* See sign for TEMPLE.

**tomorrow** *n., adv.*

■ [The sign moves forward into the future] Move the palm side of the right *10 hand,* palm facing left, from the right side of the chin forward while twisting the wrist.

**tonight** *n.* See sign for NIGHT.

**too much** See signs for EXCESS, OVER[1].

**tooth** *n.*

■ [Location of a tooth] Touch a front tooth with the extended right index finger, palm facing in.

**toothbrush** *n.*

■ [Mime the action of brushing one's teeth] Move the extended right index finger, palm facing down and finger pointing left, up and down with a repeated movement in front of the front teeth.

# top

**top** *n., adj.*
- [The location on the top of something] Bring the palm of the right *open hand*, palm facing down and fingers pointing left, downward on the finger tips of the left *open hand* held in front of the chest, palm facing right and fingers pointing up.

**topic** *n.* See sign for TITLE.

**torn** *adj.* See sign for TEAR.

**tornado** *n.*
- [Shows the circular winds occurring during a tornado] Beginning with the extended right index finger pointing down in front of the right side of the chest, palm facing down, and the extended left index finger pointing up in front of the chest, palm facing up, move the hands in small circles around each other in opposite directions as the hands move from right to left in front of the chest.

**tortoise** *n.* See sign for TURTLE.

**torture** *n., v.* Same sign used for: **abuse, haze, maltreatment, mutilate, persecute, persecution, probation, prosecute, prosecution.**
- [Striking against another] Shove the little-finger side of the right *X hand*, palm facing left, forward across the index-finger side of the left *X hand*, palm facing right, while moving the left hand upward to repeat the left hand movement over the right hand with a double movement.

**toss** *v.* See sign for THROW.

**total**[1] *v.* See sign for ADD[1].

**total**[2] *adj.* See sign for ALL THE TIME.

**touch** *v., n.*
- [Demonstrates touching something, with the middle finger used frequently to indicate feelings] Bring the bent middle finger of the right hand, palm facing down, downward to touch the back of the left *open hand* held in front of the body, palm facing down.

**tough**[1] *adj.*

■ [Shows a rough surface] Slide the little-finger side of the right *bent V hand*, palm facing in, in an arc to the right off the back of the left *S hand* held in front of the body, palm facing down.

**tough**[2] *adj.* See signs for GANG, MEANNESS, STURDY[1].

**tour** *n.* See signs for RUN AROUND, TRIP.

**tow** *v.* See signs for DRAG, HAUL[1].

**toward** *prep.*

■ [Demonstrates a movement toward something] Beginning with the extended right index finger in front of the right shoulder, palm facing left, move the hand in an arc to the left, ending with the right extended index finger touching the left extended index finger pointing up in front of the left side of the body, palm facing right.

**towel** *n.*

■ [Mime drying one's back with a towel] Beginning with the right *S hand* above the right shoulder, palm facing forward, and the left *S hand* near the left hip, palm facing back, move the hands simultaneously upward and downward at an angle with a repeated movement.

**town** *n.* Same sign used for: **community, village.**

■ [Represents the rooftops in a town] Tap the fingertips of both *open hands* together in front of the chest with a double movement, palms facing each other at an angle.

**trade** *v.* Same sign used for: **budget, exchange, replace, substitute, substitution, swap, switch.**

■ [Demonstrates moving something into another thing's place] Beginning with both *F hands* in front of the body, palms facing each other and right hand somewhat forward of the left hand, move the right hand back toward the body in an upward arc while moving the left hand forward in a downward arc.

## trade places

**trade places** Same sign used for: **change places, swap places, switch places.**

- [Directional sign representing a person trading places with the referent toward whom the sign is formed] Beginning with the right *V hand* near the right side of the waist, palm facing down and fingers pointing forward, flip the hand over, ending with the palm facing up.

**tradition** *n.* Related form: **traditional** *adj.*

- [Initialized sign similar to sign for **habit**] With the heel of the right *T hand,* palm facing forward, on the back of the left *S hand,* palm facing down, move both hands downward in front of the chest.

**traffic** *n.*

- [Represents many vehicles moving quickly past each other in both directions] With both *5 hands* in front of the chest, palms facing each other and fingers pointing up, move the right hand forward and the left hand back with a repeated alternating movement, brushing palms as they pass each time.

**tragedy** *n.* Related form: **tragic** *adj.*

- [Initialized sign similar to sign for **tears**] Beginning with both *T hands* near each cheek, palms facing each other, bring the hands downward simultaneously.

**trail** *v.* See sign for FOLLOW.

**trailer** *n.* See sign for TRUCK.

**train** *n.* Same sign used for: **go by train, railroad, travel by train.**

- [Represents the crossties on a railroad track] Rub the fingers of the right *H hand* back and forth with a repeated movement on the fingers of the left *H hand* held in front of the body, both palms facing down.

**training** *n*. See sign for PRACTICE.

**tranquil** *adj*. See sign for QUIET.

**transfer** *v., n*.
- [Represents a person's legs moving to another place] Beginning with both *bent V hands* in front of the left side of the body, palms facing down, swing the hands to the right.

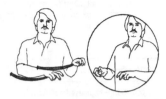

**transform** *v*. See sign for TRANSLATE.

**translate** *v*. Related form: **translation** *n*. Same sign used for: **transform.**
- [Initialized sign similar to sign for **change**[1]] Beginning with the palms of both *T hands* together in front of the chest, right hand over the left hand, twist the wrists to exchange positions.

**transparent** *adj*. See sign for VISIBLE.

**transport** *v*. See sign for BRING.

**trapped** *adj*. See sign for STUCK.

**trash** *n*. See sign for GARBAGE.

**travel** *v*. See signs for RUN AROUND, TRIP.

**travel by train** See sign for TRAIN.

**tree** *n*.
- [Represents a tree trunk and branches at the top] Beginning with the elbow of the bent right arm resting on the back of the left *open hand* held across the body, twist the right *5 hand* forward and back with a small repeated movement.

**trespass** *n*. See sign for SIN.

**trial** *n*. See sign for JUDGE.

# tribute

**tribute** *n.* See sign for GIFT.

**trick** *n.*, *v.* Same sign used for: **con, fool.**
- [Symbolizes "hitting on someone"] Tap the knuckles of the right *A hand*, palm facing forward, with a double movement against the extended left index finger held up in front of the body, palm facing right.

**trim** *v.* See sign for PRUNE.

**trip** *n.* Same sign used for: **journey, mobilize, tour, travel.**
- [Represents legs moving as if on a trip] Move the right *bent V hand*, palm facing down, from in front of the right side of the body upward and forward in an arc, ending with the palm facing forward.

**triumph** *n.* See sign for SUCCESSFUL.

**trophy**[1] *n.* Same sign used for: **award.**
- [The shape of a trophy] Tap the thumbs and little fingers of both *Y hands*, palms facing in, together in front of the body with a double movement.

**trophy**[2] *n.* See sign for CHAMPION.

**trouble**[1] *n.* Same sign used for: **anxious, care, concern, worry.**
- [Represents problems coming from all directions] Beginning with both *B hands* near each side of the head, palms facing each other, bring the hands toward each other with a repeated alternating movement, crossing the hands in front of the face each time.

**trouble**[2] *n.* See sign for DIFFICULT.

**trousers** *pl. n.* See sign for PANTS.

**truck** *n.* Same sign used for: **trailer.**
- [Initialized sign similar to sign for **bus**] Beginning with the little-finger side of the right *T hand*, palm facing left, touching the index-finger side of the left *T hand*, palm facing right, move the right hand back toward the chest while the left hand moves forward.

**trudge** *v.* See sign for PLOD.

**true** *adj.* Same sign used for: **actual, actually, certain, certainly, truly.**

- [Represents words coming from the mouth] Move the side of the extended right index finger from in front of the mouth, palm facing left and finger pointing up, forward in an arc.

**truly** *v.* See signs for ABSOLUTE, TRUE.

**trust** *n.* See sign for CONFIDENT.

**truth** *n.* Same sign used for: **fact, really.**

- [Represents the truth coming straight from the mouth] Move the extended right index finger from pointing up in front of the mouth, palm facing left, forward with a deliberate movement.

**try** *v.* Same sign used for: **attempt, strive.**

- [The hands push forward indicating effort] Move both *S hands* from in front of each side of the body, palms facing each other, downward and forward in simultaneous arcs.

**tubal ligation** *n.* See sign for STERILIZATION.

**Tuesday** *n.*

- [Initialized sign] Move the right *T hand*, palm facing in, in a circle in front of the right shoulder.

**turkey** *n.*

- [Represents the action of a turkey's wattle] With the thumb side of the right *G hand* under the chin, palm and fingers pointing down, wiggle the fingers from side to side with a repeated movement.

# turn

**turn** *n.* See also sign for CHANGE[1]. Same sign used for: **alternate, next.**

■ [Indicates alternating positions in order to take turns] Move the right *L hand* from in front of the body, palm angled left, to the right by flipping the hand over, ending with the palm facing up.

**turn down** *v. phrase.* See signs for DECLINE[3], REJECT[1].

**turn into** *v. phrase.* See sign for BECOME.

**turn off** *v. phrase.* Same sign as for **turn on** but the wrist twists in the opposite direction.

**turn on** *v. phrase.*

■ [Mime turning a knob so as to turn something on or off] While holding an imaginary switch between the thumb and bent index finger of the right *X hand* held in front of the right side of the body, palm facing up, twist the wrist, ending with the palm facing down.

**turn over** *v. phrase.* See sign for COOK.

**turn up** *v. phrase.* See sign for SHOW UP.

**turtle** *n.* Same sign used for: **tortoise.**

■ [Represents a turtle's head coming from under the shell] Cup the left palm over the right *A hand*, palm facing left, and wiggle the right thumb with a repeated movement.

**twenty-five cents** *pl. n.* See sign for QUARTER[2].

**twin** *n.*

■ [Initialized sign] Touch the index-finger side of the right *T hand*, palm facing left, first to the right side of the chin and then to the left side of the chin.

**two dollars** *pl. n.* See sign for SECOND[2].

**two weeks** *n. phrase* See sign for BIWEEKLY.

**type**[1] *v.* Related form: **typing** *v.*
- [Mime typing] Beginning with both *curved 5 hands* in front of the body, palms facing down, wiggle the fingers with a repeated movement.

**type**[2] *n.* See sign for FAVORITE[1]. Related form: **typical** *adj.*

**type**[3] *n.* See sign for KIND[2].

---

**ugly** *adj.*

- Beginning with the extended right index finger in front of the left side of the face, palm facing left and finger pointing left, move the hand to the right side of the face while bending the index finger to form an *X hand*.

---

**umbrella** *n.*

- [Mime raising an umbrella] Beginning with the little-finger side of the right *A hand* on the index-finger side of the left *A hand* in front of the chest, palms facing in opposite directions, raise the right hand upward in front of the head.

---

**unaware** *adj.* See sign for DON'T KNOW.

---

**uncertain** *adj.* See signs for INDECISION, RESIST.

---

**uncle** *n*

- [Initialized sign formed near the male area of the head] Shake the right *U hand,* palm facing forward and fingers pointing up, near the right side of the forehead.

---

**unconscious** *adj.* See sign for DON'T KNOW.

---

**undecided** *adj.* See sign for INDECISION.

---

**under** *prep.*

- [Shows a location under something else] Move the right *10 hand,* palm facing left, from in front of the chest downward and forward under the left *open hand* held in front of the chest, palm facing down and fingers pointing right.

---

**underclothes** *n.* See sign for UNDERWEAR.

**understand** *v.* Same sign used for: **apprehend, comprehend, perceive.**

■ [Comprehension seems to pop into one's head] Beginning with the right *S hand* near the right side of the forehead, palm facing left, flick the right index finger upward with a sudden movement.

**underwear** *n.* Same sign used for: **underclothes.**

■ [Location of underwear worn on the body] Beginning with the fingertips of both *bent hands* touching each side of the abdomen, palms facing in, twist the wrists upward, ending with both *open hands* in front of each side of the waist, palms facing down and fingers pointing forward.

**undress** *v.* See sign for TAKE OFF.

**unfair** *adj.*

■ [Nicking or bumping into another] Bring the fingertips of the right *F hand*, palm facing left, downward, striking the fingertips of the left *F hand*, palm facing right, as it passes.

**uniform** *n.* See sign for ALIKE[2].

**union** *n.* See sign for COOPERATION.

**unique** *adj.* See sign for SPECIAL.

**unite** *v.* See sign for BELONG[1].

**unity** *n.* See sign for COOPERATION.

**universal** *adj.* See sign for COOPERATION.

**university** *n.*

■ [Initialized sign similar to sign for **college**] Beginning with the palm side of the right *U hand* on the left *open hand* in front of the chest, palm facing up, move the right hand in a circular movement upward and forward.

# unknown

**unknown** *adj.* See sign DON'T KNOW.

---

**unskilled** *adj.* Same sign used for: **clumsy, inexperienced.**

- [Being held back from doing work] While grasping the thumb of the right *5 hand,* palm facing in and fingers pointing down, with the left *S hand,* palm facing down, twist the right wrist to move the right fingers upward, ending with the palm facing forward.

---

**until** *prep., conj.*

- [Uses a movement indicating the passage of time] Move the extended right index finger, palm facing left, in an arc to meet the extended left index finger in front of the left side of the chest, palm facing right and finger pointing up.

---

**unusual** *adj.* See sign for STRANGE.

---

**unwanted** *adj.* See sign for DON'T WANT.

---

**up** *adv., prep.*

- [Points up] With the right extended index finger pointing up in front of the right shoulder, palm facing forward, move the right hand upward a short distance.

---

**update** *v., n.* Same sign used for: **conversion, sequel.**

- [The hand catches up, bringing it up to date] Beginning with the right *10 hand* in front of the right side of the chest, palm facing down, and the left *10 hand* in front of the left side of the chest, palm facing right, twist the right wrist to the right to turn the palm left. Then bring the knuckles of the right hand against the heel of the left hand, pushing it forward.

---

**upset**[1] *v., adj., n.*

- [The stomach seems to turn over as when upset] Beginning with the right *P hand* in front of the abdomen, palm facing down, twist the wrist forward, ending with the palm facing up.

---

**upset**[2] *v.* See sign for DISGUSTED[1].

**upstairs** *adv.* Same sign as for UP but made with a double movement. Same sign used for: **upward.**

**up to** See sign for MAXIMUM.

**urge** *v.* Same sign used for: **persuade.**

■ [Shaking another to impose one's will] With both *modified X hands* in front of each side of the chest, palms facing each other and right hand closer to the chest than the left hand, move the hands forward with a short double movement.

**urgent** *adj.* See signs for HURRY, NOW.

**urine** *n.* See sign for PENIS.

**us** *pron.*

■ [Initialized sign similar to sign for **we**] Touch the index-finger side of the right *U hand*, palm facing left and fingers pointing up, to the right side of the chest. Then twist the wrist and move the hand around to touch the little-finger side of the right *U hand* to the left side of the chest, palm facing right.

**use** *v.*

■ [Initialized sign] Move the right *U hand*, palm facing forward and fingers pointing up, in a repeated circle over the back of the left *S hand* held in front of the chest, palm facing down, hitting the heel of the right hand on the left hand each time as it passes.

**used** *adj.* See sign for SECOND-HAND.

**used to** *adj. phrase.* Same sign used for: **usual, usually.**

■ [Initialized sign similar to sign for **habit**] With the heel of the right *U hand*, palm facing forward and fingers pointing up, on the back of the left *S hand* held in front of the chest, palm facing down, move both hands downward.

**use up** *v. phrase.* See sign for RUN OUT OF.

**usual** *adv.* See signs for DAILY, USED TO. Related form: **usually** *adv.*

**vacant** *adj.* See sign for EMPTY. Related form: **vacancy** *n.*

**vacation** *n.*
- [Thumbs in the straps of one's overalls as a symbol of leisure] With the thumbs of both *5 hands* near each armpit, palms facing in and fingers pointing toward each other, wiggle the fingers with a repeated movement.

**vaccinate** *v.* Related form: **vaccination** *n.*
- [Shows the traditional location the upper arm for vaccinations] With the bent index finger and thumb of the right hand pinched together, rub the right hand downward with a double movement on the upper left arm.

**vaccine** *n.* See sign for SHOT.

**vacuum** *v.*
- [Demonstrates the action of a vacuum drawing in dirt] With the fingertips of the right *flattened C hand* on the fingers of the left *open hand* held in front of the chest, palm facing up and fingers pointing forward, close the right fingers with a double movement while sliding across the left palm, forming a *flattened O hand* each time.

**vague** *adj.* Same sign used for: **ambiguous, blurry, fade, hazy, illegible.**
- [Represents a blurring of the facts] With the palms of both *5 hands* together at angles in front of the chest, move both hands in circular movements going in opposite directions rubbing the palms against each other.

**vain** *adj.* Related form: **vanity.**
- [Initialized sign] Beginning with both *V hands* in front of each shoulder, palms facing in and fingers pointing up, move the fingers backward toward each shoulder with a double movement.

**valley** *n.*

- [Shows the shape of a valley] Beginning with the index-finger sides of both *B hands* held up in front of both shoulders, palms facing down and fingers pointing forward, bring the right hand downward and then upward again, ending with the index-finger sides of both hands touching in front of the left shoulder.

**value** *adj.* See signs for COST², IMPORTANT.

**vanilla** *n.*, *adj.*

- [Initialized sign] Shake the right *V hand*, palm facing forward and fingers pointing up, from side to side with a small double movement in front of the right shoulder.

**vanish** *v.* See sign for DISAPPEAR¹.

**vanquish** *v.* See sign for DEFEAT.

**vapor** *n.* See sign for RAPTURE.

**variety** *n.* Same sign used for: **and so-forth, random, range.**

- [Pointing out many things] Beginning with the extended index fingers of both hands touching in front of the chest, palms facing down, move the hands apart while bending the index fingers downward, forming *X hands* with a repeated movement, ending with the hands in front of each side of the chest.

**vasectomy** *n.* See sign for STERILIZATION.

**vegetable** *n.*

- [Initialized sign] Beginning with the index finger of the right *V hand*, palm facing forward, touching the right side of the chin, twist the wrist to turn the palm back and touch the middle finger to the right side of the chin, ending with the palm facing back.

### vending machine *n.*

- [**machine** + mime putting money in a vending machine and pulling a knob for one's selection] With the fingers of both *curved 5 hands* loosely meshed together, palms facing in, move the hands up and down in front of the chest with a repeated movement. Then with the right thumb holding down the bent left index finger in front of the right shoulder, palm facing left, quickly flick the index finger up. Then with the right thumb tucked under the bent right index finger, palm facing left, pull the right hand back toward the right side of the body.

### venetian blinds *n.* See sign for BLINDS.

### vengeance *n.* See sign for REVENGE.

### versus *prep.* See sign for CHALLENGE.

### very *adv.*

- [Initialized sign similar to sign for **much**] Beginning with the fingertips of both *V hands* touching in front of the chest, palms facing each other, bring the hands apart to in front of each shoulder.

### veto *v.* See sign for REJECT[1].

### via *prep.* See sign for THROUGH.

### vibrate *v.* See sign for BEAT[2]. Related form: **vibration** *n.*

### vice president *n.*

- [Abbreviation **v-p**] Beginning with the right *V hand* in front of the right side of the forehead, palm facing forward and fingers pointing up, move the hand downward by twisting the wrist, forming a *P hand* in front of the right shoulder.

### video camera *n.* See sign for MOVIE CAMERA.

### videotape[1] *n., v.*

- [Abbreviation **v-t**] Beginning with the index-finger side of the right *V hand,* palm facing forward and fingers pointing up, against the open left palm held up in front of the chest, move the right hand forward in a circular movement while changing into a *T hand* as the hand moves.

**videotape²** *v.* (alternate sign) Same sign used for:
**camcorder.**

- [Represents the fluttering pictures on a videotape]
  With the index-finger side of the right *C hand*
  against the palm of the left *open hand* held in front
  of the chest, palm facing right and fingers pointing
  up, bend the right fingers and thumb with a quick
  repeated movement.

**videotape³** *v.* See sign for MOVIE CAMERA.

**view** *v.* See sign for LOOK OVER.

**viewpoint** *v.* See sign for PERSPECTIVE.

**village** *n.* See sign for TOWN.

**violin** *n.* Same sign used for: **fiddle.**

- [Mime playing a violin] While holding the left *curved
  hand* in front of the left shoulder, palm facing in,
  move the right *F hand* forward and back toward
  the left side of the chest with a swinging movement, palm facing down.

**virtual** *adj.*

- [Initialized sign similar to sign for **dream**] Beginning
  with the index-finger side of the right *V hand*
  touching the right side of the forehead, palm
  facing left, move the hand forward in a double arc.

**visible** *adj.* Same sign used for: **transparent.**

- [see + through] Move the right *V hand*, palm
  facing down and fingers pointing forward,
  from near the right side of the face forward
  between the index finger and middle finger
  of the left *5 hand* held in front of the face,
  palm facing in and fingers pointing right.

**visit** *v., n.*

- [Initialized sign] Beginning with both *V hands* in front of
  each side of the chest, palms facing in and fingers pointing
  up, move the hands in alternating repeated movements.

# visualize

**visualize** *adj.* See sign for SEE.

---

**vocabulary** *n.*

- [Initialized sign similar to sign for **word**] Tap the fingertips of the right *V hand,* palm facing down, with a double movement on the extended left index finger held in front of the body, palm facing in and finger pointing right.

---

**voice** *n.* Related forms: **vocal, vocalize.**

- [Initialized sign showing the location of one's voice] Move the fingertips of the right *V hand,* palm facing down, upward on the throat with a double movement.

---

**void** *adj.* See sign for EMPTY.

---

**volleyball** *n.*

- [Mime hitting a volleyball] Beginning with both *open hands* near each side of the head, palms facing forward and fingers pointing up, push the hands upward and forward with a double movement.

---

**volunteer** *v.* See sign for APPLY².

---

**vomit** *v. n.* Same sign used for: **throw up.**

- [Represents food being expelled from the mouth] Beginning with the right *5 hand* near the mouth, palm facing left and fingers pointing forward, and the left *5 hand* forward of the right hand, palm facing right and fingers pointing forward, move both hands upward and forward in large arcs.

488

**vote** *n., v.* Same sign used for: **elect, election.**

- [Represents putting one's vote into a ballot box] Insert the fingertips of the right *F hand,* palm facing down, with a double movement in the hole formed by the left *O hand* held in front of the chest, palm facing in.

**vow** *n., v.* See also sign for PROMISE. Same sign used for: **assurance, assure, commit, commitment, obligate, pledge, swear, sworn.**

- [Natural gesture for making a pledge] Beginning with the extended right index finger in front of the mouth, palm facing left and finger pointing up, move the right hand forward with a deliberate movement while opening into an *open hand,* palm facing forward and fingers pointing up, and hitting the right forearm against the index-finger side of the left *open hand* held across the body, palm facing down and fingers pointing right.

**wacky** *Slang. adj.* See sign for CRAZY.

**wager** *n.* See sign for BET.

**wages** *pl. n.* See signs for EARN, INCOME[1].

**wait** *v., n.*

■ [Seems to be twiddling the finger while waiting impatiently] Beginning with both *curved 5 hands* in front of the body, palms facing up, wiggle the middle fingers with a repeated motion.

**waive** *v.* See sign for DISMISS.

**wake up** *v. phrase.* See sign for AWAKE[1].

**walk** *v.* Same sign used for: **stroll, wander.**

■ [Represents a person's legs moving when walking] Beginning with both *open hands* in front of each side of the body, left palm facing in and fingers pointing down and right palm facing down and fingers pointing forward, move the fingers of both hands up and down with an alternating movement by bending the wrists.

**wall** *n.* See sign for BOARD[1].

**wander** *v.* See signs for ROAM, WALK.

**want** *v.* Same sign used for: **desire, passion.**

■ [Represents bringing a wanted thing toward oneself] Beginning with both *5 hands* in front of the body, palms facing up and fingers pointing forward, bring the hands back toward the chest while constricting the fingers toward the palms.

**war** *n*. See sign for BATTLE.

**warm** *adj*. Related form: **warmth** *n*.

■ [Using one's breath to warm the hand] Beginning with the fingers of the right *E hand* near the mouth, palm facing in, move the hand forward in a small arc while opening the fingers into a *C hand.*

**warn** *v*. Related form: **warning** *n*. Same sign used for: **caution, rebuke.**

■ [Indicates tapping someone on the hand as a warning] Tap the palm of the right *open hand* with a double movement on the back of the left *open hand* held in front of the chest, both palms facing down.

**was**¹ *v*. Same sign used for: **past, were.**

■ [The hand gestures toward the past] Bring the fingertips of the right *bent hand,* palm facing back, down on the right shoulder.

**was**² *v*. See sign for AGO.

**wash** *v*. Same sign used for: **rub.**

■ [Demonstrates the action of rubbing something to wash it] Rub the palm side of the right *A hand* with a repeated movement across the palm side of the left *A hand,* palms facing each other.

**wash one's hair** See sign for SHAMPOO.

**washer** *n*. See sign for WASHING MACHINE.

**washing machine** *n*. Same sign used for: **washer.**

■ [Indicates the action of a washing machine's agitator] Beginning with the right *curved 5 hand* over the left *curved 5 hand* in front of the chest, palms facing each other, twist the hands with a repeated movement in opposite directions.

# washroom

**washroom** *n.* See sign for TOILET.

**waste** *n., v.*

- [The hand seems to toss waste away] Beginning with the back of the right *S hand,* palm facing up, in the palm of the left *open hand* held in front of the chest, palm facing up, move the right hand forward while opening into a *5 hand.*

**watch**[1] *n.* Same sign used for: **timepiece, wristwatch.**

- [The shape of a watch's face] Place the palm side of the right *F hand* on the back of the left wrist.

**watch**[2] *v.*

- [Represents the eyes looking at something] Beginning with the right *V hand* in front of the right side of the face, palm facing down and fingers pointing forward, move the hand forward.

**watch**[3] *v.* See sign for ATTENTION.

**watch out** *v. phrase.* See sign for LOOK OUT.

**water** *n.*

- [Initialized sign] Tap the index-finger side of the right *W hand,* palm facing left, against the chin with a double movement.

**watermelon** *n.*

- [water + pumpkin] Tap the index-finger side of the right *W hand,* palm facing left, against the chin with a double movement. Then with a double movement flick the middle finger of the right *8 Hand,* palm facing down, off the back of the left *S hand,* palm facing down, bouncing the right hand up slightly each time.

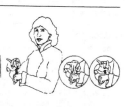

**way**[1] *n.*
- [Initialized sign similar to sign for **road**] Beginning with both *W hands* in front of each side of the body, palms facing each other, move the hands straight forward.

**way**[2] *n.* See sign for ROAD.

**we** *pron.*
- [Points to self and encompasses others in near area] Touch the extended right index finger, palm facing down, first to the right side of the chest and then to the left side of the chest.

**weak** *adj.* Related form: **weakness** *n.* Same sign used for: **fatigue, feeble.**
- [The fingers collapse as if weak] Beginning with the fingertips of the right *5 hand,* palm facing in, touching the palm of the left *open hand* held in front of the chest, move the right hand downward with a double movement, bending the fingers each time.

**wealth** *n.* See sign for RICH.

**wear** *v.*
- [Initialized sign formed with *U hand* for **use**] the right *U hand,* palm facing forward and fingers pointing up, in a circle in front of the right side of the body with a double movement.

**wear out** *v. phrase.* Same sign used for: **decay, rot, rotten.**
- [Shows something coming apart] Beginning with both *S hands* together in front of the chest, palms facing up, move the hands forward with a sudden movement while opening into *5 hands,* palms facing up.

**weary** *adj.* See sign for TIRED.

# weather

## weather *n.*

- [Initialized sign] With the fingertips of both *6 hands* together in front of the chest, palms facing each other, twist the hands in opposite directions with a double movement.

## wedding *n.* Related form: **wed** *v.*

- [Represents bringing the bride's and groom's hands together during a wedding] Beginning with both *open hands* hanging down in front of each side of the chest, palms facing in and fingers pointing down, bring the fingers upward toward each other, meeting in front of the chest.

## Wednesday *n.*

- [Initialized sign] Move the right *W hand,* palm facing in and fingers pointing up, in a circle in front of the right shoulder.

## week *n.* Same sign used for: **one week.**

- [The finger moves along the days of one week on an imaginary calendar] Slide the palm side of the right *1 hand* from the heel to the fingers of the left *open hand* held in front of the chest, palm facing in.

## weekend *n.*

- [**week + end**[1]] Slide the palm side of the right *1 hand* from the heel to the fingertips of the left *open hand* held in front of the chest, palm facing in. Then move the palm side of the right *open hand* downward along the fingertips of the left *open hand* held in front of the chest, palm facing right.

**weep** *v.* See sign for CRY[1].

**weigh** *v.* Related form: **weight** *n.* Same sign used for: **pound.**

- [The fingers seem to balance something as if on a scale] With the middle-finger side of the right *H hand* across the index-finger side of the left *H hand,* palms angled toward each other, tip the right hand up and down with a repeated movement.

**weird** *adj.* See also sign for STRANGE.

- [Initialized sign] Move the right *W hand,* palm facing down and fingers pointing left, across the front of the face, bending the fingers as the hand moves.

**welcome** *v., n., adj., interj.* See sign for INVITE.

**welfare** *n.* See sign for PENSION.

**well**[1] *adj., adv.* Same sign used for: **bold, cure, heal, healthy, strength, strong.**

- [The hands seem to pull health from the body] Beginning with the fingertips of both *5 hands* on each side of the chest, palms facing in and fingers pointing up, bring the hands forward with a deliberate movement while closing into *S hands.*

**well**[2] *adj.* See sign for GOOD.

**were** *v.* See signs for AGO, WAS[1].

**west** *n., adj., adv.*

- [Initialized sign showing a west direction on a map] Move the right *W hand,* palm facing forward and fingers pointing up, to the left in front of the right side of the chest.

**wet** *adj.* Same sign used for: **damp, dew, humid, misty, moist, moisten, moisture.**

- [The hands seem to feel something wet] Beginning with the right *5 hand* near the right side of the chin, palm facing left, and the left *5 hand* in front of the left side of the chest, palm facing up, bring the hands downward while closing the fingers to the thumbs.

# whack

**whack** *v.* See sign for SPANK.

## what *pron.*

■ [The fingers on the left hand are choices pointed out by the right hand] Bring the extended right index finger, palm facing left, downward across the left *open hand* held in front of the chest, palm facing up.

**whatever** *pron.* See sign for ANYWAY.

## what for?

■ [**for** formed with a repeated movement] Beginning with the extended right index finger touching the right side of the forehead, palm facing down, twist the hand forward with a double movement, pointing the index finger forward each time.

## what's happening? Same sign used for: **thrilling.**

■ [Feelings well up in the body] Beginning with the bent middle fingers of both *5 hands* touching the chest, palms facing in, bring the hands upward and forward with a quick double movement.

## what's the matter?

■ [Similar to sign for **wrong**] Bring the knuckles of the right *Y hand*, palm facing in, against the chin with a deliberate movement while wrinkling the forehead.

## when *adv.*

■ [A continuous movement showing duration of time] Beginning with the extended right index finger in front of the chest, palm facing down and finger pointing forward, and the left extended index finger in front of the lower chest, palm facing in and finger pointing right, move the right index finger in a circular movement down to land on the left index finger.

## where *adv.*

■ [Indicates one direction and then another] Move the extended right index finger, palm facing forward and finger pointing up, with a short double movement from side to side in front of the right shoulder.

**whether** *pron.* See sign for WHICH.

**whew**[1] *interj.*
- [Natural gesture used to wipe sweat from the forehead] Wipe the index-finger side of the right *B hand,* palm facing down, from left to right across the forehead, and then throw the right hand downward to in front of the right shoulder, ending with the palm facing in and fingers pointing down.

**whew**[2] *interj.* See sign for FINEST.

**which** *pron., adj.* Same sign used for: **either, whether.**
- [The movement indicates indecision] Beginning with both *10 hands* in front of each side of the chest, palms facing each other and right hand higher than the left hand, move the hands up and down in front of the chest with an alternating movement.

**while** *conj.* See sign for DURING.

**while ago, a**[1] Same sign used for: **few minutes ago, a.**
- [The finger moves only slightly into the past] Beginning with the little-finger side of the right *1 hand,* palm angled left, on the left *open hand* in front of the chest, palm facing up, move the right index finger back toward the chest by pivoting on the left hand.

**while ago, a**[2] See signs for JUST, RECENTLY[1].

**whip** *n., v.* See sign for SPANK. Related form: **whipping** *n.*

**whiskey** *n.* Same sign used for: **brandy, liquor.**
- [The size of a jigger] With the index fingers and little fingers of both hands extended, tap the little finger of the right hand with a double movement on the index finger of the left hand, palms facing in opposite directions.

**whistle** *n., v.* See sign for REFEREE.

# white

**white** *adj.*

- [The downy breast of a swan] Beginning with the fingertips of the right *5 hand* on the chest, palm facing in, pull the hand forward while closing the fingers into a *flattened O hand*.

**whiz** *n. Informal.* See sign for ADROIT.

**who** *pron.* Same sign used for: **whom.**

- [Outlines the verbal formation of the word **who**] With the thumb of the *modified C hand* touching the chin, palm facing left, bend the index finger up and down with a double movement.

**whole** *adj., n.* See sign for ALL.

**whom** *pron.* See sign for WHO.

**whore** *n.* See sign for PROSTITUTE.

**why**¹ *adv.*

- [Taking information and presenting it for examination] Beginning with the fingertips of the right *bent hand* touching the right side of the forehead, palm facing down, move the hand forward with a deliberate movement while changing into a *Y hand*.

**why**² *adv.* (alternate sign)

- [An abbreviated form of **why**¹] With the right index finger, little finger, and thumb extended, palm facing in, wiggle the bent middle fingers with a small repeated movement in front of the forehead.

**wicked** *adj.* See sign for BAD.

**wide** *adj.* Same sign used for: **broad, general.**

- [Indicates a wide space] Beginning with both *open hands* in front of each side of the body, palms facing each other and fingers pointing forward, move the hands away from each other outward to the sides of the body.

**wiener** *n.* See sign for SAUSAGE.

**wife** *n.*

- [The hand moves from near the female area of the head + **marry**] Move the right *curved hand* from near the right side of the chin, palm facing forward, downward to clasp the left *curved hand* held in front of the body.

---

**wild** *adj.* See sign for RAVE.

**will**[1] *n.*

- [Initialized sign similar to sign for **against**] Hit the index-finger side of the right *W hand*, palm facing forward, against the left *open hand* held in front of the chest, palm facing right and fingers pointing up.

---

**will**[2] *v.*

- [The hand moves into the future] Move the right *open hand*, palm facing left and fingers pointing up, from the right side of the chin forward while turning the fingers forward.

---

**willing** *adj.* See sign for ADMIT[1].

**will not** See sign for WON'T.

**win** *v., n.*

- [Grabbing the golden ring on a carousel] Beginning with the right *5 hand* in front of the right shoulder, palm facing forward and fingers pointing up, and the left *5 hand* in front of the body, palm facing right and fingers pointing forward, sweep the right hand downward in an arc across the index-finger side of the left hand while changing both hands into *S hands* and bringing the right hand upward in front of the chest.

---

**wind** *n.* Same sign used for: **storm.**

- [Represents the action of wind blowing] Beginning with both *5 hands* in front of the left side of the body, palms facing each other and fingers pointing forward, move the hands back and forth in front of the chest with a repeated movement.

---

**wind up** *v. phrase.* See sign for END[1].

# window

**window** *n.*
- [Represents closing a window] Bring the little-finger side of the right *open hand* down sharply with a double movement on the index-finger side of the left *open hand,* both palms facing in and fingers pointing in opposite directions.

**wine** *n.*
- [Initialized sign] Move the right *W hand,* palm facing left, in a small circle near the right side of the chin.

**wings** *pl. n.,* See signs for ANGEL, FLY.

**winter**[1] *n*
- [Initialized sign similar to sign for **cold**[2]] Beginning with both *W hands* in front of the body, palms facing each other, move the hands toward each other with a shaking repeated movement.

**winter**[2] *n.* See sign for COLD[2].

**wipe** *v.* Same sign used for: **rub.**
- [Demonstrates the action of wiping something] Wipe the palm side of the right *A hand* with a repeated movement back and forth on the left *open hand* held in front of the body, palm facing up.

**wire** *n.* See sign for CORD.

**wise** *adj.* Related form: **wisdom** *n.*
- [Shows the depth of wisdom in the brain] Move the right *X hand,* palm facing left, up and down with a double movement in front of the right side of the forehead.

**wish** *v., n.* Same sign used for: **desire.**
- [The fingers outline the path of craving for something] Move the fingers of the right *C hand,* palm facing in, downward on the chest a short distance.

### witch *n.*

■ [Represents the traditional hooked nose of a witch] Move the bent index finger of the right *X hand* from near the right side of the nose, palm facing left, downward in front of the nose, ending with the palm facing down.

### with *prep.*

■ [Indicates two things coming together so they are with one another] Beginning with both *A hands* in front of the chest, palms facing each other, bring the hands together.

### withdraw[1] *v.*

■ [Abbreviation **w-d**] Beginning with the right *W hand* in front of the right shoulder, palm facing forward, bring the hand back toward the right shoulder while changing into a *D hand*.

**withdraw**[2] *v.* See signs for DISCONNECT, FORSAKE[1], LEAVE[1].

**within** *prep.* See sign for INCLUDE.

### without *prep.*

■ [**with** + releasing the hands to indicate the opposite meaning] Beginning with the palm sides of both *A hands* together in front of the chest, bring the hands apart while opening into *5 hands*, palms facing each other.

### woman *n.*

■ [A gesture beginning near the female area of the head + **polite**] Beginning with the extended thumb of the right *open hand* touching the right side of the chin, palm facing left, bring the hand downward to touch the thumb again in the center of the chest.

# wonder

**wonder** *v.* Same sign used for: **consider, contemplate, meditate, ponder, reflect, think, think about, thinking.**

■ [Represents thoughts going around in one's head] Move the extended right index finger, palm facing in, in a small circle near the right side of the forehead with a repeated movement.

**wonderful** *adj.* Same sign used for: **amaze, excellent, fantastic, great, incredible, marvel, marvelous, remarkable.**

■ [A gesture of awe and wonder] Move both *5 hands,* palms facing forward and fingers pointing up, from in front of each side of the head forward with a short double movement.

**won't** *contraction.* Same sign used for: **refuse, will not.**

■ [Natural gesture for refusing to do something] Beginning with the right *10 hand* in front of the right shoulder, palm facing left, move the hand deliberately back toward the shoulder while twisting the wrist up.

**wood** *n., adj.* Same sign used for: **saw.**

■ [Shows action of sawing wood] Slide the little-finger side of the right *open hand,* palm facing left and fingers pointing forward, forward and back with a double movement on the index–finger side of the left *open hand* held in front of the chest, palm facing in and fingers pointing right.

**woods** *pl. n.* See sign for FOREST.

**word** *n.* Same sign used for: **text.**

■ [Measures the size of a word] Tap the extended fingers of the right *G hand,* palm facing left, with a double movement against the extended left index finger pointing up in front of the left side of the chest, palm facing right.

**work** *n., v.* Same sign used for: **employment, job, labor, occupation, task.** See also sign for ACTIVE[1].

■ [Demonstrates repetitive action] Tap the heel of the right *S hand,* palm facing forward, with a double movement on the back of the left *S hand* held in front of the body, palm facing down.

**work hard** See sign for WORKAHOLIC.

**work out** See sign for EXERCISE[1].

**workaholic** *n.* Same sign used for: **toil, work hard, working.**
- [**work** formed with a repeated circular movement] Bring the heel of the right *A hand,* palm facing forward, in a double circular movement down across the back of the left *S hand* held in front of the chest.

**working** *adj.* See sign for WORKAHOLIC.

**workshop** *n.*
- [Abbreviation **w-s**] Beginning with the thumbs of both *W hands* together in front of the chest, palms facing each other, move the hands outward in arcs while closing into *S hands,* ending with the little fingers of both *S hands* touching in front of the body, palms facing in.

**world** *n.*
- [Initialized sign indicating the movement of the earth around the sun] Beginning with both *W hands* in front of the body, palms facing each other, move the right hand upward and forward in an arc as the left hand moves back and upward around the right hand, exchanging positions.

**worry** *v.* See sign for TROUBLE[1].

**worse** *adj.*
- [Similar to sign for **multiply** to indicate a bad condition multiplied] Beginning with both *V hands* in front of each shoulder, palms facing in, push the hands past each other in front of the chest, brushing the little-finger side of the right hand across the index-finger side of the left hand.

# worship

**worship**[1] *n., v.* Same sign used for **adore, beg, please, pray.**

■ [Similar to sign for **amen** except with a double movement] With the right fingers cupped over the left *A hand*, bring the hands downward and in toward the chest with a double movement.

**worship**[2] *v.* See sign for HAIL[2].

**worth** *n., prep.* See signs for COST[2], IMPORTANT.

**wound** *v., n.* See signs for HURT[1,2].

**wow** *interj.*

■ [Natural gesture] Swing the right *5 hand,* palm facing in, limply up and down in front of the right side of the body.

**wrench** *n.* Same sign used for: **maintenance.**

■ [Shows twisting action of a wrench] With the extended left index finger inserted between the index finger and middle finger of the right *3 hand,* both palms angled in, twist the right hand up and down with a double movement.

**wristwatch** *n.* See sign for WATCH[1].

**write** *v.* Related form: **written** *adj.* Same sign used for: **edit, scribble.**

■ [Mime writing on paper] Bring the fingers of the right *modified X hand,* palm facing left, with a wiggly movement from the heel to the fingers of the left *open hand* held in front of the body, palm facing up.

**wrong** *adj.* Same sign used for: **incorrect.**

■ [Similar to sign for **mistake** but with a single movement] Place the middle fingers of the right *Y hand,* palm facing in, against the chin with a deliberate movement.

### xylophone *n.*

■ [Mime playing a xylophone] Beginning with the palms of both *modified X hands* facing each other in front of each side of the body, move the hands up and down with an alternating movement.

---

**yawn** *v.*, *n.*

■ [Natural gesture used to cover the mouth when yawning] Bring the fingers of the right *open hand,* palm facing in and fingers pointing up, back against the mouth with a double movement.

---

**yeah** *adv. Informal.* See sign for YES.

---

**year** *n.*

■ [Represents the movement of the earth around the sun] Beginning with the right *S hand,* palm facing left, over the left *S hand,* palm facing right, move the right hand forward in a complete circle around the left hand while the left hand moves in a smaller circle around the right hand, ending with the little-finger side of the right hand on the thumb side of the left hand.

---

**yearlong** *adj.* See sign for YEAR-ROUND.

---

**year-round** *adj.*, *adv.* Same sign used for: **cycle, orbit, yearlong.**

■ [Represents the movement of the earth around the sun] Beginning with both extended index fingers pointing toward each other in front of the chest, right hand slightly higher than the left hand and both palms facing down, move the right index finger in a complete circle around the left finger.

---

**yearn** *v.* See sign for HUNGRY.

---

**yell** *v.* See signs for CALL², SCREAM.

---

**yellow** *adj.*

- [Initialized sign] Move the right *Y hand,* palm facing left, with a twisting double movement.

**yes** *adv.* Same sign used for: **yeah** *(informal).*

- [Represents a person's head nodding in approval] Move the right *S hand,* palm facing forward, up and down in front of the right shoulder by bending the wrist with a repeated movement.

**yesterday** *n., adv.*

- [Initialized sign moving back into the past] Move the thumb of the right *Y hand,* palm facing forward, from the right side of the chin up to the right cheek.

**yet** *adv.* See also sign for STILL[1].

- [The hand gestures back into the past] Bend the wrist of the right *open hand,* palm facing back and fingers pointing down, back with a double movement near the right side of the waist.

**yield** *v.* See signs for GIVE UP, LOOK OUT.

**you** *pron.*

- [Point toward the referent] Point the extended right index finger, palm facing down, toward the person being talked to.

# young

**young** *adj.* Same sign used for: **youth.**
- [Represents bringing up youthful feelings in the body] Beginning with the fingers of both *bent hands* on each side of the chest, palms facing in, brush the fingers upward with a double movement.

**your** *pron.* Related form: **yours** *pron.*
- [The hand moves toward the referent] Push the palm of the right *open hand,* palm facing forward and fingers pointing up, toward the person being talked to.

**you're too late.** See sign for MISS[2].

**yourself** *pron.*
- [This hand shape is used for reflexive pronouns and moves toward the referent] Push the extended thumb of the right *10 hand,* palm facing left, forward with a double movement toward the person being talked to.

**youth** *n.* See sign for YOUNG.

**zap** *v. Informal, n.* Same sign used for: **got you!** or **gottcha!**

■ [The fingers mime zapping something] Beginning with the right *H hand* in front of the chest, palm facing forward and fingers pointing up, move the fingers forward and then back again with a quick movement.

**zeal** *n.* Same sign used for: **aspiration, aspire, eager, enthusiastic, motivation, motive.**

■ [Rubbing the hands together in eagerness] Rub the palms of both *open hands*, palms facing each other, back and forth against each other with a double alternating movement.

**zero** *n.* See sign for NONE[2].

**zip** *v.* Same sign as for **zipper** but formed with a single movement.

**zipper** *n.*

■ [Mime pulling a zipper up and down] With the right *modified X hand,* palm facing down, move the right hand up and down with a double movement in front of the chest.

**zoom**[1] *v.* Same sign used for: **set off.**

■ [Represents something getting smaller as it goes off into the distance] Beginning with the thumb of the right *G hand,* palm facing forward, at the base of the extended left index finger held in front of the chest, palm facing down and finger pointing right, move the right thumb across the length of the left index finger, closing the right index finger and thumb together as the hand moves to the right.

**zoom**[2] *v.* See sign for SHOOT UP.

# Manual Alphabet

The American Manual Alphabet is a series of handshapes used to represent each letter of the English alphabet. Many countries have their own manual alphabets, just as they have their own sign languages. It is important to note that although English is spoken in the United States and in England, the English Manual Alphabet, which is formed by using two hands, is very different from the American Manual Alphabet.

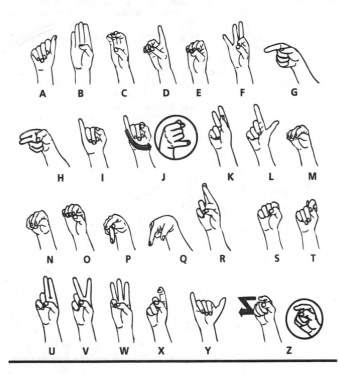

# Numbers:
# Cardinals and Ordinals

## Cardinal Numbers

Numbers are formed by holding the dominant hand comfortably in front of the shoulder with the palm either forward or in, depending on the context for using the number. When counting objects up to five, the palm should face in toward the signer. However, when expressing age or time, the palm should face forward.

The following are the signs for numbers from zero to 30. From the numbers from 31 to 99, the signs follow a regular pattern. For those numbers, sign each digit of the numeral moving the hand slightly to the right, such as for 34, sign *3* followed by *4*. For 60, sign *6* followed by *zero*. For numbers where both digits are the same (e.g., 44), bounce the hand slightly in place while holding the four handshape.

**Cardinal Numbers**

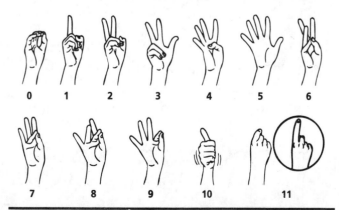

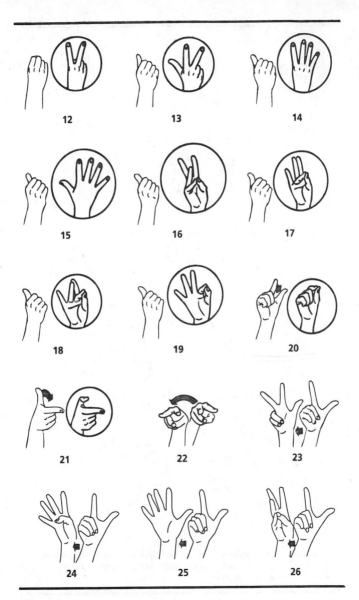

12

13

14

15

16

17

18

19

20

21

22

23

24

25

26

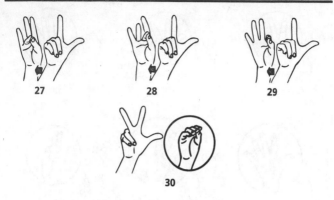

**27**  **28**  **29**

**30**

The following are signs for hundred, thousand, and million. When signing numbers over one hundred, the numbers are signed just as they are spoken. For example, 283 is signed *two-hundred + eighty + three*. Similarly, 5,690 is signed *five-thousand + six-hundred + ninety*.

*one-hundred*          *thousand*

*million*

When giving an address, sign the numbers in the manner in which an address is usually spoken. For example, 3812 Charles Avenue is signed *thirty-eight + twelve*.

Money is also signed in the same order that it is spoken, except for dollar amounts under ten dollars, which are signed by using the corresponding ordinal (see p. 516). For example, "eight dollars" is signed with the sign used for *eighth*. For larger amounts, the sign *dollar* is used after the dollar amount, just as it is spoken. For example, $86.17 is signed *eighty-six + dollar + seventeen*. For cents under a dollar, sign the cents sign followed by the amount. For example, 45¢ is signed *cents + forty-five*.

*dollar*

Fractions are formed by signing the top number of the fraction and then dropping the hand slightly to form the bottom number of the fraction. The following are a few examples of fractions.

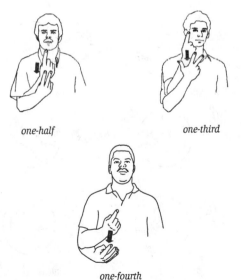

*one-half*

*one-third*

*one-fourth*

## Ordinal Numbers

The following signs are used when expressing order or rank in a series. Hold the hand comfortably in front of the right shoulder, twisting the wrist when forming each sign. The same signs are used for dollar amounts under ten dollars.

**Ordinal Numbers**

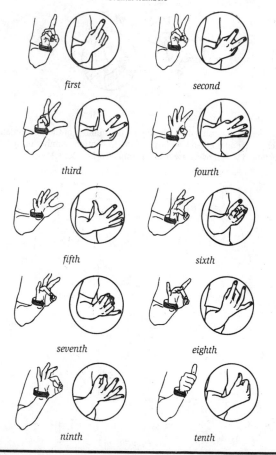

first

second

third

fourth

fifth

sixth

seventh

eighth

ninth

tenth